bauhaus, modernism and the illustrated book

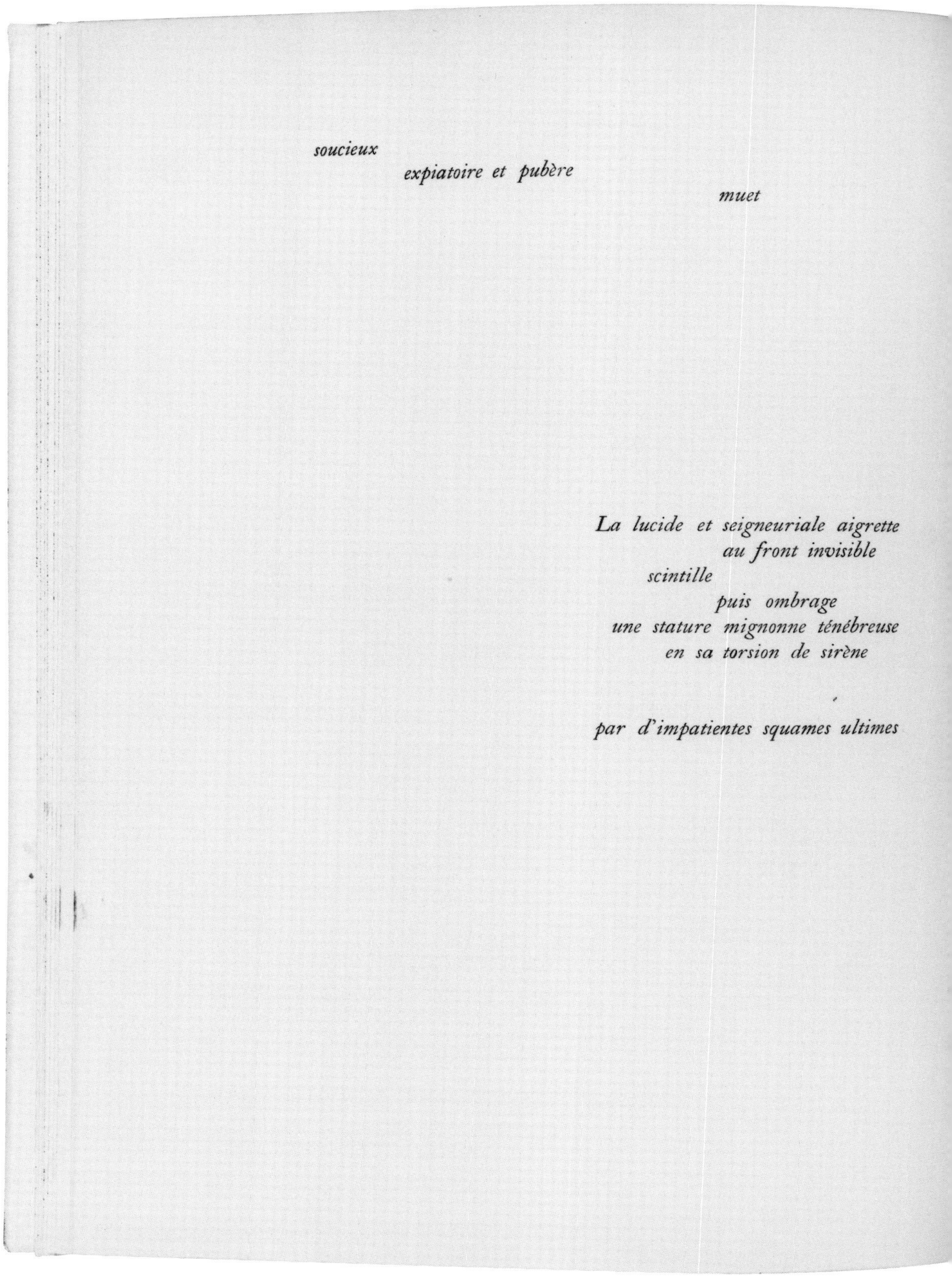

soucieux
expiatoire et pubère
muet

La lucide et seigneuriale aigrette
au front invisible
scintille
puis ombrage
une stature mignonne ténébreuse
en sa torsion de sirène

par d'impatientes squames ultimes

Stéphane Mallarmé
Un Coup de dés
(A Throw of the Dice)
Paris, 1914
Illustrated at 66% actual size

rire

que

SI

de vertige

debout

le temps
de souffleter
bifurquées

un roc

faux manoir
tout de suite
évaporé en brumes

qui imposa
une borne à l'infini

SOIT
que

l'Abîme

blanchi
étale
furieux
sous une inclinaison
plane désespérément

d'aile

la sienne
par

avance retombée d'un mal à dresser le vol
et couvrant les jaillissements
coupant au ras les bonds

très à l'intérieur résume

l'ombre enfouie dans la profondeur par cette voile alternative

jusqu'adapter
à l'envergure

sa béante profondeur en tant que la coque

d'un bâtiment

penché de l'un ou l'autre bord

Alan Bartram

bauhaus, modernism and the illustrated book

You may be surprised, Reader
that a story of modernism should begin with pages from 1897
But Stéphane Mallarmé's *Un Coup de dés*
(although not given this typographic form until 1914)
exemplifies many fundamental principles of that story
An arrangement of text dictated by meaning
not formal constraints
the elegant use of space to achieve this
(and which here is an integral part of the poetry)
the two pages treated as one, not as independent designs
the overall simplicity
the restraint
the lightness of touch
only the modern structural grid is missing
But the grid (geometric in its basis, very twentieth century)
is merely a convenient and practical way of unifying different elements
Here, the structure is formed by meaning
and artificial frameworks are unnecessary

Yale University Press 2004

Published in North America by
Yale University Press
P.O. Box 209040
New Haven, CT 06520-9040

First published 2004 by
The British Library
96 Euston Road
London NW1 2DB
Great Britain

Library of Congress Control Number:
2003114795

ISBN 0-300-10117-1

Designed by Alan Bartram
Typeset in Monotype Fournier
and Franklin Gothic Heavy
by Norman Tilley Graphics, Northampton
Scanning origination by
The Heyford Press Ltd, Wellingborough
Printed in Great Britain at
the University Press, Cambridge

THE USUAL SUSPECTS, AND OTHERS
Once again, I have rounded up some familiar names for assistance, and added a few new ones. I am extremely grateful for the help they have given me. In particular, I must mention Diana Allen, Harold Bartram, Ron Costley, Paul Gumn, Richard Hendel, Richard Hollis, Gordon House, Lucy Myers, Rick Poynor, Pat Schleger and Nick Tite. Also Faber and Faber, Lund Humphries, Oxford University Press, The Royal Academy of Arts and St Bride Printing Library. Also my publisher David Way, together with Lara Speicher and Kate Hampson of the Publishing Office.

contents

Shelfmarks [in square brackets] are those of The British Library. Other items are from private collections.

preface

It is a rash narrator who claims a tale can only be told one way, or that it can have only one conclusion.

John Fowles gave his novel *The French Lieutenant's Woman* three possible endings, the final one signalled by the resetting of a watch. This present work departs from the plot of my *Five Hundred Years of Book Design* around the late nineteenth century, to follow a very different storyline. While I have tried to make it factual, personal preferences govern the selection of examples, and thus the plot. The factors influencing those choices might be of interest.

My first job was as an assistant to Herbert Spencer. My brother Harold had been taught by Anthony Froshaug and Spencer at the Central School of Arts and Crafts, but I went to the Royal College of Art. The two schools could not have been more different in their approach to typography: uncompromising modernism at the Central, elegant twentieth-century traditionalism at the College. For me, there was no conflict: I was firmly in the modernist camp, quietly undermining (I hoped) the decorative-typefaces-and-borders approach favoured by (but not insisted upon – it was far too civilised a place for such authoritarianism) the staff at the RCA. To encourage the modernist faction, a beacon shone from distant Switzerland: hard-edge design, all grids and grots, the post-war New Order made visible. Later, Spencer's particular interest in Dutch design (his wife was Dutch) probably coloured my appreciation of the rather different work of Willem Sandberg.

A far more difficult conflict to resolve was that between Swiss and Italian design, both then at their zenith. The exuberance of work by such Italians as Max Huber and Franco Grignani was very seductive. (Although Swiss-born and trained, Huber found Italy a less constraining place to work in.) Stores – La Rinascente; firms – Olivetti (I typed the text of this book on my Lettera 22, designed by Marcello Nizzoli in 1950) and AGIP (*supercortemaggiore!* Who, having scootered around Italy in those days, could forget the elegant and well-mannered service stations, with daringly cantilevered canopies, fronted by six-legged dragons breathing fire?); car designers – Pinin Farina; magazines – *Domus*, *Casabella*, *Stile Industria* (the contents of all three, even to a mere graphic designer, were immensely stimulating); Vespas, Lambrettas, espresso machines (and their coffee), architecture, museum design, furniture, films; everything Italians touched seemed to set the pace. No wonder that, like many British designers, and especially one so enthusiastic about things Italian as me, I eventually became weary of Swiss perfectionism, and attempted to de-grid my work. But not being Italian, I had neither the confidence nor the flair, and returned to the grid. Were this book about my life as a designer, a section on Italian graphics would have been essential. But my story mainly concerns north and central European typography. And soon one realised that the basics of the practical Swiss system are surprisingly resilient and adaptable. This book attempts to demonstrate its ongoing development; but its foundations lie in the very different work of the early pioneers.

This is not a comprehensive history of modern book design, merely stabs at significant moments in its evolution; an approach that results in a jerky curve, like a silent film run at the wrong speed. The story is part of the history of the life of our times: its architecture, its society, its bursts of utopian vision and disillusionment. Book design can no longer be viewed in isolation.

This is not a novel. Unlike Fowles's foppish impresario negligently leaning against the Embankment parapet, adjusting his watch, I have not, here, provided an alternative ending. *Five Hundred Years of Book Design*, concerned with the more or less classical tradition, stops before 1950. But if its plot were continued to the present day, like the very different plot of this book, it would show refinements, but few significant developments, during those fifty years. So *that* account could be read as having my alternative ending.

Both books follow paths as truthful as I can make them, but historical facts are as selectable, as manipulatable as characters in any novel. Some can be emphasised, others played down. Designers on their AppleMacs may feel that Tschichold's stylistic 'rules', which Max Bill disparaged as 'recipes', and my emphasis on structure and the 'architecturally good' book, are out-of-fashion and irrelevant. For them, yet another book needs to be written, with a plot springing still from Futurist typography, but glancing at Tschichold's pre-1928 work, including his film posters, which I have ignored; continuing along Italian and French paths, and guided by a different set of facts. Such a plot might discover freer and more dynamic principles (or 'recipes') appropriate to new technology.

But I will get into the landau so kindly provided by John Fowles, and draw briskly away.

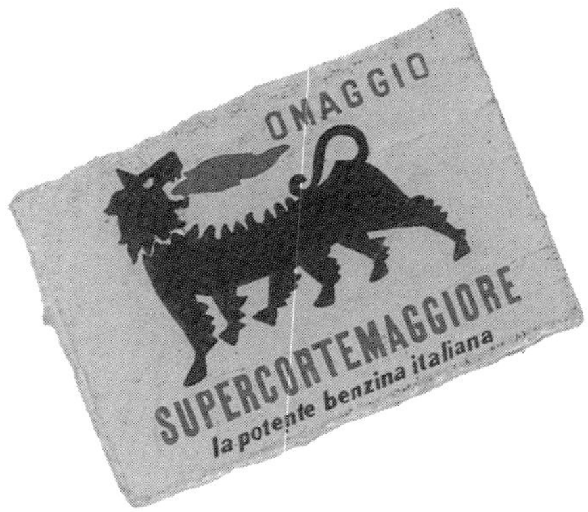

... to educate men and women
to understand the world they live in
and to invent and create forms
symbolizing that world

The aims of the Bauhaus, declared by Gropius in 1923 remain pertinent eighty years later

'Well, I lay it down that a book quite unornamented can look actually and positively beautiful, if it be so to say, architecturally good.' William Morris's approach to book design is not mine, but I applaud his sentiments. This book celebrates the evolution of the form of modern book which relates text to integrated illustrations by means of a consistent structure; has controlled, almost severe typography; shows consideration for the reader with its clarity of design; and makes positive use of space. It is the pre-eminent achievement of twentieth-century book design. A lot of its most crucial development coincided with my early days as a designer: it was happening in front of my eyes. For many designers in the twenty-first century, it is history – remote, obscure and not easily accessible. While this book is not a fully fledged analysis, it does aim to provide enough background for an understanding of the ideas that underpin today's design, so allowing an appreciation of how and why we have got where we are. Over 115,000 new titles a year are published in the UK alone; unsurprisingly, many, or most, are visually unsatisfying. But the best – we should judge any period only by the best – are exemplars of book production.

Until the 1920s, there was no serious attempt to relate the various forms of visual expression. Only the 'spirit of the times' gave them any coherence. The Bauhaus, and the slightly earlier de Stijl group, changed that. Both deliberately sought principles which could be applied to all design, marrying art, architecture and industry in a way never before attempted. Although the unity of architecture, painting and sculpture in Bavarian baroque and rococo churches is a wonder, everyday artefacts of the period bore little or no relation to them. Artists, architects and craftsmen working in the art nouveau manner shared a common vocabulary, one which embraced book design and illustration; but the Bauhaus, under Walter Gropius, set out to create an academic, theoretical and practical synthesis of all forms of visual expression. Gropius: 'The approach toward any kind of design – of a chair, a building, a whole town or a regional plan – should be essentially identical, not only in respect to their relationship in space but to social aspects as well.' Although the Bauhaus existed for only fourteen years, its thinking influenced the appearance of almost every kind of artefact throughout the twentieth century, and continues to do so in the twenty-first, despite occasional reactions against its modernist ethic.

I use the terms 'modernist' and 'modernism' to cover the wide variety of twentieth-century movements, many of which overlap chronologically, some of which interacted with or conflicted with others, and most of which, like the Bauhaus, appeared during or just after the First World War.

Modernism affected all visual disciplines from architecture and design to painting and pottery. Such wide-ranging interests were a defining characteristic of all the different factions. Anti-historicist, against traditional forms of visual expression, these groups tried to develop a new broadly-based aesthetic in tune with the character of the twentieth century. Modernism's most significant period was the late 1920s and the 1930s, especially in continental Europe. The factor common to all its disparate factions was visionary. It grew out of the mechanical, industrialised culture of the day, and tried to improve it as well as reflect it. It has been repeatedly attacked by totalitarian states, and disliked by the general public, especially in Britain, for being supposedly too pure, too serious, too inhuman. Nonetheless, its influence over our lives is pervasive (its enemies might say pernicious), and it refuses to go away. My use of the term is vague and all-inclusive, because the idea of modernism is that.

Gropius, founder of the Bauhaus in 1919, was an architect, and his initial impulse was to create buildings which embraced architecture and sculpture and painting in one unity; although the Bauhaus architecture department, under Hannes Meyer, was not established until 1927. But, as Gropius said later, 'What the Bauhaus preached in practice was the common citizenship of all forms of creative work, and their logical interdependence on one another in the modern world … The object of the Bauhaus was not to propagate any style, system or dogma, but simply to exert a revitalising influence on design.' Much of the print produced went to extremes in its determination to overturn the existing mediocrity. But the underlying philosophy of the teaching was so well founded that it could be reinterpreted without becoming debased.

While it is tempting to suggest that the quest for a New Art for the New Life was prompted by the disasters of the First World War – and these probably played some part – the de Stijl group, the first movement that need concern us, was born in neutral Holland in 1917. It was founded by Piet Mondrian and Theo van Doesburg, and hoped to replace the dying 'brown world' of lyricism, vagueness and sentimentality (no mention there of Flanders mud) with a brave new 'white world', declaring a need for clarity, certainty and order. Its aims were to create a collective style embracing painting, furniture, the applied arts and architecture, and at the same time to promote a utopian vision; one, in Mondrian's struggling phrases, 'reducing natural forms to the constant elements of form, the laws governing nature's basic structure'. Some of us might have difficulty in identifying any elements of even the most simplistic idea of nature's structure in his paintings after about 1916. In a more down-to-earth manner, Richard Weston, in *Modernism*, remarks that Mondrian's compositions are all-over, from edge to edge, asymmetric and de-centred. This seems rather a good description of the modern illustrated book.

Jan Tschichold, who belonged to no group although a prime player in the New Typography, put Mondrian's thoughts rather more clearly when he declared that 'the final and most pure form of a necessary item is always constructed of geometric shapes' – a fundamental tenet of the time. In 1920, the painter Amédée Ozenfant, with Le Corbusier, launched the magazine *L'Esprit Nouveau*, claiming 'we now aspire to serious rigour … art must tend always to precision'. They agreed with Plato: 'By beauty of shapes … I mean straight lines and circles, and shapes – plane or solid – made from them by lathe, rule and square. These are not, like other things, beautiful relatively, but always and absolutely'. One of the great icons of the twentieth century, Le Corbusier's Villa Savoye of 1928-31, exhibits 'in full song, architecture's purest gift – mathematical lyricism' (Richard Weston again). Would de Stijl have approved of *this* lyricism, seeing as it was mathematical?

The emphasis on untainted geometric severity was found in the work of de Stijl, Le Corbusier, and the products of the Bauhaus. It is a utopian and possibly naive vision; but it is understandable that, after the horrors of the war, this vision of a 'white world' became haunting. The architect Peter Behrens said, in 1920, 'What is most depressing is not the scarcities we have to face, not the inflation, not the neglect of the streets and means of public transport, but the demoralisation of broad sections of the population. The stealing, the lying and cheating … the unscrupulous money-making … A transformation must emerge from this tragedy … A passionate, moral renewal of puritanical severity.'

This slightly frightening vision could sometimes be found in Le Corbusier's declarations, although in his actual work poetry usually broke through. Some of the modernists could be a little alarming: even Corb had his trademark heavy, black-framed, round glasses. Machine-mad László Moholy-Nagy, a major Bauhaus figure, in red industrial overalls and nickel-framed spectacles, with pugnacious jaw and swept-back hair, was the archetypal and slightly sinister modern rationalist.

The Bauhaus, which had what eventually became a somewhat fraught relationship with the de Stijl group and its co-founder Theo van Doesburg, has been probably the longest-lasting, certainly the best-known, influence on applied design that we have yet seen. The convincing logic, high-powered teaching and unwavering belief in its own ideas were difficult to ignore. But the often assertive design, and the typography that emerged from this hothouse, was too excited (and exciting) for adaptation to the general run of books. That image of Moholy-Nagy as the clinical metal-bashing technician is a little too accurate. We must look elsewhere for a more sympathetic influence.

The propagation and dissemination of modernist architectural theory owed a lot to Le Corbusier and his heroic prose style, especially notable in *Vers une Architecture* of 1923, one of the most influential books on architecture ever published. As an architect and as a writer he was continually provocative, but he had his romantic side: 'Architecture must bring to the men of our new mechanical civilisation, not just strict utility, but joy itself.' He described his Villa Savoye as 'poetry produced by technology'. *He* never ignored the attraction of the inexplicable.

This more sophisticated modernism of the 1930s can be defined as being precise, logical and unsentimental, with geometry overtly playing a key role, creating purity of form; generally asymmetric, reflecting needs and purpose; restrained; sensitive to materials, respecting their intrinsic qualities or nature;

meticulous in the attention paid to details, which were reduced to a minimum; and notable for its transparency and light. Jan Tschichold's New Typography and its later developments, with their aspirations to 'exactitude and order' (Le Corbusier's phrase), could be described in this way, too.

While Swiss architects – who contributed to the development of a new and slightly later typographic system evolved by their fellow designers – were proficient in their use of modernist principles, none (except the great Corb himself, and the bridge engineer Robert Maillart) were true innovators. Some find the Swiss hard-edge typography of the 1940s (which in its rigour *was* innovative) chilly and too intellectual – and these tendencies were certainly an inherent danger – but it was fundamentally calm and ordered, avoiding the extremes of Bauhaus work. This may be the secret of its success. Also, its logic was easily understood, if not so easily applied; for (illogical) aesthetic skill was also required.

In many ways, architecturally, visually and socially, 1945 was a more significant turning point – in Britain, at least – than 1918. Although a lot of architectural/social theorising went on in continental Europe during the 1920s and 1930s, much of it remained on paper. Throughout the war-torn Europe of 1945, the new and more widespread destruction offered modernist architects and designers, especially those in Britain (encouraged by government social policies), an opportunity which they felt wonderfully well-equipped to respond to: the rebuilding, on a rational basis, not just of towns and cities, but of society itself. This optimism was reflected in a new and vital typography. In Britain, pre-war typography had generally remained traditionally classical. Now, largely imported from continental Europe, was a style truly for the twentieth century.

It was fifteen years before the very different American agenda took over from the excitement of that vision. The war had taught American industry how to produce; the problem now was to sell. The answer lay in advertising, consumerism, and quickly outmoded styling – anathema to modernist (and often socialist) Europeans. Their severe 'white world' was out of place in a gaudy consumer economy driven by manufactured desires rather than by need. Even the bland – or sometimes serenely beautiful – towers derived from Mies van der Rohe's poetic minimalism are symbols of this capitalist economy, for they are massive advertisements of corporate power, not a response to social obligations.

This new society – a far cry from the one that the European modernists of the 1940s and 1950s had hoped to create – was responsible for the confusion of styles devised by egocentric and competitive architects. Individuality replaced groups and movements marching together towards the new dawn. Formalism, where shapes and styling came before function, resulted in what the architect and designer Max Bill described as 'a riot of anti-social waste'. For him, this concern with the decorative was opposed to the true spirit of architecture, 'the social art above all others'. The dream was destroyed; optimism and confidence disappeared with it. Architects had made many errors in their attempts at social engineering, errors exacerbated by the use of poor post-war materials. But there was excitement in the air.

(Many of Le Corbusier's buildings also suffered from his experiments with untried technology. If materials did not behave as he expected, he was undeterred by such details, for like the younger post-war architects he was attempting to build a better world. The conflict between the dreams and the reality of modernism – or any architecture – was nothing new. When the owners of a Lutyens house complained that the roof leaked onto their table, what should they do? Lutyens replied 'Move the table'.

Of course, Corb's buildings, like those of Lutyens, had poetry, even if they leaked.)

The Hochschule für Gestaltung at Ulm, Germany, was set up in 1953 with Max Bill as Director. It marked modernism's last real attempt to unite industrial design and genuine social reform. Bill's vision was of the artist-designer elevating design as a vehicle of culture, not commerce. While younger members of his staff, such as Tomas Maldonado, shared his belief in 'the needs of the people instead of the demands of luxury' – a belief advanced by Gropius's successor at the original Bauhaus, Hannes Meyer – they thought design should be scientifically based: ergonomics, product management and systems analysis, not art, would be its foundation. Bill resigned; Maldonado took over. The new approach resulted, for instance, in a collaboration with the electrical goods firm Braun, and also the corporate styling of Lufthansa. But the 'crisis of functionalism' in the late 1960s was an obstacle too many. The disbandment of the school in 1968 ended the last concerted attempt to rethink the role of design in society. With its demise, the fundamental de Stijl and Bauhaus precept – a common vocabulary and philosophy for all forms of design – has died with it.

After 1960 it becomes increasingly difficult to relate the now disparate, even contradictory, architectural scenes to book design. For the rectangular pages of books always keep a check on what goes on in them. (Well, almost always. Children's books in the shape of Rupert Bear, or pop-up books exploding in all directions, are not part of my story.) And while consumerism, and the huge number of books scrambling for attention in the market place, has challenged many long-cherished ideals in bookmaking, the result, in certain subject areas, is a new professionalism. Some of the design may be deliberately intended to catch the eye, but much of it holds to modernist principles. Even in architecture, these refuse to go away, and geometric certainties have seen off what Sigfried Giedion has called 'playboy architecture'. (We have had playboy book design, too.) The original modernist purity has sometimes been abandoned – not least by Corb himself enriching it with sculptural forms which often become brutal and overpowering when attempted by other architects. But it does seem to be a stayer. The Royal Festival Hall, completed in 1951 at the height of post-war English modernism, has what is still one of the most satisfying interiors in London. It is to be sensitively restored. The design of the numerous gallery or museum extensions carried out around the turn of the millennium, refuting such earlier follies as the tricksy exterior of the National Gallery's Sainsbury Wing, or the mannerism of the Tate's Clore Gallery, are designed in a straight-speaking modernism, quietly updated for the late twentieth century. Such public examples, and countless others throughout Britain and elsewhere, both in the field of architecture and in glassware, ceramics, industrial design for instance, or the reproduction of many classic furniture designs of the 1920s and 1930s (providing appropriate pieces for newly created modernist or minimalist interiors), do not suggest that modernism has had its day. Rather, its sound principles of logic, function, simplicity, the visual effect relying on clarity of form, not decoration or historicism; these seem to provide an answer to one of the twentieth century's dilemmas: how to establish a tradition which can develop without relying on historical styles.

Many hitherto unacceptably time-consuming or undesirable practices in bookmaking have been made possible by the new technology. This has encouraged designers to explore alternative approaches which challenge the earlier orthodoxies. Yet, at the same time, the rational principles based on analysis and function, evolved fifty years ago in Switzerland, have shown themselves capable of being developed in ways sympathetic to readers' needs, while remaining true to the logic and discipline of those idealistic innovators. But the spirit of hope, the utopian vision of design as a unified force embracing *all* its forms including architecture, and leading to a better society, a better world, has vanished – like a golden landscape at nightfall. As Alexander Herzen says in Stoppard's trilogy of plays *The Coast of Utopia*, we always want the story to end in universal bliss; but nobody's got the map.

The impact modernism had on book design is best demonstrated by first showing the decorative typography it opposed.

For 450 years the basic assumptions behind the appearance of books were rarely challenged. Slightly off-centre text (inner margins smaller than outer, top margins smaller than bottom), the frequent use of decorative borders, headbands, initials; a concern with pattern-making in headings displacing logic; little interest in analysing the particular requirements of the text; no attempt to assist the reader by typographically structuring this in order to clarify meaning: in these books, a general classical calm and serenity prevailed, only slightly disturbed in the late nineteenth century. Tradition ruled, originality (beyond subtle refinements of type design, encouraged by improved printing techniques) frowned upon. Any change was slow, barely perceptible at the time.

Early twentieth-century developments in printing (type set by machine, not by hand, improved presses, allowing faster and more even printing) did not of themselves demand a different approach to design. But society had changed. For those 450 years the printer himself had arranged the page. Now, poets, writers, architects, artists, from a background outside the printing industry, challenged the old ways. From the Futurists onwards, the feeling grew that a changed world, a new society, demanded new approaches which would radically affect the printed page, especially if it included illustrations. Writers or artists, especially those belonging to one of the all-embracing modernist movements such as de Stijl or constructivism, increasingly concerned themselves with print design. So a new profession evolved: the specialist *designer*, who, with a proper understanding of printing techniques, could provide a visual guide for the printer. The latter, with his technical knowledge, his skill and sensitivity in typesetting, continued to make a considerable contribution. But the overall appearance of books has never undergone such a radical rethink as that which developed over the twentieth century. The Futurists were to call the kinds of books shown in this section 'passéist'. But they also occasionally contain the seeds of modern book design, even if modernism itself is entirely absent.

Early Italian printers had often dispensed with any form of decoration. But from the first half of the sixteenth century until the mid-eighteenth, French printers (who had taken the lead from the Italians), while still working within the classical concept of a formal, often constrictive symmetry, were governed by a different tradition. They produced books which were primarily decorative, rather than a means of communication. Many of their ornaments or frills, and even illustrations, were re-used for quite different books, willy-nilly, with no attempt to create new designs pertinent to the new text. Any old headband or decorative initial would do: economies in production were important even then. Similarly, the mise-en-page of many books today derives not solely from an analysis of the material in order to present it coherently (which is what we tell the publisher). Aesthetic judgements in positioning are today's equivalent of those earlier decorations. 'It looks nicer that way' (which, after all, was the reason for those frills) is not a very convincing argument, especially if the publisher says 'I don't think so'. Yet for the modern designer, as for the early printers, it is the reason for doing more than is needed for simple communication.

Baskerville, that astonishing mid-eighteenth-century 'amateur', was the first printer since the early Italians to dispense with decoration almost entirely. Bodoni completed his revolution, bringing logic to the arrangement of headings. Baskerville had been content to let headings amble down the page; but the Italian grouped phrases by sense, using space and subtle changes of type size. In this he showed a more modern approach to design than did his French rivals the Didots, who had also been influenced by the simplicity of Baskerville's work.

After Baskerville and Bodoni, both of whom I would claim as harbingers of many twentieth-century ideals, there followed little development in book design for about twenty years. Indeed it slipped back slightly, for neither John Bell nor William Bulmer, great exploiters of the spacious layout, appreciated Bodoni's subtle heading designs. And by about 1850 standards generally had fallen dreadfully, as more books were produced for the popular market.

In the 1890s, books were being designed in the style known as art nouveau. This wide-ranging aesthetic attempted a harmonisation of art and artefacts, but its imitation of natural forms was a blind alley. Nonetheless, many books in this manner showed a refreshing originality of approach, and were especially notable for the freedom with which they used space. The contemporaneous and equally short-lived aesthetic movement (pursuing beauty for its own sake, with no moral or instructional overtones) showed a similar daring. Here, Whistler was famous – or notorious – for his bold, even startling layouts. In a decade or two, very different artist-designers, in France, Italy and Russia, and elsewhere, would create very different pages; but, like him, their means consisted solely of type and space.

Philippe de Commines: *Memoires*
Jean de Tournes, Lyons, 1559
Illustrated at 44% actual size

This attractive spread by one of the great sixteenth-century French printers shows many of the practices that modernist typographers deplored. Typographic pattern-making regardless of sense or function, with heading lines illogically broken; unleaded text in overlong lines; irrelevant and distracting decoration: Jan Tschichold was an eloquent critic of all this. De Tournes's spread is less perverse than many examples I could have shown, even by the same printer. Part of the tradition of the time, the long-continued use of such devices became a tiresome formula. Today, they are regarded as hindrances to what responsible designers consider the prime object of book design: communication.

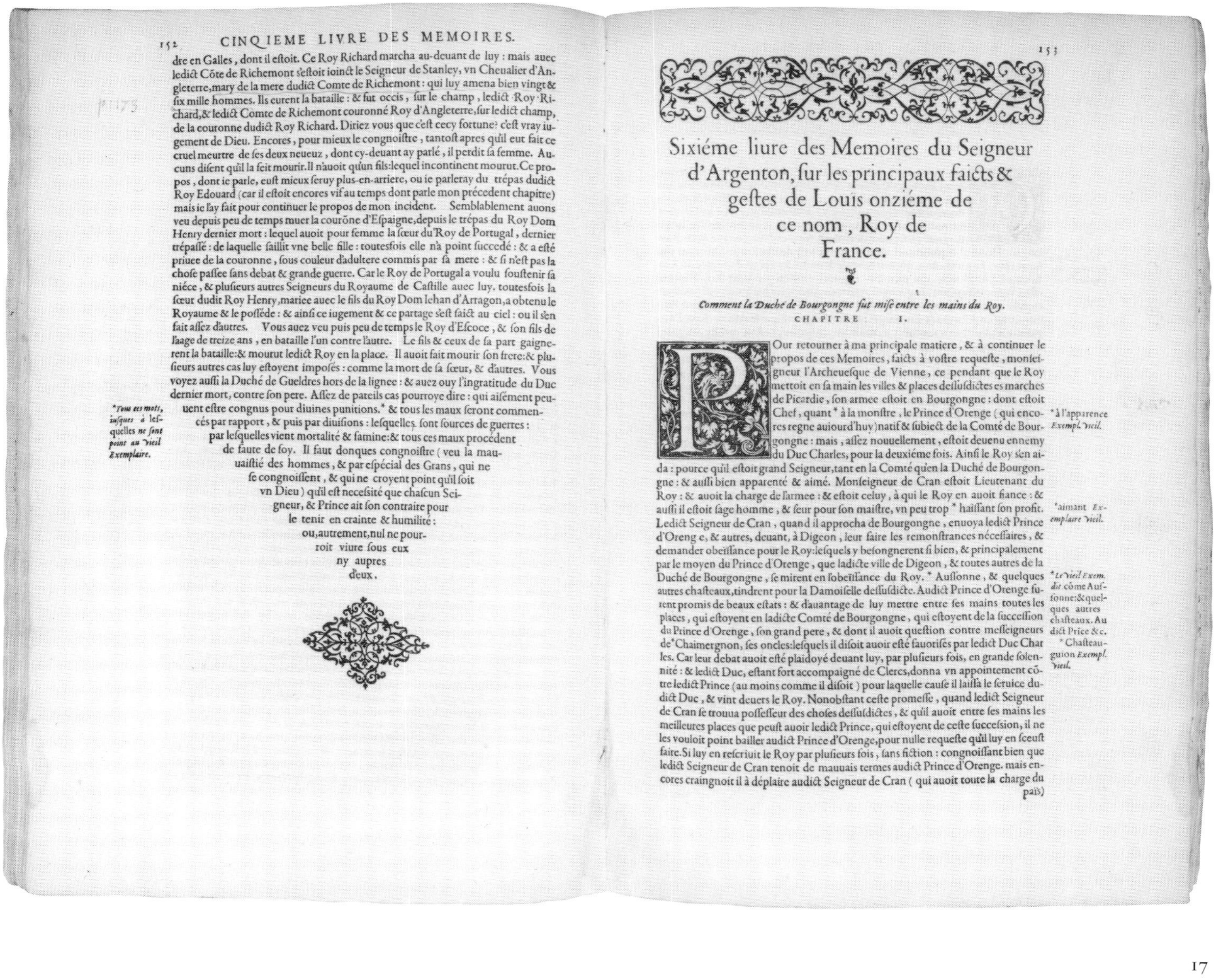

152 CINQUIEME LIVRE DES MEMOIRES.

dre en Galles, dont il estoit. Ce Roy Richard marcha au-deuant de luy : mais auec ledict Côte de Richemont s'estoit ioinct le Seigneur de Stanley, vn Cheualier d'Angleterre, mary de la mere dudict Comte de Richemont : qui luy amena bien vingt & six mille hommes. Ils eurent la bataille : & fut occis, sur le champ, ledict Roy Richard, & ledict Comte de Richemont couronné Roy d'Angleterre, sur ledict champ, de la couronne dudict Roy Richard. Diriez vous que c'est cecy fortune? c'est vray iugement de Dieu. Encores, pour mieux le congnoistre, tantost apres qu'il eut fait ce cruel meurtre de ses deux neueuz, dont cy-deuant ay parlé, il perdit sa femme. Aucuns disent qu'il la feit mourir. Il n'auoit qu'un fils: lequel incontinent mourut. Ce propos, dont ie parle, eust mieux seruy plus-en-arriere, ou ie parleray du trépas dudict Roy Edouard (car il estoit encores vif au temps dont parle mon précedent chapitre) mais ie l'ay fait pour continuer le propos de mon incident. Semblablement auons veu depuis peu de temps muer la courõne d'Espaigne, depuis le trépas du Roy Dom Henry dernier mort : lequel auoit pour femme la sœur du Roy de Portugal, dernier trépassé : de laquelle saillit vne belle fille : toutesfois elle n'a point succedé : & a esté priuee de la couronne, sous couleur d'adultere commis par sa mere : & si n'est pas la chose passee sans debat & grande guerre. Car le Roy de Portugal a voulu soustenir sa niéce, & plusieurs autres Seigneurs du Royaume de Castille auec luy. toutesfois la sœur dudit Roy Henry, mariee auec le fils du Roy Dom Iehan d'Arragon, a obtenu le Royaume & le possède : & ainsi ce iugement & ce partage s'est faict au ciel : ou il s'en fait assez d'autres. Vous auez veu puis peu de temps le Roy d'Escoce, & son fils de l'aage de treize ans, en bataille l'un contre l'autre. Le fils & ceux de sa part gaignerent la bataille: & mourut ledict Roy en la place. Il auoit fait mourir son frere: & plusieurs autres cas luy estoyent imposés : comme la mort de sa sœur, & d'autres. Vous voyez aussi la Duché de Gueldres hors de la lignee : & auez ouy l'ingratitude du Duc dernier mort, contre son pere. Assez de pareils cas pourroye dire : qui aisément peuuent estre congnus pour diuines punitions.* & tous les maux seront commencés par rapport, & puis par diuisions : lesquelles sont sources de guerres : par lesquelles vient mortalité & famine: & tous ces maux procédent de faute de foy. Il faut donques congnoistre (veu la mauaistié des hommes, & par espécial des Grans, qui ne se congnoissent, & qui ne croyent point qu'il soit vn Dieu) qu'il est necesité que chascun Seigneur, & Prince ait son contraire pour le tenir en crainte & humilité : ou, autrement, nul ne pourroit viure sous eux ny aupres d'eux.

Tous ces mots, iusques à lesquelles ne sont point au Vieil Exemplaire.

153

Sixiéme liure des Memoires du Seigneur d'Argenton, sur les principaux faicts & gestes de Louis onziéme de ce nom, Roy de France.

Comment la Duché de Bourgongne fut mise entre les mains du Roy.

CHAPITRE I.

POur retourner à ma principale matiere, & à continuer le propos de ces Memoires, faicts à vostre requeste, monseigneur l'Archeuesque de Vienne, ce pendant que le Roy mettoit en sa main les villes & places dessusdictes es marches de Picardie, son armee estoit en Bourgongne : dont estoit Chef, quant * à la monstre, le Prince d'Orenge (qui encores regne auiourd'huy) natif & subiect de la Comté de Bourgongne : mais, assez nouuellement, estoit deuenu ennemy du Duc Charles, pour la deuxiéme fois. Ainsi le Roy s'en aida : pource qu'il estoit grand Seigneur, tant en la Comté qu'en la Duché de Bourgongne : & aussi bien apparenté & aimé. Monseigneur de Cran estoit Lieutenant du Roy : & auoit la charge de l'armee : & estoit celuy, à qui le Roy en auoit fiance : & aussi il estoit sage homme, & seur pour son maistre, vn peu trop * haissant son profit. Ledict Seigneur de Cran, quand il approcha de Bourgongne, enuoya ledict Prince d'Oreng e, & autres, deuant, à Digeon, leur faire les remonstrances nécessaires, & demander obeïssance pour le Roy: lesquels y besongnerent si bien, & principalement par le moyen du Prince d'Orenge, que ladicte ville de Digeon, & toutes autres de la Duché de Bourgongne, se mirent en l'obeïssance du Roy. * Aussonne, & quelques autres chasteaux, tindrent pour la Damoiselle dessusdicte. Audict Prince d'Orenge furent promis de beaux estats : & d'auantage de luy mettre entre ses mains toutes les places, qui estoyent en ladicte Comté de Bourgongne, qui estoyent de la succession du Prince d'Orenge, son grand pere, & dont il auoit question contre messeigneurs de *Chaimergnon, ses oncles: lesquels il disoit auoir esté fauorisés par ledict Duc Charles. Car leur debat auoit esté plaidoyé deuant luy, par plusieurs fois, en grande solennité : & ledict Duc, estant fort accompaigné de Clercs, donna vn appointement cõtre ledict Prince (au moins comme il disoit) pour laquelle cause il laissa le seruice dudict Duc, & vint deuers le Roy. Nonobstant ceste promesse, quand ledict Seigneur de Cran se trouua possesseur des choses dessusdictes, & qu'il auoit entre ses mains les meilleures places que peust auoir ledict Prince, qui estoyent de ceste succesion, il ne les vouloit point bailler audict Prince d'Orenge, pour nulle requeste qu'il luy en sceust faire. Si luy en rescriuit le Roy par plusieurs fois, sans fiction : congnoissant bien que ledict Seigneur de Cran tenoit de mauuais termes audict Prince d'Orenge. mais encores craingnoit il à déplaire audict Seigneur de Cran (qui auoit toute la charge du païs)

*à l'apparence *Exempl. Vieil.*

*aimant *Exemplaire Vieil.*

**Le Vieil Exem. dit* cõme Aussonne: & quelques autres chasteaux. Audict Prĩce &c.

*Chasteauguion *Exempl. Vieil.*

Guillaume de la Perrière
Théâtre de Bons Engins
Denys Janot, Paris, 1539
Illustrated at 87% actual size

Less sophisticated than the previous example, although printed only twenty years before it, the irregularity of the type echoes the ingenuous woodcut decorations to create a happy unity. All-round borders, a hangover from manuscript books, were a favourite device of French printers until at least 1560. Although usually of smaller-scale patterns than these, they could be extremely distracting, crowding the text on all sides. Here, the effect is undeniably agreeable, with – unlike many examples, early or late – space on three sides of the text, allowing it, and the reader, to breathe.

Such a decorative approach is, of course, forbidden to modernists; and any attempt to imitate it would, in any case, fail, lacking conviction, continuity of traditional skills, or meaningful relationship to life today.

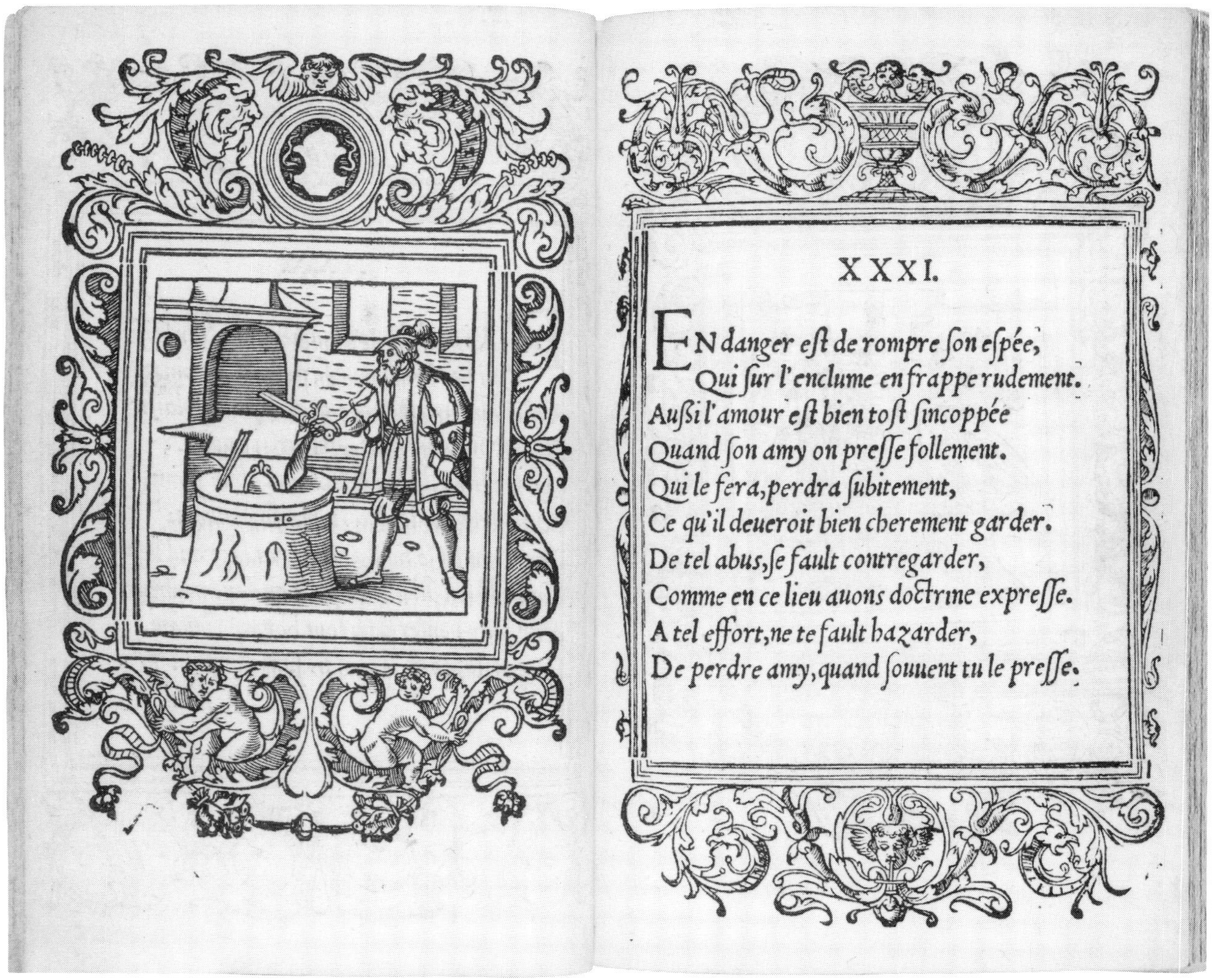

XXXI.

EN danger eſt de rompre ſon eſpée,
Qui ſur l'enclume en frappe rudement.
Auſsi l'amour eſt bien toſt ſincoppée
Quand ſon amy on preſſe follement.
Qui le fera, perdra ſubitement,
Ce qu'il deueroit bien cherement garder.
De tel abus, ſe fault contregarder,
Comme en ce lieu auons doctrine expreſſe.
A tel effort, ne te fault hazarder,
De perdre amy, quand ſouuent tu le preſſe.

Molière: *Oeuvres*
Pierre Pault, Paris, 1734
Illustrated at 47% actual size

While the illustration, from a design by François Boucher, gives a big boost to this spread, it has a hard time fighting off the busy clunking heading facing it. The printer seems to have a horror of space, continually changing type sizes and letterspacing to avoid it as far as possible. Yet he was happy to leave the OU of the second line dangling in mid-air. While the rule divides main heading from act details, neither have been well thought out, with relationships of phrases and words undifferentiated spatially. The unnecessarily large type not only detracts from the illustration, it hinders a more logical layout; the decorative initial adds to the confusion.

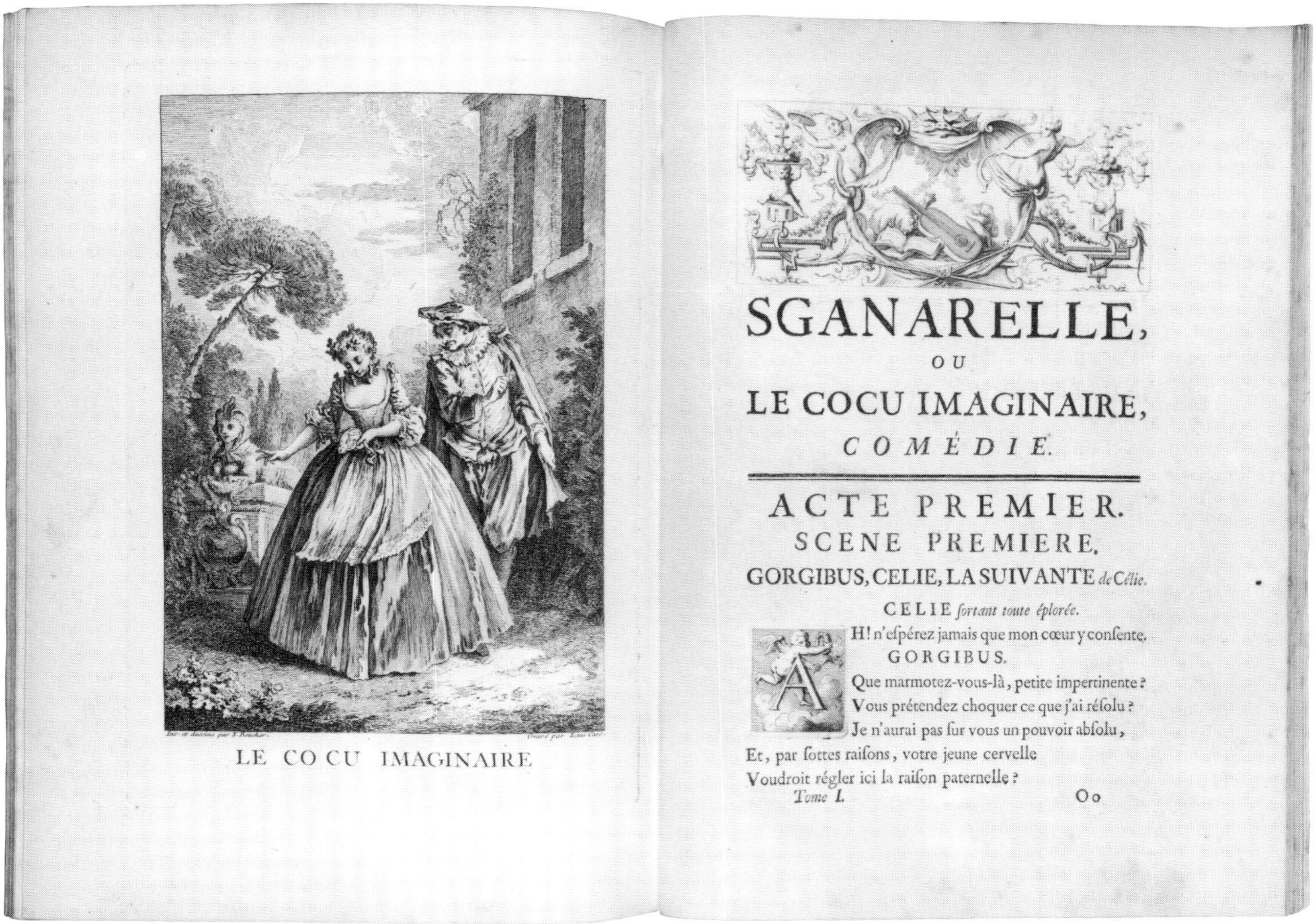
LE COCU IMAGINAIRE

SGANARELLE,
OU
LE COCU IMAGINAIRE,
COMÉDIE.

ACTE PREMIER.
SCENE PREMIERE.
GORGIBUS, CELIE, LA SUIVANTE *de Célie.*

CELIE *ſortant toute éplorée.*
AH! n'eſpérez jamais que mon cœur y conſente.
GORGIBUS.
Que marmotez-vous-là, petite impertinente?
Vous prétendez choquer ce que j'ai réſolu?
Je n'aurai pas ſur vous un pouvoir abſolu,
Et, par ſottes raiſons, votre jeune cervelle
Voudroit régler ici la raiſon paternelle?
Tome I. Oo

Joseph Addison: *Works*
John Baskerville, Birmingham, 1761
Illustrated at 54 and 43% actual size

Baskerville's first book, his *Virgil* of 1751, like many of his subsequent publications, has no decoration of any kind. This title page, perhaps one of his most elegant, uses rules carefully and functionally. The discreet triangulations of type are organised by sense, and the differing sizes needed to achieve the shape in the first group are logical.

There are unnecessary changes of type style or size within the lines, and, as so often in Baskerville's work, some overwide letter-spacing; yet, despite the design being spread more or less evenly down the page (or maybe because of this), the whole has a serene and airy unity. Baskerville's own sharply cut type adds to the distinction, and to the sense that we have entered a new world, where clarity and space – used one way or another – become conscious and essential ingredients.

That is also apparent in the spread opposite. Again the rule is functional, not merely decorative; there is a logical progression of type sizes from running head, scene number and characters' names, with italic of the same size to head their speeches. In its avoidance of anything to distract from the text, and its consideration for the reader, this is a foretaste of modernist principles in a classical format.

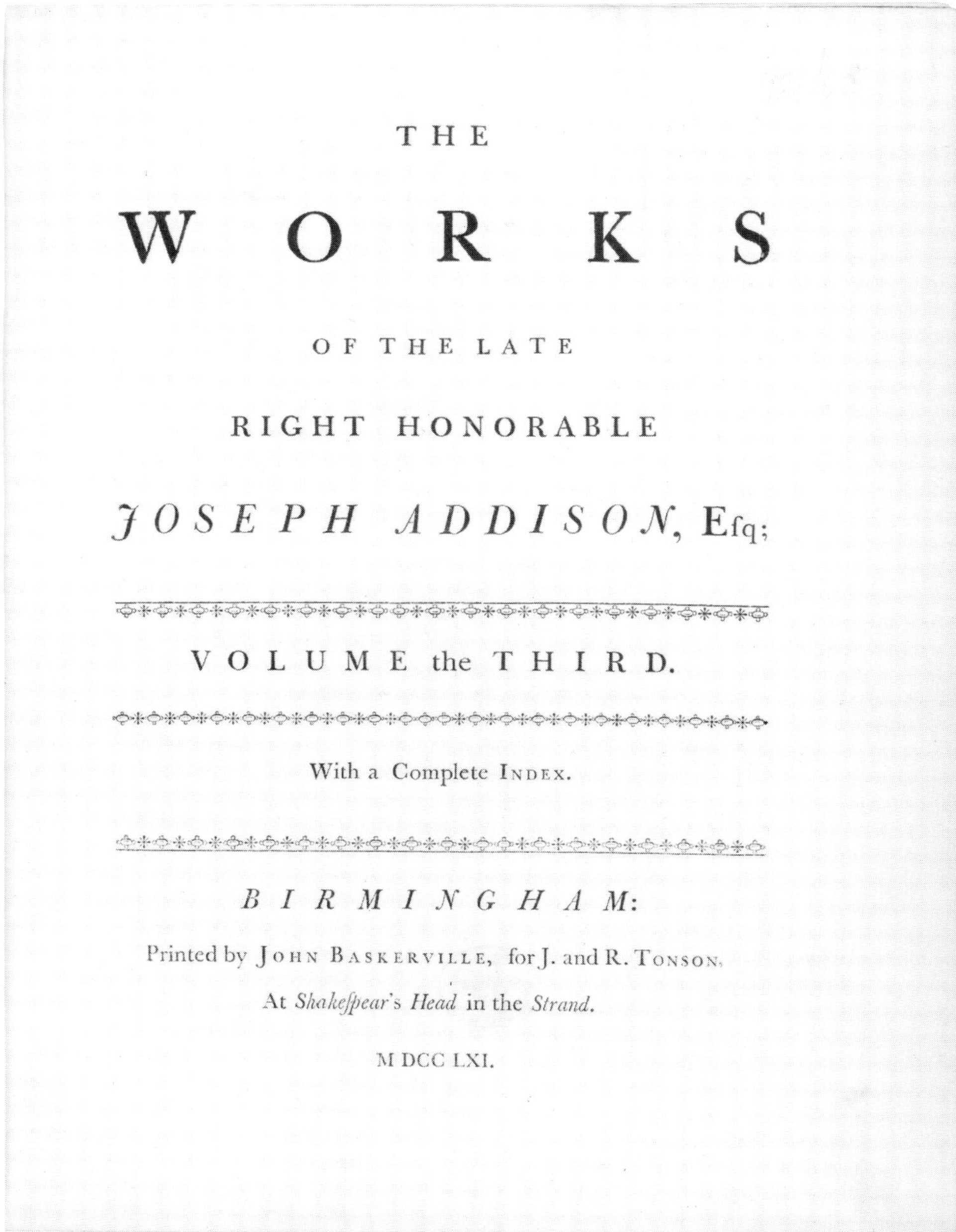

THE

WORKS

OF THE LATE

RIGHT HONORABLE

JOSEPH ADDISON, Efq;

VOLUME the THIRD.

With a Complete INDEX.

BIRMINGHAM:

Printed by JOHN BASKERVILLE, for J. and R. TONSON,
At *Shakefpear's Head* in the *Strand*.

M DCC LXI.

Thou might'ſt as well court the pale trembling Veſtal,
When ſhe beholds the holy flame expiring.

SEMPRONIUS.

The more I ſee the wonders of thy race,
The more I'm charm'd. Thou muſt take heed, my *Portius!*
The world has all its eyes on *Cato*'s ſon.
Thy father's merit ſets thee up to view,
And ſhews thee in the faireſt point of light,
To make thy virtues, or thy faults, conſpicuous.

PORTIUS.

Well doſt thou ſeem to check my ling'ring here
On this important hour — I'll ſtraight away,
And while the Fathers of the Senate meet
In cloſe debate to weigh th' events of war,
I'll animate the ſoldiers' drooping courage
With love of freedom, and contempt of life:
I'll thunder in their ears, their country's cauſe,
And try to rouſe up all that's *Roman* in 'em.
'Tis not in mortals to Command ſucceſs,
But we'll do more, *Sempronius;* we'll Deſerve it. [*Exit.*

SEMPRONIUS ſolus.

Curſe on the Stripling! how he apes his Sire!
Ambitiouſly ſententious! — but I wonder
Old *Syphax* comes not; his *Numidian* genius
Is well diſpoſed to miſchief, were he prompt
And eager on it; but he muſt be ſpurr'd,
And every moment quick'ned to the courſe.

—— *Cato*

— *Cato* has us'd me ill: he has refuſed
His daughter *Marcia* to my ardent vows.
Beſides, his baffled arms, and ruined cauſe,
Are bars to my ambition. *Cæſar*'s favor,
That ſhow'rs down greatneſs on his friends, will raiſe me
To *Rome*'s firſt honors. If I give up *Cato,*
I claim in my reward his captive daughter.
But *Syphax* comes! —

SCENE III.

SYPHAX, SEMPRONIUS.

SYPHAX.

— *Sempronius,* all is ready,
I've founded my *Numidians,* man by man,
And find 'em ripe for a revolt: they all
Complain aloud of *Cato*'s diſcipline,
And wait but the command to change their maſter.

SEMPRONIUS.

Believe me, *Syphax,* there's no time to waſte;
Even whilſt we ſpeak, our Conqueror comes on,
And gathers ground upon us every moment.
Alas! thou knoweſt not *Cæſar*'s active ſoul,
With what a dreadful courſe he ruſhes on
From war to war: in vain has nature form'd

Mountains

Aesop: *Fables*
John Baskerville, Birmingham, 1761
Illustrated at 82% actual size

This octavo volume shows all the care and skill that Baskerville lavished on his quartos. Again his own type creates a distinguished and readable page. His characteristic italic running heads are a little strong, although, in the interests of unity, he has made them the same size as the (overspaced) cap headings. (Why did he not also letterspace the roman numerals?) Myself, I would have made the fable *title* the important part of the heading and closed up the two lines a little, thereby increasing the space between the previous fable and the new heading. Well, such refinements had to wait for Bodoni to think things out more logically.

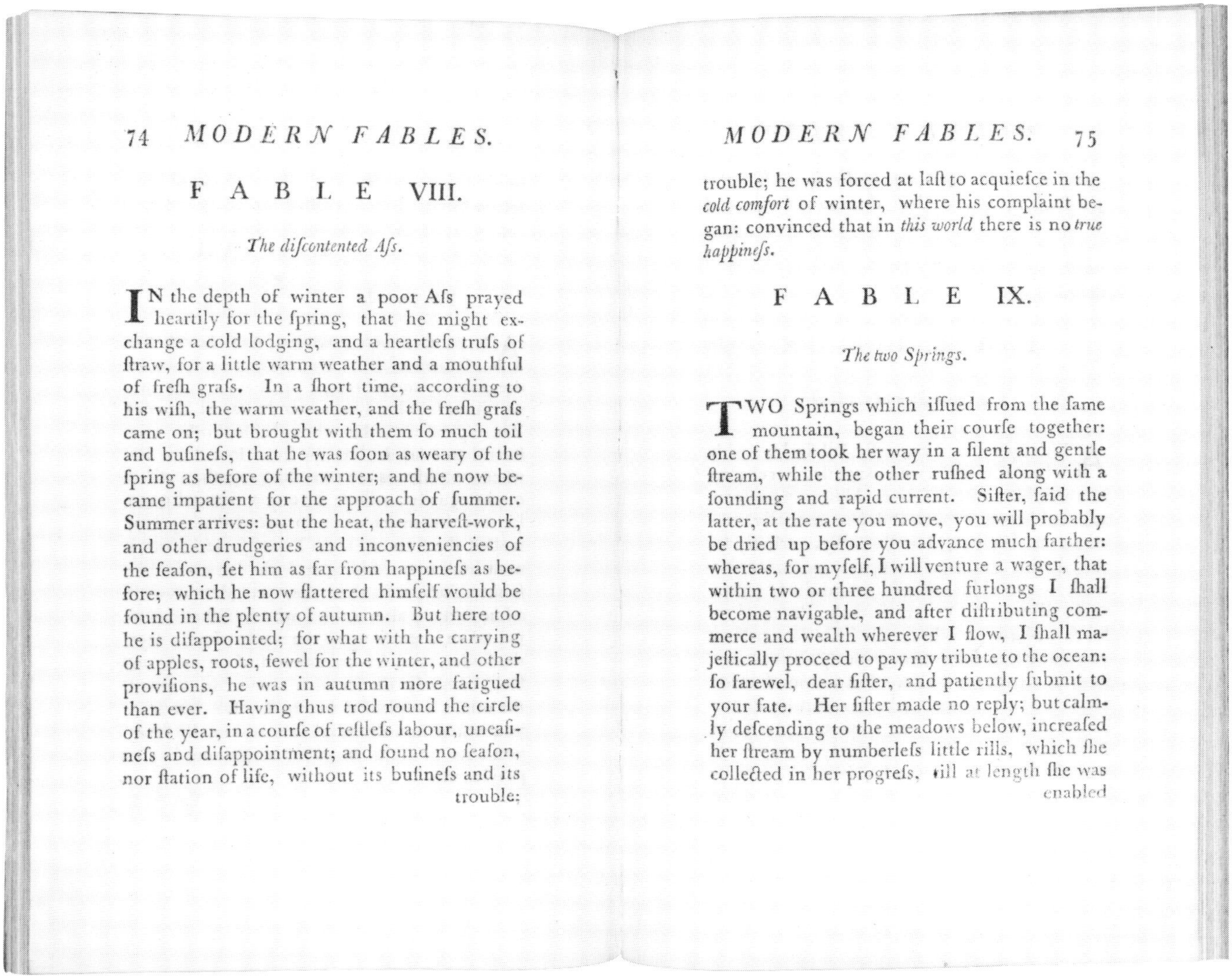

74 *MODERN FABLES.*

FABLE VIII.

The diſcontented Aſs.

IN the depth of winter a poor Aſs prayed heartily for the ſpring, that he might exchange a cold lodging, and a heartleſs truſs of ſtraw, for a little warm weather and a mouthful of freſh graſs. In a ſhort time, according to his wiſh, the warm weather, and the freſh graſs came on; but brought with them ſo much toil and buſineſs, that he was ſoon as weary of the ſpring as before of the winter; and he now became impatient for the approach of ſummer. Summer arrives: but the heat, the harveſt-work, and other drudgeries and inconveniencies of the ſeaſon, ſet him as far from happineſs as before; which he now flattered himſelf would be found in the plenty of autumn. But here too he is diſappointed; for what with the carrying of apples, roots, fewel for the winter, and other proviſions, he was in autumn more fatigued than ever. Having thus trod round the circle of the year, in a courſe of reſtleſs labour, uneaſineſs and diſappointment; and found no ſeaſon, nor ſtation of life, without its buſineſs and its trouble:

MODERN FABLES. 75

trouble; he was forced at laſt to acquieſce in the *cold comfort* of winter, where his complaint began: convinced that in *this world* there is no *true happineſs*.

FABLE IX.

The two Springs.

TWO Springs which iſſued from the ſame mountain, began their courſe together: one of them took her way in a ſilent and gentle ſtream, while the other ruſhed along with a ſounding and rapid current. Siſter, ſaid the latter, at the rate you move, you will probably be dried up before you advance much farther: whereas, for myſelf, I will venture a wager, that within two or three hundred furlongs I ſhall become navigable, and after diſtributing commerce and wealth wherever I flow, I ſhall majeſtically proceed to pay my tribute to the ocean: ſo farewel, dear ſiſter, and patiently ſubmit to your fate. Her ſiſter made no reply; but calmly deſcending to the meadows below, increaſed her ſtream by numberleſs little rills, which ſhe collected in her progreſs, till at length ſhe was enabled

Lodovico Ariosto: *Orlando Furioso*
John Baskerville, Birmingham, 1773
Illustrated at 64% actual size

Baskerville frequently published his classics in two sizes, quarto and octavo, the latter achieved by reducing margins. All type remained exactly the same. This octavo edition might be compared with the Molière opening on page 19. Its illustration, by Charles Eisen, is old-fashioned, unsympathetic to Baskerville's new ways, and compares badly with Boucher's gentle poetry. But the headings are more spacious, restrained and logical than those in the Molière. Bringing LUDOVICO ARIOSTO up to the level of DI and combining them in one line (thereby creating more space beneath) would further improve things. This, of course, would be in a different and more modern idiom than the one in which Baskerville worked.

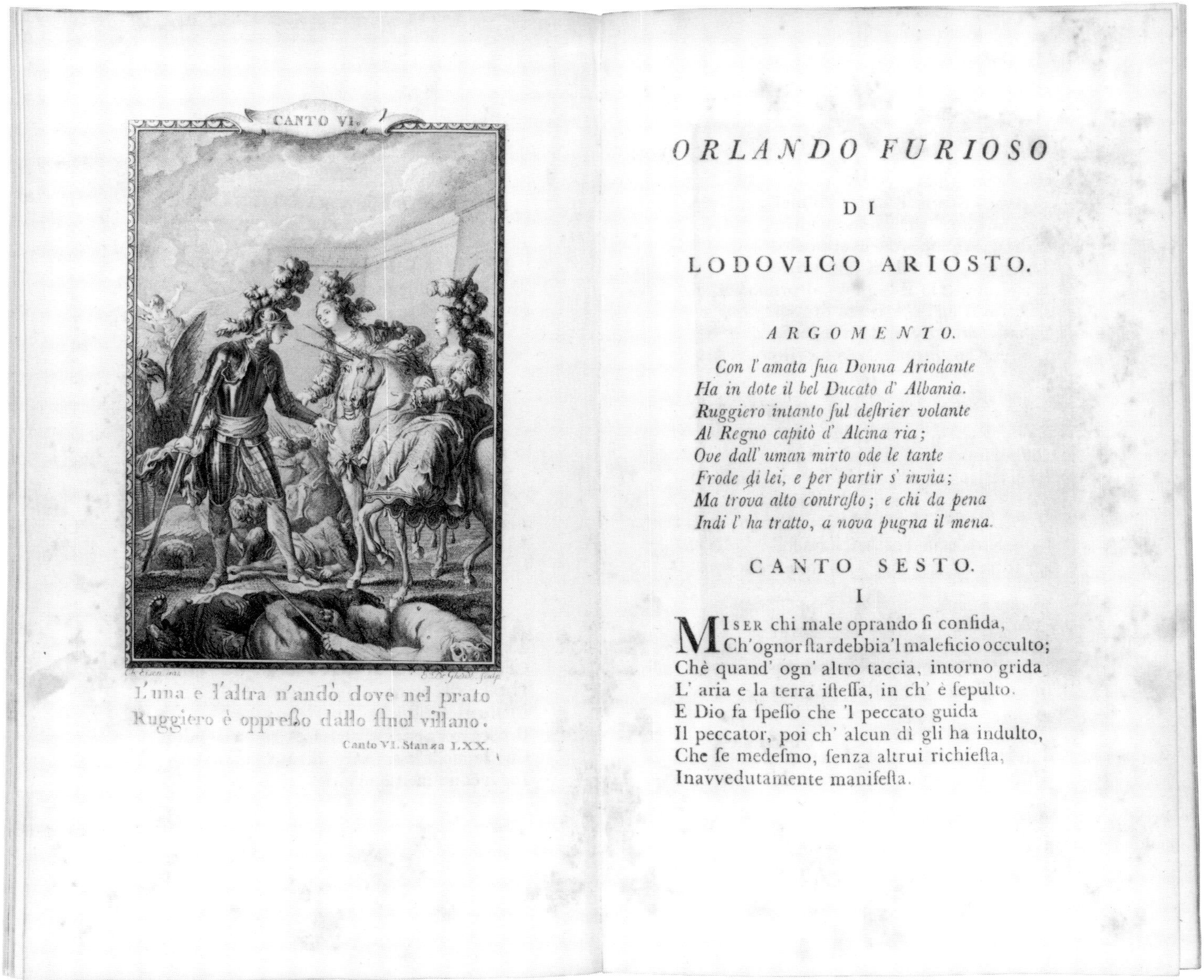

CANTO VI.

L'una e l'altra n'andò dove nel prato
Ruggiero è oppreſſo dallo ſtuol villano.

Canto VI. Stanza LXX.

ORLANDO FURIOSO

DI

LODOVICO ARIOSTO.

ARGOMENTO.

Con l' amata ſua Donna Ariodante
Ha in dote il bel Ducato d' Albania.
Ruggiero intanto ſul deſtrier volante
Al Regno capitò d' Alcina ria;
Ove dall' uman mirto ode le tante
Frode di lei, e per partir s' invia;
Ma trova alto contraſto; e chi da pena
Indi l' ha tratto, a nova pugna il mena.

CANTO SESTO.

I

MISER chi male oprando ſi confida,
Ch' ognor ſtar debbia 'l maleficio occulto;
Chè quand' ogn' altro taccia, intorno grida
L' aria e la terra iſteſſa, in ch' è ſepulto.
E Dio fa ſpeſſo che 'l peccato guida
Il peccator, poi ch' alcun dì gli ha indulto,
Che ſe medeſmo, ſenza altrui richieſta,
Inavvedutamente maniſeſta.

W Jackson: *The Beauties of Nature*
John Baskerville, Birmingham, 1769
Illustrated at 81% actual size

This simple little book follows Baskerville's usual pattern, although his characteristic running heads are absent. The bracketed folios might have been less distracting placed below the text. Like the even smaller book opposite, it was privately printed for the author. Was Baskerville's heart *quite* in either of them? The headings here have inconsistent spacing around them, that on the recto looking a little cramped. (Strict uniformity never seemed a serious concern with this printer, even in his carefully produced *Virgil*.) The presswork, too, is a little uneven. The typical dropped caps give colour to the page, perhaps too much for this small format, although they are only two lines deep, as was Baskerville's standard practice, so could hardly be smaller.

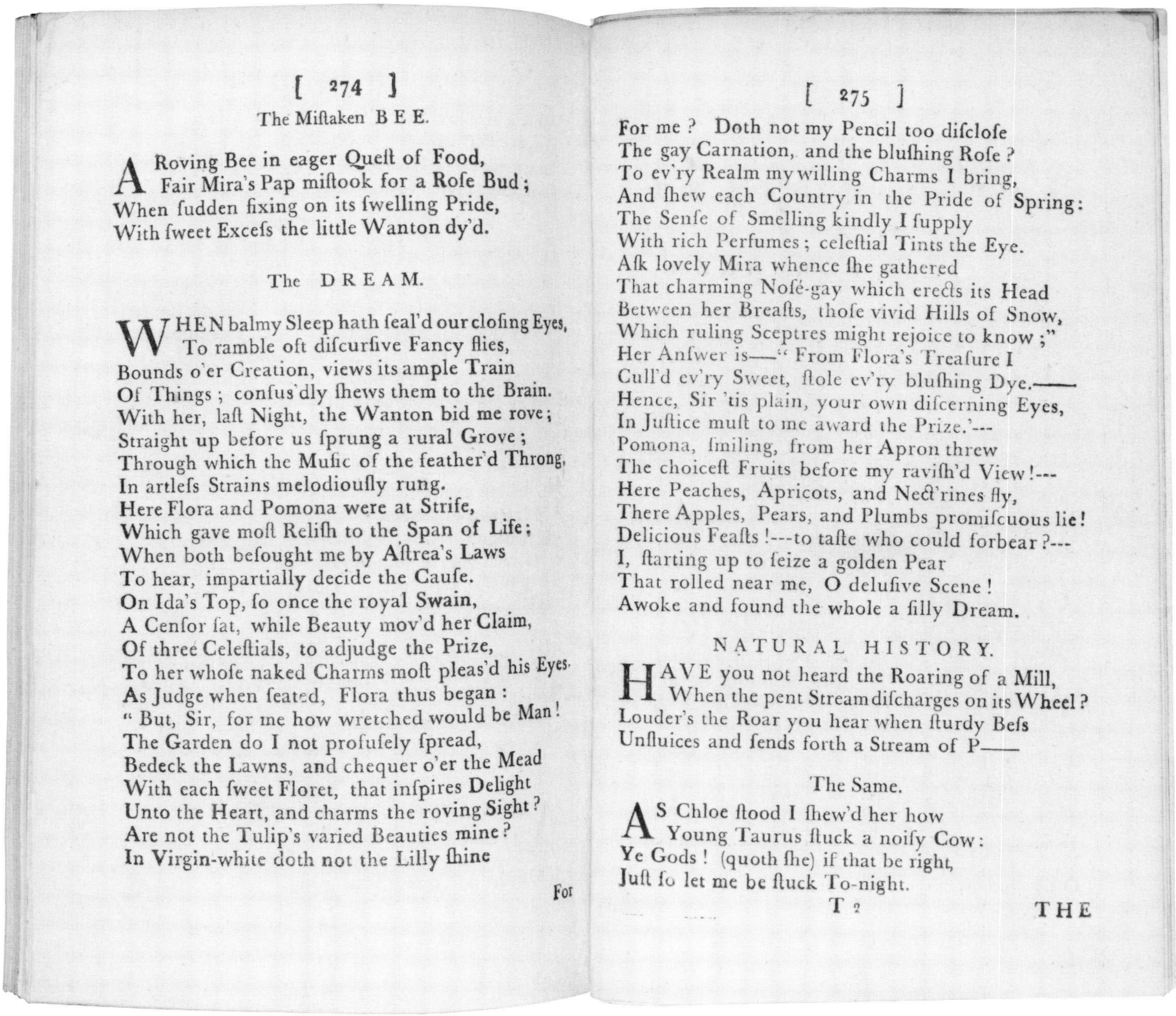

[274]

The Miſtaken BEE.

A Roving Bee in eager Queſt of Food,
Fair Mira's Pap miſtook for a Roſe Bud;
When ſudden fixing on its ſwelling Pride,
With ſweet Exceſs the little Wanton dy'd.

The DREAM.

WHEN balmy Sleep hath ſeal'd our cloſing Eyes,
To ramble oft diſcurſive Fancy flies,
Bounds o'er Creation, views its ample Train
Of Things; confus'dly ſhews them to the Brain.
With her, laſt Night, the Wanton bid me rove;
Straight up before us ſprung a rural Grove;
Through which the Muſic of the feather'd Throng,
In artleſs Strains melodiouſly rung.
Here Flora and Pomona were at Strife,
Which gave moſt Reliſh to the Span of Life;
When both beſought me by Aſtrea's Laws
To hear, impartially decide the Cauſe.
On Ida's Top, ſo once the royal Swain,
A Cenſor ſat, while Beauty mov'd her Claim,
Of three Celeſtials, to adjudge the Prize,
To her whoſe naked Charms moſt pleas'd his Eyes.
As Judge when ſeated, Flora thus began:
" But, Sir, for me how wretched would be Man!
The Garden do I not profuſely ſpread,
Bedeck the Lawns, and chequer o'er the Mead
With each ſweet Floret, that inſpires Delight
Unto the Heart, and charms the roving Sight?
Are not the Tulip's varied Beauties mine?
In Virgin-white doth not the Lilly ſhine

For

[275]

For me? Doth not my Pencil too diſcloſe
The gay Carnation, and the bluſhing Roſe?
To ev'ry Realm my willing Charms I bring,
And ſhew each Country in the Pride of Spring:
The Senſe of Smelling kindly I ſupply
With rich Perfumes; celeſtial Tints the Eye.
Aſk lovely Mira whence ſhe gathered
That charming Noſé-gay which erects its Head
Between her Breaſts, thoſe vivid Hills of Snow,
Which ruling Sceptres might rejoice to know;"
Her Anſwer is—" From Flora's Treaſure I
Cull'd ev'ry Sweet, ſtole ev'ry bluſhing Dye.——
Hence, Sir 'tis plain, your own diſcerning Eyes,
In Juſtice muſt to me award the Prize.'---
Pomona, ſmiling, from her Apron threw
The choiceſt Fruits before my raviſh'd View!---
Here Peaches, Apricots, and Nect'rines fly,
There Apples, Pears, and Plumbs promiſcuous lie!
Delicious Feaſts!---to taſte who could forbear?---
I, ſtarting up to ſeize a golden Pear
That rolled near me, O deluſive Scene!
Awoke and found the whole a ſilly Dream.

NATURAL HISTORY.

HAVE you not heard the Roaring of a Mill,
When the pent Stream diſcharges on its Wheel?
Louder's the Roar you hear when ſturdy Beſs
Unſluices and ſends forth a Stream of P——

The Same.

AS Chloe ſtood I ſhew'd her how
Young Taurus ſtuck a noiſy Cow:
Ye Gods! (quoth ſhe) if that be right,
Juſt ſo let me be ſtuck To-night.

T 2 THE

Charles Bowlker: *The Art of Angling*
John Baskerville, Birmingham, 1774
Illustrated at 89% actual size

This late book – Baskerville died the following year, aged 69 – is, by modern standards, unnecessarily complicated. The rules are a touch obtrusive, aggravating the problem of an already chopped-up text. It might have been wiser, also, to omit those dropped initials – for once. (Like the French printers, Baskerville, too, had his formulas.) A twentieth-century designer – say, Hans Schmoller – would have sorted all this out far more simply, as a glance at Pevsner's *Buildings of England* will show. Schmoller designed that series within the classical tradition, shunning the use of bolds. They, and other modernist devices, facilitate the presentation of information, which, essentially, is what was required here.

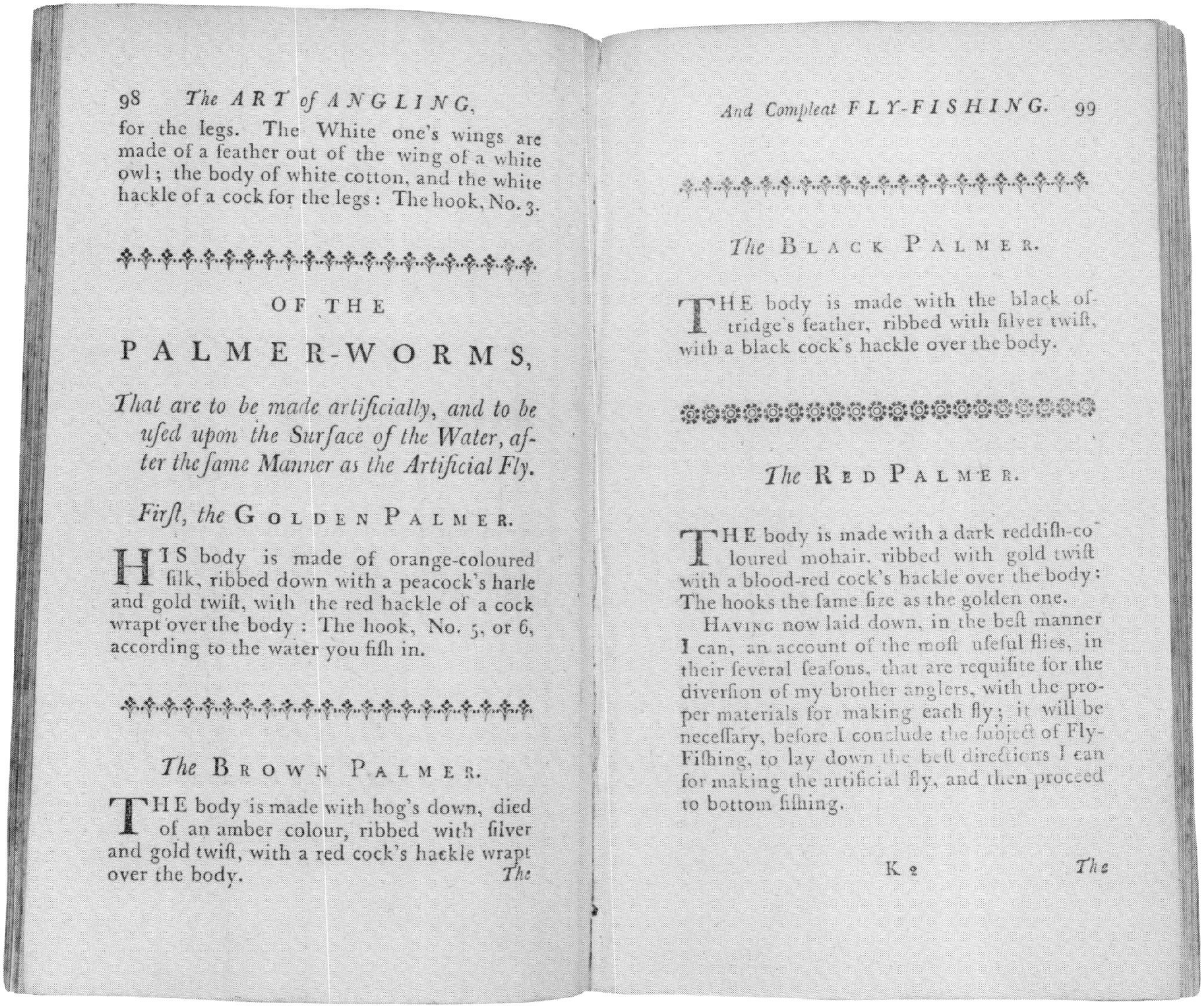

98 *The* ART *of* ANGLING,

for the legs. The White one's wings are made of a feather out of the wing of a white owl; the body of white cotton, and the white hackle of a cock for the legs: The hook, No. 3.

OF THE

PALMER-WORMS,

That are to be made artificially, and to be uſed upon the Surface of the Water, after the ſame Manner as the Artificial Fly.

Firſt, the GOLDEN PALMER.

HIS body is made of orange-coloured ſilk, ribbed down with a peacock's harle and gold twiſt, with the red hackle of a cock wrapt over the body: The hook, No. 5, or 6, according to the water you fiſh in.

The BROWN PALMER.

THE body is made with hog's down, died of an amber colour, ribbed with ſilver and gold twiſt, with a red cock's hackle wrapt over the body. *The*

And Compleat FLY-FISHING. 99

The BLACK PALMER.

THE body is made with the black oſtridge's feather, ribbed with ſilver twiſt, with a black cock's hackle over the body.

The RED PALMER.

THE body is made with a dark reddiſh-coloured mohair, ribbed with gold twiſt with a blood-red cock's hackle over the body: The hooks the ſame ſize as the golden one.

HAVING now laid down, in the beſt manner I can, an account of the moſt uſeful flies, in their ſeveral ſeaſons, that are requiſite for the diverſion of my brother anglers, with the proper materials for making each fly; it will be neceſſary, before I conclude the ſubject of Fly-Fiſhing, to lay down the beſt directions I can for making the artificial fly, and then proceed to bottom fiſhing.

K 2 *The*

Tasso: *Aminta Favola Boschereccia*
Giambattista Bodoni, Parma, 1789
Illustrated at 59 and 48% actual size

Bodoni's grander books, such as this, frequently had elaborate dedications, often in italic caps. This one is distinguished by the use of caps in italic script. These caps reappear in the act and scene headings of the book itself (opposite). Despite the overall decorative effect, the design shows Bodoni's characteristic disdain for rules or ornaments. Almost anyone else would have put some device between the EC.EC. and his name.

Bodoni quickly absorbed the significance of Baskerville's new typography, and it profoundly affected his work. In the spread opposite, the beauty of his own sharply-cut type is enhanced by the careful and well-leaded setting, the simple layout, good margins and excellent printing. The effect is one of airy grandeur, with a delicate balance between text and space.

For the heading, Bodoni allowed himself the use of two rules, plus the decorative caps used in the dedication page. Yet the rules are used functionally, both to assist the sense and to strengthen the layout. But it was to be a few years before Bodoni realised that speakers' names would be better related to their speech if a little more space was inserted above them – as, six years later, he was to do in the Dante shown on page 29.

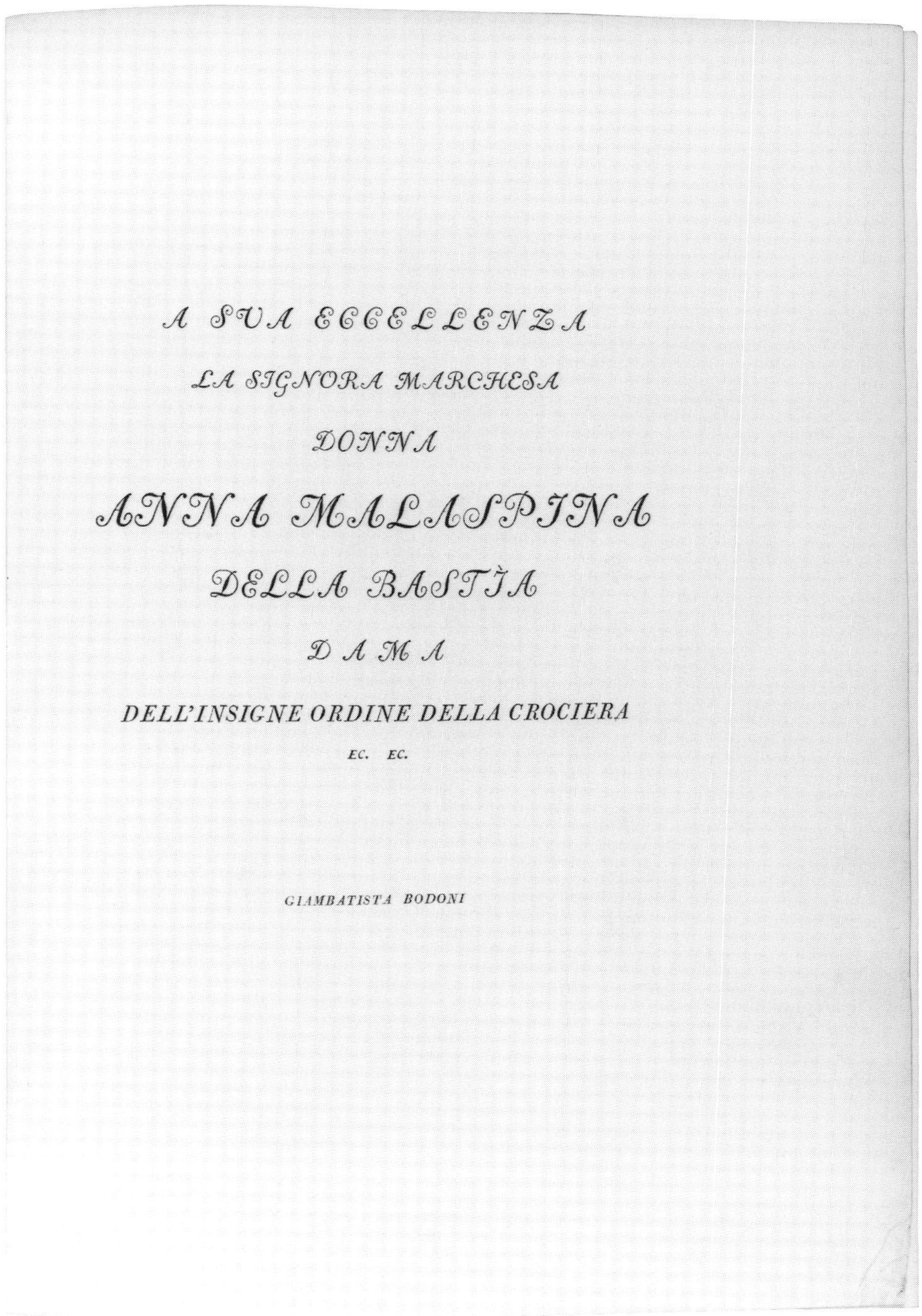
A SUA ECCELLENZA
LA SIGNORA MARCHESA
DONNA
ANNA MALASPINA
DELLA BASTÌA
DAMA
DELL'INSIGNE ORDINE DELLA CROCIERA
EC. EC.

GIAMBATISTA BODONI

TIRSI

Dio faccia, ch'ei non sia tra questi rari.

CORO

Non sarà, no.

TIRSI

Io voglio irmene all'antro
Del saggio Elpino: ivi, s'è vivo, forse
Sarà ridotto, ove sovente suole
Raddolcir gli amarissimi martiri
Al dolce suon della sampogna chiara,
Ch'ad udir trae dagli alti monti i sassi,
E correr fa di puro latte i fiumi,
E stillar mele dalle dure scorze.

SCENA II

AMINTA, DAFNE, NERINA.

AMINTA

Dispietata pietate
Fu la tua veramente, o Dafne, allora
Che ritenesti il dardo;
Però che 'l mio morire
Più amaro sarà, quanto più tardo.
Ed or perchè m'avvolgi
Per sì diverse strade, e per sì varj
Ragionamenti invano? Di che temi?
Ch'io non m'uccida? Temi del mio bene.

DAFNE

Non disperar, Aminta,
Chè io lei ben conosco;
Sola vergogna fu, non crudeltate,
Quella che mosse Silvia a fuggir via.

Anacreon: *L'Odi di Anacronte*
Giambattista Bodoni, Parma, 1793
Illustrated at 81% actual size

This attractive little book shows Bodoni in a more feminine mood, as befits the subject, a celebration of love. It is distinguished not merely by its delicate type placed within generous margins. The heading is subtly treated, the title (damn that full point) is slightly bolder than ODE (although the same size) and carefully positioned. Space is as important here as, in different ways, it is in modernist work. The folios in their decorative boxes (one of many that Bodoni held, always sparingly used) play a surprisingly important part in the overall effect of these otherwise purist pages. That tiny rule at the end of the verse is worthy of Tschichold.

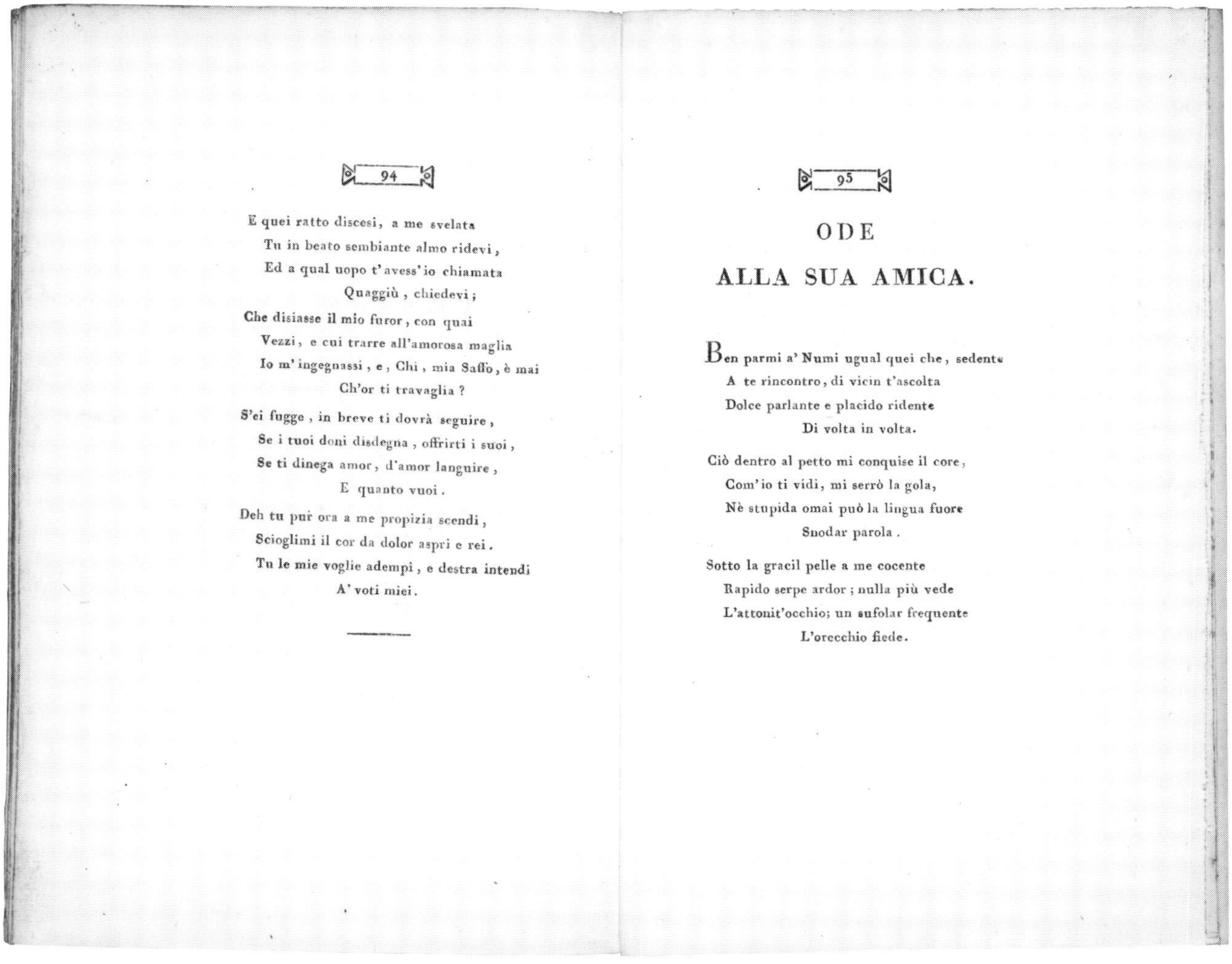

94

E quei ratto discesi, a me svelata
Tu in beato sembiante almo ridevi,
Ed a qual uopo t'avess' io chiamata
Quaggiù, chiedevi;

Che disiasse il mio furor, con quai
Vezzi, e cui trarre all'amorosa maglia
Io m' ingegnassi, e, Chi, mia Saffo, è mai
Ch'or ti travaglia?

S'ei fugge, in breve ti dovrà seguire,
Se i tuoi doni disdegna, offrirti i suoi,
Se ti dinega amor, d'amor languire,
E quanto vuoi.

Deh tu pur ora a me propizia scendi,
Scioglimi il cor da dolor aspri e rei.
Tu le mie voglie adempi, e destra intendi
A' voti miei.

95

ODE

ALLA SUA AMICA.

Ben parmi a' Numi ugual quei che, sedente
A te rincontro, di vicin t'ascolta
Dolce parlante e placido ridente
Di volta in volta.

Ciò dentro al petto mi conquise il core,
Com' io ti vidi, mi serrò la gola,
Nè stupida omai può la lingua fuore
Snodar parola.

Sotto la gracil pelle a me cocente
Rapido serpe ardor; nulla più vede
L'attonit'occhio; un sufolar frequente
L'orecchio fiede.

Dante: *La Divina Commedia*
Giambattista Bodoni, Parma, 1795
Illustrated at 35% actual size

Bodoni, having looked carefully at Baskerville's work, came to realise that it still had shortcomings in need of correction. Chief of these was the treatment of headings. Acknowledging their relative importance, and taking a more sophisticated approach to their positioning, were key elements of the solution. In this spread, carefully letterspaced caps create running heads which are clearly that, with a half-line space separating them from the text; canto numbers are a little larger, in italic caps, and – crucially – with more space above than below, so that they relate to the relevant text rather than dangling in mid-air. It is such subtleties that distinguish the really great typographers. Tschichold knew this too.

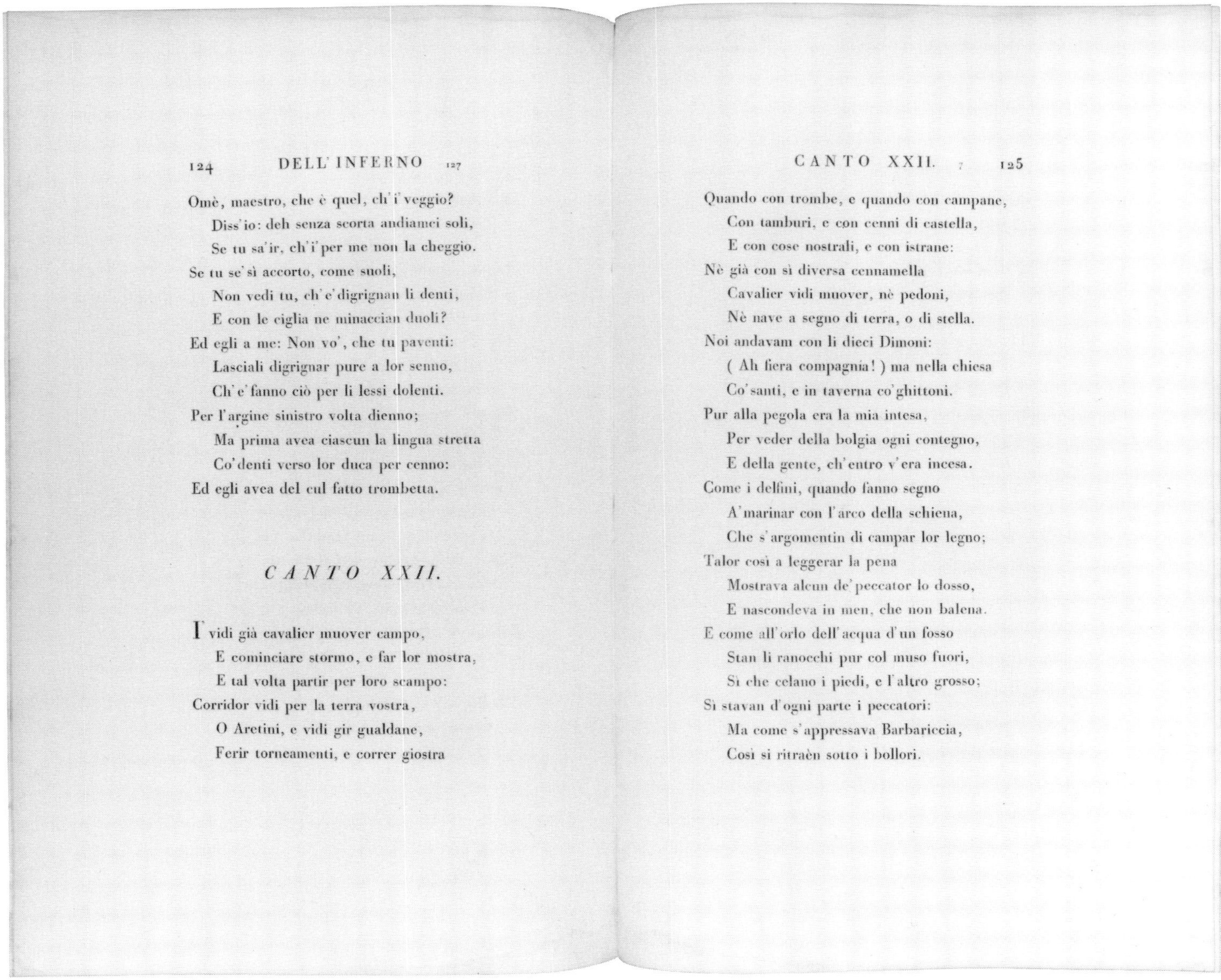

124 DELL' INFERNO 127

Omè, maestro, che è quel, ch' i' veggio?
Diss' io: deh senza scorta andiamci soli,
Se tu sa' ir, ch' i' per me non la cheggio.
Se tu se' sì accorto, come suoli,
Non vedi tu, ch' e' digrignan li denti,
E con le ciglia ne minaccian duoli?
Ed egli a me: Non vo', che tu paventi:
Lasciali digrignar pure a lor senno,
Ch' e' fanno ciò per li lessi dolenti.
Per l' argine sinistro volta dienno;
Ma prima avea ciascun la lingua stretta
Co' denti verso lor duca per cenno:
Ed egli avea del cul fatto trombetta.

CANTO XXII.

I vidi già cavalier muover campo,
E cominciare stormo, e far lor mostra,
E tal volta partir per loro scampo:
Corridor vidi per la terra vostra,
O Aretini, e vidi gir gualdane,
Ferir torneamenti, e correr giostra

CANTO XXII. 7 125

Quando con trombe, e quando con campane,
Con tamburi, e con cenni di castella,
E con cose nostrali, e con istrane:
Nè già con sì diversa cennamella
Cavalier vidi muover, nè pedoni,
Nè nave a segno di terra, o di stella.
Noi andavam con li dieci Dimoni:
(Ah fiera compagnia!) ma nella chiesa
Co' santi, e in taverna co' ghittoni.
Pur alla pegola era la mia intesa,
Per veder della bolgia ogni contegno,
E della gente, ch' entro v' era incesa.
Come i delfini, quando fanno segno
A' marinar con l' arco della schiena,
Che s' argomentin di campar lor legno;
Talor così a leggerar la pena
Mostrava alcun de' peccator lo dosso,
E nascondeva in men, che non balena.
E come all' orlo dell' acqua d' un fosso
Stan li ranocchi pur col muso fuori,
Sì che celano i piedi, e l' altro grosso;
Sì stavan d' ogni parte i peccatori:
Ma come s' appressava Barbariccia,
Così si ritraèn sotto i bollori.

Longus: *Daphnis and Chloe*
Vale Press, London, 1893
Printed by Ballantyne Press
London and Edinburgh
Designed by Charles Ricketts
Illustrated at 45% actual size

Dismayed by the decline of standards which had occurred over the previous fifty years, William Morris and the private presses set about reviving an interest in good printing and book design; but the results were often questionable, heavy with nostalgia and denying the industrialisation of the printing industry. Here, Aldus Manutius's *Hypnerotomachia Poliphili* of 1499 is the obvious model, even if the actual result is a mere echo of that wonderful book. Viewed on its own merit, spacious margins mitigate the density of the text. The illustrations and decorations, by Charles Ricketts and Charles Shannon, are an eclectic mix of art nouveau, renaissance pastiche and William Morris/Burne-Jones. Reflecting Morris's influence, these pages, overseen by a designer, are a considerable improvement on the earlier, effete Victorian productions; but they come as a bit of a shock after looking at Bodoni's work of a century earlier, despite the equally generous margins.

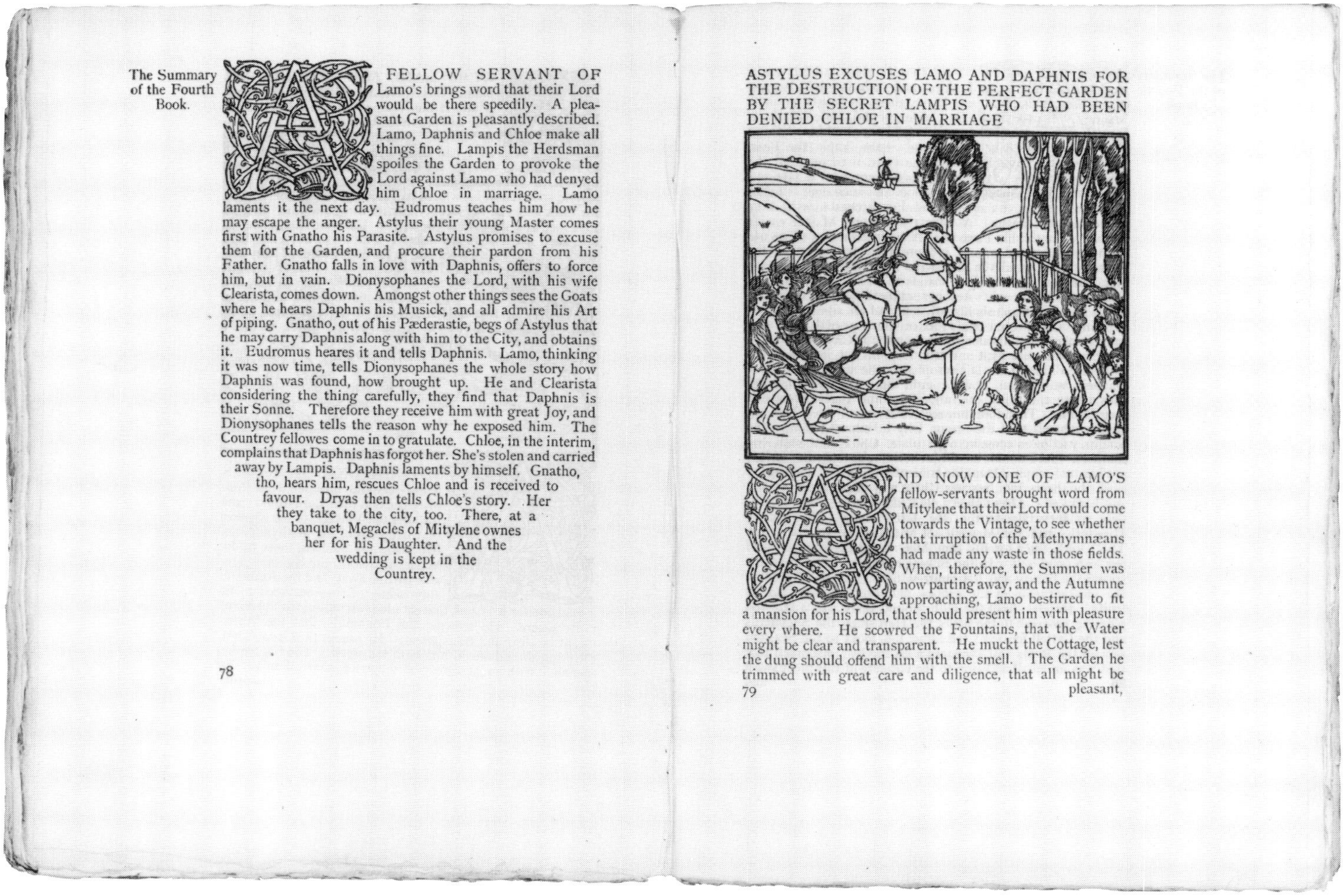

The Summary of the Fourth Book.

A FELLOW SERVANT OF Lamo's brings word that their Lord would be there speedily. A pleasant Garden is pleasantly described. Lamo, Daphnis and Chloe make all things fine. Lampis the Herdsman spoiles the Garden to provoke the Lord against Lamo who had denyed him Chloe in marriage. Lamo laments it the next day. Eudromus teaches him how he may escape the anger. Astylus their young Master comes first with Gnatho his Parasite. Astylus promises to excuse them for the Garden, and procure their pardon from his Father. Gnatho falls in love with Daphnis, offers to force him, but in vain. Dionysophanes the Lord, with his wife Clearista, comes down. Amongst other things sees the Goats where he hears Daphnis his Musick, and all admire his Art of piping. Gnatho, out of his Pæderastie, begs of Astylus that he may carry Daphnis along with him to the City, and obtains it. Eudromus heares it and tells Daphnis. Lamo, thinking it was now time, tells Dionysophanes the whole story how Daphnis was found, how brought up. He and Clearista considering the thing carefully, they find that Daphnis is their Sonne. Therefore they receive him with great Joy, and Dionysophanes tells the reason why he exposed him. The Countrey fellowes come in to gratulate. Chloe, in the interim, complains that Daphnis has forgot her. She's stolen and carried away by Lampis. Daphnis laments by himself. Gnatho, tho, hears him, rescues Chloe and is received to favour. Dryas then tells Chloe's story. Her they take to the city, too. There, at a banquet, Megacles of Mitylene ownes her for his Daughter. And the wedding is kept in the Countrey.

78

ASTYLUS EXCUSES LAMO AND DAPHNIS FOR THE DESTRUCTION OF THE PERFECT GARDEN BY THE SECRET LAMPIS WHO HAD BEEN DENIED CHLOE IN MARRIAGE

AND NOW ONE OF LAMO'S fellow-servants brought word from Mitylene that their Lord would come towards the Vintage, to see whether that irruption of the Methymnæans had made any waste in those fields. When, therefore, the Summer was now parting away, and the Autumne approaching, Lamo bestirred to fit a mansion for his Lord, that should present him with pleasure every where. He scowred the Fountains, that the Water might be clear and transparent. He muckt the Cottage, lest the dung should offend him with the smell. The Garden he trimmed with great care and diligence, that all might be pleasant,

79

Thomas Malory: *Le Morte d'Arthur*
J M Dent, London, 1893
Printed by Turnbull and Spears, Edinburgh
Illustrated at 52% actual size

The decorations of this book, developed from William Morris's work, almost parodying it (he was not amused) were by Aubrey Beardsley. They depict art nouveau mannerisms at their most heady and distracting. The use of black letter for chapter headings – although one appreciates its relevance to the subject – is disconcerting as a companion to those over-poweringly unmedieval borders. Timeless they are not: today they probably look even less medieval, more fin-de-siècle, than they did when they were created. Disparity between illustration style and the 'antique' text; poor relationship between parts; the way decoration takes precedence over consideration for the reader; despite all the good intentions of illustrator and publisher, such failings, characteristic of the period, and the style, are sadly retrogressive – no matter how attractive some may find those borders.

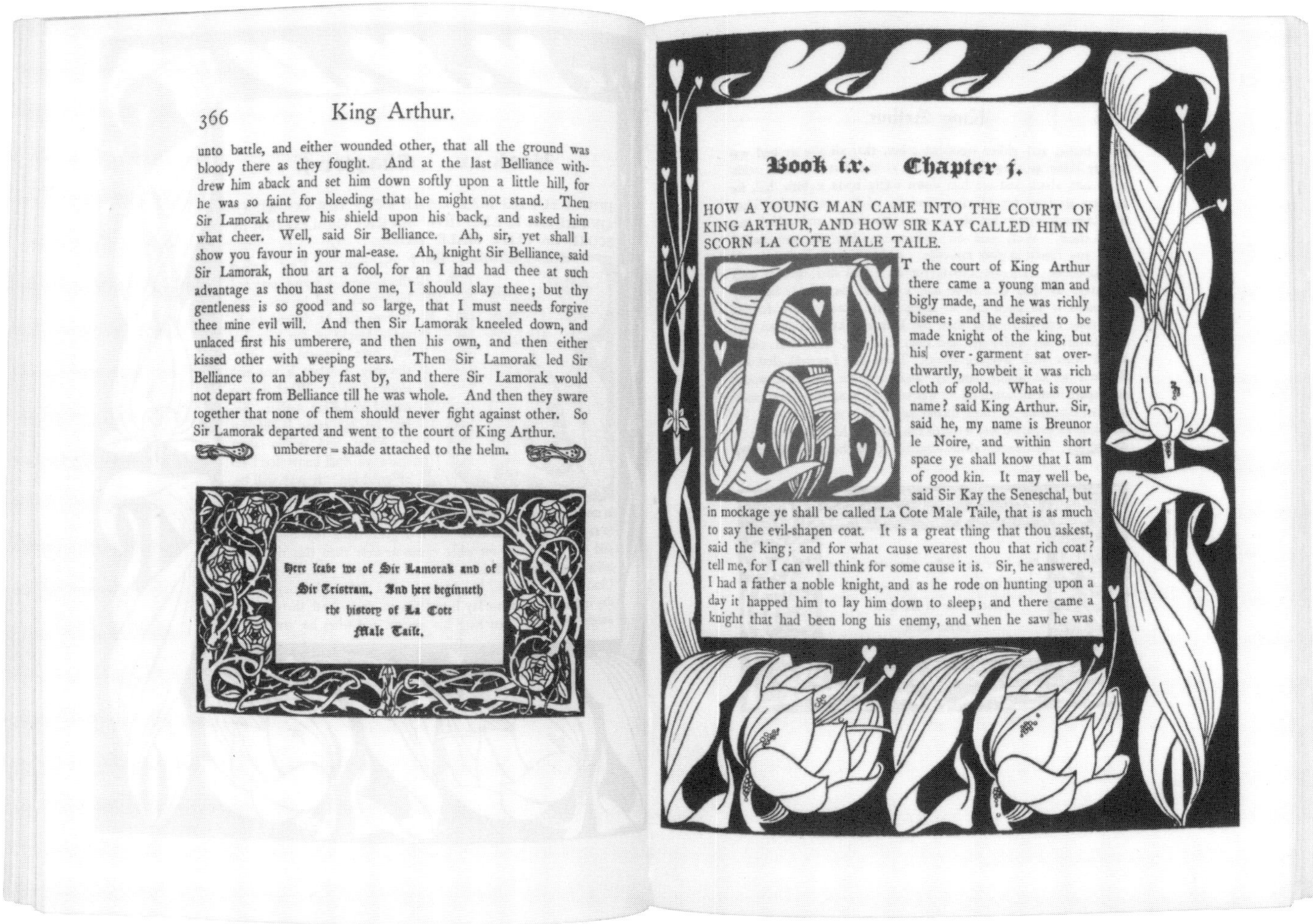

366 King Arthur.

unto battle, and either wounded other, that all the ground was bloody there as they fought. And at the last Belliance withdrew him aback and set him down softly upon a little hill, for he was so faint for bleeding that he might not stand. Then Sir Lamorak threw his shield upon his back, and asked him what cheer. Well, said Sir Belliance. Ah, sir, yet shall I show you favour in your mal-ease. Ah, knight Sir Belliance, said Sir Lamorak, thou art a fool, for an I had had thee at such advantage as thou hast done me, I should slay thee; but thy gentleness is so good and so large, that I must needs forgive thee mine evil will. And then Sir Lamorak kneeled down, and unlaced first his umberere, and then his own, and then either kissed other with weeping tears. Then Sir Lamorak led Sir Belliance to an abbey fast by, and there Sir Lamorak would not depart from Belliance till he was whole. And then they sware together that none of them should never fight against other. So Sir Lamorak departed and went to the court of King Arthur.

umberere = shade attached to the helm.

Here leave we of Sir Lamorak and of Sir Tristram. And here beginneth the history of La Cote Male Taile.

Book ix. Chapter j.

HOW A YOUNG MAN CAME INTO THE COURT OF KING ARTHUR, AND HOW SIR KAY CALLED HIM IN SCORN LA COTE MALE TAILE.

AT the court of King Arthur there came a young man and bigly made, and he was richly bisene; and he desired to be made knight of the king, but his over-garment sat overthwartly, howbeit it was rich cloth of gold. What is your name? said King Arthur. Sir, said he, my name is Breunor le Noire, and within short space ye shall know that I am of good kin. It may well be, said Sir Kay the Seneschal, but in mockage ye shall be called La Cote Male Taile, that is as much to say the evil-shapen coat. It is a great thing that thou askest, said the king; and for what cause wearest thou that rich coat? tell me, for I can well think for some cause it is. Sir, he answered, I had a father a noble knight, and as he rode on hunting upon a day it happed him to lay him down to sleep; and there came a knight that had been long his enemy, and when he saw he was

Oscar Wilde: *A House of Pomegranates*
Charles Ricketts and Charles Shannon
London, 1891
Illustrated at 56% actual size

I am no great enthusiast for art nouveau works (you may have realised), but this book, another production from the Ricketts/Shannon partnership – here, pre-Vale Press – is altogether more original than their *Daphnis and Chloe* that we saw on page 30. It reveals no stylistic influence other than art nouveau either in layout or decoration. I can't say I like it much, or at all, with the text squeezed into gaps left by illustrations like putty keeping window panes from rattling. Ricketts, the designer, seems to have deliberately created perverse typographic problems, not least with those two small and puzzling illustrations. It is unfortunate that, while commendably departing from traditional symmetry, his feeling for space and the relationship of parts was not up to the job. Asymmetry is not the easy option.

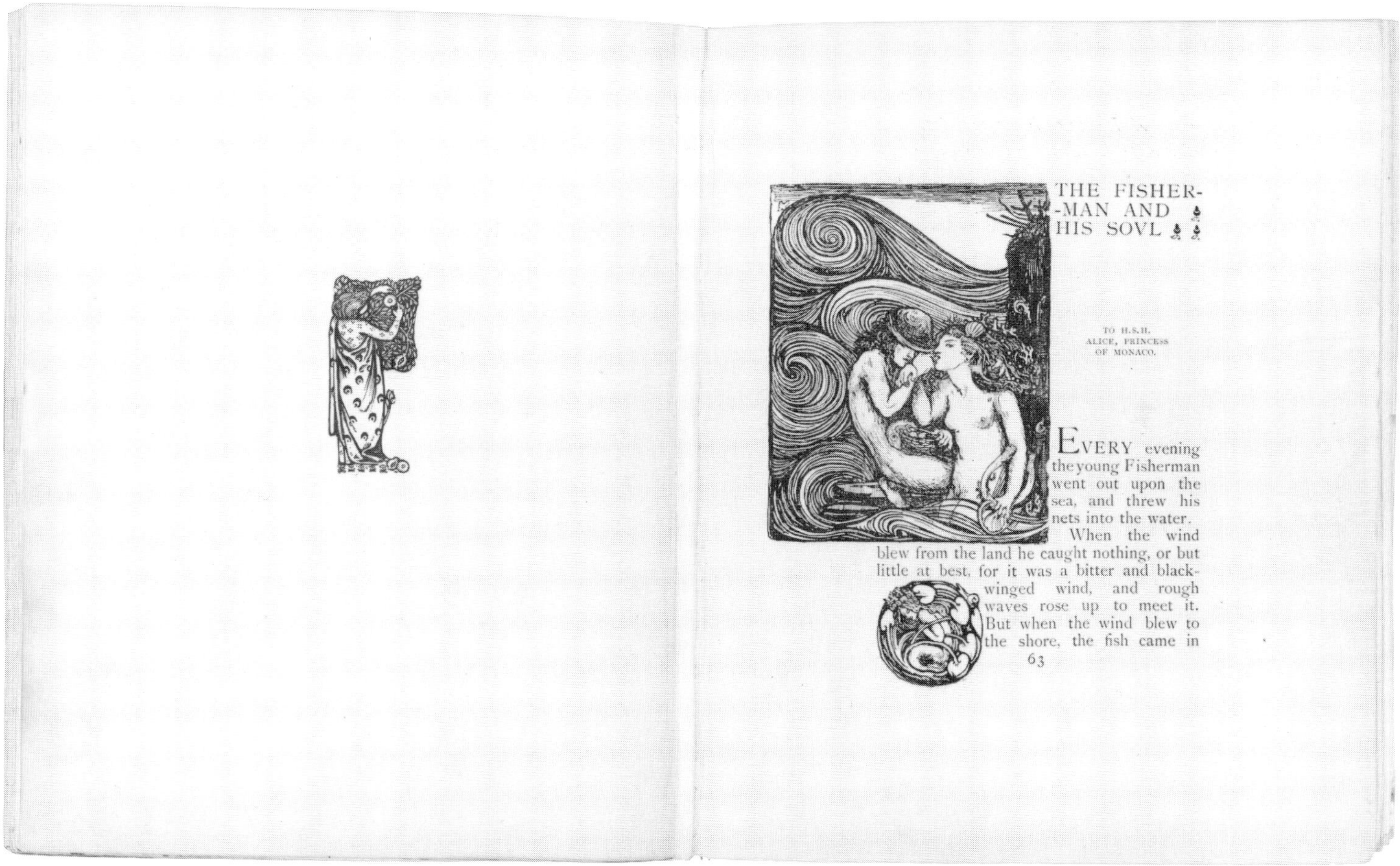

THE FISHER-
-MAN AND
HIS SOVL

TO H.S.H.
ALICE, PRINCESS
OF MONACO.

EVERY evening the young Fisherman went out upon the sea, and threw his nets into the water.
When the wind blew from the land he caught nothing, or but little at best, for it was a bitter and black-winged wind, and rough waves rose up to meet it. But when the wind blew to the shore, the fish came in

63

Oscar Wilde: *The Picture of Dorian Gray*
Charles Carrington, Paris, 1908
Illustrated at 49% actual size

James McNeill Whistler
The Baronet and the Butterfly
R H Russell, New York, 1899
Printed by Valentine, Paris
Designed by James McNeill Whistler
Illustrated at 60% actual size

The title page for Wilde's book is as perverse as Whistler's; but it lacks the American's spatial control and confidence. Type sizes jump around, with rules included in the hope that they will anchor things down. The imprint, in quite a different idiom from the rest of the design, makes a pleasing symmetrical group in itself, although the repeat of the building number is odd. The three groups of type are scattered, disparate in style, and unrelated in position; but nice try.

Whistler's book designs show the strong influence upon him of Japanese prints and their unWestern handling of space. Although this is particularly overt in his paintings, it also emerges, in a less direct manner, in his typography: the extremely lavish margins and daringly organised title pages are evidence. Whereas Carrington's title page for Oscar Wilde has self-contained blocks of type, Whistler has treated his groups freely, allowing the space of the page to flow in and amongst the lines of type. The result is a precariously balanced unity rather than three isolated incidents.

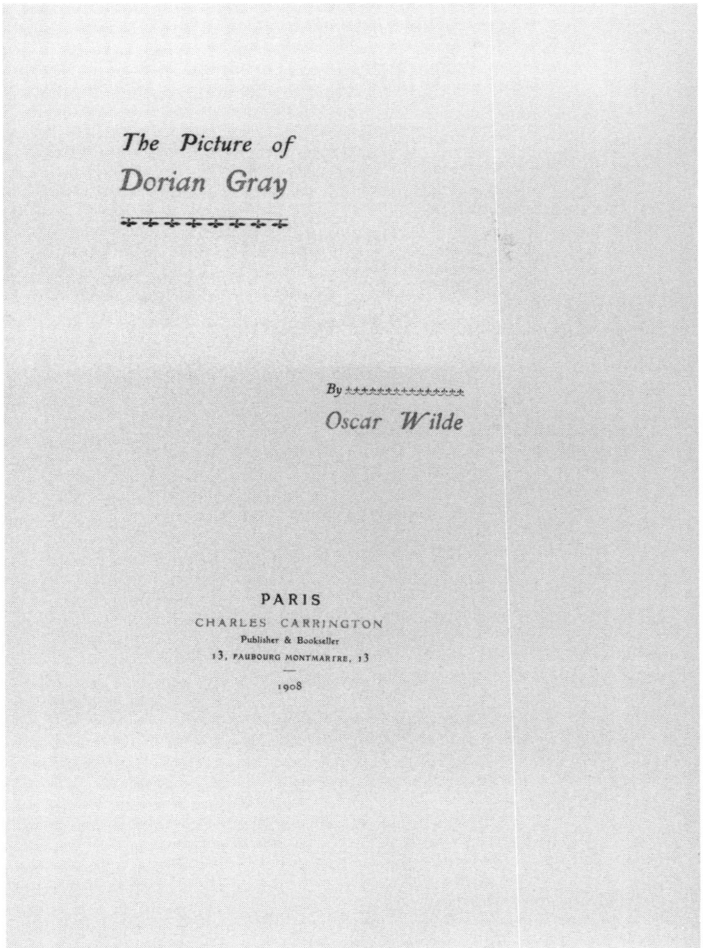
The Picture of
Dorian Gray

By
Oscar Wilde

PARIS
CHARLES CARRINGTON
Publisher & Bookseller
13, FAUBOURG MONTMARTRE, 13

1908

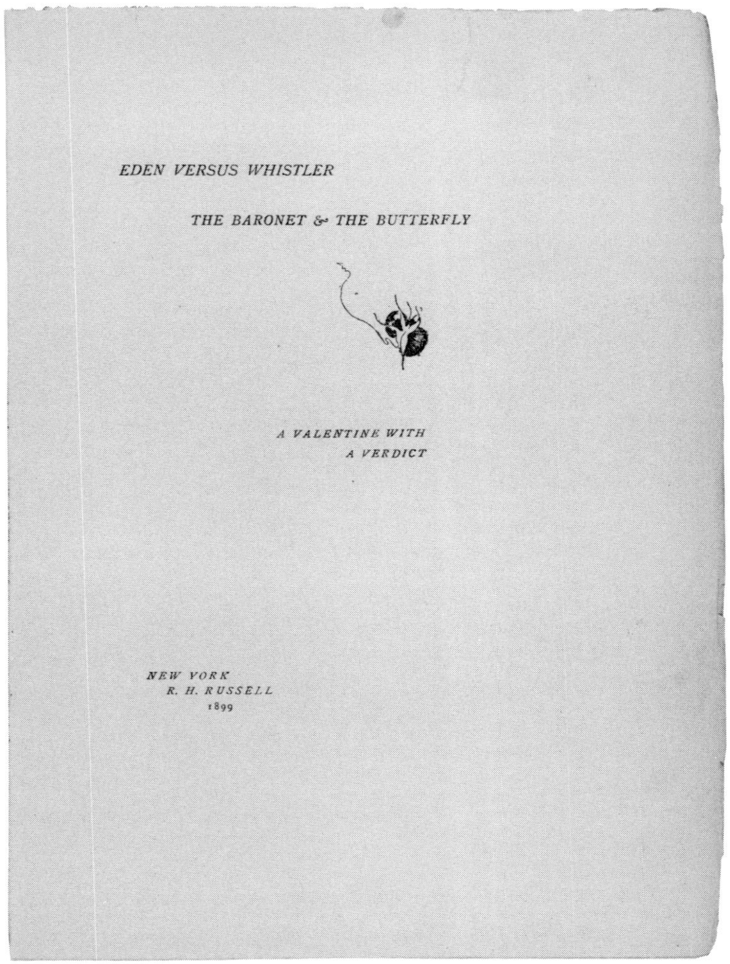
EDEN VERSUS WHISTLER

THE BARONET & THE BUTTERFLY

A VALENTINE WITH
A VERDICT

NEW YORK
R. H. RUSSELL
1899

Christina Rossetti: *Goblin Market*
Macmillan, London, 1893
Printed by R & R Clark, Edinburgh
Illustrated at 55% actual size

The illustrations, by Laurence Housman, are art nouveau in style, but the typography seems more closely related to the aesthetic movement in its almost extravagant use of space. Even the larger illustrations, not seen here, occupy only the text area. The short lines, well-leaded text, and overall simplicity achieve a serenity unusual for the time.

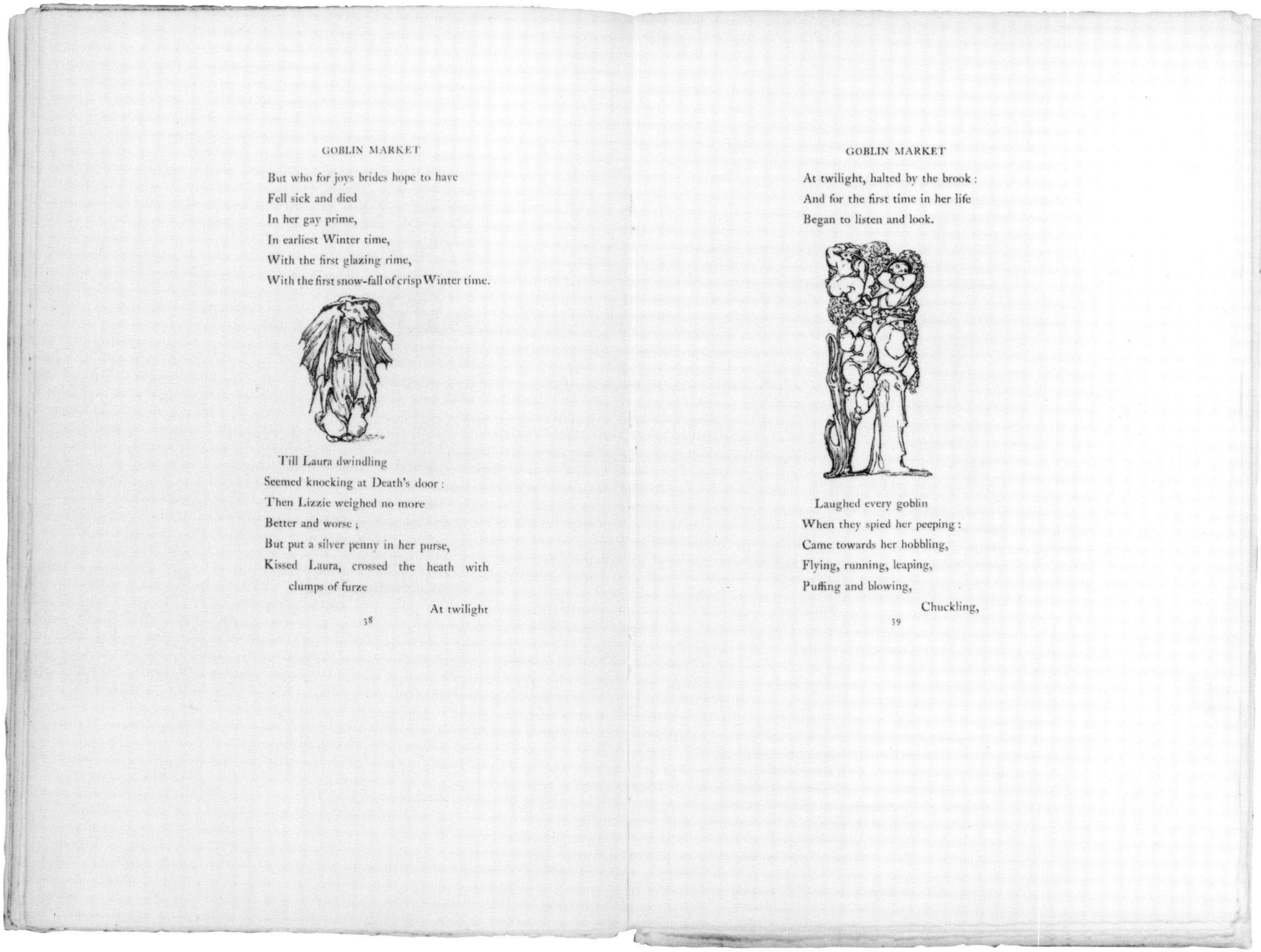

GOBLIN MARKET

But who for joys brides hope to have
Fell sick and died
In her gay prime,
In earliest Winter time,
With the first glazing rime,
With the first snow-fall of crisp Winter time.

Till Laura dwindling
Seemed knocking at Death's door:
Then Lizzie weighed no more
Better and worse;
But put a silver penny in her purse,
Kissed Laura, crossed the heath with
clumps of furze

At twilight

38

GOBLIN MARKET

At twilight, halted by the brook:
And for the first time in her life
Began to listen and look.

Laughed every goblin
When they spied her peeping:
Came towards her hobbling,
Flying, running, leaping,
Puffing and blowing,

Chuckling,

39

James McNeill Whistler
The Baronet and the Butterfly
R H Russell, New York, 1899
Printed by Valentine, Paris
Designed by James McNeill Whistler
Illustrated at 60% actual size

In this book Whistler repeats a trick he played in *The Gentle Art of Making Enemies* of 1890: using his wide margins as repositories for notes, references and (often) sarcastic comments relating to the text. His originality has transformed what are normally tiresome excrescencies into a visually appealing pattern which is nonetheless functional – even if a slight headache for the printer. Perhaps a mere quarter of the pages use the margins in this way, so the book, like that opposite, is spacious, but unpretentious.

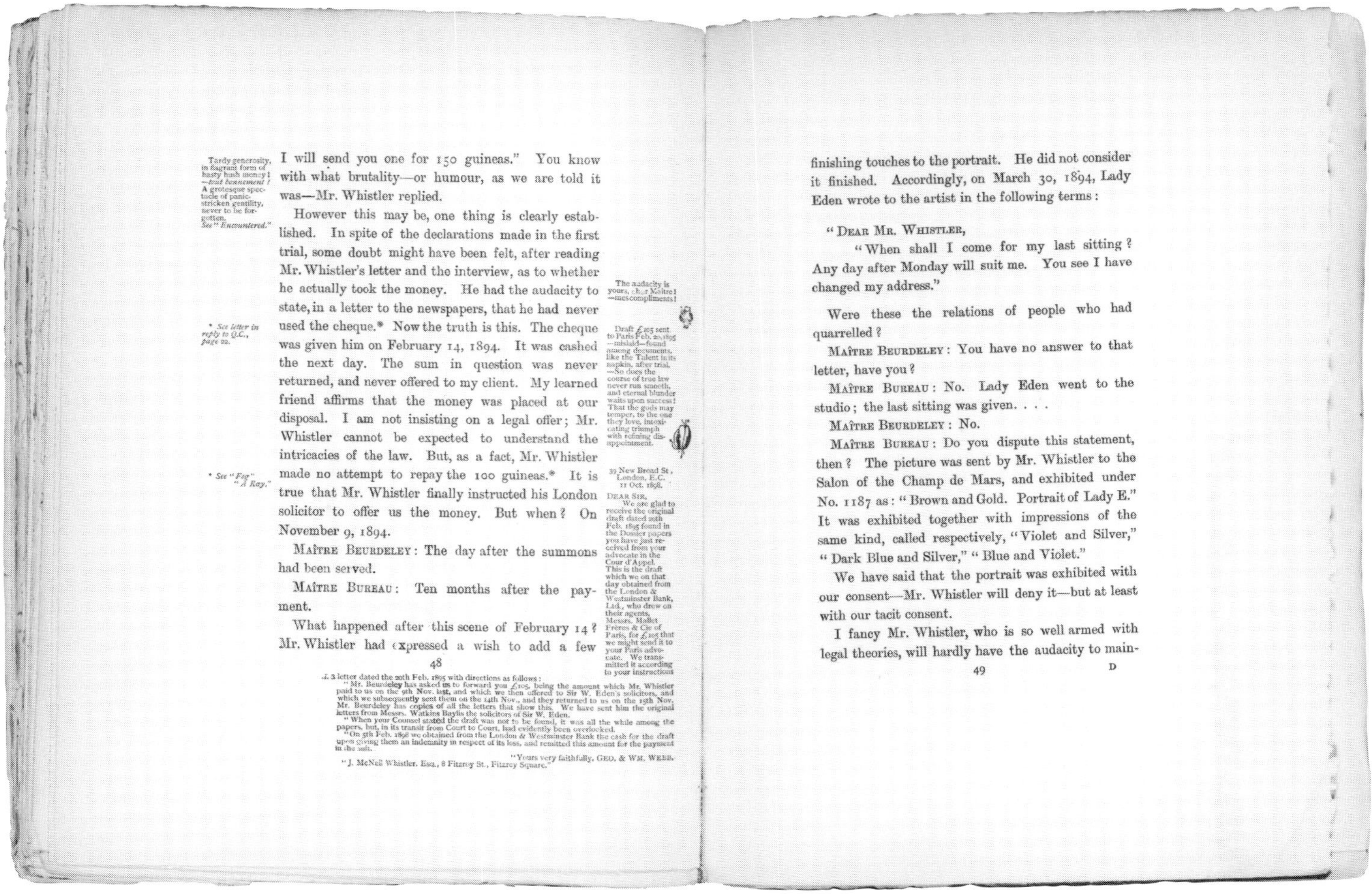

Tardy generosity, in flagrant form of hasty hush money! —*tout bonnement!* A grotesque spectacle of panic-stricken gentility, never to be forgotten. *See "Encountered."*

I will send you one for 150 guineas." You know with what brutality—or humour, as we are told it was—Mr. Whistler replied.

However this may be, one thing is clearly established. In spite of the declarations made in the first trial, some doubt might have been felt, after reading Mr. Whistler's letter and the interview, as to whether he actually took the money. He had the audacity to state, in a letter to the newspapers, that he had never used the cheque.* Now the truth is this. The cheque was given him on February 14, 1894. It was cashed the next day. The sum in question was never returned, and never offered to my client. My learned friend affirms that the money was placed at our disposal. I am not insisting on a legal offer; Mr. Whistler cannot be expected to understand the intricacies of the law. But, as a fact, Mr. Whistler made no attempt to repay the 100 guineas.* It is true that Mr. Whistler finally instructed his London solicitor to offer us the money. But when? On November 9, 1894.

The audacity is yours, cher Maître! —mes compliments!

* *See letter in reply to Q.C., page 22.*

Draft £105 sent to Paris Feb. 20, 1895 —mislaid—found among documents, like the Talent in its napkin, after trial. —So does the course of true law never run smooth, and eternal blunder waits upon success! That the gods may temper, to the one they love, intoxicating triumph with refining disappointment.

* *See "Fog" "A Ray."*

Maître Beurdeley: The day after the summons had been served.

Maître Bureau: Ten months after the payment.

What happened after this scene of February 14? Mr. Whistler had expressed a wish to add a few

48

39 New Broad St., London, E.C. 11 Oct. 1898.

Dear Sir,
We are glad to receive the original draft dated 20th Feb. 1895 found in the Dossier papers you have just received from your advocate in the Cour d'Appel. This is the draft which we on that day obtained from the London & Westminster Bank, Ltd., who drew on their agents, Messrs. Mallet Frères & Cie of Paris, for £105 that we might send it to your Paris advocate. We transmitted it according to your instructions in a letter dated the 20th Feb. 1895 with directions as follows:

"Mr. Beurdeley has asked us to forward you £105, being the amount which Mr. Whistler paid to us on the 9th Nov. last, and which we then offered to Sir W. Eden's solicitors, and which we subsequently sent them on the 14th Nov., and they returned to us on the 15th Nov. Mr. Beurdeley has copies of all the letters that show this. We have sent him the original letters from Messrs. Watkins Baylis the solicitors of Sir W. Eden.

"When your Counsel stated the draft was not to be found, it was all the while among the papers, but, in its transit from Court to Court, had evidently been overlooked.

"On 5th Feb. 1896 we obtained from the London & Westminster Bank the cash for the draft upon giving them an indemnity in respect of its loss, and remitted this amount for the payment in the suit.

"Yours very faithfully, Geo. & Wm. Webb.

"J. McNeill Whistler, Esq., 8 Fitzroy St., Fitzroy Square."

finishing touches to the portrait. He did not consider it finished. Accordingly, on March 30, 1894, Lady Eden wrote to the artist in the following terms:

"Dear Mr. Whistler,

"When shall I come for my last sitting? Any day after Monday will suit me. You see I have changed my address."

Were these the relations of people who had quarrelled?

Maître Beurdeley: You have no answer to that letter, have you?

Maître Bureau: No. Lady Eden went to the studio; the last sitting was given. . . .

Maître Beurdeley: No.

Maître Bureau: Do you dispute this statement, then? The picture was sent by Mr. Whistler to the Salon of the Champ de Mars, and exhibited under No. 1187 as: "Brown and Gold. Portrait of Lady E." It was exhibited together with impressions of the same kind, called respectively, "Violet and Silver," "Dark Blue and Silver," "Blue and Violet."

We have said that the portrait was exhibited with our consent—Mr. Whistler will deny it—but at least with our tacit consent.

I fancy Mr. Whistler, who is so well armed with legal theories, will hardly have the audacity to main-

49 D

the typography of artists and writers

The deliberately provocative and experimental typography created by coteries of artists and writers before and just after the First World War – Italian and Russian Futurists, Russian Constructivists, Polish writers and others – was to exert a strong influence on the Bauhaus artist-designers. Coming from outside the normally conservative printing industry, and so unaffected by its traditional constraints, those earlier pioneers realised that, as owners, so to speak, of their words, they had the right to manipulate them as they wished, rather than leave them to the printer. Usual formulas could be avoided; more expressive and adventurous layouts reflecting the meaning would enhance communication. It is the opposite of the French sixteenth- and seventeenth-century tradition, where lines of type were forced into patterns regardless of meaning.

Perhaps the first serious manifestation of modernism, and this new spirit of making design more expressive of content, is Mallarmé's poem *Un Coup de dés* (see pages 2-5 and opposite). Here, he exploited his spatial arrangement to point up verbal connections throughout the poem, and used changes from roman to italic to create dynamic contrasts. He sought to avoid the dulling effect of reading normal text, which required 'successive, incessant, back and forth movement of our eyes'. His attempt to elucidate meaning fortuitously creates a visually satisfying pattern. The poet/publisher Stefan Themerson was to carry this analysis of the text even further in the 1950s and 1960s; but the use of space to enhance sense or content is, in different ways, a cardinal principal of all modernism.

The Italian Futurists, led by the poet Filippo Tommaso Marinetti, had violent aims which were very different from what he called 'the decorative and precious style of Mallarmé … his static ideal. My reformed typesetting allows me to treat words like torpedoes and hurl them forth at all speeds.' Traditional, long-accepted values were attacked in a re-ordered language, where normal syntax had itself been destroyed. This was aggravated by the use of mathematical symbols and other non-alphabetic signs infiltrated into the text (given half a chance, as in display work, typographers have loved doing this ever since). By exploiting the expressive potential of typography, Marinetti aimed to create a mechanistic, impersonal poetry of immediacy; one which seems to attempt the direct shock to the nervous system that Francis Bacon aimed for in his paintings fifty years later.

Marinetti demanded a revolution against 'the idiotic and nauseating concept of the outdated and conventional book' with its 'typographic harmony of the page'. The writings of the Futurists were full of onomatopoeia effects, where the sound of the word itself is imitative of the sound of the act or object denoted. They carried this further by making the *appearance* of the word add an extra element of imitation. Different typefaces, changes of size or weight, repetition of vowels or consonants, and freedom of layout all played their part. The result was a lively, even deliberately chaotic, page. Sometimes an image was created by the word pattern, something Apollinaire also played around with in his famous calligrammes of 1917, especially *Il Pleut*. Such effects bear some relationship to the word- or letter-play of concrete poetry, although purists refute any notion that this manipulation of text in order to imitate natural appearances belongs to the movement of that name. But I am reluctant to open that can of worms.

Although I have grouped them together, a distinction must be made between the Futurist poets (and Mallarmé, too, together with esoteric Russian poet-designers such as Ilia Zdanevich) who attempted to give words added force by visual means, and work by Constructivists (and other avant-garde Russians) who aimed to evolve a radical visual language, with words and letters exploited for their pattern-making potential. They used type like paint. In many cases the end result had a practical purpose – poster or book cover; the effect (and intention), though, was more 'fine art' than 'graphic design' as we now know it. They were no less effective for that. Large, often wood, type and type matter, such as rules, squares, circles, boxes and other geometric shapes, were combined with prolific invention. The final design was usually printed by lithography, and photomontage was often incorporated.

These avant-garde artists and writers made type an expressive medium: one with which, as Futurists, they could attack 'old-fashioned, passéist' values in art, culture and society; or, as Constructivists, one which reflected the new revolutionary spirit. Combined with photographs or photomontage, it became an ideal means of creating propaganda. The vitality, even violence, of the Russian designs was more suited to display work than to bookwork; the creations of the Italian Futurists have only a little more direct relevance. So why include these wild men in this book?

Because their work was so influential on de Stijl and the Bauhaus. They demonstrated how dynamic and painterly the hitherto solemn world of print could become. It was sometimes *too* dynamic for normal commerce, which lacked the nerve of the earlier Russian publishers (although Zdanevich, in his later reincarnation as a publisher of *livres d'artiste* in Paris, under the name of Iliadz, lost none of his daring); but it broke through a sort of log jam of old ways, and initiated new creative thinking around the subject. The sequence is clear: Futurists; Constructivists and other Russian avant-garde artist/designers; de Stijl and the Bauhaus; Jan Tschichold and the New Typography; Swiss design. The end of the sequence bears no relation to the work of those pioneers; but it was they who opened doors.

Stéphane Mallarmé: *Un Coup de dés*
(*A Throw of the Dice*)
Paris, 1914
Illustrated at 40% actual size

See also pages 2-5

Although not published in this form until 1914, long after his death in 1898, Mallarmé's poem of 1897 is generally regarded as the pioneering experiment in the visual presentation of poetic language. Its original form used a more varied range of types (often bold), and had a more scattered appearance. It had been closely supervised by the poet. We shall just have to imagine the cursing that went on in the print shop as compositors struggled to interpret Mallarmé's manuscript indications into metal type. (Apollinaire's calligrammes of 1917 would present even greater challenges.) Here, for the first time, the white of the paper – that is, space – became part of the poem (Mallarmé thought the mystery of this blank space was like silence). With letterpress printing, that space could only be created by filling the chase holding the type with below-type-high metal or furniture. A tiresome task with such an irregular arrangement. Today's poets, working on their AppleMacs, can now, themselves, play such spatial tricks, or vary type sizes and styles at will. But, without real typographic training, would they have the skill to achieve such visually pleasing effects? Specialist skills or advice can enhance and intensify the author's intentions. How much input, or how many suggestions, did the printers offer Mallarmé, to arrive at the original result? And who finalised this later slightly simplified and more elegant version?

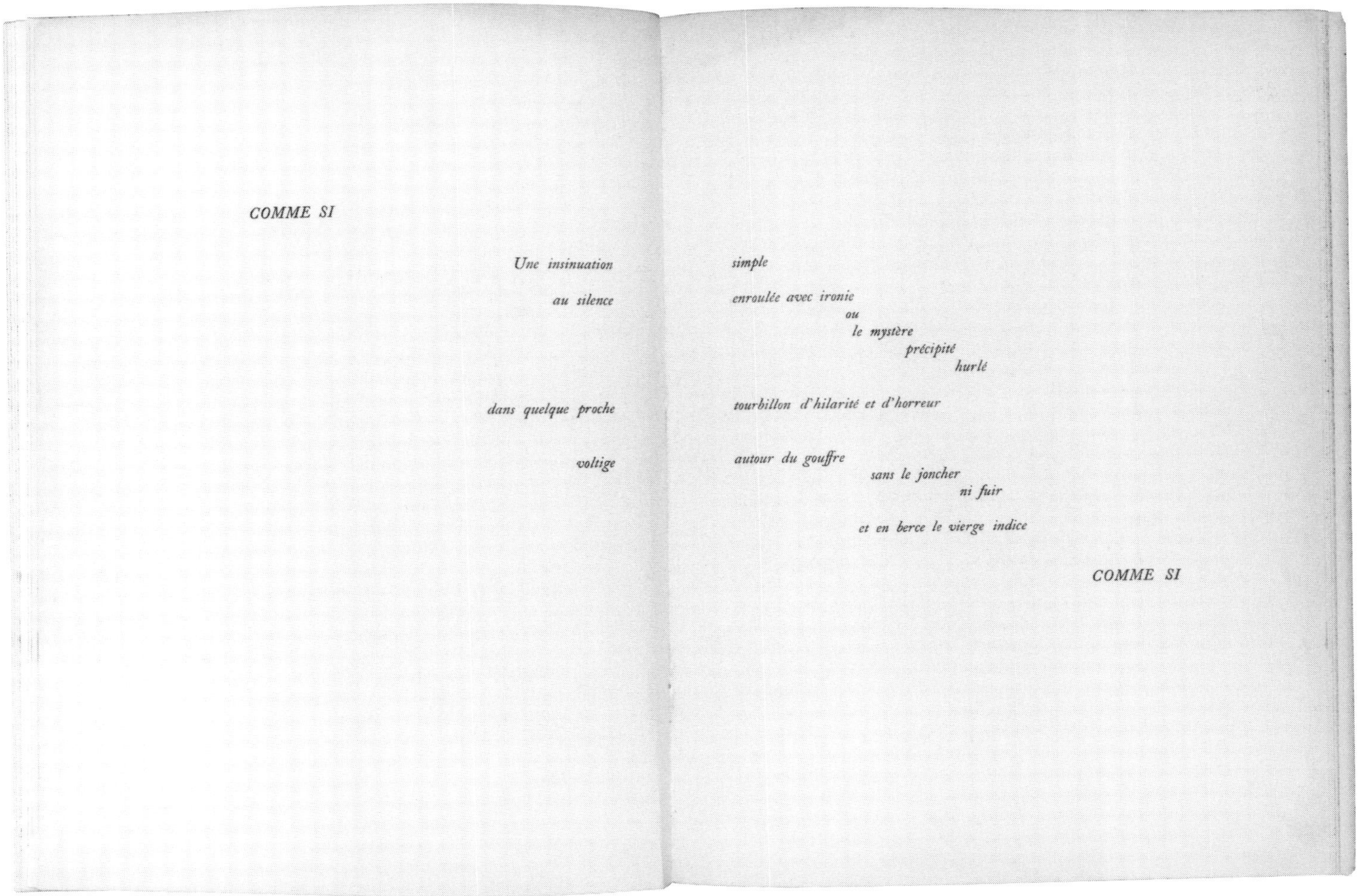

COMME SI

Une insinuation

au silence

dans quelque proche

voltige

simple

enroulée avec ironie
ou
le mystère
précipité
hurlé

tourbillon d'hilarité et d'horreur

autour du gouffre
sans le joncher
ni fuir

et en berce le vierge indice

COMME SI

Filippo Tommaso Marinetti: *Zang Tumb Tumb*
Edizioni Futuriste de Poesia, Milan, 1914
Designed by F T Marinetti
Illustrated at 75% actual size

As a reporter during the Balkan War, Marinetti witnessed the siege of Turkish Adrianopoli by the Bulgarians. This book is a novel based on his experiences. The chance to attempt to create warlike images in type was too good for a lover of violence and chaos to miss.

The cover is 'words in liberty' design in display mode, here created solely by type. (For later and more chaotic designs, Marinetti created a collage with drawn shapes and cut-up pieces of print patched in.) The text, however, is (for me) more original and far more interesting in its effect of 'visual onomatopoeia'. Like other writings of his, the book was declaimed by Marinetti in deliberately rowdy performances – often in London variety theatres, where music hall traditions could cope with Futurist uproar.

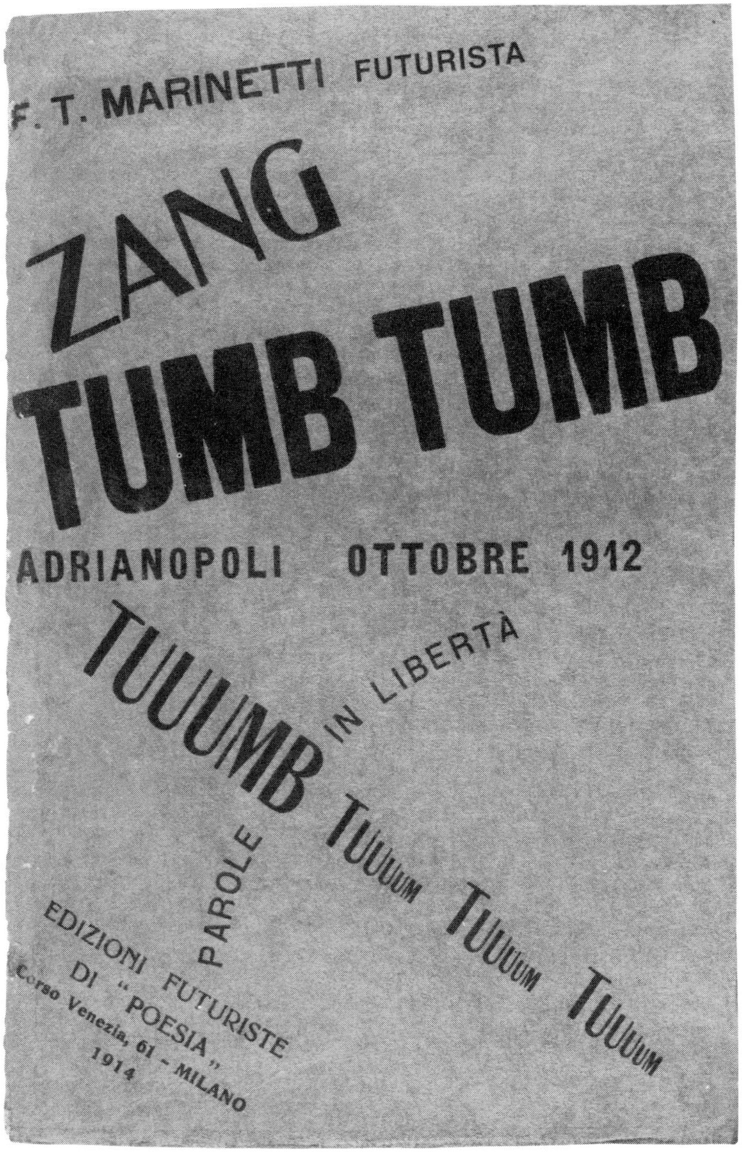

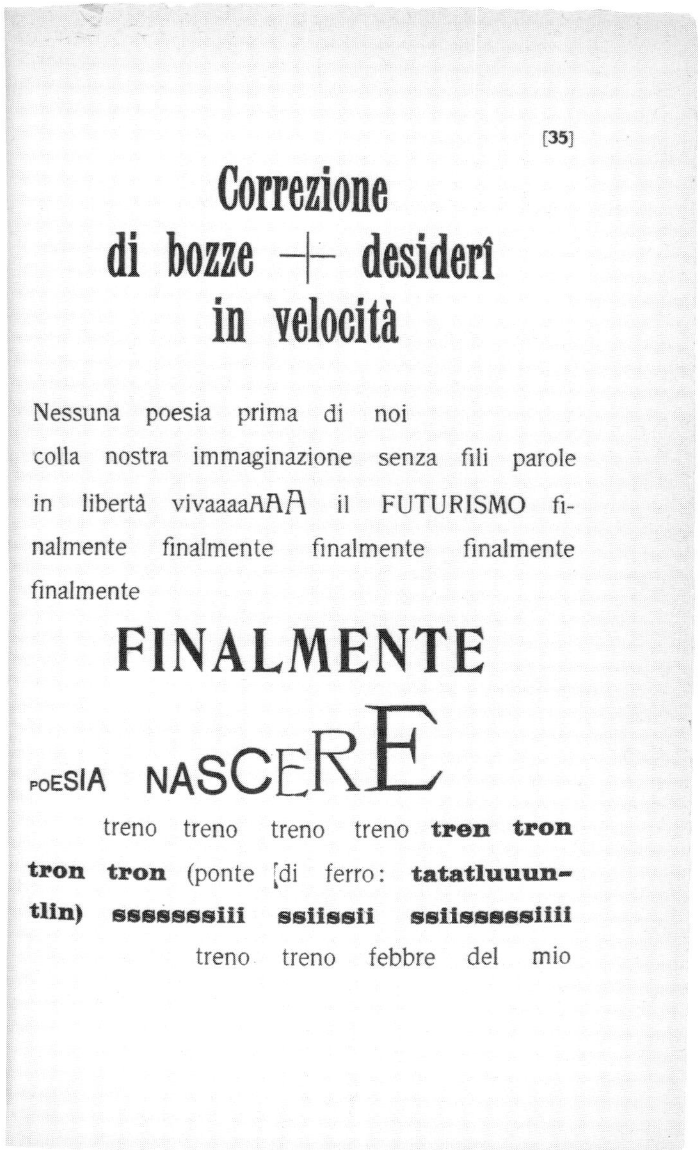
[35]

Correzione
di bozze + desiderî
in velocità

Nessuna poesia prima di noi
colla nostra immaginazione senza fili parole in libertà vivaaaaAAA il FUTURISMO finalmente finalmente finalmente finalmente finalmente

FINALMENTE

POESIA NASCERE

treno treno treno treno **tren tron tron tron** (ponte [di ferro: **tatatluuuntlin) sssssssiii ssiissii ssiisssssiiii**
treno treno febbre del mio

[36]

treno express-express-expresssssssss press-press press-press-press-press-press-press-press-press-press-press-pressssssss punzecchiato dal sale marino aromatizzato dagli aranci cercare mare mare mare balzare balzare rotaie rott-tttaie balzare roooooottttaie roooooooottaie (***GOLOSO SALATO PURPUREO FALOTICO INEVITABILE INCLINATO IMPONDERABILE FRAGILE DANZANTE CALAMITATO***) spiegherò queste parole voglio dire che cielo mare montagne sono golosi salati purpurei ecc. e che io sono goloso salato purpureo ecc. tutto ciò fuori di me ma **anche in me** totalità simultaneità sintesi assoluta = superiorità della mia poesia su tutte le altre stop Villa San Giovanni cattura + pesca + ingoiamento del treno-pescecane immagliarlo spingerlo nel

[37]

ferry-boat-balena partenza della stazione galleggiante solidità del mare di quercia piallata indaco ventilazione (***INSENSIBILE QUOTIDIANO METODICO SERICO IMBOTTITO METALLICO TREPIDANTE RITAGLIATO IMPACCHETTATO CESELLATO NUOVO***) accensione di un veliero = lampada a petrolio + 12 paralumi bianchi + tappeto verde + cerchio di solitudine serenità famiglia

metodo d'un secondo veliero prua lavorare al tornio il metallo del mare

trucioli di schiuma abbassarsi della temperatura = 3 ventagli al disopra dei Monti Calabri (***AZZZZZZURRRRRRO LENTO INDULGENTE SCETTICO***)

Macerie di Messina nello stretto

Zang Tumb Tumb continued

The image is of a Turkish captive balloon. Such attempts to imitate reality, together with the 'visual sounds', were criticised at the time. Art should, it was claimed, be a transforming process, a form of alchemy. Picasso, 'a most intelligent man … uses all kinds of material … but does not use wood to imitate wood'. Well, the Futurists aimed to transform type, making it represent not itself, but sound or emotion. And I cannot help thinking that both the sound and the appearance of the Italian language aided the aspirations of these poets.

The very wide wordspacing in the 'normal' text of this book seems to add to its effectiveness. I hope the typesetter entered into the spirit of the thing.

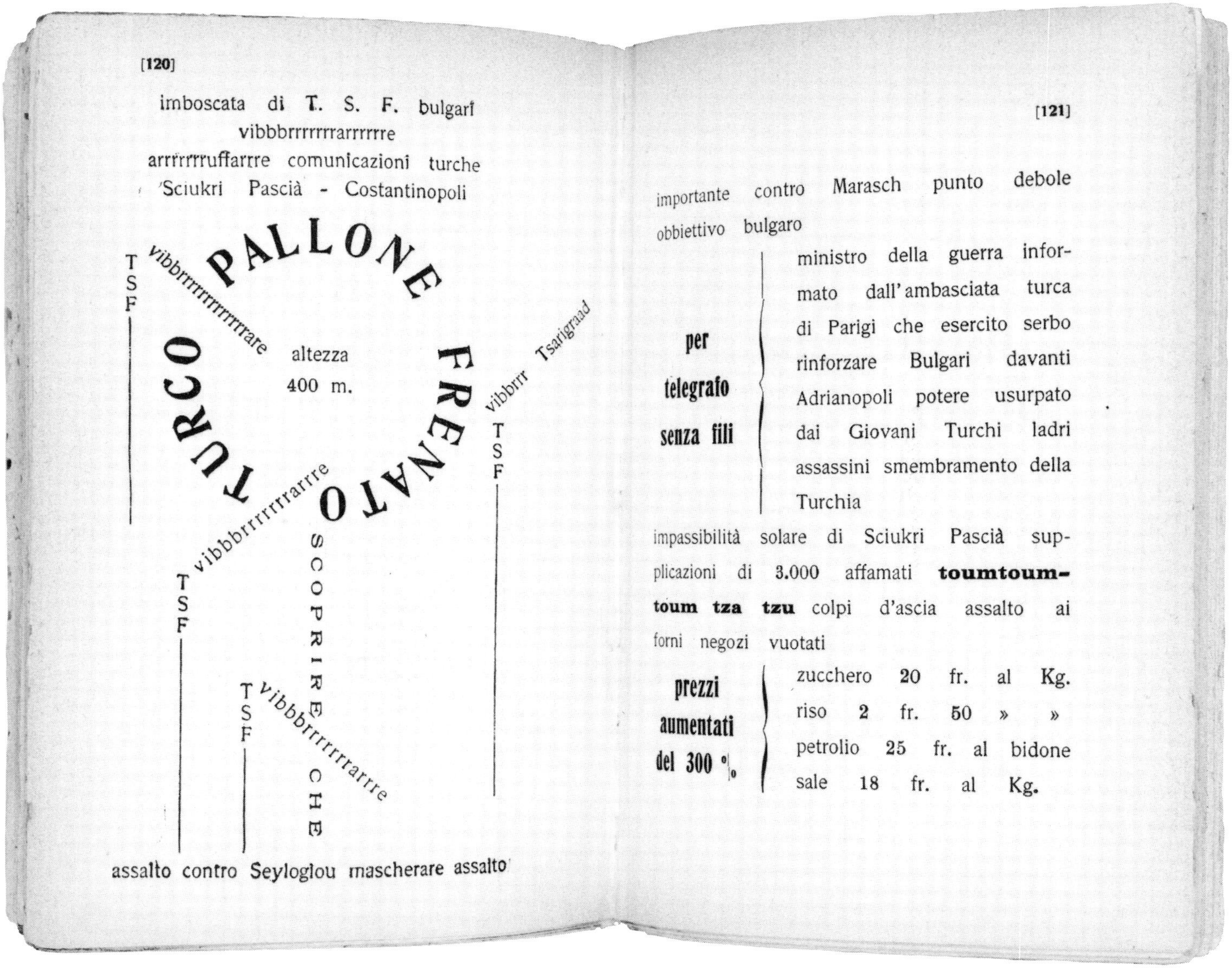
[120]

imboscata di T. S. F. bulgari
vibbbrrrrrrrarrrrrre
arrrrrrruffarrre comunicazioni turche
'Sciukri Pascià - Costantinopoli

PALLONE FRENATO TURCO
vibbrrrrrrrrrrrrrare
altezza
400 m.
vibbrrr Tsarigraad
vibbbrrrrrrrarrre
SCOPRIRE CHE
vibbbrrrrrrrarrre
TSF
TSF
TSF
TSF
TSF

assalto contro Seyloglou mascherare assalto

[121]

importante contro Marasch punto debole obbiettivo bulgaro

per telegrafo senza fili

ministro della guerra informato dall'ambasciata turca di Parigi che esercito serbo rinforzare Bulgari davanti Adrianopoli potere usurpato dai Giovani Turchi ladri assassini smembramento della Turchia

impassibilità solare di Sciukri Pascià supplicazioni di 3.000 affamati **toumtoum-toum tza tzu** colpi d'ascia assalto ai forni negozi vuotati

prezzi aumentati del 300 %

zucchero 20 fr. al Kg.
riso 2 fr. 50 » »
petrolio 25 fr. al bidone
sale 18 fr. al Kg.

fucilare immediatamente

TUTTI (100) TUTTI (300) TUTTI (2000)

soldati che hanno assaltata la regìa dei tabacchi

BOOOOOOOMBAAAARDAMENTO

BOOOOOMBOOOOOMBAAAAARDAAAMENTO

24 Marzo 25 Marzo 26 Marzo	**BUM BUM BUM**

fame disperazione terrore dei Turchi ripiegarsi sui forti Kavkaz Aivaz Bata

vendere le armi per pezzo di pane sfondare botteghe Sciukri Sciukri Sciukri

UBIQUITA' DI SCIUKRI

razione degli abitanti ridotta a 75 gr. di pane (miglio paglia sorgo polvere)

3 OBICI

5 obici

2 obici

4 obici 3 obici **8 oBici**

su Stambul-Youlou su giardino Rechadié

su Istituto delle suore d'Agram (edificio + solidità = schiumarola)

traslochi precipitosi di Khalil-bey

7 della mattina ingresso della cavalleria bulgara dalla parte di Kaik

Filippo Tommaso Marinetti
Nuovi Poeti Futuristi
Rome, 1925
Illustrated at 75% actual size (*Treno* 43%)

This book consists of writings by various Futurist poets. Like Marinetti, its editor, they aimed to short-circuit passéist forms, manipulating type to make mere words more vivid. *Treno in Corsa*, a fold-out 'poem' by Cesare Simonetti, attempts to reproduce the sound of a steam locomotive hissing and puffing at the beginning of its journey before rumbling across clacking rails and points. It is neither concrete poetry nor related to Apollinaire's calligrammes. It can be considered an equivalent in words of Honegger's musical 'poem' *Pacific 231* of one year earlier. Trains, trams, cars, traffic violence: these are archetypal subjects for Futurist poets, and painters too. The modern metropolis with its great crowds – workers, pleasure-seekers, rioters; insatiable stations swallowing the smoking serpents of their trains, deep-chested locomotives that paw the ground with their wheels – this could only be Marinetti speaking – the modern metropolis was their muse; and the architectural visions of Antonio Sant'Elia suggested the form The New City should take.

This is heady stuff. In the real world, manipulating type in this way, forcing the reader to take notice of it rather than allowing the author's voice to be heard neutrally,

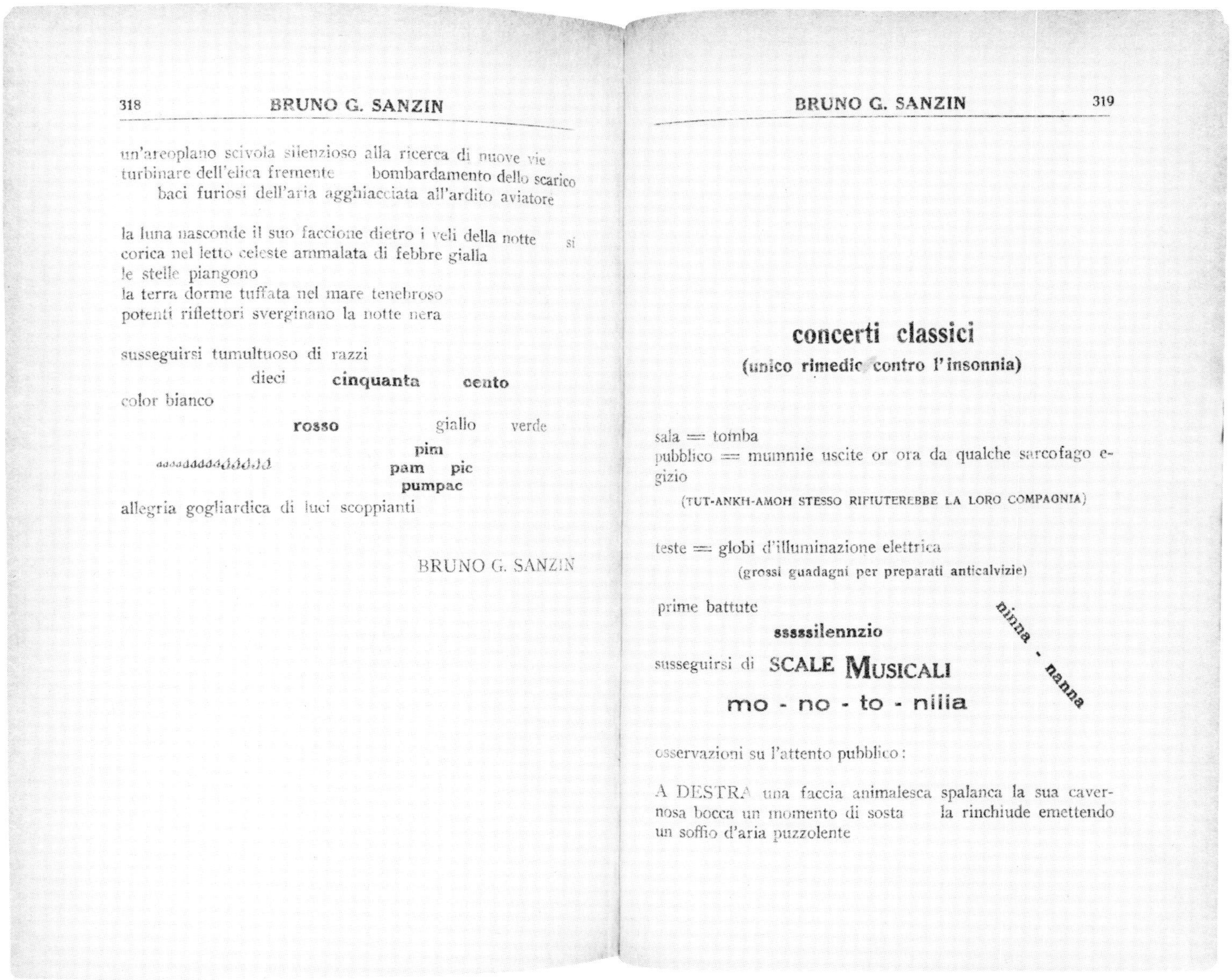

318 BRUNO G. SANZIN

un'areoplano scivola silenzioso alla ricerca di nuove vie
turbinare dell'elica fremente bombardamento dello scarico
baci furiosi dell'aria agghiacciata all'ardito aviatore

la luna nasconde il suo faccione dietro i veli della notte si
corica nel letto celeste ammalata di febbre gialla
le stelle piangono
la terra dorme tuffata nel mare tenebroso
potenti riflettori sverginano la notte nera

susseguirsi tumultuoso di razzi
dieci **cinquanta** **cento**
color bianco
rosso giallo verde
dddddddddddddd **pim**
pam **pic**
pumpac
allegria gogliardica di luci scoppianti

BRUNO G. SANZIN

BRUNO G. SANZIN 319

concerti classici
(unico rimedio contro l'insonnia)

sala = tomba
pubblico = mummie uscite or ora da qualche sarcofago egizio
(TUT-ANKH-AMOH STESSO RIFIUTEREBBE LA LORO COMPAGNIA)

teste = globi d'illuminazione elettrica
(grossi guadagni per preparati anticalvizie)

prime battute
sssssilennzio ninna - nanna
susseguirsi di **SCALE MUSICALI**
mo - no - to - niiia

osservazioni su l'attento pubblico:

A DESTRA una faccia animalesca spalanca la sua cavernosa bocca un momento di sosta la rinchiude emettendo un soffio d'aria puzzolente

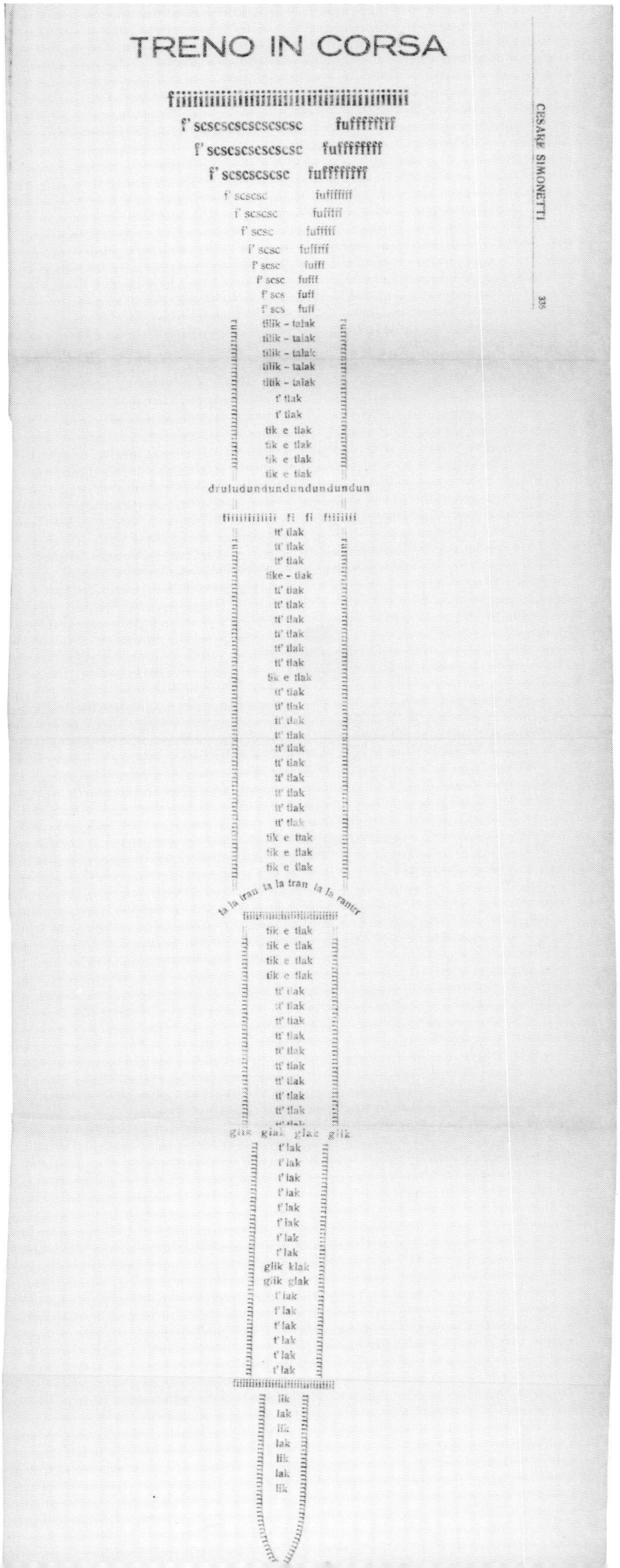

TRENO IN CORSA

CESARE SIMONETTI

335

fiiiiiiiiiiiiiiiiiiiiiiiiiiiiiiiiiiii
f' scscscscscscscsc fuffffffff
f' scscscscscscsc fuffffffff
f' scscscscsc fuffffffff
f' scscsc fuffffff
f' scscsc fuffff
f' scsc fuffff
f' scsc fuffff
f' scsc fufff
f' scsc fufff
f' scs fuff
f' scs fuff
tilik - talak
tilik - talak
tilik - talak
tilik - talak
tilik - talak
f' tlak
f' tlak
tik e tlak
tik e tlak
tik e tlak
tik e tlak
druludundundundundundundun
fiiiiiiiiii fi fi fiiiiii
tt' tlak
tt' tlak
tt' tlak
tike - tlak
tt' tlak
tt' tlak
tt' tlak
tt' tlak
tt' tlak
tt' tlak
tik e tlak
tt' tlak
tt' tlak
tt' tlak
tt' tlak
tt' tlak
tt' tlak
tt' tlak
tt' tlak
tt' tlak
tt' tlak
tik e ttak
tik e tlak
tik e tlak
ta la tran ta la tran ta la ranttr
fiiiiiiiiiiiiiiiiiiiiii
tik e tlak
tik e tlak
tik e tlak
tik e tlak
tt' tlak
tt' tlak
tt' tlak
tt' tlak
tt' tlak
tt' tlak
tt' tlak
tt' tlak
tt' tlak
glik glak glak glik
f' lak
f' lak
f' lak
f' lak
f' lak
f' lak
f' lak
f' lak
glik klak
glik glak
f' lak
f' lak
f' lak
f' lak
f' lak
f' lak
fiiiiiiiiiiiiiiiiiiiiii
lik
lak
lik
lak
lik
lak
lik

without interpretation, is a dangerous game to play with extended texts. But it helped to give a jolt to the straight-laced typographic conventions of the day. Even the generally unadventurous Stanley Morison declared (in the 1930s) that 'despite the printer, type should be treated like rubber' – extending the phrase out into the margin to make his point. Of course, these heretics had greater influence on much more significant designers than scholarly English gentlemen.

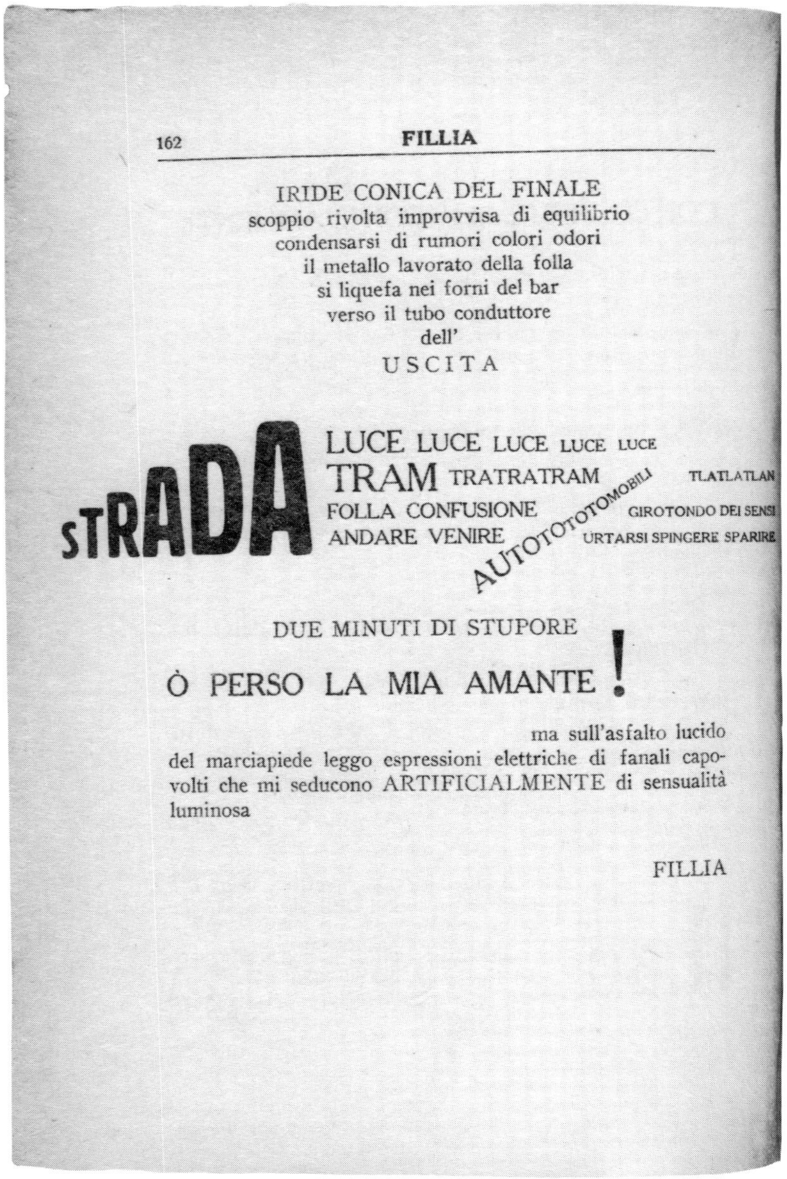

162 FILLIA

IRIDE CONICA DEL FINALE
scoppio rivolta improvvisa di equilibrio
condensarsi di rumori colori odori
il metallo lavorato della folla
si liquefa nei forni del bar
verso il tubo conduttore
dell'
USCITA

sTRADA
LUCE LUCE LUCE LUCE LUCE
TRAM TRATRATRAM
FOLLA CONFUSIONE
ANDARE VENIRE
AUTOTOTOTOMOBILI
TLATLATLAN
GIROTONDO DEI SENSI
URTARSI SPINGERE SPARIRE

DUE MINUTI DI STUPORE

Ò PERSO LA MIA AMANTE !

ma sull'asfalto lucido del marciapiede leggo espressioni elettriche di fanali capovolti che mi seducono ARTIFICIALMENTE di sensualità luminosa

FILLIA

Two designs by Theo van Doesburg, 1921
as shown in *Kunst van Heden in het Stedelijk*
by Willem Sandberg and H L C Jaffé
Stedelijk Museum, Amsterdam, 1961

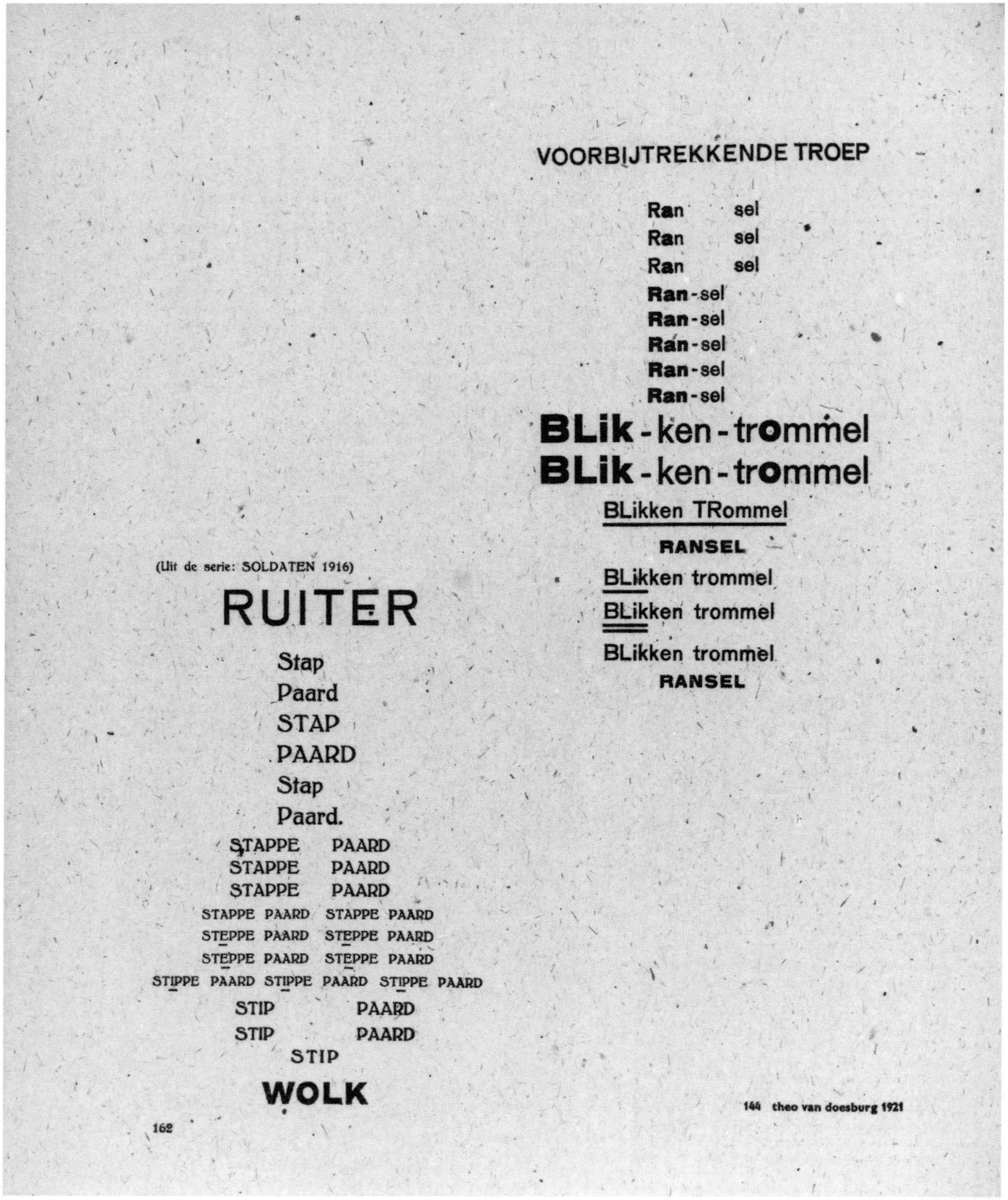
(Uit de serie: SOLDATEN 1916)

RUITER

Stap
Paard
STAP
PAARD
Stap
Paard.
STAPPE PAARD
STAPPE PAARD
STAPPE PAARD
STAPPE PAARD STAPPE PAARD
STEPPE PAARD STEPPE PAARD
STEPPE PAARD STEPPE PAARD
STIPPE PAARD STIPPE PAARD STIPPE PAARD
STIP PAARD
STIP PAARD
STIP
WOLK

162

VOORBIJTREKKENDE TROEP

Ran sel
Ran sel
Ran sel
Ran-sel
Ran-sel
Ran-sel
Ran-sel
Ran-sel
BLik-ken-trommel
BLik-ken-trommel
BLikken TRommel
RANSEL
BLikken trommel
BLikken trommel
BLikken trommel
RANSEL

144 theo van doesburg 1921

OPPOSITE

Other designers besides the Futurists were playing around with typographic pattern-making, articulating the text. The aims of de Stijl, in which van Doesburg was a key figure, were geometrical order and clarity – almost the converse of Futurist mayhem. Yet these two designs opposite share many characteristics with the Italian work, even if all the type is horizontal. But these were formal games, not attempts to give poetry (words) added force by visual means.

The brave new 'white world' sometimes needed rather black type with which to express itself.

RIGHT

Two designs by El Lissitzky, 1922-3
as shown in *Die Neue Typographie*
by Jan Tschichold
Berlin, 1928

These two spreads shown by Jan Tschichold illustrate the famous book of thirteen Mayakovsky poems (*For the Voice*) which El Lissitzky illustrated using only type, rules and other devices from the typesetter's repertoire. The peripatetic Lissitzky, who has been described as the Constructivists' travelling salesman, or ambassador-at-large, here pioneers the kind of typographic freedoms which were so influential in Bauhaus work. Type set vertically or at an angle, the use of bold rules and geometric shapes, with exuberant and forceful pattern-making taking precedence over sense, even logic: artist-designers such as Moholy-Nagy, enthralled by this approach, were convinced this was the way forward. But although Jan Tschichold showed these examples in his book with apparent approval, in his own work – even in his film posters – any influence was thoroughly digested and transformed.

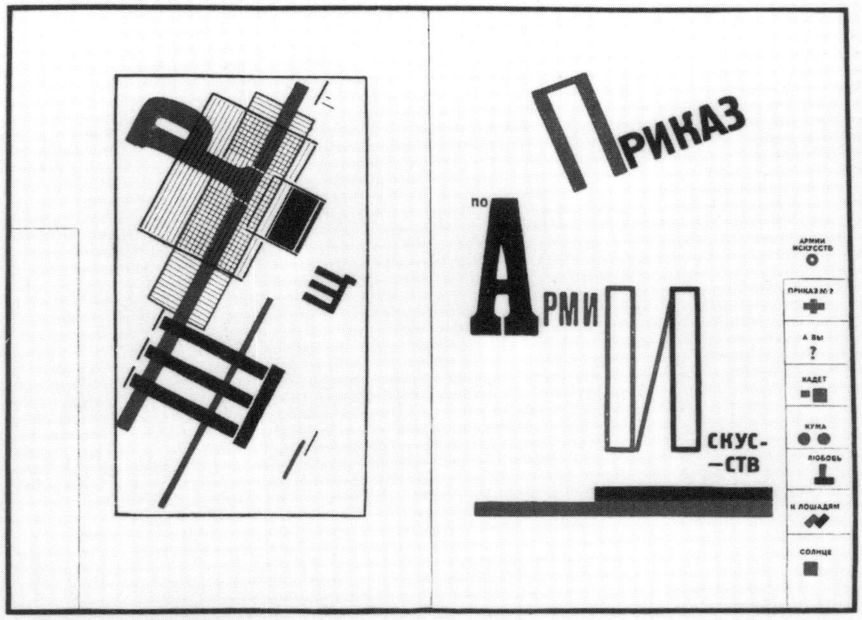

EL LISSITZKY (1922-1923):
Zwei Seiten (Gedichttitel) aus Majakowsky, Dlja Gólossa (Zum Vorlesen)

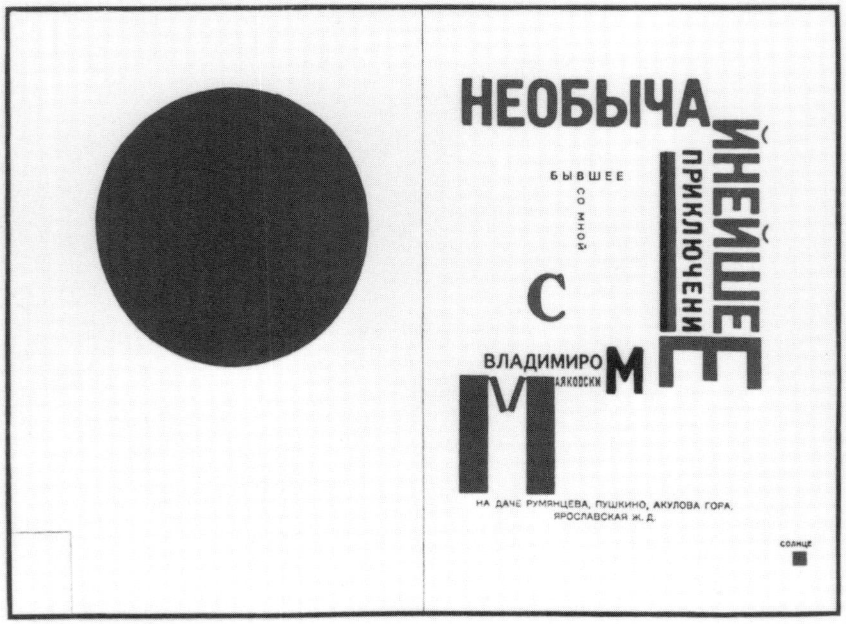

EL LISSITZKY (1922-1923):
Zwei Seiten (Gedichttitel) aus Majakowsky, Dlja Gólossa (Zum Vorlesen)

V Mayakovsky: *Thirteen Years of Work*
Volume 1, Moscow, 1923
Cover design by Anton Lavinsky
Illustrated at 73% actual size

S P Bobrov: *Revolt of the Misanthropes*
Moscow, 1922
Cover design by Liubov Popova
Illustrated at 79% actual size

El Lissitzky, like many Constructivists, essentially a designer rather than an artist, used type and type matter freely, creating designs more mechanistic than those by many of his fellow Russians. In contrast, Lavinsky's design here incorporates hand-drawn letterforms – perhaps cut from paper. Many of these avant-garde artist-designers were carrying on a tradition begun by the earlier Russian Futurists, whose books were often hand-made (with tipped-in pages, glued-on labels and different coloured papers), often hand-written, and which incorporated high-spirited etchings, lithographs, lino-cuts or drawings.

These avant-garde Russian artists gradually moved towards what we today would call 'graphic design'. Lurking behind the overwhelming and somewhat disordered type of Popova's design is a photograph of a gun. A space has been carefully contrived to reveal the gunner, but it cannot be said that the integration of type and image is particularly skilful.

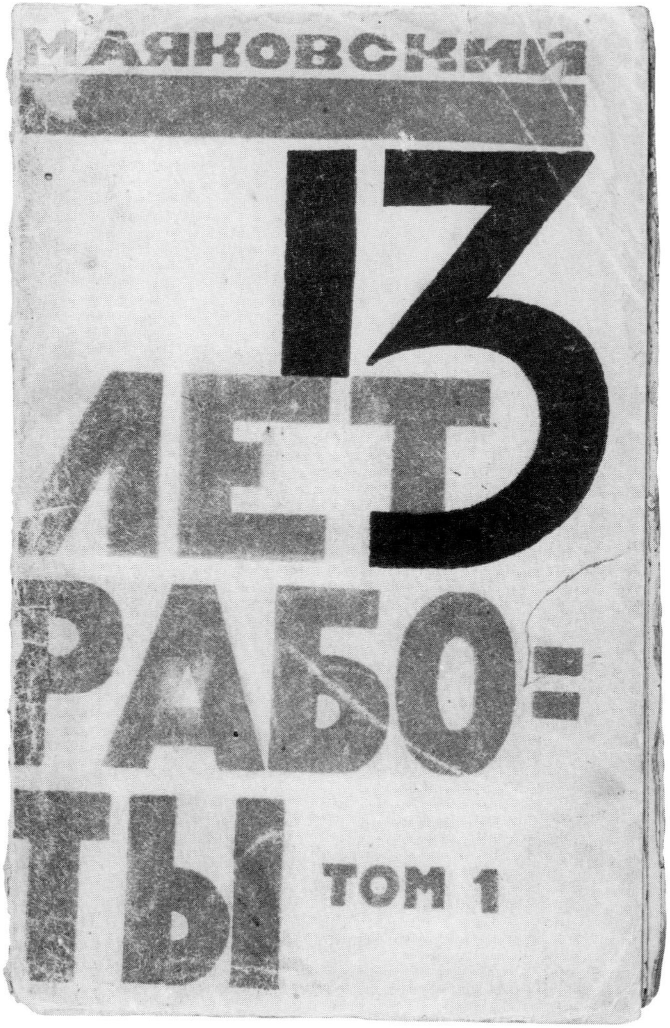

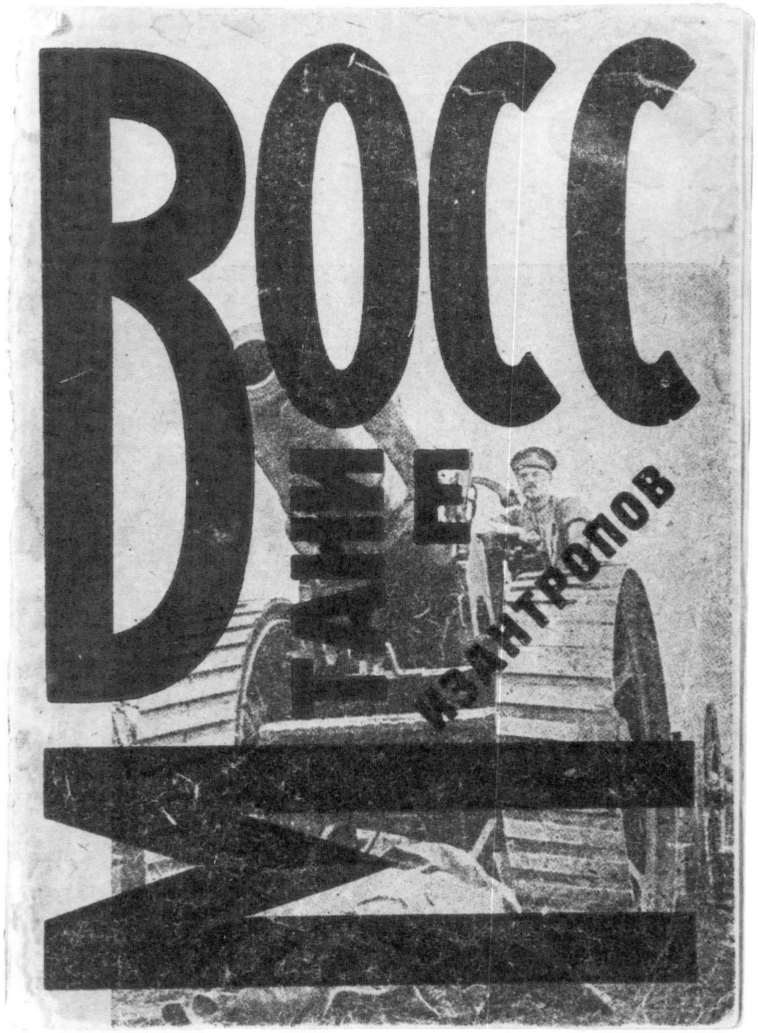

Vkhutemas Architecture
Moscow, 1927
Cover design by El Lissitzky
Illustrated at 79% actual size

Contemporary Architecture No 5
Moscow, 1930
Title page designed by Solomon Telingater
Illustrated at 45% actual size

The Vkhutemas Art School was as experimental and innovative as the Bauhaus. In this cover design, El Lissitzky shows how to seriously combine image and type. Although he had used this photograph at least once before, in 1924, he has here closely integrated the typography with it. All has been carefully planned, with nothing left to chance. Not that chance has no part to play in even fully developed graphic design – it can add the unexpected fillip; but here, only the idiosyncrasies of a human hand are allowed to break out into uncontrollable territory.

For Lissitzky, there was no division between his work as a Constructivist artist and his graphic design: the same principles applied to both.

Telingater's title page, from which all trace of the early 'folk art' elements has been eliminated, could be mistaken for a Bauhaus design but for the Russian words. The architectural subject does, of course, immediately refer one to the kind of work extensively illustrated in, for instance, the Bauhaus journal; but the treatment of the logo CA 5, the boxed line of type beneath it, and the careful integration of architectural plan, drawing, and typography – all this is exemplary Bahauserie. Perhaps, by 1930, the influence was beginning to flow the other way.

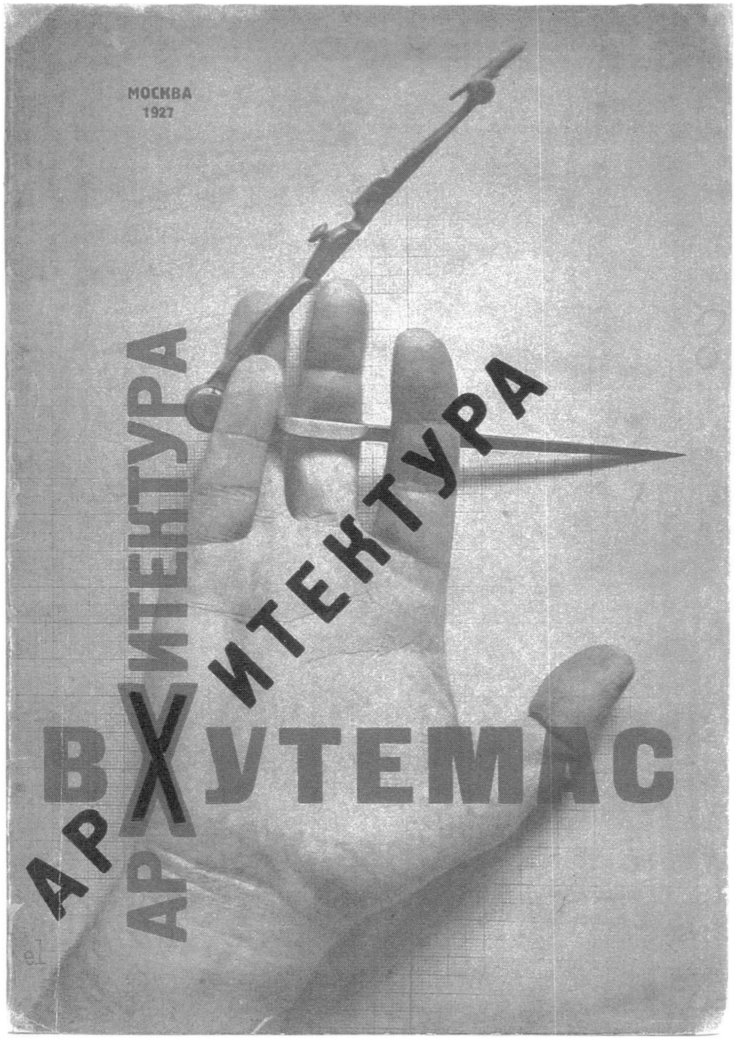

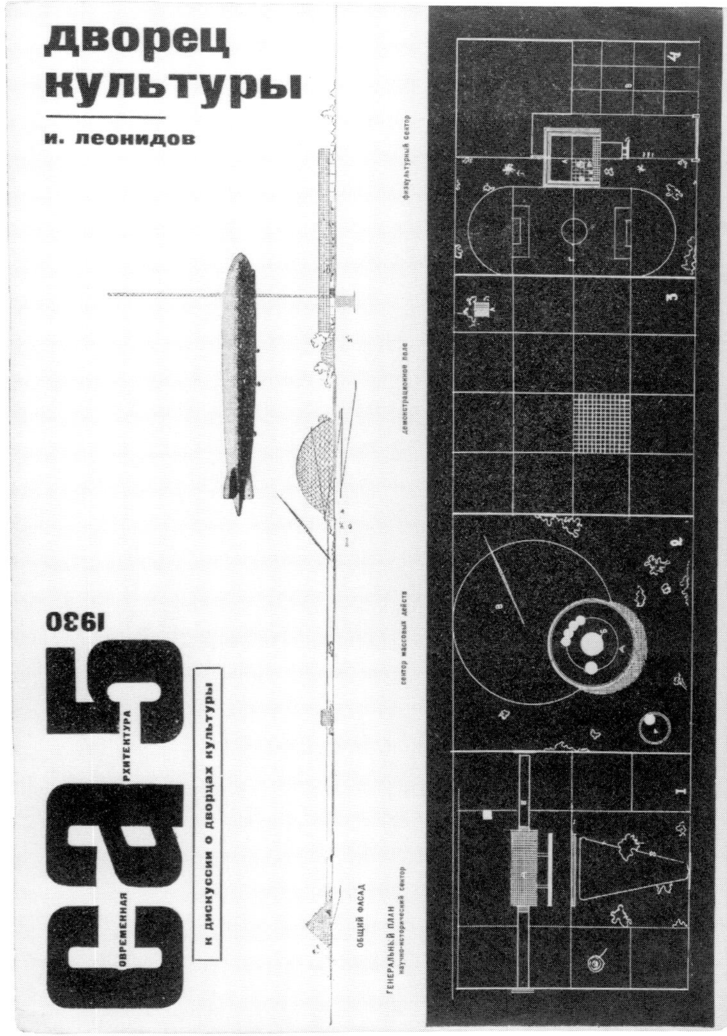

While the production of volumes designed, printed and priced for bibliophiles continues, even today, the growth of a literate but far less wealthy alternative society in the nineteenth century created a demand for less imposing and more popularly priced books. Technical advances in the printing industry allowed this demand to be met. Cheaper books could now be produced, and more speedily; but this resulted in a drop in both design and production standards. William Morris, disgusted by the state of the trade, set up his Kelmscott Press in 1891, giving unstinting attention to design, type, illustration, materials and printing. He, and the private presses that followed him, created very expensive, backward-looking books serving, as he himself put it, 'the swinish luxury of the rich'.

It was just such handcraft-based productions that the Bauhaus so sternly rejected as quite inappropriate for the twentieth century. They were not opposed to craftsmanlike work – far from it. But while Morris took one route and opposed the machine, the Bauhaus saw this as defeatist, and wrong. They believed the machine should be exploited, creatively. Gropius's solution was to insist that each student was instructed by both a 'master of form' and a 'master of craft', with the aim of producing designers who combined both skills. These would pass on their dual knowledge to *their* students.

In its early years the school had no specialist typography teacher. Artists such as László Moholy-Nagy developed the visionary pioneering work of Italian Futurists and Russian Constructivists, urging a similar expressive presentation of content through imaginative form. It has been claimed that the Futurist typographic vocabulary owed something to advertising (I am not convinced). But certainly the Bauhaus vocabulary was fundamentally an advertising language. This new language was also employed even then (with some success) not only for stationery but also for the series of 'Bauhaus Books' designed by Moholy-Nagy and Herbert Bayer – an architect who had studied typography at the Bauhaus and later taught it there. Those books were of a kind for which the rather aggressive Bauhaus style was suited. Nonetheless, the predisposition towards advertising design later became even more explicit under Joost Schmidt.

Many of the principles underlying the new book design, initially worked out at the Bauhaus, then advanced by the later Swiss designers, came about through the development of advertising design. But unlike the Bauhaus, the Swiss devised a *system* which was almost universally applicable, or adaptable. It fulfilled Gropius's hopes and aims, expressed later, not to create a fixed style. The Bauhaus idea 'will only remain alive so long as it does not congeal into a static form, so long as it seeks the essence of life in continual change'.

Not all Bauhaus typography is reader-friendly, despite the attempts at a logical approach. While, importantly, space in design became 'dynamic' (a very Bauhaus word), some of the more extreme pronouncements (mainly by Herbert Bayer) were distinctly unhelpful. No capital letters, no signalling of new paragraphs by indents or line spaces, unleaded text. The use of grotesque (sanserif) typefaces in text is still contentious today. The most obvious marks of Bauhauserie: the use of aggressive heading type; large numerals; heavy rules, squares, circles, triangles and arrows; type set vertically or at an angle; these are used in bookwork nowadays mainly for allusive effects. They are thought of, to some extent correctly, as being a (superficial) shorthand for 'Bauhaus'. How Gropius would have hated that.

The aims and ideals of designers are often not realised, and this is so with the Bauhaus visionaries. While their goal of design which looked thoroughly twentieth century was attained (in spades), a belief in 'expressive presentation of content' is not always entirely conducive to clarity of communication. In advertising design, getting the reader's attention is of first importance. Nonetheless, the typography taught in Bauhaus advertising courses was to affect bookwork both then and later, especially through its influence on the young Jan Tschichold. Book design was never a subject in its own right at the Bauhaus, and has always been a poor relation in art schools ever since. In books, unlike in advertising, typographic clarity and 'sorting out the text' (how often one has to do that) are of primary importance. Yet much of Herbert Bayer's teaching was applicable to both fields. He made serious attempts to analyse the text. Both Bayer and Moholy-Nagy believed that the design should be governed by the relative significance of words or phrases, whether or not these were arranged horizontally, vertically or angled, although Moholy's concern for 'expressive presentation' sometimes worked against a more detailed articulation. It was probably Bayer, too, who introduced the sophisticated use of a structural grid which, in primitive form, is a device as old as printing. A means of controlling the elements of a page, and relating one part to another, it was to be developed yet further by Swiss designers as a major and defining component of their design ethic.

In the complicated equation that is bookwork, designers can easily be seduced by aesthetic considerations, or 'expressive presentation', which sometimes conflicts with the readability factor. Aesthetics must play their part: the book needs to look attractive to the possible purchaser as well as to the reader. It is a question of balance, which the Bauhaus approach, despite its beneficial influence in attempting to harness logic, function, analysis and aesthetics to typography in general – a craft hitherto rather dismissive, even ignorant, of such ideas – did not completely answer. In truth, we are still struggling with the equation; and nowhere more so than in book design.

While the direct impact of the iconoclastic Bauhaus typography on bookwork is limited, its indirect influence, encouraging designers such as Jan Tschichold to re-examine the whole tradition of typography and its relationship to twentieth-century life, is difficult to overestimate. The work of many designers today ultimately derives from Bauhaus thinking, even if it shows scant resemblance to what must now be considered the period character of the original. Would things have turned out differently without the Bauhaus? It is inconceivable that, with architects like Le Corbusier or Mies van der Rohe around, similar ideas about the need for an industrially based theory of design would not have evolved. (Mies actually became the school's last director, in 1930.) Yet, despite it being such a fighting community, its radical ideas were only slowly taken up. Perversely, it may have been the closure of the school by the Nazi regime in 1933, resulting in the dispersal of its powerful teachers, that helped eventually to spread its gospel.

Two notable designers, both Dutch, whose work relates to and refines that of the Bauhaus, were the near-contemporaries Paul Schuitema and Piet Zwart. The latter's varied career included furniture and interior design, architecture (as assistant to H P Berlage), and then – most importantly – advertising, where he integrated typography and photographs (often his own words and his own photographs) in a strikingly original way. He had been in contact with both de Stijl (as assistant to Jan Wils, a member of the group) and the Constructivists (through El Lissitzky); in 1931 he was briefly a guest-teacher at the Bauhaus. Thus he was a link between three major early movements. As Herbert Spencer writes, 'the whole uninhibited pioneering enthusiasm of his attack suddenly charged the printed page with a new power, a new tension, and gave it in effect a new dimension'.

The work of the slightly younger Schuitema, equally vigorous, also shows photography integrated into the design in a free and imaginative way. It perhaps reflected the Bauhaus influence more closely. In 1930s Switzerland, designers such as Anton Stankowsky, Heiri Steiner and Ernst Keller were also affected by it, again incorporating photographs and photomontage. The Swiss skills we shall see later were a culmination of a long tradition.

Neue Arbeiten der Bauhauswerkstätten
Bauhausbücher 7, 1924
Designed by László Moholy-Nagy
Illustrated at 55% actual size

The use of a bold expanded grotesque, the heavy rule, and the swinging sideways of page 11, give these pages the dynamic effect that Bauhaus principles demanded; but – especially in pages 110 and 111 opposite – there is a good control of space. That spread is firmly held together by the alignment of the two bottom lines. Even in the spread on this page, which is less unified, the top of the rule aligns with the half-tone on its opposite page. The determined asymmetry is of course a policy statement.

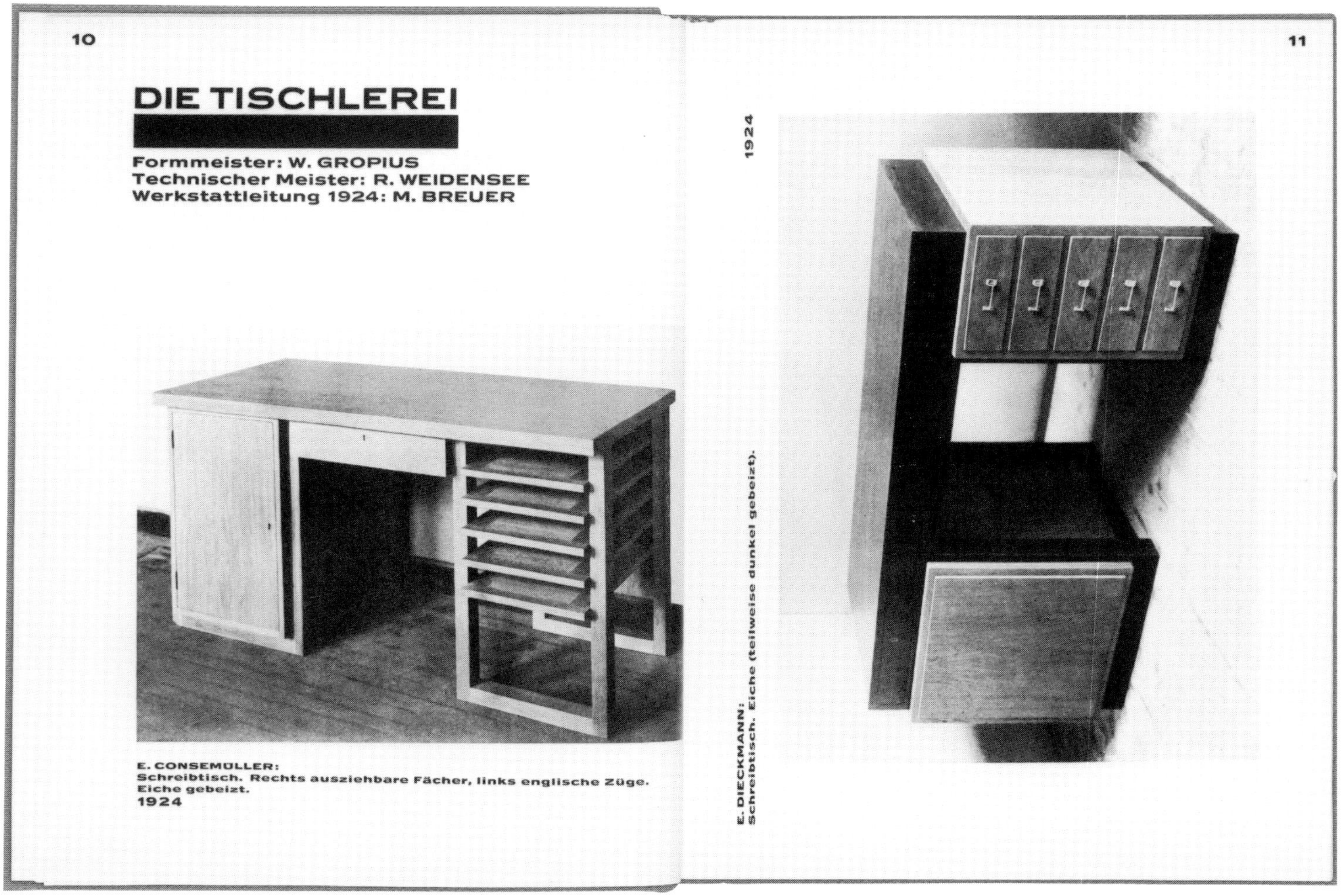
10

DIE TISCHLEREI

Formmeister: W. GROPIUS
Technischer Meister: R. WEIDENSEE
Werkstattleitung 1924: M. BREUER

E. CONSEMÜLLER:
Schreibtisch. Rechts ausziehbare Fächer, links englische Züge.
Eiche gebeizt.
1924

11

1924

E. DIECKMANN:
Schreibtisch. Eiche (teilweise dunkel gebeizt).

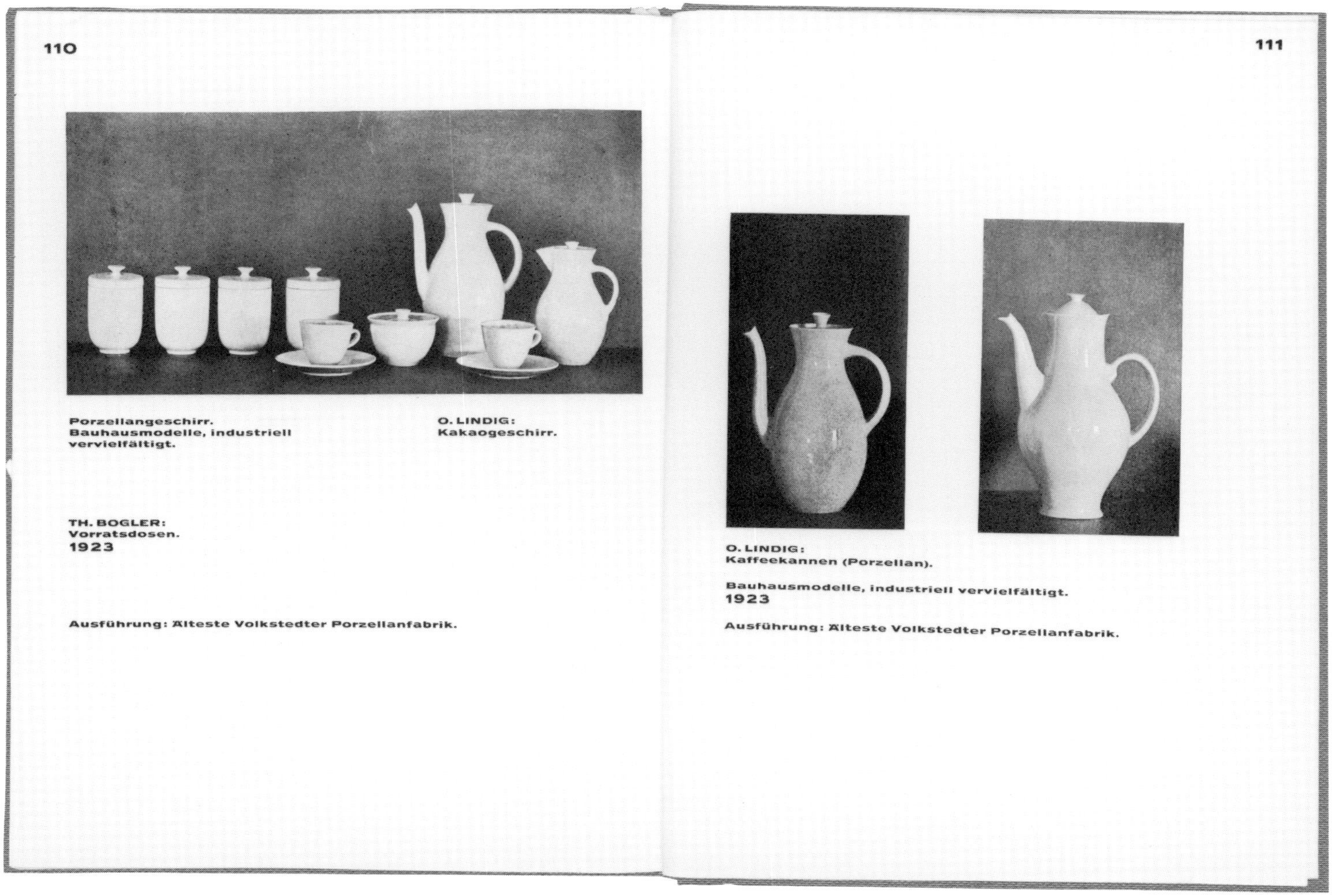

110

Porzellangeschirr.
Bauhausmodelle, industriell vervielfältigt.

O. LINDIG:
Kakaogeschirr.

TH. BOGLER:
Vorratsdosen.
1923

Ausführung: Älteste Volkstedter Porzellanfabrik.

111

O. LINDIG:
Kaffeekannen (Porzellan).

Bauhausmodelle, industriell vervielfältigt.
1923

Ausführung: Älteste Volkstedter Porzellanfabrik.

László Moholy-Nagy
Malerei Photographie Film
Bauhausbücher 8, 1925
Designed by László Moholy-Nagy
Illustrated at 55% actual size

Moholy-Nagy's approach to Typography for Modern Times differs from Herbert Bayer's quieter meditations on the subject, seen on pages 57 and 58-9. Moholy's two spreads here are industrial strength. His pages 12 and 13, below, with their strong folios, heavy rules both horizontal and vertical, odd intrusions of bold type instead of italic, and bold blobs – the one on page 12 just a blob, that on page 13 signalling a footnote – are strong stuff. Pages 116 and 117, opposite, are especially daunting, an unwise attempt to translate a Mondrian painting into the spread of a book. The outer margins in this copy seem to have been over-trimmed during rebinding, and some inner margin has been lost; even so, the effect, with 'restraining' rules which do precisely the opposite, must always have been over-dynamic and restless, intensified, perhaps, by the use of both roman and extended grotesque typefaces. The calm, cool geometry of Mondrian has here been transformed into a hectic unrest, an almost Futurist chaos.

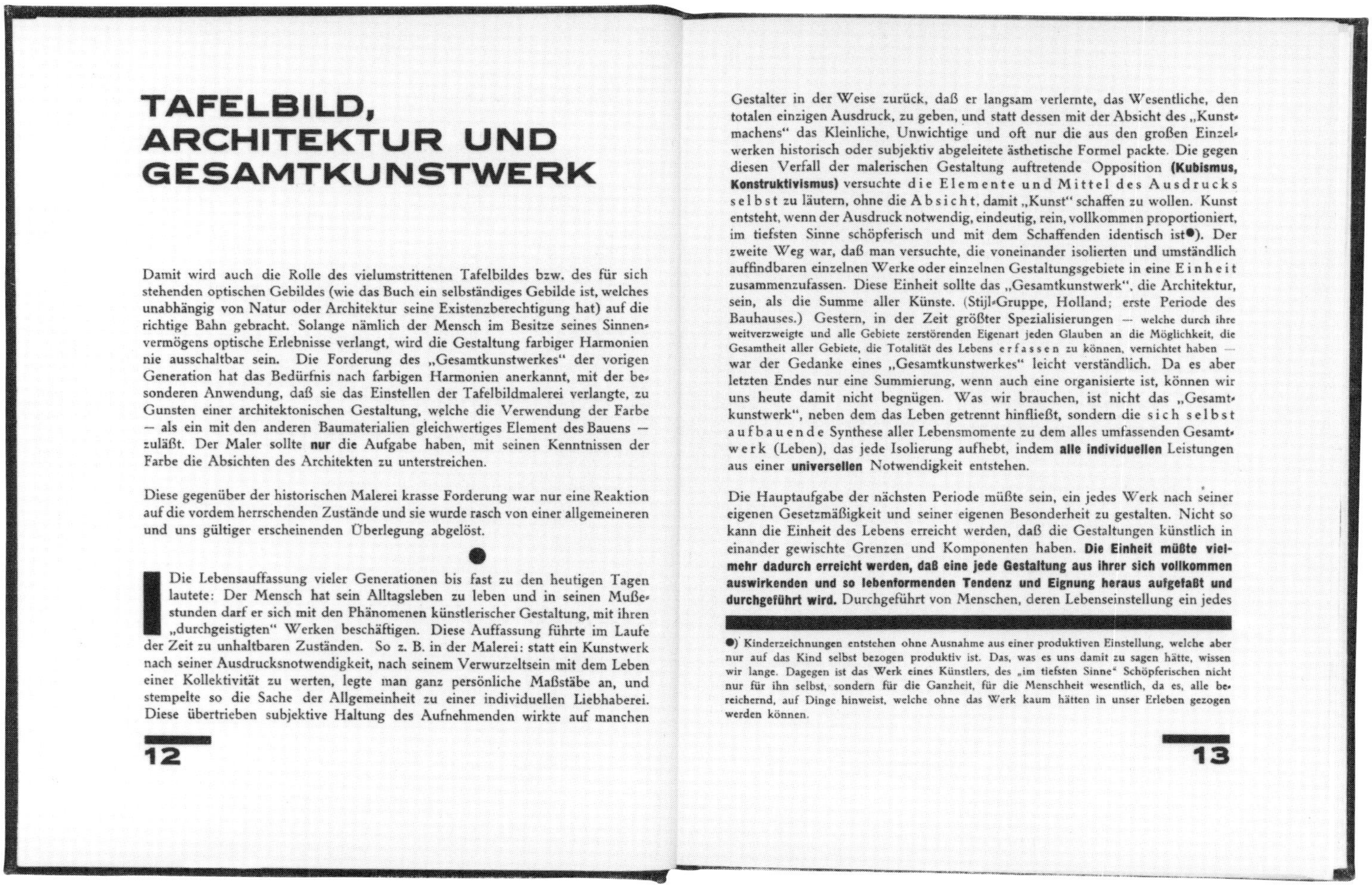

TAFELBILD, ARCHITEKTUR UND GESAMTKUNSTWERK

Damit wird auch die Rolle des vielumstrittenen Tafelbildes bzw. des für sich stehenden optischen Gebildes (wie das Buch ein selbständiges Gebilde ist, welches unabhängig von Natur oder Architektur seine Existenzberechtigung hat) auf die richtige Bahn gebracht. Solange nämlich der Mensch im Besitze seines Sinnenvermögens optische Erlebnisse verlangt, wird die Gestaltung farbiger Harmonien nie ausschaltbar sein. Die Forderung des „Gesamtkunstwerkes" der vorigen Generation hat das Bedürfnis nach farbigen Harmonien anerkannt, mit der besonderen Anwendung, daß sie das Einstellen der Tafelbildmalerei verlangte, zu Gunsten einer architektonischen Gestaltung, welche die Verwendung der Farbe – als ein mit den anderen Baumaterialien gleichwertiges Element des Bauens – zuläßt. Der Maler sollte **nur** die Aufgabe haben, mit seinen Kenntnissen der Farbe die Absichten des Architekten zu unterstreichen.

Diese gegenüber der historischen Malerei krasse Forderung war nur eine Reaktion auf die vordem herrschenden Zustände und sie wurde rasch von einer allgemeineren und uns gültiger erscheinenden Überlegung abgelöst.

●

Die Lebensauffassung vieler Generationen bis fast zu den heutigen Tagen lautete: Der Mensch hat sein Alltagsleben zu leben und in seinen Mußestunden darf er sich mit den Phänomenen künstlerischer Gestaltung, mit ihren „durchgeistigten" Werken beschäftigen. Diese Auffassung führte im Laufe der Zeit zu unhaltbaren Zuständen. So z. B. in der Malerei: statt ein Kunstwerk nach seiner Ausdrucksnotwendigkeit, nach seinem Verwurzeltsein mit dem Leben einer Kollektivität zu werten, legte man ganz persönliche Maßstäbe an, und stempelte so die Sache der Allgemeinheit zu einer individuellen Liebhaberei. Diese übertrieben subjektive Haltung des Aufnehmenden wirkte auf manchen

12

Gestalter in der Weise zurück, daß er langsam verlernte, das Wesentliche, den totalen einzigen Ausdruck, zu geben, und statt dessen mit der Absicht des „Kunstmachens" das Kleinliche, Unwichtige und oft nur die aus den großen Einzelwerken historisch oder subjektiv abgeleitete ästhetische Formel packte. Die gegen diesen Verfall der malerischen Gestaltung auftretende Opposition **(Kubismus, Konstruktivismus)** versuchte die Elemente und Mittel des Ausdrucks selbst zu läutern, ohne die Absicht, damit „Kunst" schaffen zu wollen. Kunst entsteht, wenn der Ausdruck notwendig, eindeutig, rein, vollkommen proportioniert, im tiefsten Sinne schöpferisch und mit dem Schaffenden identisch ist●). Der zweite Weg war, daß man versuchte, die voneinander isolierten und umständlich auffindbaren einzelnen Werke oder einzelnen Gestaltungsgebiete in eine Einheit zusammenzufassen. Diese Einheit sollte das „Gesamtkunstwerk", die Architektur, sein, als die Summe aller Künste. (Stijl-Gruppe, Holland; erste Periode des Bauhauses.) Gestern, in der Zeit größter Spezialisierungen — welche durch ihre weitverzweigte und alle Gebiete zerstörenden Eigenart jeden Glauben an die Möglichkeit, die Gesamtheit aller Gebiete, die Totalität des Lebens erfassen zu können, vernichtet haben — war der Gedanke eines „Gesamtkunstwerkes" leicht verständlich. Da es aber letzten Endes nur eine Summierung, wenn auch eine organisierte ist, können wir uns heute damit nicht begnügen. Was wir brauchen, ist nicht das „Gesamtkunstwerk", neben dem das Leben getrennt hinfließt, sondern die sich selbst aufbauende Synthese aller Lebensmomente zu dem alles umfassenden Gesamtwerk (Leben), das jede Isolierung aufhebt, indem **alle individuellen** Leistungen aus einer **universellen** Notwendigkeit entstehen.

Die Hauptaufgabe der nächsten Periode müßte sein, ein jedes Werk nach seiner eigenen Gesetzmäßigkeit und seiner eigenen Besonderheit zu gestalten. Nicht so kann die Einheit des Lebens erreicht werden, daß die Gestaltungen künstlich in einander gewischte Grenzen und Komponenten haben. **Die Einheit müßte vielmehr dadurch erreicht werden, daß eine jede Gestaltung aus ihrer sich vollkommen auswirkenden und so lebenformenden Tendenz und Eignung heraus aufgefaßt und durchgeführt wird.** Durchgeführt von Menschen, deren Lebenseinstellung ein jedes

●) Kinderzeichnungen entstehen ohne Ausnahme aus einer produktiven Einstellung, welche aber nur auf das Kind selbst bezogen produktiv ist. Das, was es uns damit zu sagen hätte, wissen wir lange. Dagegen ist das Werk eines Künstlers, des „im tiefsten Sinne" Schöpferischen nicht nur für ihn selbst, sondern für die Ganzheit, für die Menschheit wesentlich, da es, alle bereichernd, auf Dinge hinweist, welche ohne das Werk kaum hätten in unser Erleben gezogen werden können.

13

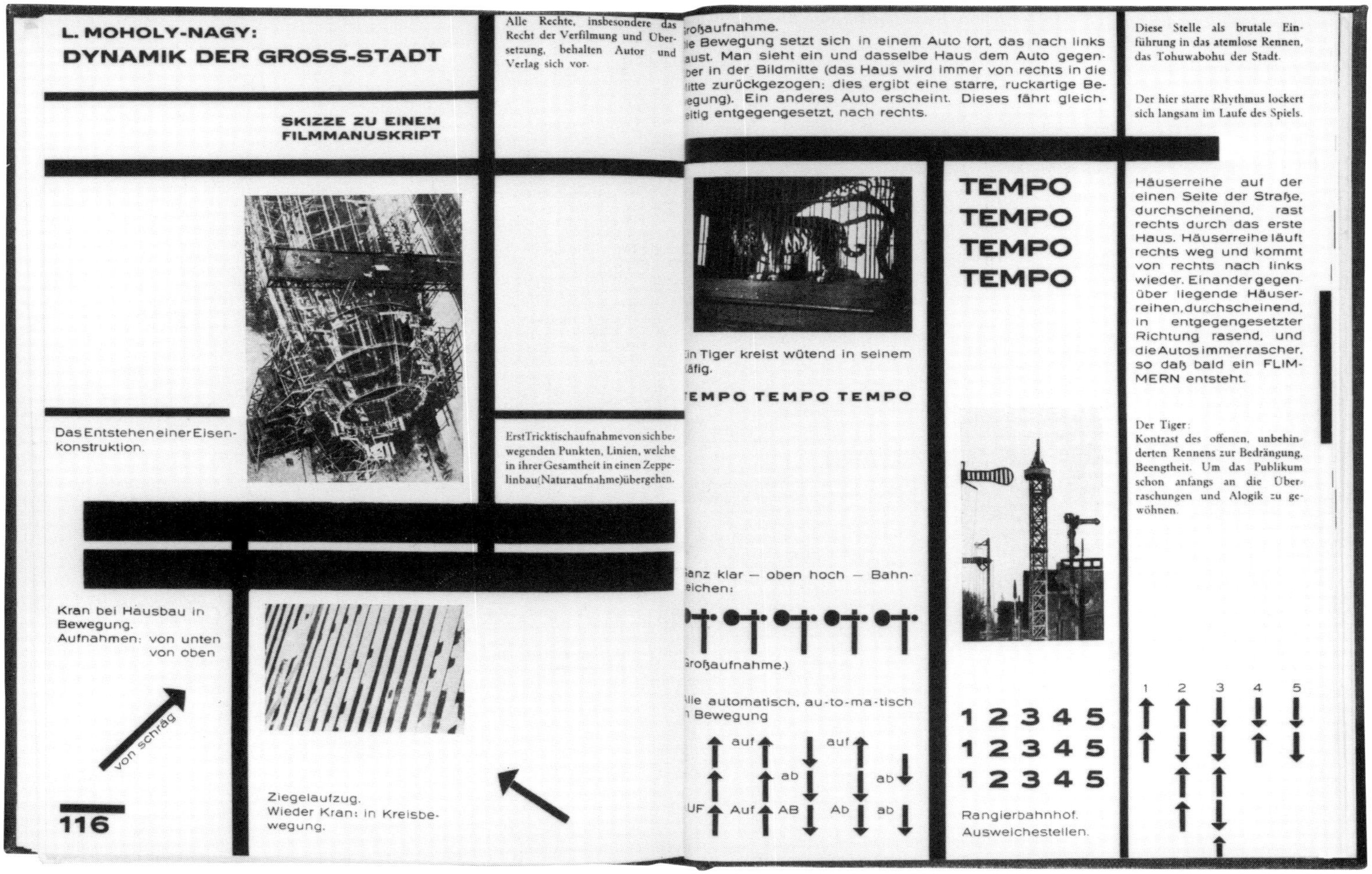

L. MOHOLY-NAGY:

DYNAMIK DER GROSS-STADT

SKIZZE ZU EINEM FILMMANUSKRIPT

Das Entstehen einer Eisenkonstruktion.

Erst Tricktischaufnahme von sich bewegenden Punkten, Linien, welche in ihrer Gesamtheit in einen Zeppelinbau (Naturaufnahme) übergehen.

Kran bei Hausbau in Bewegung.
Aufnahmen: von unten
von oben

von schräg

Ziegelaufzug.
Wieder Kran: in Kreisbewegung.

116

Großaufnahme.
Die Bewegung setzt sich in einem Auto fort, das nach links saust. Man sieht ein und dasselbe Haus dem Auto gegenüber in der Bildmitte (das Haus wird immer von rechts in die Mitte zurückgezogen; dies ergibt eine starre, ruckartige Bewegung). Ein anderes Auto erscheint. Dieses fährt gleichzeitig entgegengesetzt, nach rechts.

Ein Tiger kreist wütend in seinem Käfig.

TEMPO TEMPO TEMPO

Ganz klar — oben hoch — Bahnzeichen:

(Großaufnahme.)

Alle automatisch, au-to-ma-tisch in Bewegung

auf auf ab ab AUF Auf AB Ab ab

TEMPO
TEMPO
TEMPO
TEMPO

1 2 3 4 5
1 2 3 4 5
1 2 3 4 5

Rangierbahnhof.
Ausweichestellen.

Diese Stelle als brutale Einführung in das atemlose Rennen, das Tohuwabohu der Stadt.

Der hier starre Rhythmus lockert sich langsam im Laufe des Spiels.

Häuserreihe auf der einen Seite der Straße, durchscheinend, rast rechts durch das erste Haus. Häuserreihe läuft rechts weg und kommt von rechts nach links wieder. Einander gegenüber liegende Häuserreihen, durchscheinend, in entgegengesetzter Richtung rasend, und die Autos immer rascher, so daß bald ein FLIMMERN entsteht.

Der Tiger:
Kontrast des offenen, unbehinderten Rennens zur Bedrängung, Beengtheit. Um das Publikum schon anfangs an die Überraschungen und Alogik zu gewöhnen.

1 2 3 4 5

László Moholy-Nagy
Vision in Motion
Paul Theobald, Chicago, 1946
Designed by László Moholy-Nagy
Illustrated at 45% actual size

The Bauhaus was closed down in 1933, but Moholy-Nagy had already left (as had Bayer) in 1928. He worked in Berlin, then Amsterdam. After two years in London, he emigrated to America in 1937. Here is his definitive statement on the illustrated book; he died the year before it was published. All the illustrations are placed where mentioned in the text, or on the opposite page. The arrangement 'also considers the impatient reader, who, at first unwilling to plow through the written arguments, may enjoy the pictorial material. Stirred by this, he may then proceed to read brief captions,

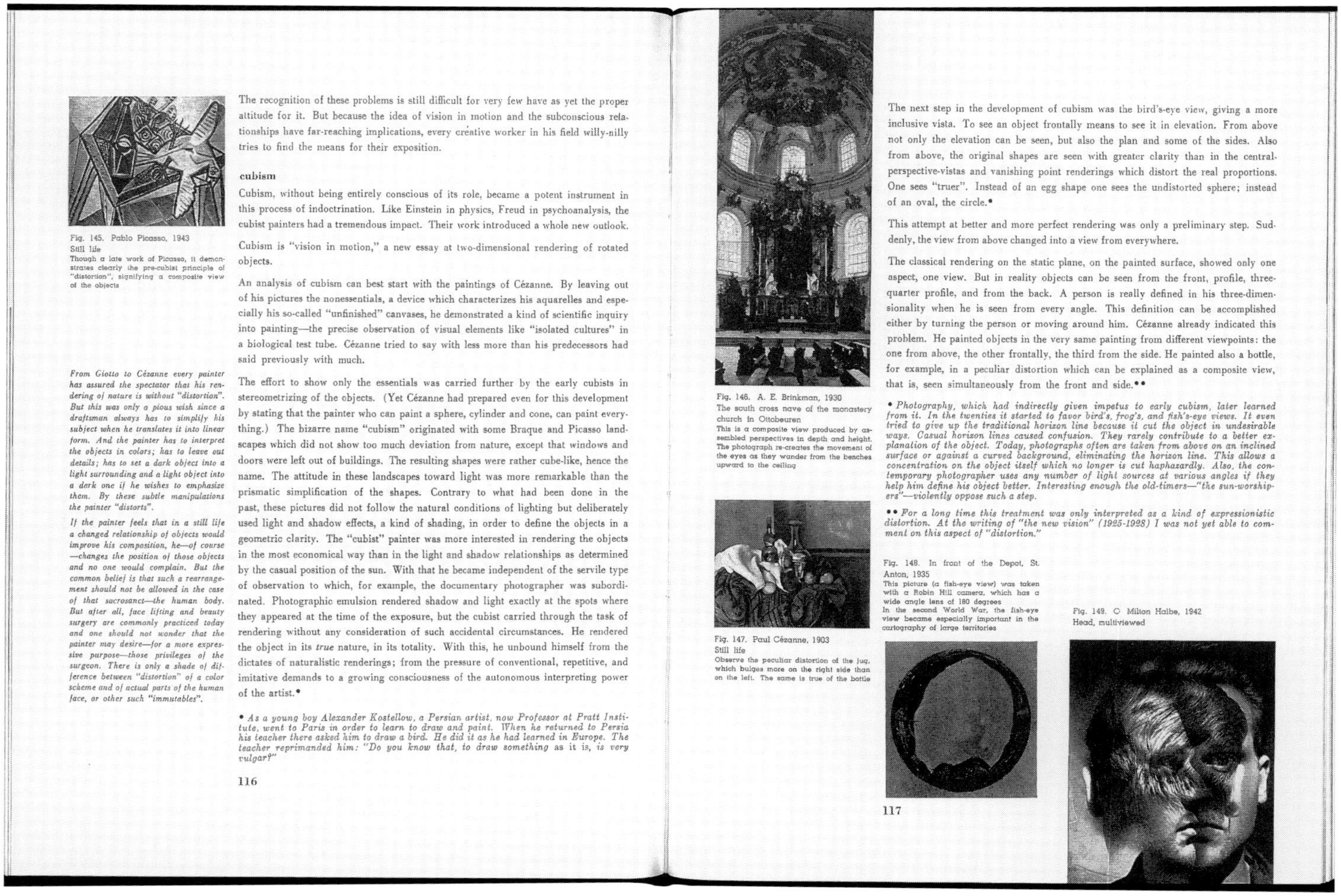

Fig. 145. Pablo Picasso, 1943
Still life
Though a late work of Picasso, it demonstrates clearly the pre-cubist principle of "distortion", signifying a composite view of the objects

The recognition of these problems is still difficult for very few have as yet the proper attitude for it. But because the idea of vision in motion and the subconscious relationships have far-reaching implications, every creative worker in his field willy-nilly tries to find the means for their exposition.

cubism

Cubism, without being entirely conscious of its role, became a potent instrument in this process of indoctrination. Like Einstein in physics, Freud in psychoanalysis, the cubist painters had a tremendous impact. Their work introduced a whole new outlook.

Cubism is "vision in motion," a new essay at two-dimensional rendering of rotated objects.

An analysis of cubism can best start with the paintings of Cézanne. By leaving out of his pictures the nonessentials, a device which characterizes his aquarelles and especially his so-called "unfinished" canvases, he demonstrated a kind of scientific inquiry into painting—the precise observation of visual elements like "isolated cultures" in a biological test tube. Cézanne tried to say with less more than his predecessors had said previously with much.

From Giotto to Cézanne every painter has assured the spectator that his rendering of nature is without "distortion". But this was only a pious wish since a draftsman always has to simplify his subject when he translates it into linear form. And the painter has to interpret the objects in colors; has to leave out details; has to set a dark object into a light surrounding and a light object into a dark one if he wishes to emphasize them. By these subtle manipulations the painter "distorts".

If the painter feels that in a still life a changed relationship of objects would improve his composition, he—of course—changes the position of those objects and no one would complain. But the common belief is that such a rearrangement should not be allowed in the case of that sacrosanct—the human body. But after all, face lifting and beauty surgery are commonly practiced today and one should not wonder that the painter may desire—for a more expressive purpose—those privileges of the surgeon. There is only a shade of difference between "distortion" of a color scheme and of actual parts of the human face, or other such "immutables".

The effort to show only the essentials was carried further by the early cubists in stereometrizing of the objects. (Yet Cézanne had prepared even for this development by stating that the painter who can paint a sphere, cylinder and cone, can paint everything.) The bizarre name "cubism" originated with some Braque and Picasso landscapes which did not show too much deviation from nature, except that windows and doors were left out of buildings. The resulting shapes were rather cube-like, hence the name. The attitude in these landscapes toward light was more remarkable than the prismatic simplification of the shapes. Contrary to what had been done in the past, these pictures did not follow the natural conditions of lighting but deliberately used light and shadow effects, a kind of shading, in order to define the objects in a geometric clarity. The "cubist" painter was more interested in rendering the objects in the most economical way than in the light and shadow relationships as determined by the casual position of the sun. With that he became independent of the servile type of observation to which, for example, the documentary photographer was subordinated. Photographic emulsion rendered shadow and light exactly at the spots where they appeared at the time of the exposure, but the cubist carried through the task of rendering without any consideration of such accidental circumstances. He rendered the object in its *true* nature, in its totality. With this, he unbound himself from the dictates of naturalistic renderings; from the pressure of conventional, repetitive, and imitative demands to a growing consciousness of the autonomous interpreting power of the artist.•

• *As a young boy Alexander Kostellow, a Persian artist, now Professor at Pratt Institute, went to Paris in order to learn to draw and paint. When he returned to Persia his teacher there asked him to draw a bird. He did it as he had learned in Europe. The teacher reprimanded him: "Do you know that, to draw something* as it is, *is very vulgar?"*

116

Fig. 146. A. E. Brinkman, 1930
The south cross nave of the monastery church in Ottobeuren
This is a composite view produced by assembled perspectives in depth and height. The photograph re-creates the movement of the eyes as they wander from the benches upward to the ceiling

The next step in the development of cubism was the bird's-eye view, giving a more inclusive vista. To see an object frontally means to see it in elevation. From above not only the elevation can be seen, but also the plan and some of the sides. Also from above, the original shapes are seen with greater clarity than in the central-perspective-vistas and vanishing point renderings which distort the real proportions. One sees "truer". Instead of an egg shape one sees the undistorted sphere; instead of an oval, the circle.•

This attempt at better and more perfect rendering was only a preliminary step. Suddenly, the view from above changed into a view from everywhere.

The classical rendering on the static plane, on the painted surface, showed only one aspect, one view. But in reality objects can be seen from the front, profile, three-quarter profile, and from the back. A person is really defined in his three-dimensionality when he is seen from every angle. This definition can be accomplished either by turning the person or moving around him. Cézanne already indicated this problem. He painted objects in the very same painting from different viewpoints: the one from above, the other frontally, the third from the side. He painted also a bottle, for example, in a peculiar distortion which can be explained as a composite view, that is, seen simultaneously from the front and side.••

• *Photography, which had indirectly given impetus to early cubism, later learned from it. In the twenties it started to favor bird's, frog's, and fish's-eye views. It even tried to give up the traditional horizon line because it cut the object in undesirable ways. Casual horizon lines caused confusion. They rarely contribute to a better explanation of the object. Today, photographs often are taken from above on an inclined surface or against a curved background, eliminating the horizon line. This allows a concentration on the object itself which no longer is cut haphazardly. Also, the contemporary photographer uses any number of light sources at various angles if they help him define his object better. Interesting enough the old-timers—"the sun-worshipers"—violently oppose such a step.*

•• *For a long time this treatment was only interpreted as a kind of expressionistic distortion. At the writing of "the new vision" (1925-1928) I was not yet able to comment on this aspect of "distortion."*

Fig. 147. Paul Cézanne, 1903
Still life
Observe the peculiar distortion of the jug, which bulges more on the right side than on the left. The same is true of the bottle

Fig. 148. In front of the Depot, St. Anton, 1935
This picture (a fish-eye view) was taken with a Robin Hill camera, which has a wide angle lens of 180 degrees
In the second World War, the fish-eye view became especially important in the cartography of large territories

Fig. 149. © Milton Halbe, 1942
Head, multiviewed

117

glossaries and footnotes until his appetite is whetted to explore the main text'. Fine and dandy, very admirable, and a true analysis of how many books are read. The result, unfortunately, looks a bit of a mess; the Swiss were to develop a far more aesthetically pleasing system. So it is interesting to compare Moholy's design with the Swiss book on Paul Klee's notebooks shown on pages 120-23.

The first spread here includes the whole battery of captions, side comments and footnotes signalled by disturbing black blobs – a device that Tschichold used in 1928, no more happily. Text is in Bodoni, side comments in Bodoni italic, footnotes in Century italic, and captions in egyptian. One can understand the thinking, but there are at least two types too many there. The page is further unsettled by the line spaces between paragraphs. And in both spreads the picture pattern is unnecessarily dispersed and ill-coordinated; although, today, the book as a whole has a lively and rather nostalgic appeal, just because it is a sincere if now dated attempt to solve the problem of integrating illustrations and varied text.

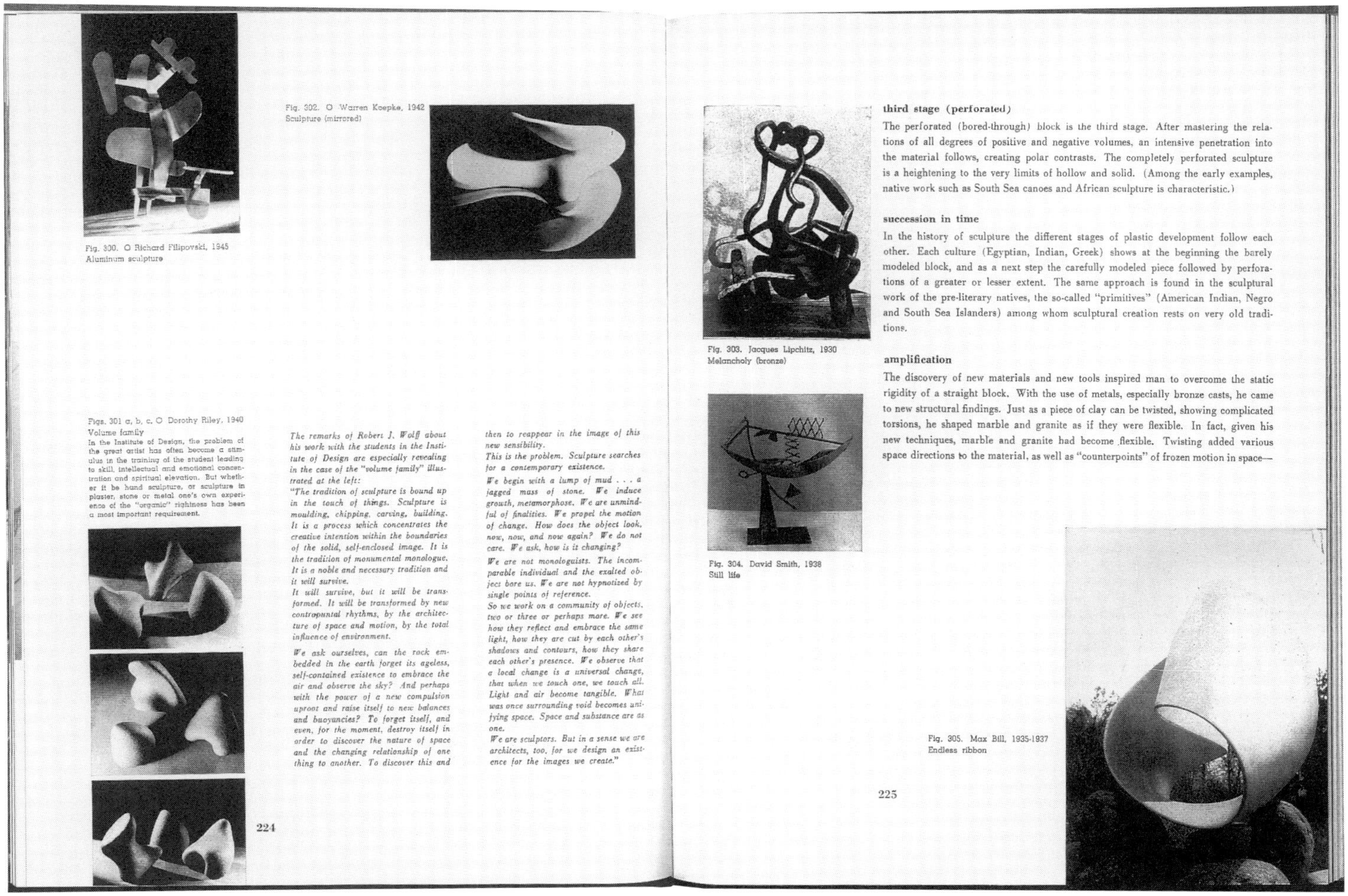

Fig. 300. © Richard Filipowski, 1945
Aluminum sculpture

Fig. 302. © Warren Koepke, 1942
Sculpture (mirrored)

Figs. 301 a, b, c. © Dorothy Riley, 1940
Volume family
In the Institute of Design, the problem of the great artist has often become a stimulus in the training of the student leading to skill, intellectual and emotional concentration and spiritual elevation. But whether it be hand sculpture, or sculpture in plaster, stone or metal one's own experience of the "organic" rightness has been a most important requirement.

The remarks of Robert J. Wolff about his work with the students in the Institute of Design are especially revealing in the case of the "volume family" illustrated at the left:
"The tradition of sculpture is bound up in the touch of things. Sculpture is moulding, chipping, carving, building. It is a process which concentrates the creative intention within the boundaries of the solid, self-enclosed image. It is the tradition of monumental monologue. It is a noble and necessary tradition and it will survive.
It will survive, but it will be transformed. It will be transformed by new contropuntal rhythms, by the architecture of space and motion, by the total influence of environment.

We ask ourselves, can the rock embedded in the earth forget its ageless, self-contained existence to embrace the air and observe the sky? And perhaps with the power of a new compulsion uproot and raise itself to new balances and buoyancies? To forget itself, and even, for the moment, destroy itself in order to discover the nature of space and the changing relationship of one thing to another. To discover this and then to reappear in the image of this new sensibility.
This is the problem. Sculpture searches for a contemporary existence.
We begin with a lump of mud . . . a jagged mass of stone. We induce growth, metamorphose. We are unmindful of finalities. We propel the motion of change. How does the object look, now, now, and now again? We do not care. We ask, how is it changing?
We are not monologuists. The incomparable individual and the exalted object bore us. We are not hypnotized by single points of reference.
So we work on a community of objects, two or three or perhaps more. We see how they reflect and embrace the same light, how they are cut by each other's shadows and contours, how they share each other's presence. We observe that a local change is a universal change, that when we touch one, we touch all. Light and air become tangible. What was once surrounding void becomes unifying space. Space and substance are as one.
We are sculptors. But in a sense we are architects, too, for we design an existence for the images we create."

224

Fig. 303. Jacques Lipchitz, 1930
Melancholy (bronze)

Fig. 304. David Smith, 1938
Still life

third stage (perforated)

The perforated (bored-through) block is the third stage. After mastering the relations of all degrees of positive and negative volumes, an intensive penetration into the material follows, creating polar contrasts. The completely perforated sculpture is a heightening to the very limits of hollow and solid. (Among the early examples, native work such as South Sea canoes and African sculpture is characteristic.)

succession in time

In the history of sculpture the different stages of plastic development follow each other. Each culture (Egyptian, Indian, Greek) shows at the beginning the barely modeled block, and as a next step the carefully modeled piece followed by perforations of a greater or lesser extent. The same approach is found in the sculptural work of the pre-literary natives, the so-called "primitives" (American Indian, Negro and South Sea Islanders) among whom sculptural creation rests on very old traditions.

amplification

The discovery of new materials and new tools inspired man to overcome the static rigidity of a straight block. With the use of metals, especially bronze casts, he came to new structural findings. Just as a piece of clay can be twisted, showing complicated torsions, he shaped marble and granite as if they were flexible. In fact, given his new techniques, marble and granite had become flexible. Twisting added various space directions to the material, as well as "counterpoints" of frozen motion in space—

Fig. 305. Max Bill, 1935-1937
Endless ribbon

225

Two postcards
as shown in *Die Neue Typographie*
by Jan Tschichold
Berlin, 1928

The top postcard is by Joost Schmidt, the bottom one by Max Burchartz and Johannes Canis. While both derive their characteristic Bauhaus vigour by opposing horizontals with verticals, by the use of bold rules, and by the dynamic handling of space, Schmidt's design is the stronger and more carefully worked out. As with the El Lissitzky designs we saw on page 45, Tschichold presumably found these postcards had qualities he could approve of, even if such designs could never be mistaken for his own work.

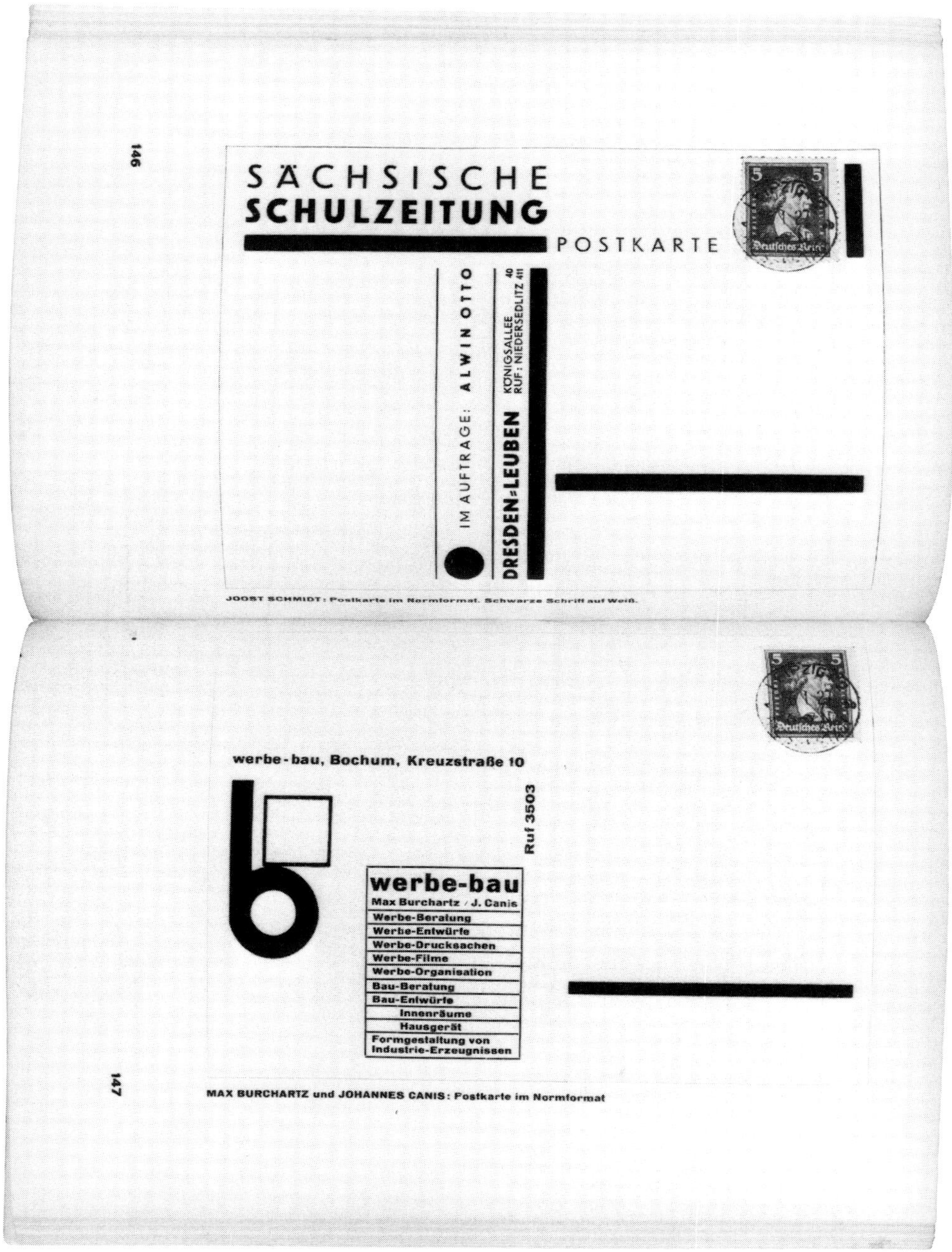

OPPOSITE
Bauhaus Journal No 1
Dessau, 1926
Illustrated at 68% actual size

Almost certainly designed by Herbert Bayer, this shows the new geometry in action, although any grid is denied by the varied picture widths. Bayer's ban on caps is enforced; grotesques are used not only in different weights, which modernism allowed, but also in different widths. These would probably have been unacceptable to Max Bill – as would those bold rules. The text above the rule is set in a seriffed face. Yet the design is unified, rigorous and strong, incorporating, in controlled form, the spirit of the pioneers. This early attempt at a design deliberately intended to reflect the industrial nature of its production, and the times, is skilfully handled, showing a restraint and a concern for function, or communication, that the Futurists, Constructivists and poet-designers had no need to bother with; or at least it was not their prime interest. The front page of the journal illustrates Gropius's iconic buildings for the Dessau Bauhaus: a potent image.

bauhaus 1

1926

die zeitschrift erscheint vierteljährlich ● bezugspreis: jährlich mk 2.—; einzelnummer 60 pfennig ●
mitglieder des „kreis der freunde des bauhauses" erhalten die zeitschrift kostenlos ●
schriftleitung: walter gropius und l. moholy-nagy ●
geschäftsstelle: bauhaus dessau ●

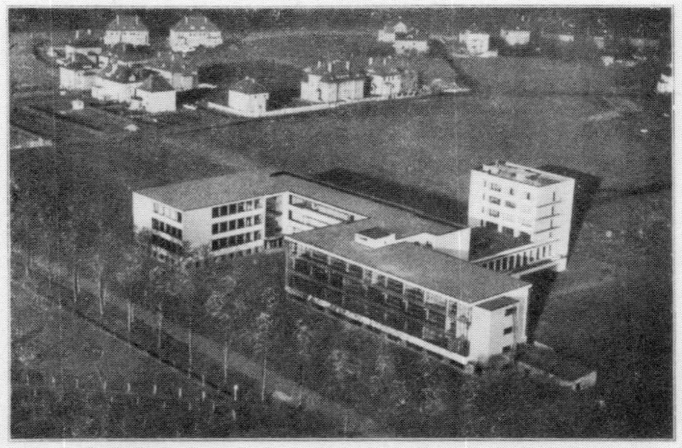

bauhausneubau dessau — junkers luftbild

statt einer vorrede:

walter gropius: bauhaus-chronik 1925/1926

weihnachten 1924 auflösungserklärung des staatlichen bauhauses weimar durch die meister des bauhauses.

april 1925 die stadt dessau, ein zentrum des mitteldeutschen braunkohlenreviers mit aufsteigender wirtschaftlicher entwicklung, faßt den beschluß, geleitet von dem kulturellen weitblick seiner stadtverwaltung, das bauhaus zu übernehmen.

alle bisherigen meister — feininger, gropius, kandinsky, klee, moholy, muche, schlemmer — verbleiben am bauhaus, mit ausnahme von marcks, der — da die keramische abteilung, die er leitet, aus räumlichen und finanziellen gründen nicht mit übernommen werden kann — eine berufung nach halle annimmt.

5 ehemalige bauhaus-studierende — albers, bayer, breuer, scheper, schmidt — werden als meister an das bauhaus berufen. mit ihrem eintritt erfährt das bauhaus-programm eine wesentliche änderung.

bauhausneubau dessau

architekt w. gropius

der bau wurde ende september vor. js. begonnen, der rohbau wurde am 21. 3. 26 fertiggestellt. das atelierhaus wurde am 1. september, die übrigen räume des bauhauses wurden am 15. oktober bezogen.

der gesamte bau bedeckt rund 2600 qm grundfläche und enthält 32000 cbm umbauten raums. bauherr ist der magistrat der stadt dessau. der preis pro cbm umbauten raums bleibt unter m. 26,-

der gesamte baukomplex besteht aus 3 teilen:

1 das **fachschulgebäude,** enthaltend die berufsschule (lehr- und verwaltungsräume, lehrerzimmer, bibliothek, fysiksaal, modellräume), [illegible] ganz ausgebautes souterrain, hochparterre und zwei obergeschosse. im ersten und zweiten obergeschoß führt eine auf 4 pfeilern über eine fahrstraße gespannte brücke, in der unten die bauhausverwaltung, oben die architekturabteilung untergebracht ist, zu dem bau

2 **laboratoriums-werkstätten** und lehrräume des bauhauses. im souterrain die bühnenwerkstatt, druckerei, färberei, bildhauerei, pack- und lagerräume, hausmannswohnung und heizkeller mit vorgelagertem kohlenbunker.

im hochparterre die tischlerei und die ausstellungsräume, großes vestibül, daran anschließend die aula mit der vorgelagerten, überhöhten bühne.

im 1. obergeschoß die weberei, die räume für die grundlehre, ein großer vortragsraum und die verbindung von bau 1 zu bau 2 durch die brücke.

im 2. obergeschoß die wandmalereiwerkstatt, metallwerkstatt, sowie zwei vortragssäle, die durch klappwand zu einem großen ausstellungssaal verändert werden können. daran anschließend die zweite brückenetage mit den räumen für die architekturabteilung und baubüro gropius.

die aula im erdgeschoß dieses baues führt in einem eingeschossigen trakt zu bau

3 **atelierhaus,** das die wohlfahrtseinrichtungen des instituts enthält. die bühne zwischen aula und speisesaal kann bei vorführungen nach beiden seiten geöffnet werden, so daß die zuschauer auf beiden

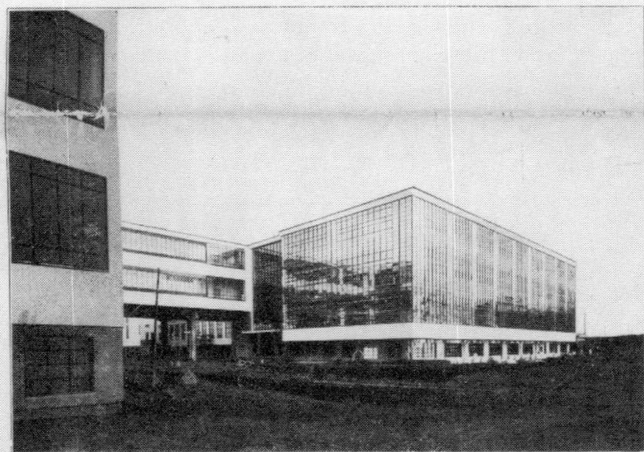

bauhausneubau · westseite — foto lucia moholy

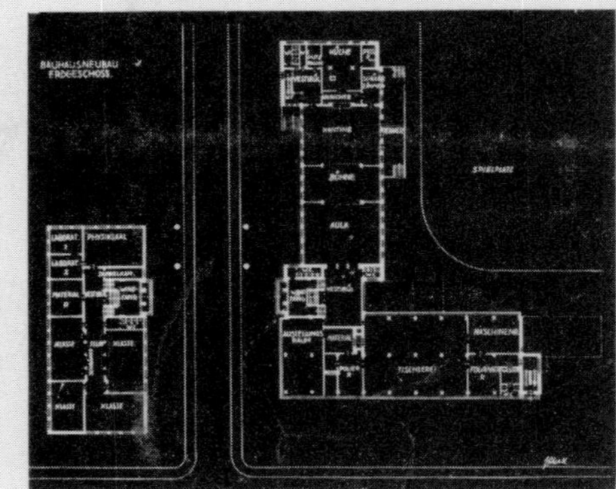

bauhausneubau dessau · grundriß des erdgeschosses

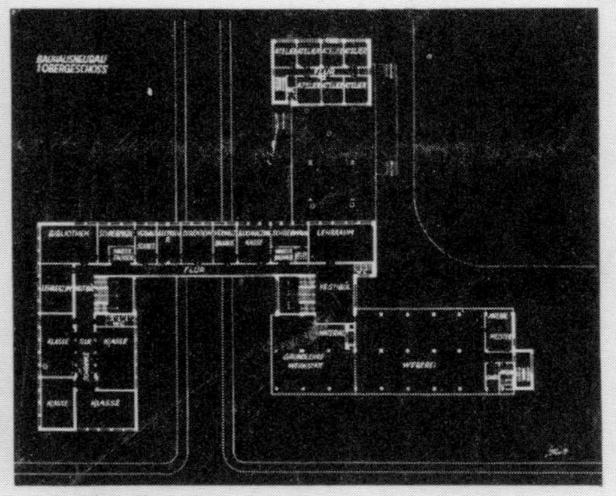

und des 1. obergeschosses

Bauhaus Journal No 4
Dessau, 1927
Illustrated at 69% actual size

Again probably designed by Bayer, this repeats the rigour of the earlier issue, but shows a free yet controlled handling of the varied illustrations which in no way diminishes the concern for geometry. While there is some evidence of a grid in their organisation, it mainly shows a good eye for pattern. The typography, using a mix of seriffed faces and grotesques (in different sizes and weights), is further articulated by rules of three weights. Strong numbers flag the captions to the illustrations; a list of Bauhaus books appears at the end. To my old-fashioned eye, the effect is as fresh as a daisy. Seventy years on, little work has such imaginative yet functional detailing; although I would have preferred a little leading.

This is a six-page journal. Page 5 folds out to reveal pages 3 and 4.

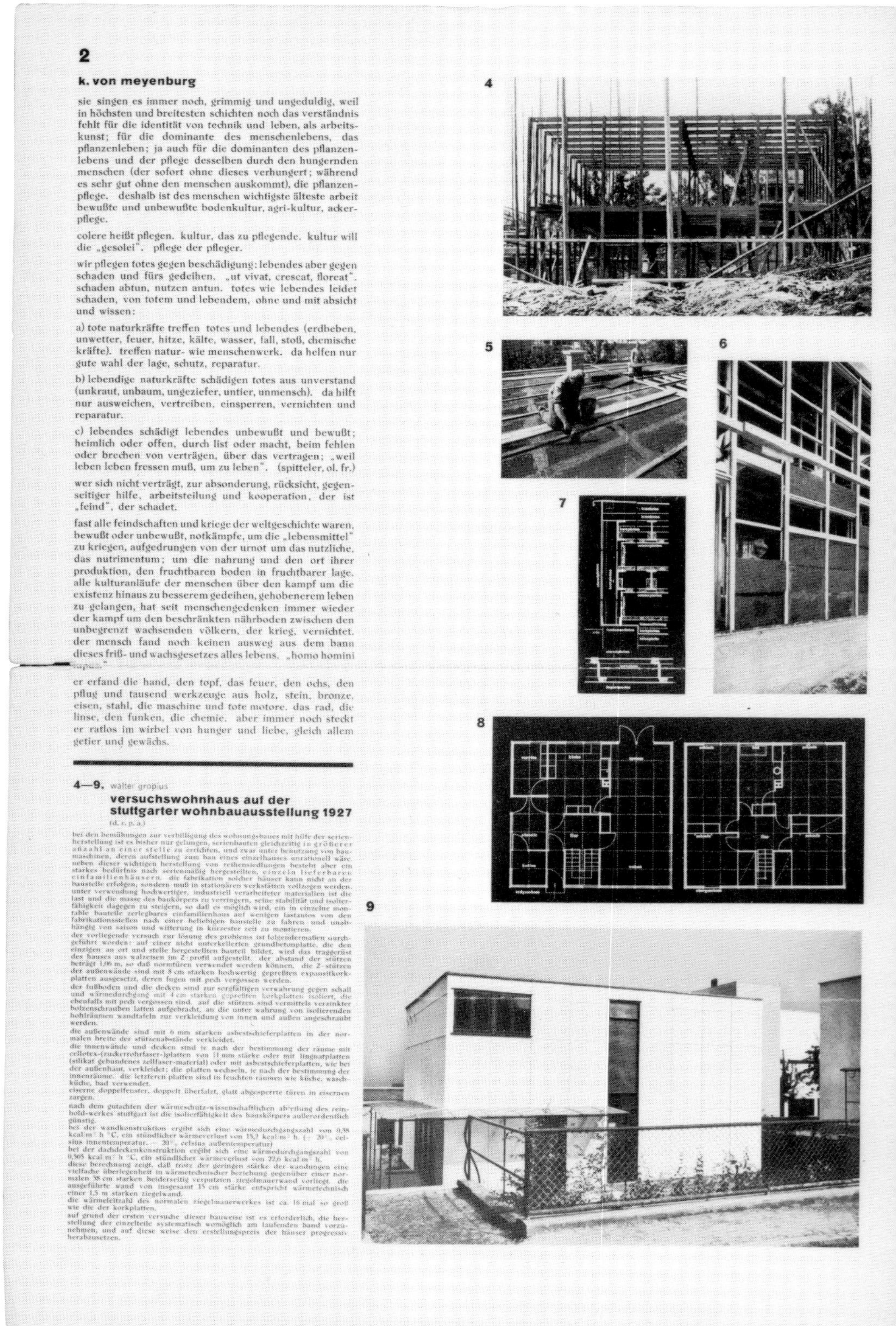

2

k. von meyenburg

sie singen es immer noch, grimmig und ungeduldig, weil in höchsten und breitesten schichten noch das verständnis fehlt für die identität von technik und leben, als arbeitskunst; für die dominante des menschenlebens, das pflanzenleben; ja auch für die dominanten des pflanzenlebens und der pflege desselben durch den hungernden menschen (der sofort ohne dieses verhungert; während es sehr gut ohne den menschen auskommt), die pflanzenpflege. deshalb ist des menschen wichtigste älteste arbeit bewußte und unbewußte bodenkultur, agri-kultur, ackerpflege.

colere heißt pflegen. kultur, das zu pflegende. kultur will die „gesolei". pflege der pfleger.

wir pflegen totes gegen beschädigung: lebendes aber gegen schaden und fürs gedeihen. „ut vivat, crescat, floreat". schaden abtun, nutzen antun. totes wie lebendes leidet schaden, von totem und lebendem, ohne und mit absicht und wissen:

a) tote naturkräfte treffen totes und lebendes (erdbeben, unwetter, feuer, hitze, kälte, wasser, fall, stoß, chemische kräfte). treffen natur- wie menschenwerk. da helfen nur gute wahl der lage, schutz, reparatur.

b) lebendige naturkräfte schädigen totes aus unverstand (unkraut, unbaum, ungeziefer, untier, unmensch). da hilft nur ausweichen, vertreiben, einsperren, vernichten und reparatur.

c) lebendes schädigt lebendes unbewußt und bewußt; heimlich oder offen, durch list oder macht, beim fehlen oder brechen von verträgen, über das vertragen; „weil leben leben fressen muß, um zu leben". (spitteler, ol. fr.)

wer sich nicht verträgt, zur absonderung, rücksicht, gegenseitiger hilfe, arbeitsteilung und kooperation, der ist „feind", der schadet.

fast alle feindschaften und kriege der weltgeschichte waren, bewußt oder unbewußt, notkämpfe, um die „lebensmittel" zu kriegen, aufgedrungen von der urnot um das nutzliche, das nutrimentum; um die nahrung und den ort ihrer produktion, den fruchtbaren boden in fruchtbarer lage. alle kulturanläufe der menschen über den kampf um die existenz hinaus zu besserem gedeihen, gehobenerem leben zu gelangen, hat seit menschengedenken immer wieder der kampf um den beschränkten nährboden zwischen den unbegrenzt wachsenden völkern, der krieg, vernichtet. der mensch fand noch keinen ausweg aus dem bann dieses friß- und wachsgesetzes alles lebens. „homo homini lupus."

er erfand die hand, den topf, das feuer, den ochs, den pflug und tausend werkzeuge aus holz, stein, bronze, eisen, stahl, die maschine und tote motore. das rad, die linse, den funken, die chemie. aber immer noch steckt er ratlos im wirbel von hunger und liebe, gleich allem getier und gewächs.

4—9. walter gropius

versuchswohnhaus auf der stuttgarter wohnbauausstellung 1927

(d. r. p. a.)

bei den bemühungen zur verbilligung des wohnungsbaues mit hilfe der serienherstellung ist es bisher nur gelungen, serienbauten gleichzeitig in größerer anzahl an einer stelle zu errichten, und zwar unter benutzung von baumaschinen, deren aufstellung zum bau eines einzelhauses unrationell wäre. neben dieser wichtigen herstellung von reihensiedlungen besteht aber ein starkes bedürfnis nach serienmäßig hergestellten, einzeln lieferbaren einfamilienhäusern. die fabrikation solcher häuser kann nicht an der baustelle erfolgen, sondern muß in stationären werkstätten vollzogen werden. unter verwendung hochwertiger, industriell verarbeiteter materialien ist die last und die masse des baukörpers zu verringern, seine stabilität und isolierfähigkeit dagegen zu steigern, so daß es möglich wird, ein in einzelne montable bauteile zerlegbares einfamilienhaus auf wenigen lastautos von den fabrikationsstellen nach einer beliebigen baustelle zu fahren und unabhängig von saison und witterung in kürzester zeit zu montieren.

der vorliegende versuch zur lösung des problems ist folgendermaßen durchgeführt worden: auf einer nicht unterkellerten grundbetonplatte, die den einzigen an ort und stelle hergestellten bauteil bildet, wird das traggerüst des hauses aus walzeisen im Z-profil aufgestellt. der abstand der stützen beträgt 1,06 m, so daß normtüren verwendet werden können. die Z-stützen der außenwände sind mit 8 cm starken hochwertig gepreßten expansitkorkplatten ausgesetzt, deren fugen mit pech vergossen werden.

der fußboden und die decken sind zur sorgfältigen verwahrung gegen schall und wärmedurchgang mit 4 cm starken gepreßten korkplatten isoliert, die ebenfalls mit pech vergossen sind. auf die stützen sind vermittels verzinkter bolzenschrauben latten aufgebracht, an die unter wahrung von isolierenden hohlräumen wandtafeln zur verkleidung von innen und außen angeschraubt werden.

die außenwände sind mit 6 mm starken asbestschieferplatten in der normalen breite der stützenabstände verkleidet.

die innenwände und decken sind je nach der bestimmung der räume mit celotex-(zuckerrohrfaser-)platten von 11 mm stärke oder mit lignatplatten (silikat gebundenes zellfaser-material) oder mit asbestschieferplatten, wie bei der außenhaut, verkleidet; die platten wechseln, je nach der bestimmung der innenräume. die letzteren platten sind in feuchten räumen wie küche, waschküche, bad verwendet.

eiserne doppelfenster, doppelt überfalzt, glatt abgesperrte türen in eisernen zargen.

nach dem gutachten der wärmeschutz-wissenschaftlichen abteilung des reinhold-werkes stuttgart ist die isolierfähigkeit des hauskörpers außerordentlich günstig.

bei der wandkonstruktion ergibt sich eine wärmedurchgangszahl von 0,58 kcal/m^2 h °C, ein stündlicher wärmeverlust von 15,7 kcal/m^2 h. (+ 20° celsius innentemperatur, − 20° celsius außentemperatur)

bei der dachdeckenkonstruktion ergibt sich eine wärmedurchgangszahl von 0,565 kcal/m^2 h °C, ein stündlicher wärmeverlust von 22,6 kcal/m^2 h.

diese berechnung zeigt, daß trotz der geringen stärke der wandungen eine vielfache überlegenheit in wärmetechnischer beziehung gegenüber einer normalen 38 cm starken beiderseitig verputzten ziegelmauerwand vorliegt. die ausgeführte wand von insgesamt 15 cm stärke entspricht wärmetechnisch einer 1,5 m starken ziegelwand.

die wärmeleitzahl des normalen ziegelmauerwerkes ist ca. 16 mal so groß wie die der korkplatten.

auf grund der ersten versuche dieser bauweise ist es erforderlich, die herstellung der einzelteile systematisch womöglich am laufenden band vorzunehmen, und auf diese weise den erstellungspreis der häuser progressiv herabzusetzen.

4

5

6

7

8

9

5

k. von meyenburg

wir werden es den lehrern wieder verständlich vor den toren der städte vormachen müssen, indem die kinder es den lehrern wieder zeigen, was leben und arbeit ist. wir werden den acker alle die städtischen vorteile der „nahen beziehungen", der motorkraft und des kurzschlusses von C, O, H, N zwischen himmel, pflanze und menschendarm genießen lassen.
wir werden, aus der angst vor der dichte der mäuler in stadt und land, die vorteile der gelockerten städte und den genuß des verdichteten landes entstehen lassen.
wir brauchen eine analyse und neusynthese unseres ganzen volkslebens, im banne des pflanzenlebens, der grundlage alles tier- und menschenlebens.
also einen besseren, sichereren kreislauf von C, O, H, N zwischen himmel, pflanze und mensch; im zeichen des kurzschlusses des nationalen kohlenstoffes.
wie im guten, älteren rom S.P.Q.R. das monogramm einer stark regierten republik war, deren oberstes gesetz die „res publica", das „gemeinwohl" war; so werde C, O, H, N das monogramm des kommenden gemeinwohles eines freien volkes, dessen bürger verstanden, daß es gilt C, O, H, N am direktesten, sichersten zu vereinen und zu kriegen; statt über 1000 unsichere glieder einer stets gefährdeten verkehrs- und handelskette.
leben ist analyse und synthese, ist arbeitstechnik; also transport und werkzeugbau dafür.

aus einer rede, gehalten auf der „gesolei", abgedruckt aus „fortschritte der landwirtschaft", 1926/18, mit erlaubnis des verlages julius springer, berlin-wien.

---

die geschäftsstelle des bauhauses teilt mit, daß die fabrikation der

beleuchtungskörper-modelle des bauhauses

von den metallwerken vorm. paul stotz a.-g., stuttgart, neckarstraße 140/142

übernommen wurde. der vertrieb erfolgt von dort aus direkt oder durch vertreter. ein katalog ist in vorbereitung und wird auch von der firma direkt zu beziehen sein.

---

17 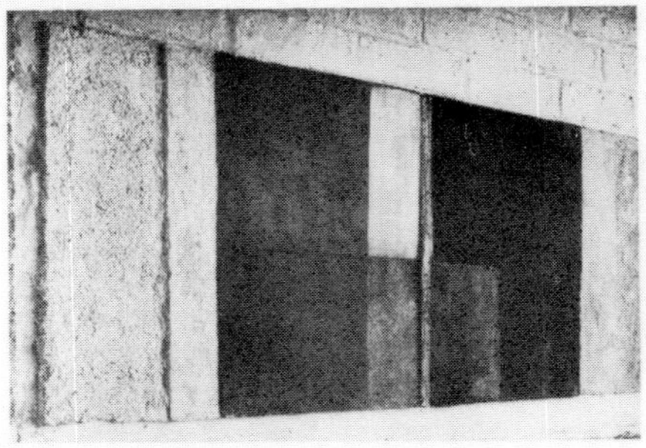

18 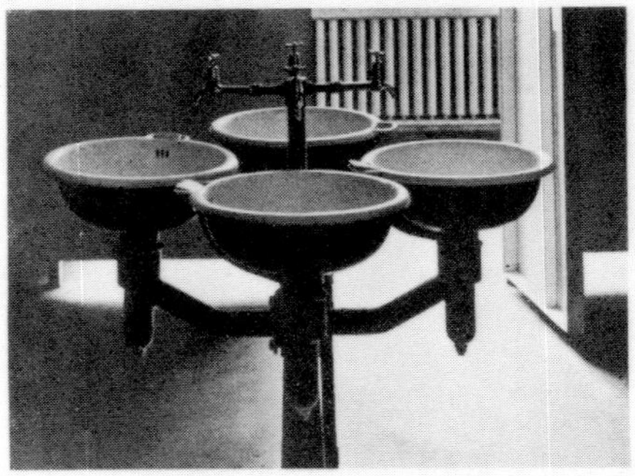

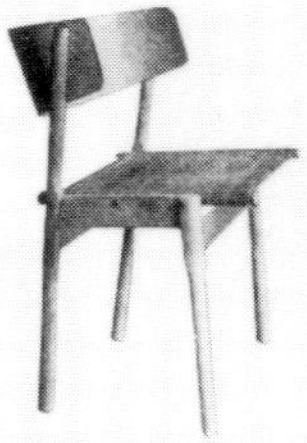

19

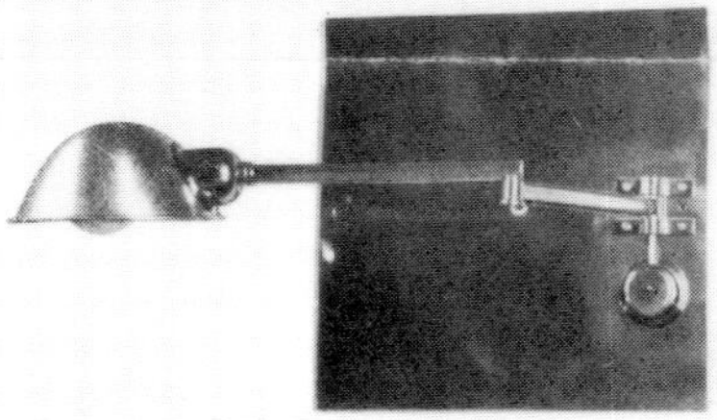

20

21 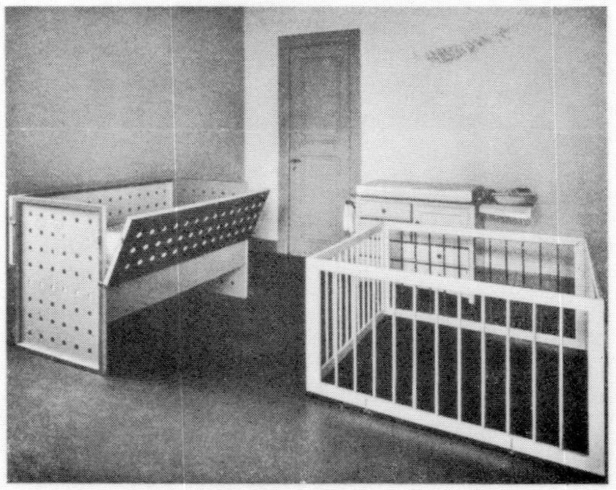

17. wandmalerei-werkstatt, bauhaus dessau putzproben · 1927 (foto consemüller)

links: kalk-marmorsandmörtel-verputz 1 : 3.
1. schicht grobkörnig, 2. schicht mittelkörnig, 3. schicht feinkörnig, 3. schicht im putz mit alkalienbeständigen farben gefärbt, zur hälfte mit dem eisen geglättet, zur hälfte halbrauh gerieben.
$^{1}/_{3}$ hiervon mit heißem wachs überzogen und eingebrannt.
rechts: kalk-sandmörtel-verputz 1 : 3.
1. schicht grobkörnig, 2. schicht mittelkörnig, 3. schicht feinkörnig zum teil halbrauh gerieben, halbrauh geschabt und mit dem eisen geglättet.
$^{1}/_{3}$ hiervon mit heißem wachs überzogen und eingebrannt.

18. waschanlage in den werkstätten des bauhauses dessau (foto consemüller)

fa.: mitteldeutsche stahlwerke a.-g.
lauchhammerwerk
lauchhammer (prov. sachsen).

19. peer bücking: leichter holzstuhl · 1927

versuchsarbeit. runde rückenlehne aus 6 mm sperrholz, mit stoffsitz.

20. marianne brandt: wandarm · 1927
beweglich, auf weißlackierter holzplatte
zu beziehen durch metallwerke vorm. paul stotz a.-g., stuttgart, neckarstr. 140/142
modell b.a. 7, vernickelt. **preis: 32.— rm.**

durch seitlich geknickte bewegung des armes und entsprechende drehung des reflektors gegen die weiße platte entsteht indirektes licht. das licht wird von der weißen fläche zurückgeworfen. neben der weißen kann noch eine schwarze fläche angebracht werden (holzplatte oder direkt auf die wand gemalt). diese ermöglicht eine wesentliche dämpfung des lichtes (verwendung vorwiegend als bettlampe, auch im krankenzimmer). druckknopfschalter auf die holzplatte montiert erleichtert das einschalten auch in halbwachem zustand.
herstellung: gießen, drücken, nieten, wenige lötstellen.

21. marcel breuer: kinderzimmer · 1927 (foto consemüller)

laufgitter (ti 136), mit zweiteiligem linoleumboden zur verwendung im freien. montage mit betthaken.

kinderbett (ti 11), seiten zum herunterklappen, mit lüftungslöchern.

---

die bauhausbücher

verlag albert langen, münchen, hubertusstraße 27

1 **walter gropius, internationale architektur** (zweite auflage) — geheftet **5** mk. leinen **7** mk.
2 **paul klee, pädagogisches skizzenbuch** — vergriffen.
3 **ein versuchshaus des bauhauses** — vergriffen.
4 **die bühne im bauhaus** — geheftet **5** mk. leinen **7** mk.
5 **piet mondrian, neue gestaltung** — vergriffen.
6 **theo van doesburg, grundbegriffe der neuen gestaltenden kunst** — vergriffen.
7 **neue arbeiten der bauhauswerkstätten** — geheftet **6** mk. leinen **8** mk.
8 **l. moholy-nagy, malerei, fotografie, film** (zweite auflage) — geheftet **7** mk. leinen **9** mk.
9 **w. kandinsky, punkt und linie zu fläche** — geheftet **15** mk. leinen **18** mk.
10 **j. j. p. oud, holländische architektur** — geheftet **6** mk. leinen **9** mk.

in vorbereitung:

11 **k. malevitsch, die gegenstandslose welt.**
12 **w. gropius, bauhausneubauten in dessau.**

die sammlung wird fortgesetzt.

Bauhaus Journal No 4
Cover. Dessau, 1928
Designed by Herbert Bayer (?)
Illustrated at 44% actual size

Bauhaus Journal No 4
Cover. Dessau, 1929
Designed by Joost Schmidt
Illustrated at 44% actual size

The change of style in the two covers reflects the change of designer, from Bayer (probably) to Joost Schmidt. The typically Bayer design incorporates a typical 'bauhausfoto' of students larking around. The more formal Schmidt cover illustrates a sculpture by Oscar Schlemmer. The change of heading may be more Bauhaus but is less attractive. Schmidt's work is usually livelier and more inventive than this almost inhibited design, which shows little influence of the early artist-designers. The boxing-up of information was a device Tschichold (and others) sometimes used.

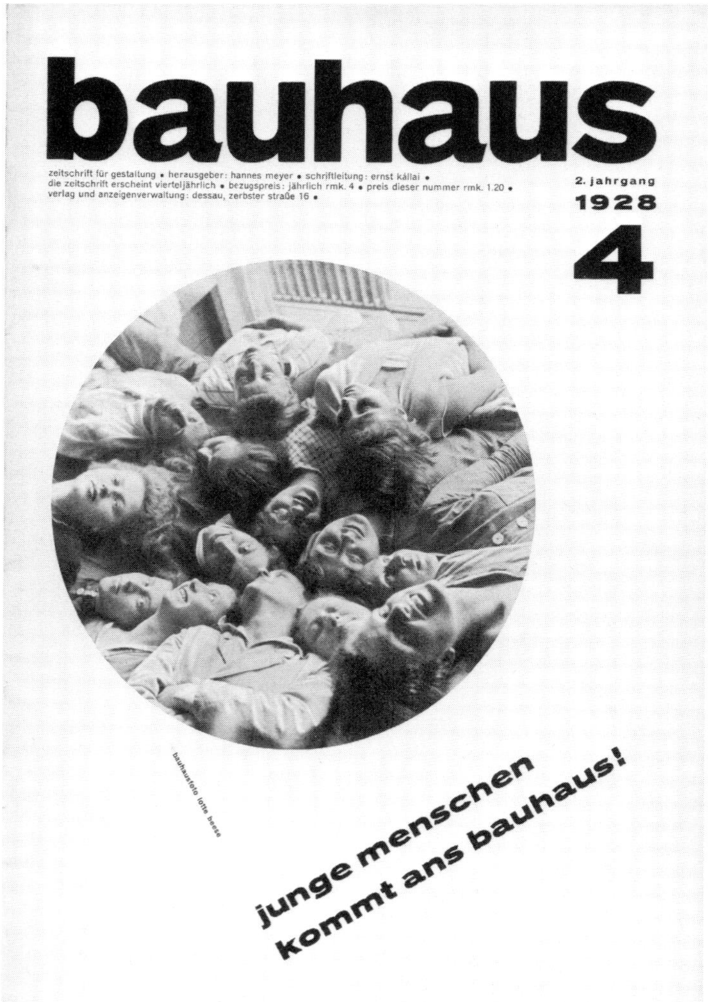

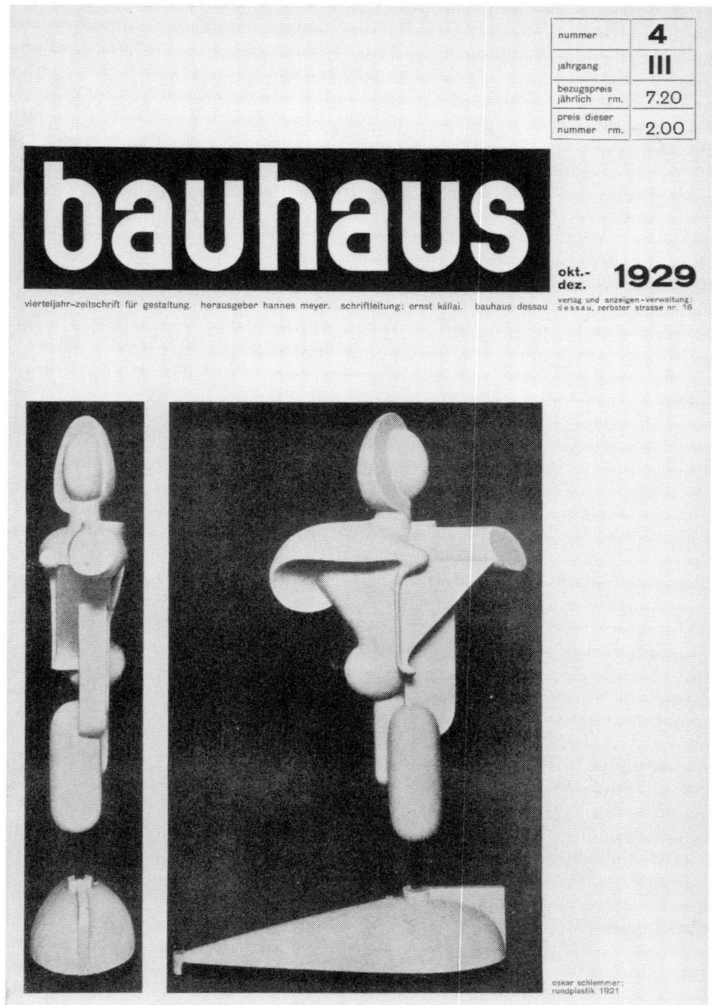

(A) Invitation card for a lecture series
Dessau, 1926
Designed by Herbert Bayer

In the most interesting of the designs shown on this page, the use of space and the relationship of parts are particularly satisfying. The conflict of horizontals and verticals creates a lively movement without the design flying apart, and the open-ended 'boxes' allow the type to appear less constrained than in Moholy's postcard. The designs of the Austrian Bayer, while tough-minded, usually had a refinement missing from the work of his Hungarian colleague.

(B) Postcard
Dessau, 1926
Designed by Moholy-Nagy

Rather more heavy-handed than the two Bayer designs here, this design refers more overtly to Mondrian's paintings, repeating the over-hectic scheme we saw in Moholy's Bauhausbücher 8 of the previous year (see page 53). There is something a little worrying about the type being imprisoned so aggressively: Moholy-Nagy could be a bit brutal in his desire to make an impact and defy convention.

(C) Catalogue of Bauhaus products
Dessau, 1925
Designed by Herbert Bayer

The use of very heavy rules and solid circles, much favoured at the Bauhaus, is one of the more obvious tricks to emulate if a 'neo-Bauhaus' design is required today. The three examples on this page show them used with verve. In this catalogue page, the contrasting light rules make an effective counterpoint, and the overall effect, despite its brio, is very controlled.

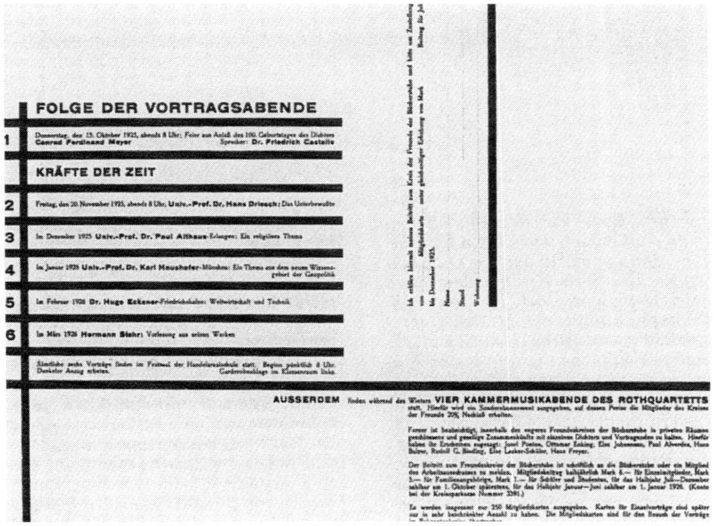

A

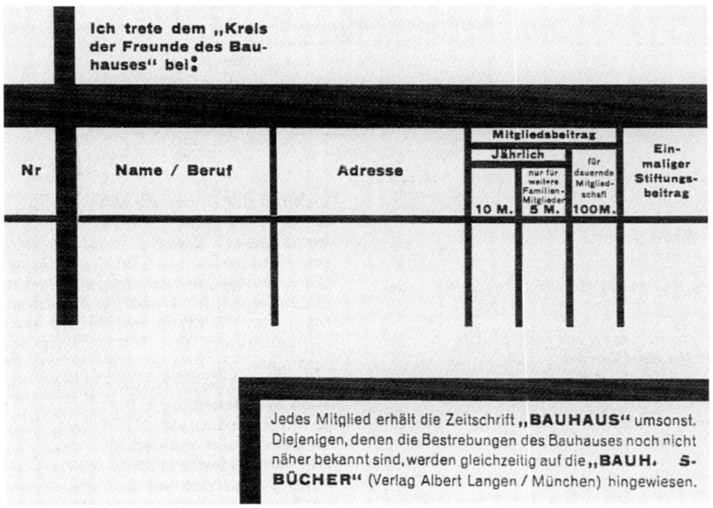

B

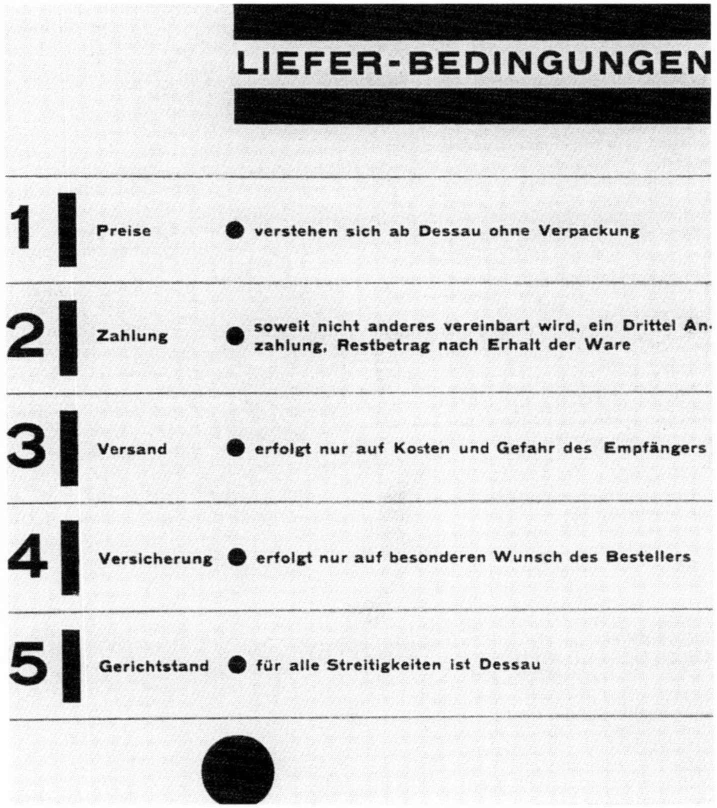

C

Bayer can be considered the Bauhaus's professional typographic designer. Schmidt's work more closely follows the approach taken by Russian artist-designers. Both these designs put abstract relationships and pattern-making before straightforward communication; yet that practical purpose is also achieved. Neither design has much relevance to modern bookwork. Despite their undeniable impact, it would be a brave publisher who found acceptable today such imaginative play with letterforms and rules, even for jackets. But designs like these play an important part in the development of modernism, and a similar exploration of the pattern-making potential to be discovered in an open-minded use of type can be found in the somewhat different work of, for instance, the Dutch designers Piet Zwart and Paul Schuitema.

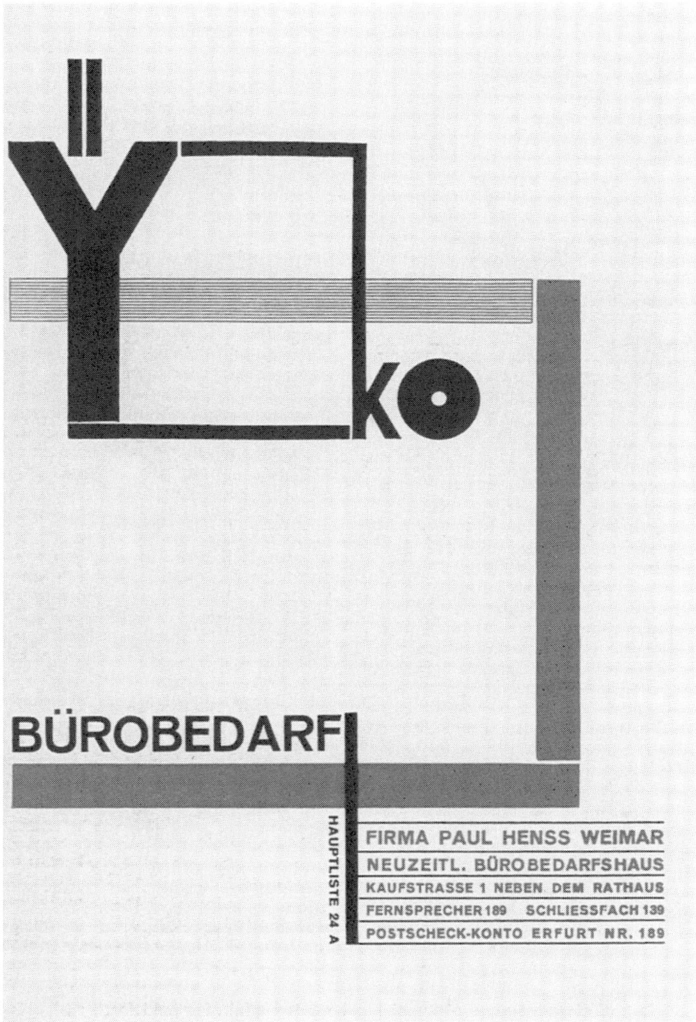

Office equipment price list, cover
Weimar, *c.*1924
Designed by Joost Schmidt
Illustrated at 56% actual size

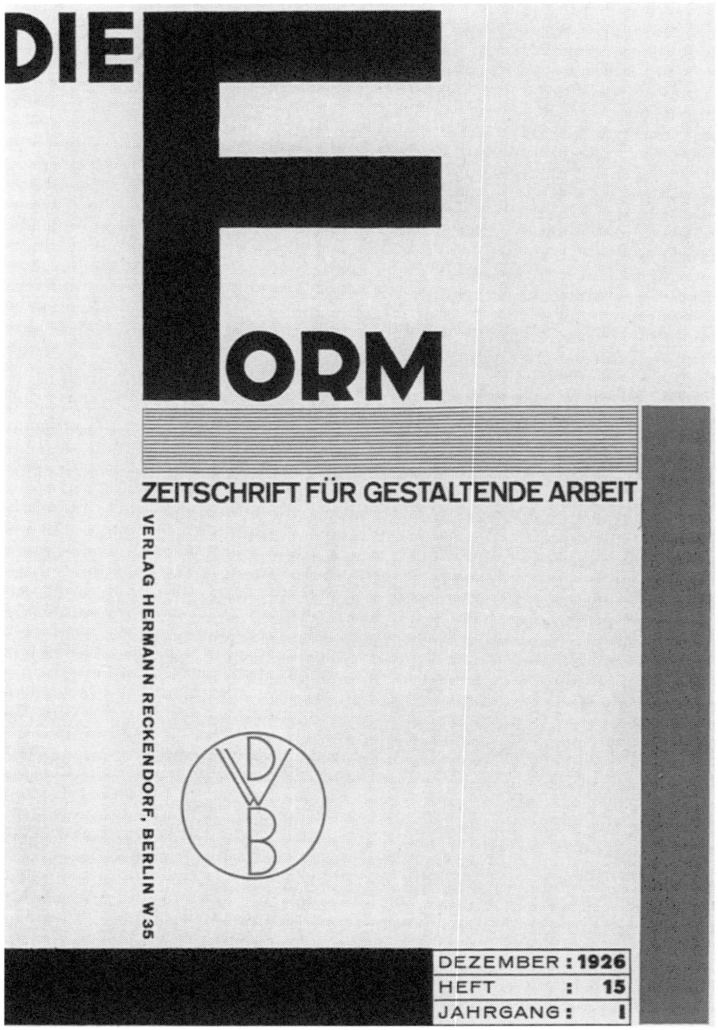

Die Form, magazine cover design
Dessau, 1926
Designed by Joost Schmidt
Illustrated at 45% actual size

Two advertisement designs by Piet Zwart, 1926
As shown in *Kunst van Heden in het Stedelijk* by Willem Sandberg and H L C Jaffé
Stedelijk Museum, Amsterdam, 1961

Both designs are for Nederlandsche Kabelfabrick, and are more strictly typographic than Schmidt's work, with little or no reliance on bars and rules. The influence of the Russians is strong: their ability to rethink the way that type could be used was a big factor in Zwart's work; but he was his own man, ingeniously interlocking different sizes and forms of type, playing one off against another. His designs were generally tighter and tougher, more coordinated, than Russian work. Astonishingly, they were accepted by commercial firms. It would be difficult to imagine that happening today.

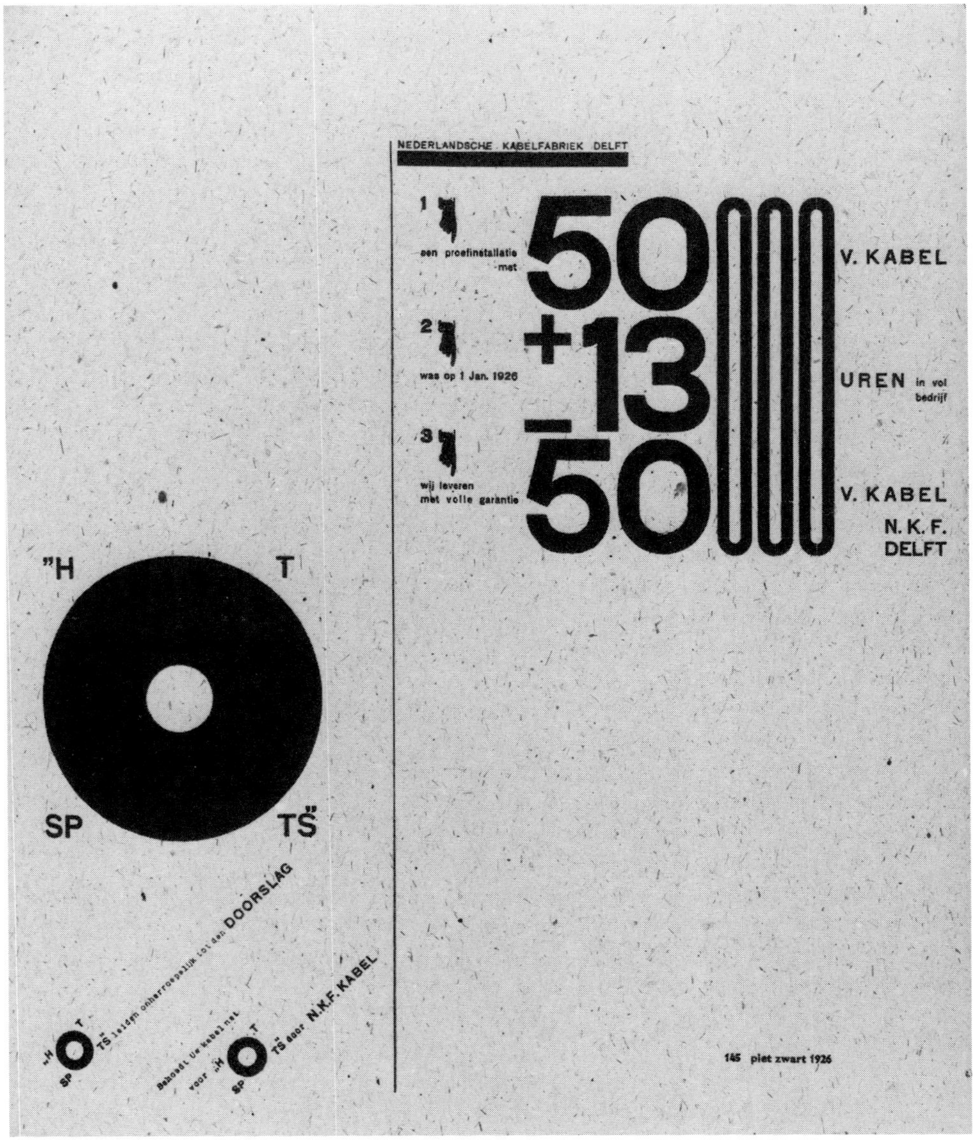

Four pages from a prospectus
for an advertising agency
Designed by Piet Zwart, 1932
as shown in *Typographica 7*
Lund Humphries, London, 1963

Zwart became a skilled user of photomontage, using his own photographs. His fondness for putting type at an angle, and overprinting type and images, gave his designs power and urgency. One could trace various sources behind his work but, like the best painters, he was influenced by everyone, and no one. His colours tended to be those of de Stijl: blue, yellow and red.

Zwart's designs had the potential of falling apart. That they never did shows his confidence and skill in the use of his material. He had clearly looked hard at work going on elsewhere; but the resulting designs, very much of their time in their absorption of many different movements from several different countries, were unique to him.

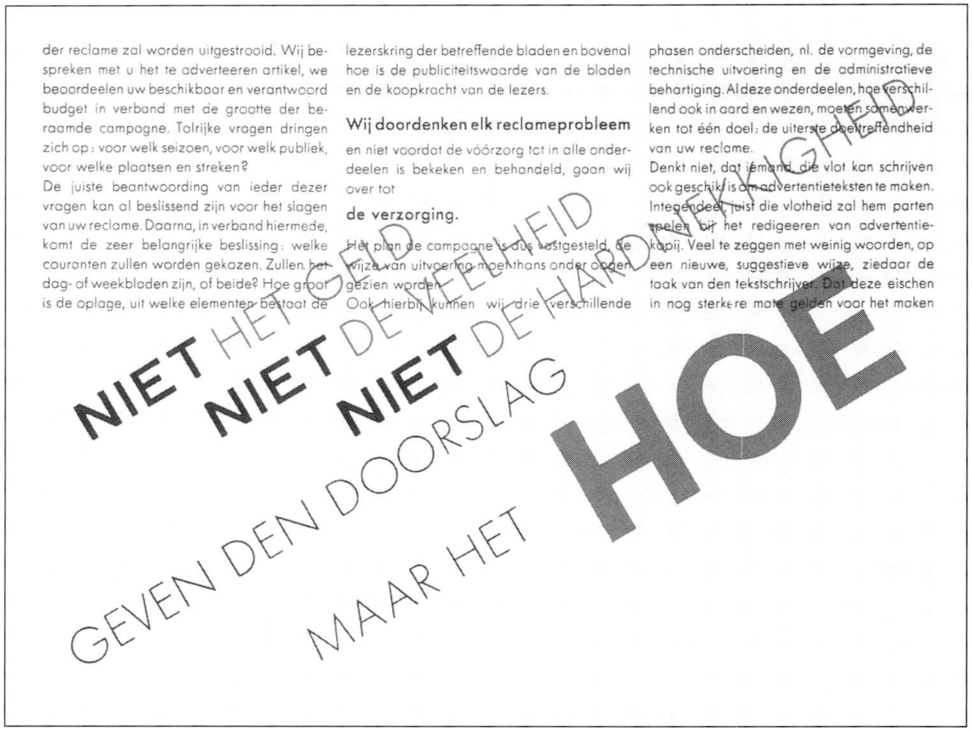

der reclame zal worden uitgestrooid. Wij bespreken met u het te adverteeren artikel, we beoordeelen uw beschikbaar en verantwoord budget in verband met de grootte der beraamde campagne. Talrijke vragen dringen zich op: voor welk seizoen, voor welk publiek, voor welke plaatsen en streken?
De juiste beantwoording van ieder dezer vragen kan al beslissend zijn voor het slagen van uw reclame. Daarna, in verband hiermede, komt de zeer belangrijke beslissing: welke couranten zullen worden gekozen. Zullen het dag- of weekbladen zijn, of beide? Hoe groot is de oplage, uit welke elementen bestaat de lezerskring der betreffende bladen en bovenal hoe is de publiciteitswaarde van de bladen en de koopkracht van de lezers.

Wij doordenken elk reclameprobleem

en niet voordat de vóórzorg tot in alle onderdeelen is bekeken en behandeld, gaan wij over tot

de verzorging.

Het plan de campagne is dus vastgesteld, de wijze van uitvoering moet thans onder oogen gezien worden.
Ook hierbij kunnen wij drie verschillende phasen onderscheiden, nl. de vormgeving, de technische uitvoering en de administratieve behartiging. Al deze onderdeelen, hoe verschillend ook in aard en wezen, moeten samenwerken tot één doel: de uiterste doeltreffendheid van uw reclame.
Denkt niet, dat iemand, die vlot kan schrijven ook geschikt is om advertentieteksten te maken. Integendeel, juist die vlotheid zal hem parten spelen bij het redigeeren van advertentiekopij. Veel te zeggen met weinig woorden, op een nieuwe, suggestieve wijze, ziedaar de taak van den tekstschrijver. Dat deze eischen in nog sterkere mate gelden voor het maken

NIET HET GELD
NIET DE VEELHEID
NIET DE HARDNEKKIGHEID
GEVEN DEN DOORSLAG
MAAR HET HOE

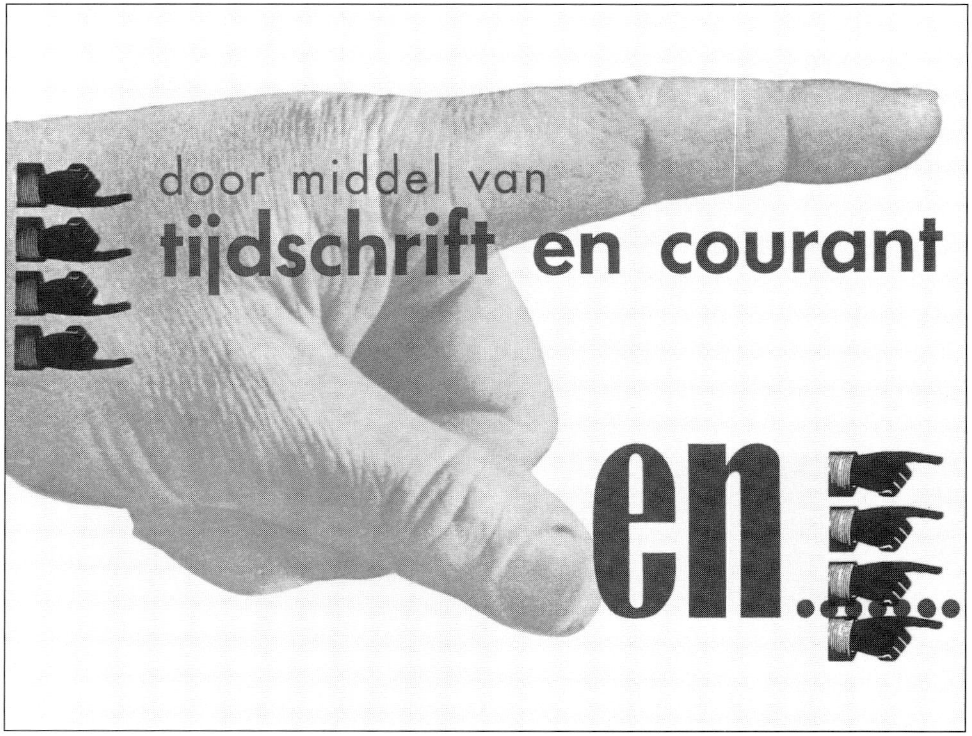

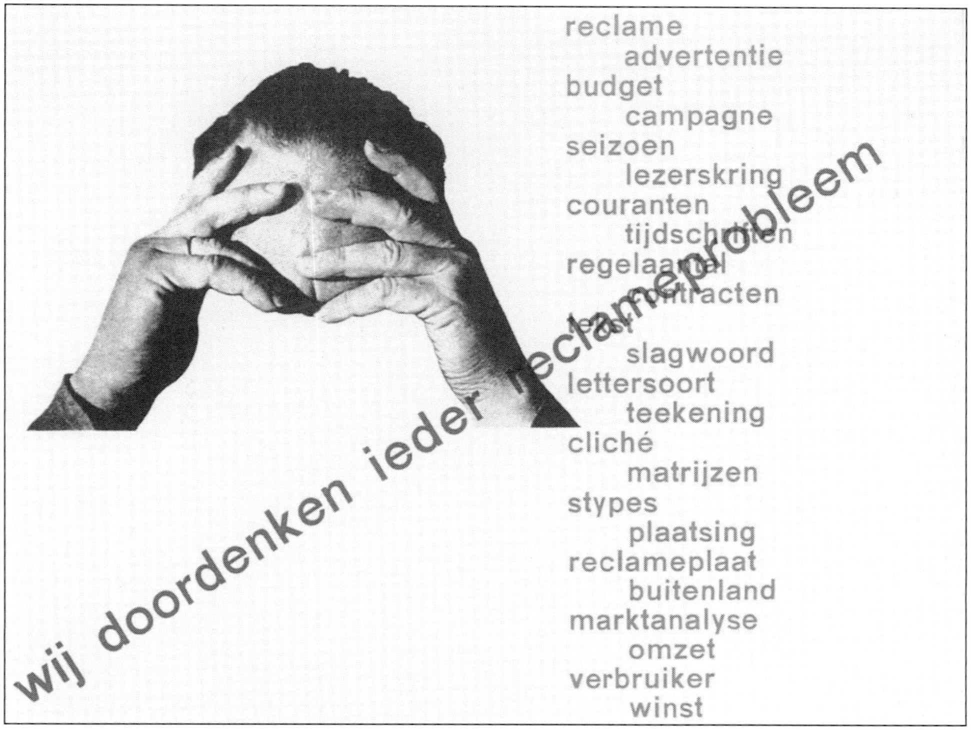
reclame
advertentie
budget
campagne
seizoen
lezerskring
couranten
slagwoord
lettersoort
teekening
cliché
matrijzen
stypes
plaatsing
reclameplaat
buitenland
marktanalyse
omzet
verbruiker
winst
wij doordenken ieder reclameprobleem

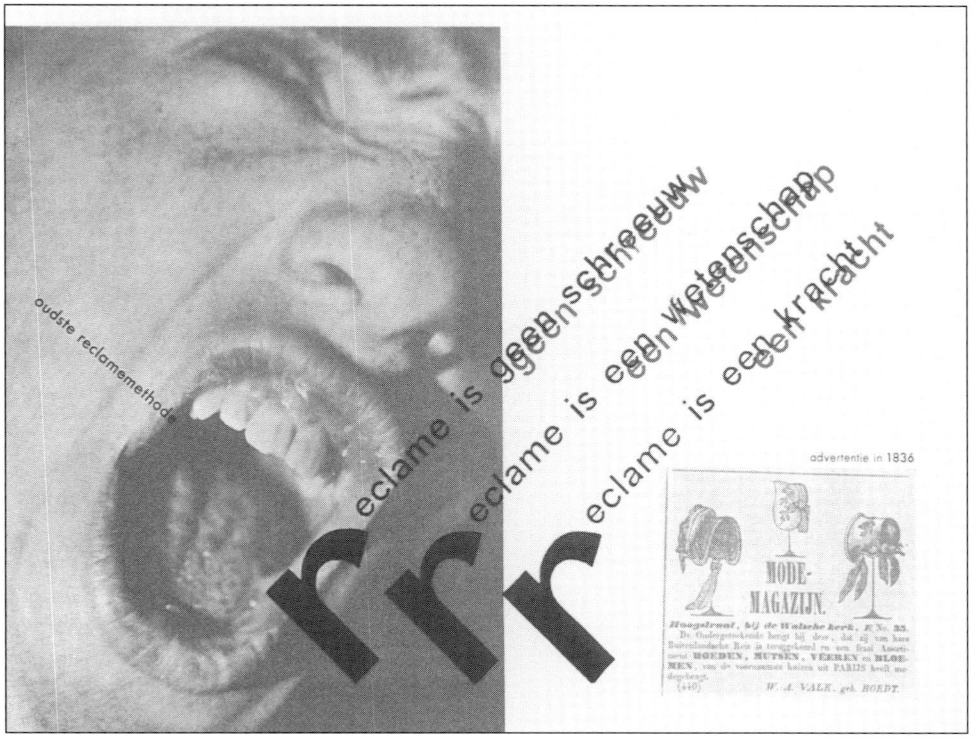
oudste reclamemethode
reclame is geen schreeuw
reclame is een wetenschap
reclame is een kracht
advertentie in 1836
MODE-MAGAZIJN.

Designs by Paul Schuitema, *c.*1930
as shown in *Neue Grafik 11*
Otto Walter, Olten, 1961
Pages illustrated at 60% actual size

The Swiss magazine *Neue Grafik/New Graphic Design/Graphisme actuel* is described in more detail on pages 96 and 107. Although showing mainly Swiss work of the time, it also carried major articles on antecedent designers and movements such as Polish design of the 1920s, Piet Zwart, and of course the Bauhaus. This spread on Paul Schuitema shows work which, like designs by his compatriot Zwart, derived from varied sources (Bauhaus, Constructivism, even Dada) but which, again like Zwart's, is entirely original. It shares with Zwart's work angled type, inventive use of photography and photomontage, and much overprinting of type and images. The illustrations are, left, a cinema prospectus; upper right, a periodical cover; lower right, a political pamphlet. The expressive vigour of the work shown contrasts with the cool precision of the magazine pages. Not that Schuitema's work lacks precision. Like Zwart, he is able to control designs that in less able hands would collapse in a formless heap of type and images.

2

Neue Typografie um 1930

Paul Schuitema, Wassenaar Holland

Es ist grundsätzlich immer schwierig, über seine eigene Arbeit zu sprechen. Vielleicht aber doch etwas leichter, wenn es sich um Arbeiten handelt, die vor 30 bis 40 Jahren entstanden sind.
Ich will mich bemühen, sowenig als möglich über mein Werk zu sprechen, und versuchen, etwas von den geistigen Hintergründen aufzuzeigen.
Die vorliegenden Arbeiten stammen aus den Jahren 1926–1933. Zu dieser Zeit ist alle Gestaltung direkt ausgerichtet. Die Farben sind primär, die Komposition unkompliziert. Man arbeitete unter seltsamen Umständen. Die Buchdrucker wußten beispielsweise nicht, ob die elementare Typografie schön oder brutal war, ob diese Ausdrucksform bleiben würde oder ob sie eine Eintagsfliege sei. Selber ist man hart, sachlich und ohne Bereitschaft, Konzessionen zu machen. ‹Take it or leave it.› Es war Verkehr in einer Richtung. Alles andere war falsch, schlapp und ungesunde Sentimentalität. Man ging geradeaus. Man hatte entweder wenige Freunde, viele Feinde, oder man wurde nicht ernst genommen. Man dachte nur international-revolutionär. Gleichgesinnte sammelten sich: Architekten, Schriftsteller, Dichter, Musiker, Maler, Bildhauer und Grafiker.
Jedes Ding, jeder Buchstabe, jedes Bild, jeder Klang, jede Farbe sollte seine Funktion haben. Auch der Künstler mußte in der Gesellschaft eine funktionelle Aufgabe haben. Man dachte kaum an Erfolg, sondern nur an die wesentlichen Werte. Alles andere wurde abgelehnt. Ein Buchstabe sollte der Funktion des Lesens, nichts anderem, dienen. Er sollte deutliche, sachliche und klare Formen haben, nicht elegant, nicht schön und nicht weiblich sein. Seine Schönheit ist seine Funktion, und nichts Geheimnisvolles sollte dahinter oder daneben gesucht werden können.

Der Krieg 1914–1918 hatte uns deutlich demonstriert, daß alles, die schönsten Aussagen, Unsinn waren. Die Romantik war in Schlamm und Blut untergegangen. Alles Schöne, Heldenmut, alle Vaterlandsliebe existierte nur um des Geldes willen, war schmutzig und lügnerisch, voll falschen Pathos. Die Kunst war Eigentum der Reichen. Der sozialistische Aufruf ‹Die Kunst dem Volk› wurde gleichfalls als sentimentaler Unsinn betrachtet. Es sollte Aufgabe und Pflicht der Gesellschaft sein, Aufträge zu erteilen. Das Volk sollte nicht die abgenützten Kleider tragen und nicht eine neue Bourgeoisie heranbilden. Eine billige Reproduktion ist nicht das gleiche wie ein Original.
Mondrian läutete die Todesglocke der Malerei, diesem Staffeleigebilde, einem Produkt der Hyperindividualisten. Die Zeit der Malerei war zu Ende. Man sollte auch keine sozialistischen Gemälde machen, weil eine solche Kunst unseres Erachtens nicht existieren konnte. Die Zeit selbst gab den Künstlern ihre Aufgabe. Eine davon bestand im Realisieren bildnerischer Möglichkeiten und der Nutzbarmachung neuer schöpferischer Erkenntnisse. Kunst sollte durch ihre Nutzanwendung wieder ihren verlorenen Platz in der Gesellschaft einnehmen. Die Aufgaben des Künstlers sollten darin bestehen, Drucksachen zu erstellen, Kostüme und Dekorationen zu entwerfen. Er sollte mit dem Proletariat marschieren und nicht ein durchtriebener Bursche sein, der es mit zwei Parteien hielt. Er sollte in Betrieben arbeiten, dort seine Aufgaben lösen und sich seiner Mission bewußt sein. Wenn er Drucksachen zu entwerfen hatte, sollte er sich bewußt sein, daß die Funktion der Reklame darin bestand, zu verkaufen. Die Dinge hatten die Wahrheit zu sagen und dem Publikum den Sinn eines Produktes deutlich zu machen. Die industriellen Erzeugnisse wurden von uns als notwendig erkannt. Der Künstler hatte die Aufgabe, sie klarer und zweckmäßiger zu gestalten. Durch unsere Arbeit in den Werkstätten und Fabriken wollten wir dem Menschen bessere und schönere Dinge geben. Schon damals leisteten wir unseren

1
Paul Schuitema
Kino-Prospekt für die Aufführung von ‹Sous les toits de Paris› 1930, Format A5, gefaltet, vierseitig, zweifarbig rot und schwarz
1
Paul Schuitema
Cinema prospectus out for the performance of "Sous les Toits de Paris", 1930, Format A5, folded, 4 pages in 2 colours, red and black
1
Paul Schuitema
Prospectus pour le film «Sous les toits de Paris» 1930
Format A5, plié, 4 pages, deux tons: rouge et noir

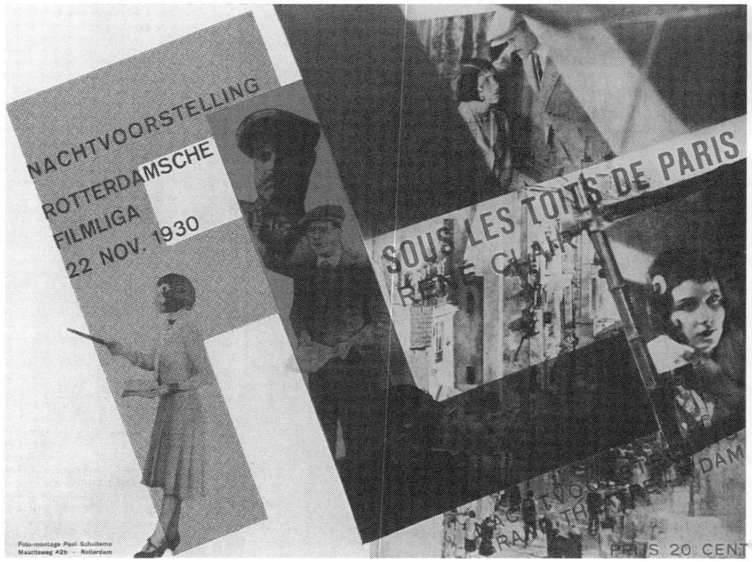

1

Neue Typografie um 1930
New Typographical Design in 1930
La «typographie nouvelle» autour de 1930

3

eitrag zur ‹industriellen Formge-
ung›, ohne daß diese Benennung da-
nals existierte. Wir hatten die Absicht,
en Produkten eine neue sachliche
orm zu geben.
n dieser Zeit arbeitete ich mit an der
ormgebung und am Bau von Waagen
nd Schneidemaschinen, entwarf Mö-
el und betätigte mich als Innenarchi-
ekt. Um uns klar und deutlich auszu-
rücken, befaßten wir uns mit vielen
orm- und Funktionsproblemen auf den
erschiedensten Gebieten. Aber man
atte nur wenig Auftraggeber, weil das
Verk wieder so persönlich war, daß
nan nur für einen sehr kleinen Kreis
rbeiten konnte. Eindeutig war das
Empfinden, ziemlich einsam zu sein
nd nur wenige Freunde zu haben, dar-
unter Architekten wie van Eesteren,
an Loghem, Stam, Oud und andere.
Später entstand der ‹Ring neuer Werbe-
gestalter› mit Schwitters, Heartfield,
Moholy-Nagy, Bill, Teige und andere,
n Holland mit Zwart.
Was wir machten, sollte spannungs-
oll sein. Rot war erste und wichtigste
arbe, die Signalfarbe. Später kamen
Gelb und Blau dazu. Stets Primärfar-
ben, keine Mischfarben. Als Schrift-
orm die Grotesk: schmal und breit,
ett und mager. Dies waren die Arbeits-
prinzipien; ebenso wesentlich war die
otomontage für uns. Man montierte
lie Foto frei auf der Ebene des Recht-

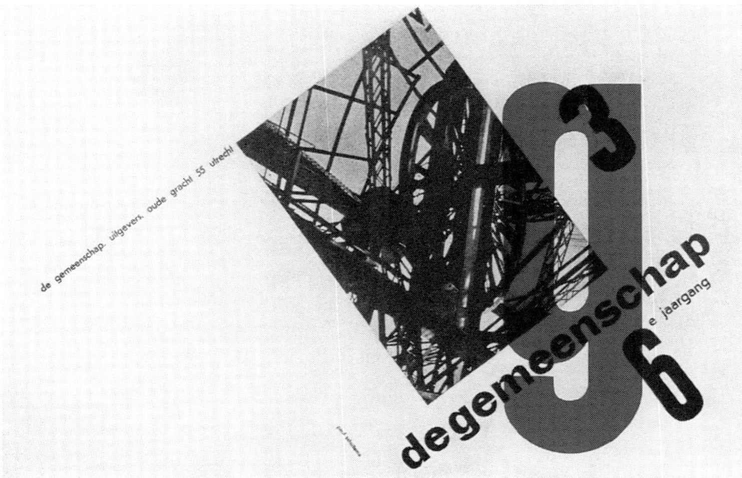

2

2
Paul Schuitema
Umschlag der Zeitschrift ‹de gemeenschap›
Format 26 × 41 cm, gefaltet, zweifarbig orange
und schwarz auf grau
2
Paul Schuitema
Cover for the periodical "de gemeenschap"
Format 26 × 41 cm, folded, in 2 colours,
orange and black on grey
2
Paul Schuitema
Couverture de la revue «de gemeenschap»
Format 26/41 cm, plié, deux tons: orange et
noir sur gris

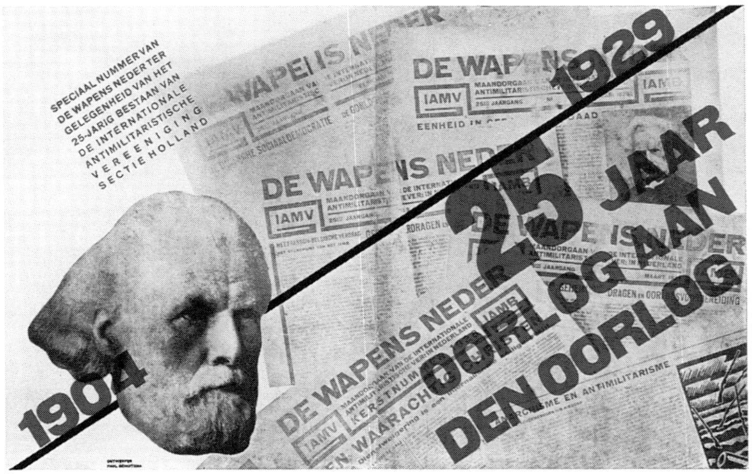

3

3
Paul Schuitema
Umschlagseite einer politischen Flugschrift
‹25 Jaar Oorlog aan den Oorlog› 1929
Format 29 × 24 cm, zweifarbig rot und schwarz
3
Paul Schuitema
Cover page of a political pamphlet "25 Jaar
Oorlog aan den Oorlog" 1929
Format 29 × 24 cm, in 2 colours, red and black
3
Paul Schuitema
Couverture d'une brochure politique
«25 Jaar Oorlog aan den Oorlog» 1929
Format 29/24 cm, deux tons: rouge et noir

The juxtaposition of these 1930s examples with the layout of the 1960s magazine says a lot about the way design developed during those thirty years. It is the difference between painterly-derived or painterly-minded work, and the professional typographic designer controlled by sterner market requirements and a philosophy of reflecting the character of a mechanised world and the needs of its society.

Even photomontage as practised in the 1930s, grafting parts of different photographs into a whole, resulted in what look like period pieces today. That it was more difficult to achieve in its heyday gave it, when successful, more character and excitement, more edge, than the productions of today's computer screens, when its impact is lost amongst all the other effects of Photoshop magic.

The young Tschichold, uncertainly pursuing undigested ideas, was won over to modernism by the first Bauhaus exhibition of 1923. While appreciating its wide-ranging philosophy, embracing all fields of design, Tschichold, as a typographer, was far more knowledgeable about book design than anyone at the Bauhaus, and he was able to bring more specific criticism, as well as more pertinent and refined solutions, to the subject. In his book *Typographische Gestaltung* of 1935 his objections to traditional centred typography (which he termed 'decorative') were made clear. It is, he wrote, inflexible, purely ornamental and entirely unfunctional, standing in the way of all true solutions to typographic problems. Pure form or pattern-making come before meaning, display lines are broken irrationally, with words or lines sometimes unpleasantly forced out by variable letterspacing. It lacks individual character, with rules and ornaments introduced in an attempt to counteract this. While the types available in the nineteenth century were often poor, it was not so much the type that needed rethinking but the way it was used. Even when better types, recut or recast from classic faces, were revived around the First World War, it was still generally thought they should only be used in the style in which they were originally employed. Such a practice was feebly inhibited.

Typographische Gestaltung was less aggressively written, more concise and refined, than Tschichold's earlier *Die Neue Typographie* of 1928, which had given its name to the principles. This book, and an earlier manifesto of 1925, had caused, according to Hans Schmoller, 'nothing short of a sensation', being 'hotly debated' throughout German and Swiss printshops. Yet neither seemed to have much practical long-term effect on their main target, the German printing industry. If the profession of typographic designer had been as common then as it was to become in the 1940s and 1950s, the impact might have been more profound. As it was, any potential influence was cut short by the Nazis, who refused to accept a style which was a practical application of laws of design being researched into by the new painters (whom they detested), and in which geometry played a key part.

Whereas the Bauhaus encouraged emotional vitality, and the Russian Constructivists, especially El Lissitzky, questioned every typographic convention, Tschichold was practical and detailed. In the 1925 manifesto he had already pronounced (in contrast to Bauhaus thinking) that order, organisation, the arrangement of the printed text, and the relationship of book to content, took precedence over expressive presentation. He refined his arguments over the next ten years. Space, asymmetry and logic were the key elements, clarity of communication the aim. The visual relationship of different elements of the page must be carefully organised. Strongly differentiated sizes, weights or typeforms could aid logical presentation. He favoured the use of grotesques for text, despite questions over their legibility. (They shared with Bodoni – the other popular 'modernist' type – the potential for being thickened-up more acceptably than classic seriffed types.) Like Herbert Bayer at the Bauhaus, he queried the use of two alphabets (caps and lower case) for the same sound, suggesting that the use of capital letters should be abandoned. (Bayer designed such an alphabet in 1926; Tschichold designed a less brutal but almost as awkward a 'single alphabet' type in 1929, together with an unhappy-looking phonetic version. Such assaults on tradition were characteristic of the period: Paul Renner's Futura of 1928-30, even Gill Sans of the same date, reflect the mood.)

For Tschichold, space – the unprinted area of the page – was as important as the printed areas. Their relationship to each other was crucial, as was their relationship to illustrations. Unlike the traditionalists of 1925, who still regarded photographs and text as incompatible, not just technically – half-tones requiring coated paper – but visually too, Tschichold welcomed photographs. Text, he believed, should be set to a constant measure, not run around illustrations, and preferably unjustified, ranged left. Type set vertically or diagonally was allowable, to create a sense of urgency. Ornament was forbidden. Any rules or geometric shapes such as squares, circles, triangles, must contribute to 'elemental presentation', and not be merely decorative.

'Economy, precision, construction with pure forms corresponding to the function of the object' – such a doctrine is also found in Le Corbusier's philosophy. The work must reflect the use of the machine in its production, and the use of DIN paper formats should be standard practice. Behind it all is the requirement that formal considerations combine with social purpose and need.

Even before Tschichold finally renounced the New Typography in the 1940s, he had become less hard-line in his doctrines. Typefaces, for instance, could be mixed (carefully) for purely aesthetic effect – as he did, startlingly, on the title page of *Typographische Gestaltung* itself. He would not have allowed himself to do this in his earlier book.

Tschichold never seemed to make much – or any – distinction between books and other kinds of print design. Good typography was good typography. Yet some book designers today think there is a schism between the two. It is not a belief to which I have ever subscribed. I am a typographic designer who has done a lot of books, that's all.

Jan Tschichold: *Die Neue Typographie*
Verlag des Bildungsverbandes, Berlin, 1928
Designed by Jan Tschichold
Illustrated at 67% actual size

Despite his youth, the twenty-six-year-old Tschichold felt fully equipped (as indeed he was) to drag the printing trade into the twentieth century. Although his books, even in his Neue Typographie period, had classical margins, what went on inside – both typographically and textually – was dynamite. This elegant and orderly spread has a unity of text, captions and illustrations, and a logical precision, which is absent from the more deliberately aggressive Bauhaus work. The use of grotesque, especially the bold, would have sent shock waves throughout the publishing world; the treatment of half-tones and their captions was similarly innovative. Youthful larks can be seen in the disturbing blobs signalling footnotes, and even the bold rule; but this is where serious modern integrated illustrated bookmaking began.

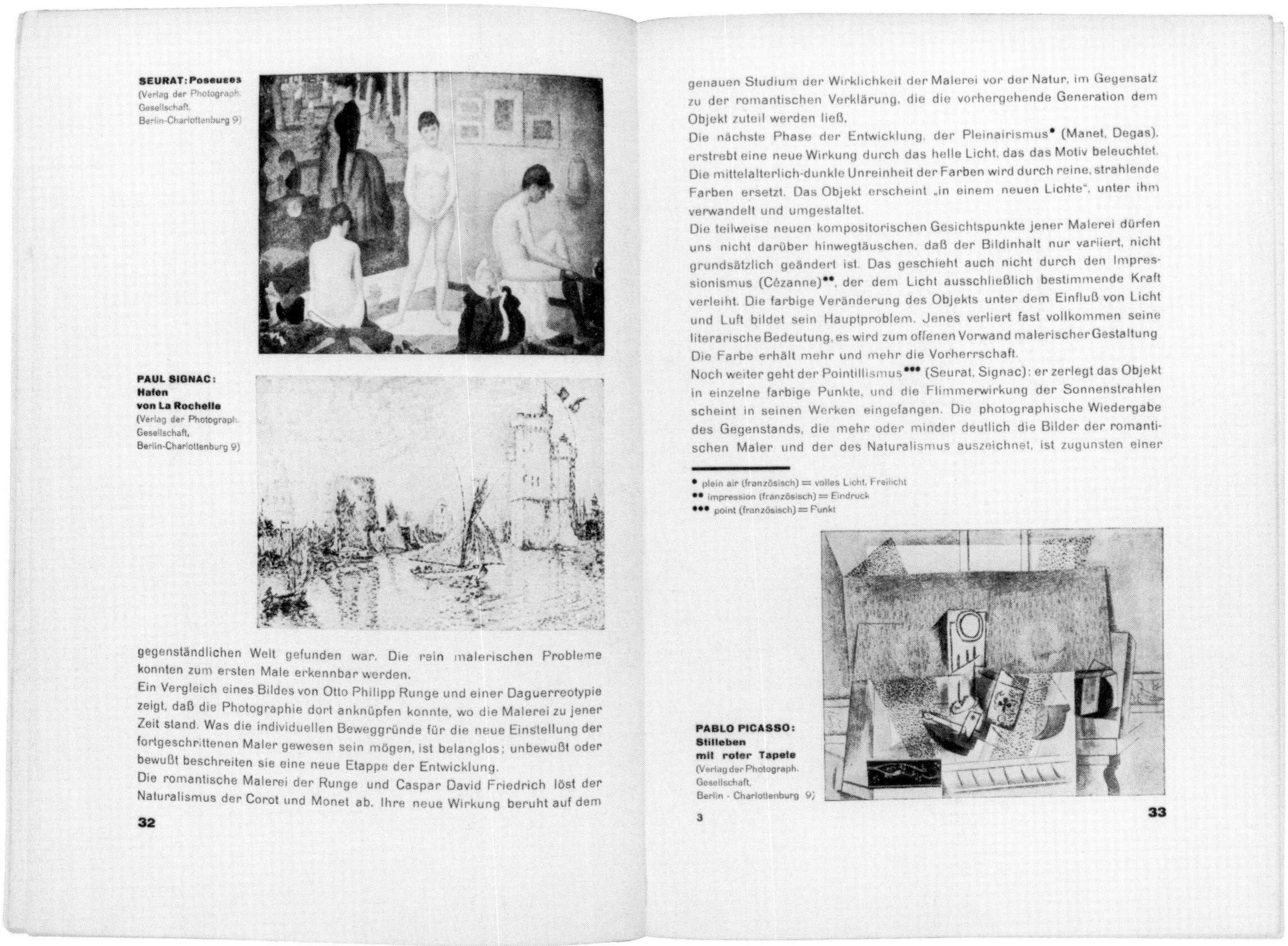

SEURAT: Poseuses
(Verlag der Photograph. Gesellschaft, Berlin-Charlottenburg 9)

PAUL SIGNAC: Hafen von La Rochelle
(Verlag der Photograph. Gesellschaft, Berlin-Charlottenburg 9)

gegenständlichen Welt gefunden war. Die rein malerischen Probleme konnten zum ersten Male erkennbar werden.
Ein Vergleich eines Bildes von Otto Philipp Runge und einer Daguerreotypie zeigt, daß die Photographie dort anknüpfen konnte, wo die Malerei zu jener Zeit stand. Was die individuellen Beweggründe für die neue Einstellung der fortgeschrittenen Maler gewesen sein mögen, ist belanglos; unbewußt oder bewußt beschreiten sie eine neue Etappe der Entwicklung.
Die romantische Malerei der Runge und Caspar David Friedrich löst der Naturalismus der Corot und Monet ab. Ihre neue Wirkung beruht auf dem

32

genauen Studium der Wirklichkeit der Malerei vor der Natur, im Gegensatz zu der romantischen Verklärung, die die vorhergehende Generation dem Objekt zuteil werden ließ.
Die nächste Phase der Entwicklung, der Pleinairismus* (Manet, Degas), erstrebt eine neue Wirkung durch das helle Licht, das das Motiv beleuchtet. Die mittelalterlich-dunkle Unreinheit der Farben wird durch reine, strahlende Farben ersetzt. Das Objekt erscheint „in einem neuen Lichte", unter ihm verwandelt und umgestaltet.
Die teilweise neuen kompositorischen Gesichtspunkte jener Malerei dürfen uns nicht darüber hinwegtäuschen, daß der Bildinhalt nur variiert, nicht grundsätzlich geändert ist. Das geschieht auch nicht durch den Impressionismus (Cézanne)**, der dem Licht ausschließlich bestimmende Kraft verleiht. Die farbige Veränderung des Objekts unter dem Einfluß von Licht und Luft bildet sein Hauptproblem. Jenes verliert fast vollkommen seine literarische Bedeutung, es wird zum offenen Vorwand malerischer Gestaltung
Die Farbe erhält mehr und mehr die Vorherrschaft.
Noch weiter geht der Pointillismus*** (Seurat, Signac): er zerlegt das Objekt in einzelne farbige Punkte, und die Flimmerwirkung der Sonnenstrahlen scheint in seinen Werken eingefangen. Die photographische Wiedergabe des Gegenstands, die mehr oder minder deutlich die Bilder der romantischen Maler und der des Naturalismus auszeichnet, ist zugunsten einer

* plein air (französisch) = volles Licht, Freilicht
** impression (französisch) = Eindruck
*** point (französisch) = Punkt

PABLO PICASSO: Stilleben mit roter Tapete
(Verlag der Photograph. Gesellschaft, Berlin - Charlottenburg 9)

3

33

Prospectus
for *Die Neue Typographie*
Designed by Jan Tschichold, 1928
Illustrated at 61% actual size

If the occasion required a more aggressive design, Tschichold could supply it. This well-known prospectus advertises the book which defines the way forward for the whole printing trade. Its design would seem to reflect some Bauhaus mannerisms: vertical and horizontal rules, bold type within normal text, arrows; all to create a deliberately lively pattern. It is thus a bridge between the school and the young independent book designer – who had, it will be remembered, been converted to modernism by the Bauhaus exhibition of 1923. Such means of giving typographic colour and force to the page, while here quite functional, had Max Bill later spitting with rage. But the design, where nothing is vulgar or slap-dash, is a practical demonstration of Tschichold's belief that even jobbing or advertising typography could, and should, obey sound typographic practice. The principles can be adapted to the requirements of the job; but they are basically the same principles.

VORZUGS-ANGEBOT

Im VERLAG DES BILDUNGSVERBANDES der Deutschen Buchdrucker, Berlin SW 61, Dreibundstr. 5, erscheint demnächst:

JAN TSCHICHOLD
Lehrer an der Meisterschule für Deutschlands Buchdrucker in München

DIE NEUE TYPOGRAPHIE

Handbuch für die gesamte Fachwelt
und die drucksachenverbrauchenden Kreise

Das Problem der neuen gestaltenden Typographie hat eine lebhafte Diskussion bei allen Beteiligten hervorgerufen. Wir glauben dem Bedürfnis, die aufgeworfenen Fragen ausführlich behandelt zu sehen, zu entsprechen, wenn wir jetzt ein Handbuch der **NEUEN TYPOGRAPHIE** herausbringen.

Es kam dem Verfasser, einem ihrer bekanntesten Vertreter, in diesem Buche zunächst darauf an, den engen Zusammenhang der neuen Typographie mit dem **Gesamtkomplex heutigen Lebens** aufzuzeigen und zu beweisen, daß die neue Typographie ein ebenso notwendiger Ausdruck einer neuen Gesinnung ist wie die neue Baukunst und alles Neue, das mit unserer Zeit anbricht. Diese geschichtliche Notwendigkeit der neuen Typographie belegt weiterhin eine kritische Darstellung der **alten Typographie**. Die Entwicklung der **neuen Malerei,** die für alles Neue unserer Zeit geistig bahnbrechend gewesen ist, wird in einem reich illustrierten Aufsatz des Buches leicht faßlich dargestellt. Ein kurzer Abschnitt „**Zur Geschichte der neuen Typographie**" leitet zu dem wichtigsten Teile des Buches, den **Grundbegriffen der neuen Typographie** über. Diese werden klar herausgeschält, richtige und falsche Beispiele einander gegenübergestellt. Zwei weitere Artikel behandeln „**Photographie und Typographie**" und „**Neue Typographie und Normung**".

Der Hauptwert des Buches für den Praktiker besteht in dem zweiten Teil „**Typographische Hauptformen**" (siehe das nebenstehende Inhaltsverzeichnis). Es fehlte bisher an einem Werke, das wie dieses Buch die schon bei einfachen Satzaufgaben auftauchenden gestalterischen Fragen in gebührender Ausführlichkeit behandelte. Jeder Teilabschnitt enthält neben **allgemeinen typographischen Regeln** vor allem die Abbildungen aller in Betracht kommenden **Normblätter** des Deutschen Normenausschusses, alle andern (z. B. postalischen) **Vorschriften** und zahlreiche Beispiele, Gegenbeispiele und Schemen.

Für jeden Buchdrucker, insbesondere jeden Akzidenzsetzer, wird „Die neue Typographie" ein **unentbehrliches Handbuch** sein. Von nicht geringerer Bedeutung ist es für Reklamefachleute, Gebrauchsgraphiker, Kaufleute, Photographen, Architekten, Ingenieure und Schriftsteller, also für alle, die mit dem Buchdruck in Berührung kommen.

INHALT DES BUCHES

typ. tschichold

Das Buch enthält über 125 Abbildungen, von denen etwa ein Viertel zweifarbig gedruckt ist, und umfaßt gegen 200 Seiten auf gutem Kunstdruckpapier. Es erscheint im Format DIN A5 (148× 210 mm) und ist biegsam in Ganzleinen gebunden.

Preis bei Vorbestellung bis 1. Juni 1928: **5.00** RM
durch den Buchhandel nur zum Preise von **6.50** RM

Bestellschein umstehend ➡

Two advertisements
Designed by Jan Tschichold, 1931

These two advertisements, the bottom one described as 'experimental' in the English edition of *Typographische Gestaltung* (*Asymmetric Typography*), in which both are shown, were designed only three years later than the prospectus opposite, yet have a new elegance, balance and feeling for space. The lower one also illustrates his new-found belief that not only could typefaces other than grotesques be used, but that they could be carefully mixed. This rapidly evolving designer was becoming remarkably subtle in his handling of type and space.

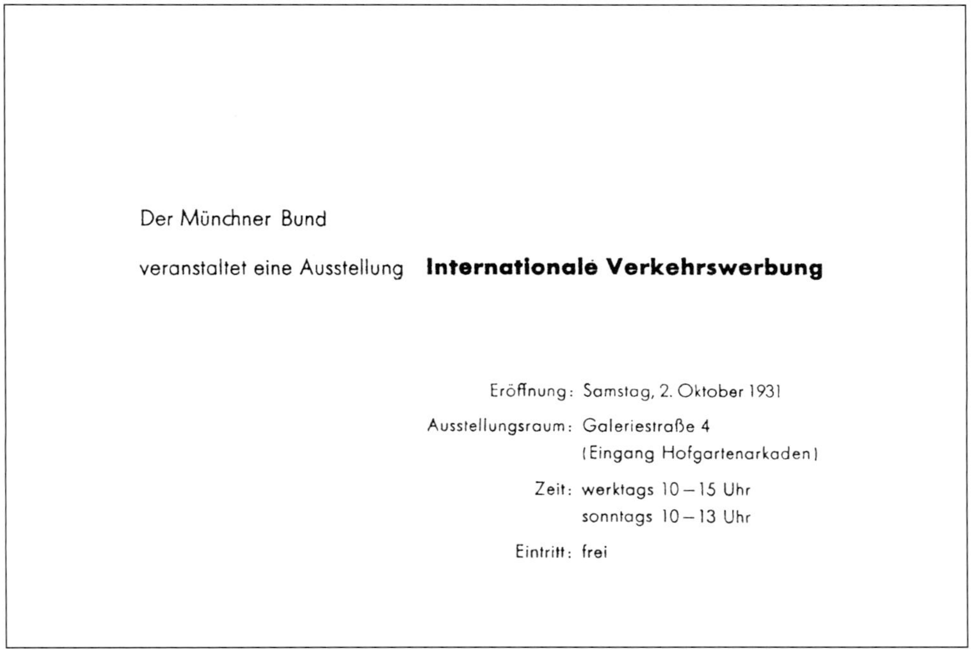

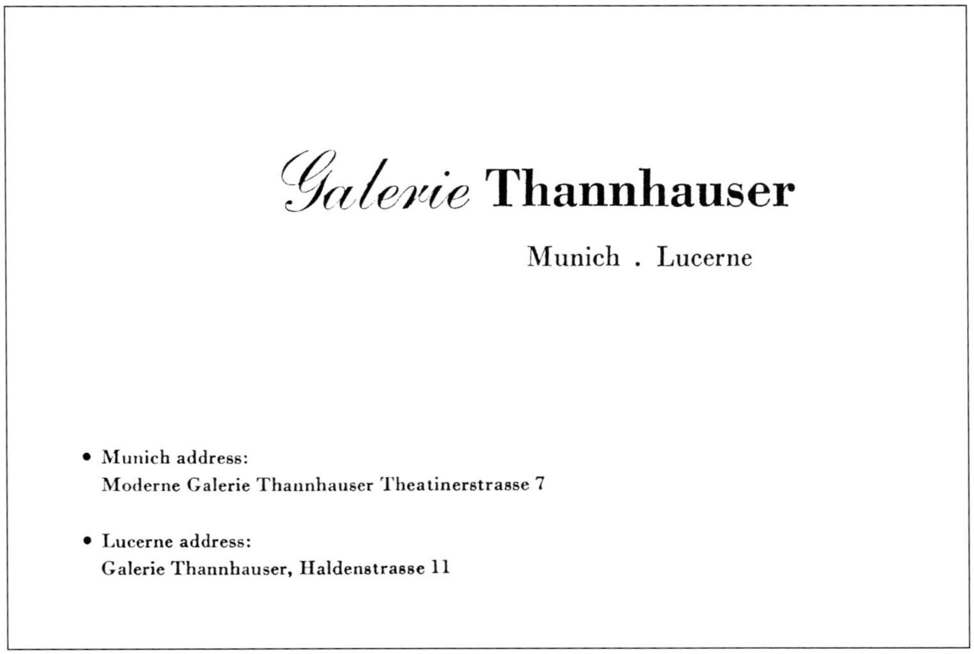

James McNeill Whistler
The Gentle Art of Making Enemies
Ballantyne Press, London and Edinburgh, 1890
Designed by James McNeill Whistler
Illustrated at 53% actual size

Jan Tschichold: *Typographische Gestaltung*
Benno Schwabe, Basel, 1935
Designed by Jan Tschichold
Illustrated at 63% actual size

Although by the time he came to write and design *Typographische Gestaltung*, in 1935, Tschichold felt able to pronounce that type mixtures were allowable, it takes a brave and confident designer to combine a script derived from eighteenth-century English writing masters with Georg Trump's slightly ungainly modernist City Medium of 1930. And get away with it. Whistler's section title looks almost tame in comparison.

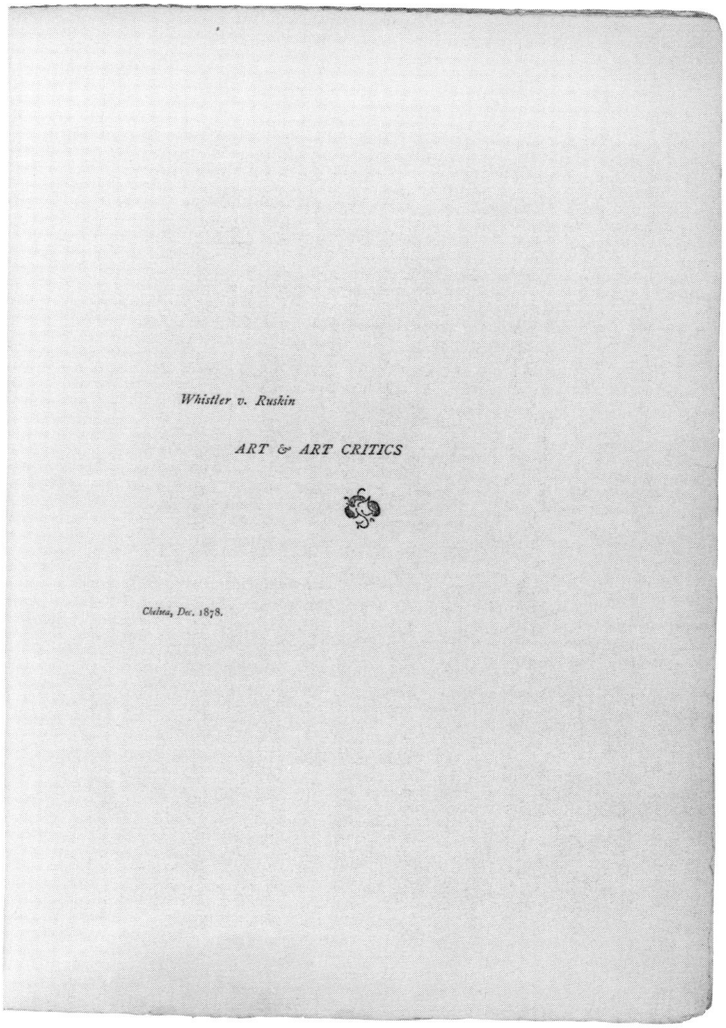

Whistler v. Ruskin

ART & ART CRITICS

Chelsea, Dec. 1878.

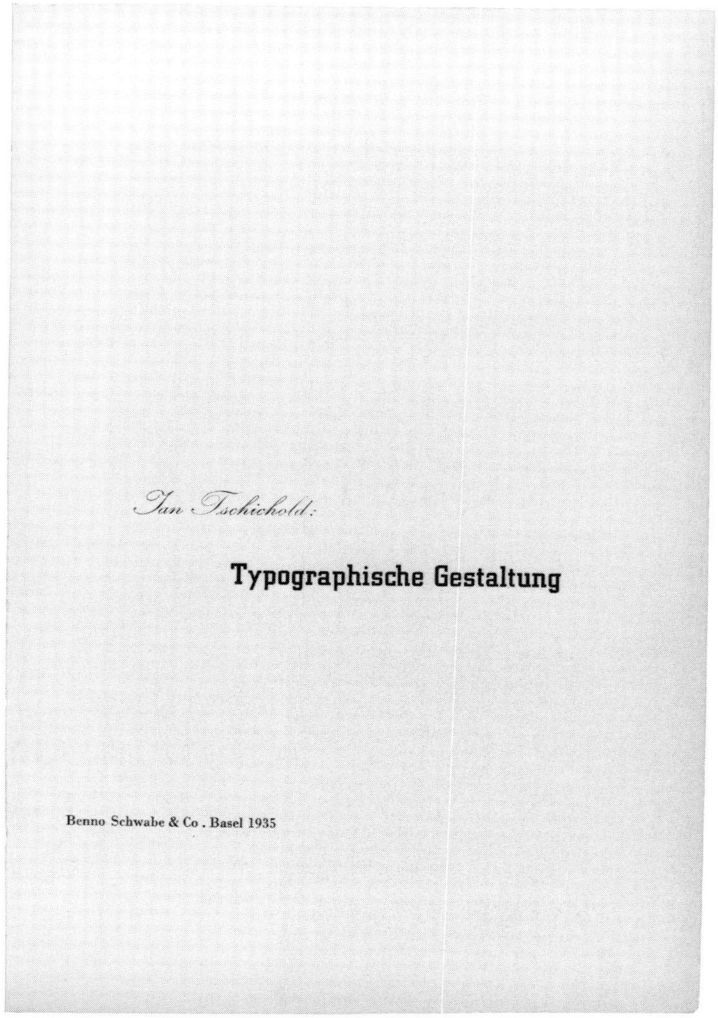

Jan Tschichold:

Typographische Gestaltung

Benno Schwabe & Co . Basel 1935

Two designs illustrated in
Typographische Gestaltung, 1935
Designed by Jan Tschichold
Illustrated at 63% actual size

It is not clear whether this title page and lecture list are from an actual publication, or merely illustrations created for his book. It is immaterial. Both, especially the title page, are fine designs. Tschichold repeats his daring combination of an English script with a bold type, here, as in the earlier advertisement shown on page 71, Bodoni. (Equally daring, Joost Schmidt had already used an English script with a modern bold upper- and lower-case – not Bodoni – in his brochure for the Dessau Travel Bureau of 1931.)

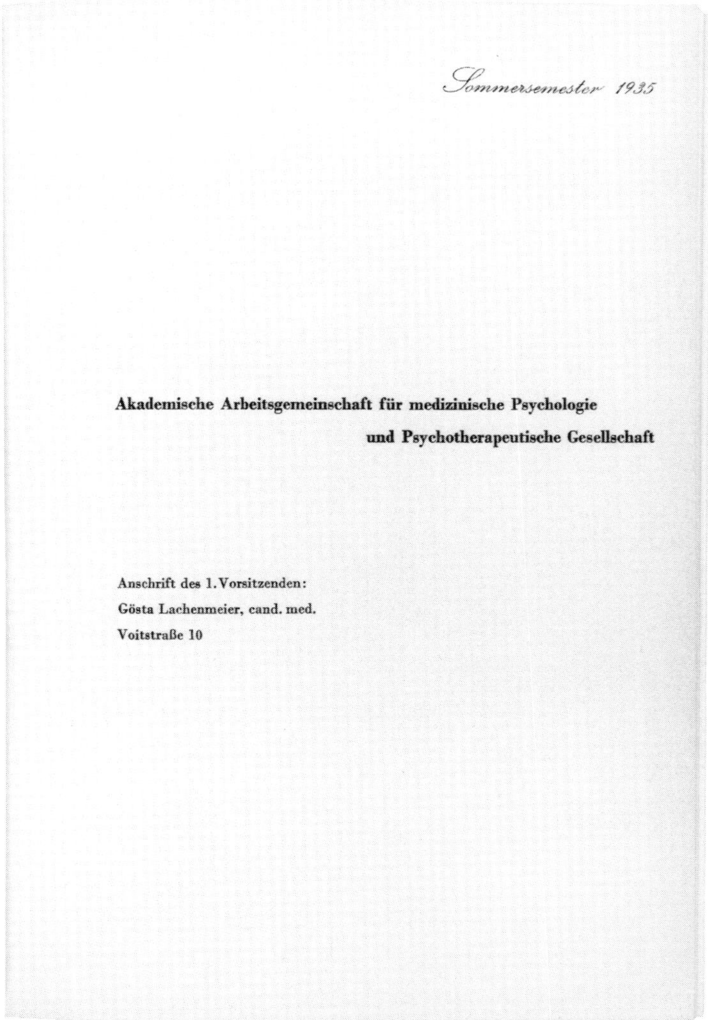

Sommersemester 1935

Akademische Arbeitsgemeinschaft für medizinische Psychologie
und Psychotherapeutische Gesellschaft

Anschrift des 1. Vorsitzenden:
Gösta Lachenmeier, cand. med.
Voitstraße 10

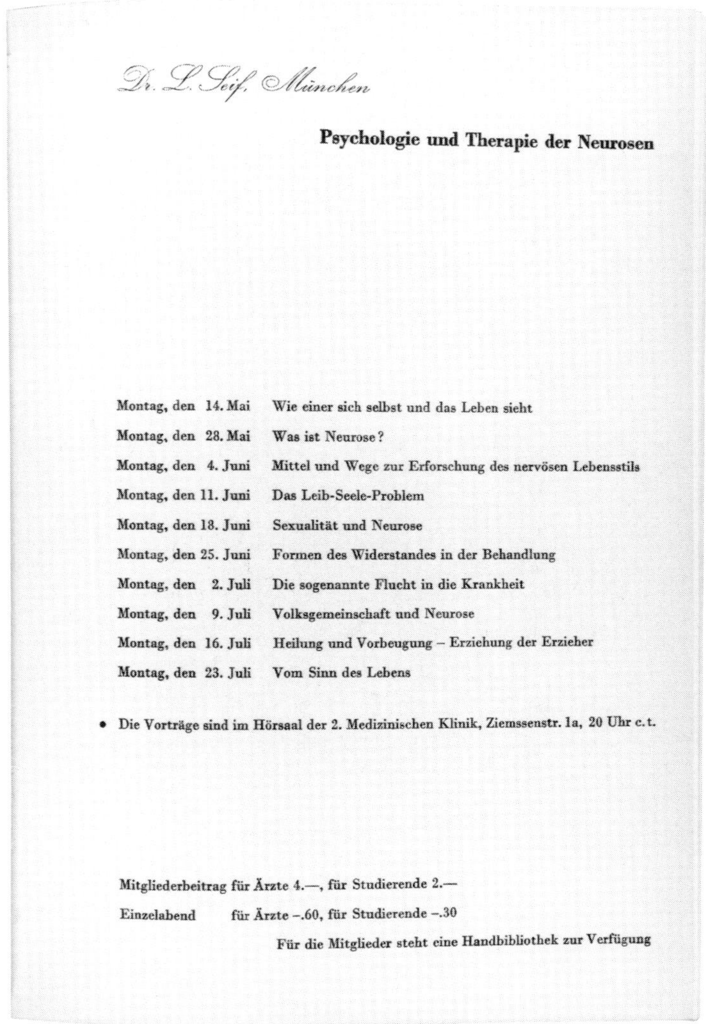

Dr. L. Seif, München

Psychologie und Therapie der Neurosen

Montag, den 14. Mai	Wie einer sich selbst und das Leben sieht
Montag, den 28. Mai	Was ist Neurose?
Montag, den 4. Juni	Mittel und Wege zur Erforschung des nervösen Lebensstils
Montag, den 11. Juni	Das Leib-Seele-Problem
Montag, den 18. Juni	Sexualität und Neurose
Montag, den 25. Juni	Formen des Widerstandes in der Behandlung
Montag, den 2. Juli	Die sogenannte Flucht in die Krankheit
Montag, den 9. Juli	Volksgemeinschaft und Neurose
Montag, den 16. Juli	Heilung und Vorbeugung – Erziehung der Erzieher
Montag, den 23. Juli	Vom Sinn des Lebens

• Die Vorträge sind im Hörsaal der 2. Medizinischen Klinik, Ziemssenstr. 1a, 20 Uhr c. t.

Mitgliederbeitrag für Ärzte 4.—, für Studierende 2.—
Einzelabend für Ärzte –.60, für Studierende –.30
Für die Mitglieder steht eine Handbibliothek zur Verfügung

Two letterheads illustrated in *Typographische Gestaltung*, 1935
Designed by Jan Tschichold
Illustrated at 92% (of A4)

The careful analysis of the copy is exemplary; the breaking down and display of the various bits of information, clearly, logically, and aesthetically pleasing, looks inevitable. But although today one may get clarity, *or* pattern-making (often confusing and ill-thought out), such an elegant combination of the two is rare. The current proliferation of addresses, telephone numbers, fax numbers, e-mail addresses and web sites is a typographic challenge, or opportunity; it is rarely taken up. Quick fixes are more common.

Filialen

Danzig
Budweis
Bukarest
Mailand

Günther Wagner Hannover

Günther Wagner Hannover

Drahtanschrift
Pelikan Hannover

Fernsprecher
66.001

Postscheckkonto
Hannover Nr. 436
Konto Nr. 74.009
bei der Hannov. Bank

ABC Code, 6. Ausgabe
Rudolf Mosse
Liebers Standard Code

Ihre Zeichen | Ihre Nachricht vom | Unser Zeichen | Tag

philobiblon eine zeitschrift für bücherliebhaber . a magazine for book-collectors

herbert reichner verlag, wien VI (vienna), strohmayergasse 6

telephon b 23854
bankkonto wiener bankverein, wien XIV
postscheckkonten leipzig 8442
wien 46469
prag 501701
zürich VII 18122

Title page illustrated in
Typographische Gestaltung, 1935
Designed by Jan Tschichold

Simplicity, elegance, subtle detailing, control of space. What more can one say?

José Ortega y Gasset

Der Einfluß der Frau auf die Geschichte

Verlag der Neuen Schweizer Rundschau, Zürich

Jan Tschichold: *Asymmetric Typography*
Faber and Faber, London, 1967
with Cooper & Beatty, Toronto
Designed by Jan Tschichold
Illustrated at 68% actual size

An English edition of *Typographische Gestaltung* (translated by Ruari McLean) had to wait thirty-two years before publication. Although, by 1967, Tschichold had long believed that asymmetry should play no part in book design, it would have been singularly perverse to use the classical mode for *this* particular book. The title spread incorporates Frank Bollinger's famous portrait of The Master approving his own work. It rather says it all. The typography is carefully related to horizontals and verticals in the photograph.

Why is he so fond of putting a colon after his name?

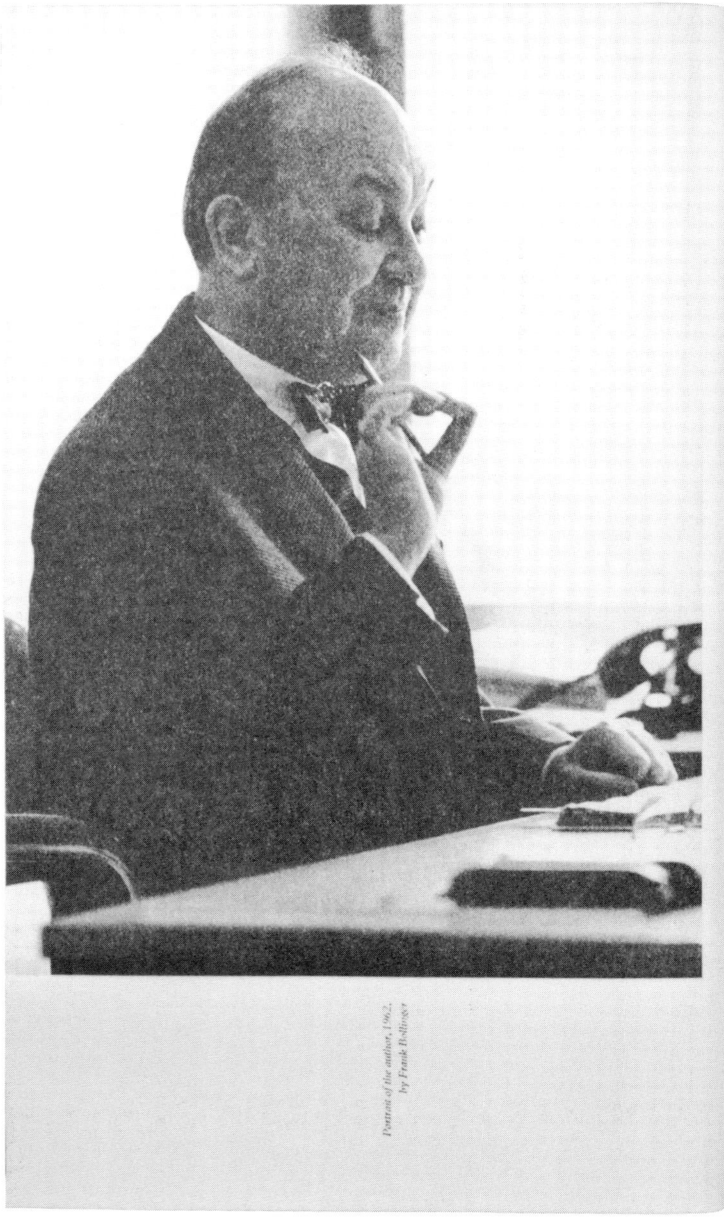
Portrait of the author, 1962, by Frank Bollinger

JAN TSCHICHOLD:

Asymmetric Typography

Published by Faber & Faber Limited
24 Russell Square, London in co-operation with
Cooper & Beatty, Limited, Toronto

This second spread from *Asymmetric Typography* is another example of how the designer favours classical margins even when the book is generally asymmetric. The gesture of that bow-tied Master is fully justified both by the elegance of these two pages, and the wonderfully balanced design of the 1937 poster he illustrates on the recto. Taking inspiration from Constructivist works, he has translated their basic elements into typography.

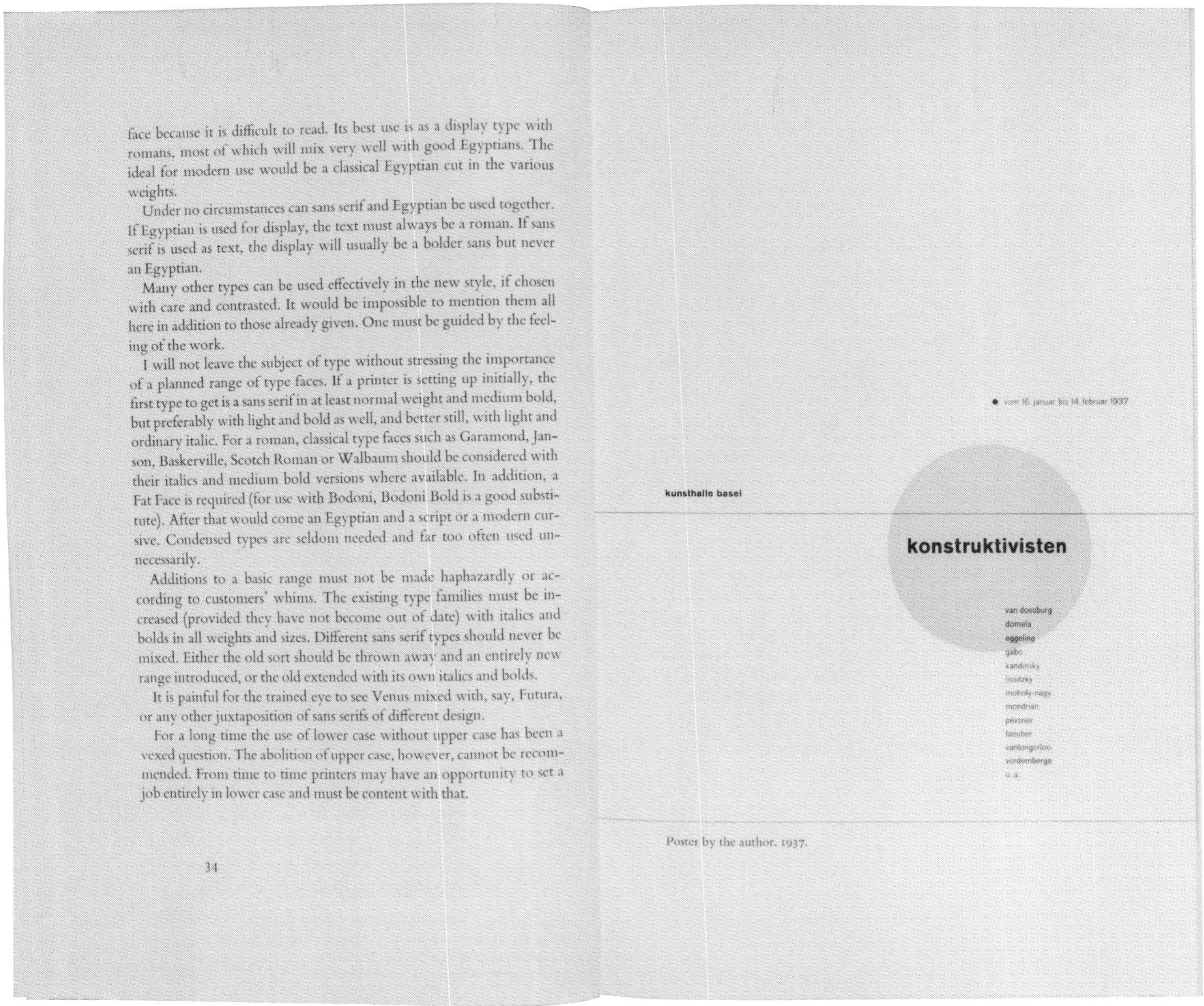

face because it is difficult to read. Its best use is as a display type with romans, most of which will mix very well with good Egyptians. The ideal for modern use would be a classical Egyptian cut in the various weights.

Under no circumstances can sans serif and Egyptian be used together. If Egyptian is used for display, the text must always be a roman. If sans serif is used as text, the display will usually be a bolder sans but never an Egyptian.

Many other types can be used effectively in the new style, if chosen with care and contrasted. It would be impossible to mention them all here in addition to those already given. One must be guided by the feeling of the work.

I will not leave the subject of type without stressing the importance of a planned range of type faces. If a printer is setting up initially, the first type to get is a sans serif in at least normal weight and medium bold, but preferably with light and bold as well, and better still, with light and ordinary italic. For a roman, classical type faces such as Garamond, Janson, Baskerville, Scotch Roman or Walbaum should be considered with their italics and medium bold versions where available. In addition, a Fat Face is required (for use with Bodoni, Bodoni Bold is a good substitute). After that would come an Egyptian and a script or a modern cursive. Condensed types are seldom needed and far too often used unnecessarily.

Additions to a basic range must not be made haphazardly or according to customers' whims. The existing type families must be increased (provided they have not become out of date) with italics and bolds in all weights and sizes. Different sans serif types should never be mixed. Either the old sort should be thrown away and an entirely new range introduced, or the old extended with its own italics and bolds.

It is painful for the trained eye to see Venus mixed with, say, Futura, or any other juxtaposition of sans serifs of different design.

For a long time the use of lower case without upper case has been a vexed question. The abolition of upper case, however, cannot be recommended. From time to time printers may have an opportunity to set a job entirely in lower case and must be content with that.

34

Poster by the author. 1937.

Jan Tschichold
Chinese Colour Prints from the Ten Bamboo Studio
Lund Humphries, London, 1972
Designed by Jan Tschichold
Illustrated at 37% actual size

Even by 1935 Tschichold had declared that centred typography was acceptable. Having fled to democratic Switzerland from Germany in 1933, he was viewing the Nazi dictatorship with increasing distaste; and, perhaps by 1940, he had dismissed the New Typography, the doctrines of which he equated with Nazism, as entirely unsuitable for bookwork. This reaction against his earlier beliefs, at a time when many architects were disapproving of classicism on the grounds that it was the favoured style of totalitarian states, was considered incomprehensible and neurotically deluded; and it led to a notorious slanging match between himself and Max Bill. ('This snake in our midst,' etc.)

This title page, the English version of the original German edition, was perhaps the last he designed, for he died two years later. It demonstrates to me that he brought to his classical work all the skills in using space, and in using type with economy and elegance, that he had learnt while designing his asymmetrical work. In comparison, title pages of Hermann Zapf, one of the most notable 'classical' designers (but who appeared not to have experienced the more demanding discipline of the New Typography) have overlarge type sprawling down the page – often not so very different in essence from Baskerville's designs. In none is his control of space anywhere as deft as Tschichold's; none has the originality shown here, the title in a small size of strong upper and lower case sensitively placed amongst delicate lines of small caps, carefully letter-spaced.

JAN TSCHICHOLD

Chinese Colour Prints from the Ten Bamboo Studio

WITH TWENTY-FOUR REPRODUCTIONS
IN FULL COLOUR FACSIMILE
OF PRINTS FROM THE MASTERPIECE
OF CHINESE COLOUR PRINTING
FROM THE MING PERIOD

LUND HUMPHRIES
LONDON

László Moholy-Nagy
The New Vision and Abstract of an Artist
Wittenborn and Company, New York, 1946
Designed by Paul Rand
Illustrated at 49% actual size

Paul Rand: *Thoughts on Design*
Wittenborn and Company, New York, 1947
Designed by Paul Rand
Illustrated at 44% actual size

Tschichold may have himself renounced his New Typography, but by the mid-1940s its influence on Swiss and British design especially was immense. It initially made less, even minimal, impact in America. Except for Paul Rand. The refinement, restraint and use of space in these two title pages, the whole general approach, show how well Rand understood Tschichold's work. Both are set, in whole or in part, in Futura, rather than the more European Akzidenz; but the restricted range of type sizes, the use of bold for emphasis, even the use of mixed type styles in *Thoughts on Design*, which the New Typography eventually permitted, are all characteristic of European thinking. The boxing-up of information in that second example follows a practice found in work by both Bayer at the Bauhaus, and Tschichold.

Rand was the most subtle of the American design pioneers, clearly appreciating the freedom with which Tschichold arranged type. He was less sympathetic to the stricter Swiss approach.

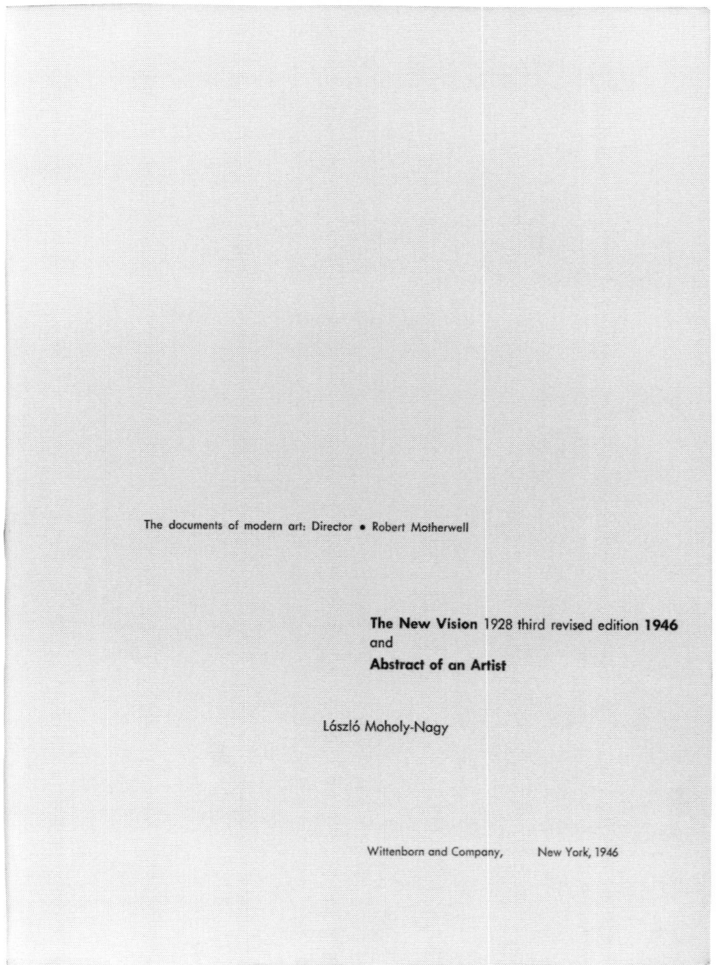
The documents of modern art: Director • Robert Motherwell

The New Vision 1928 third revised edition **1946**
and
Abstract of an Artist

László Moholy-Nagy

Wittenborn and Company, New York, 1946

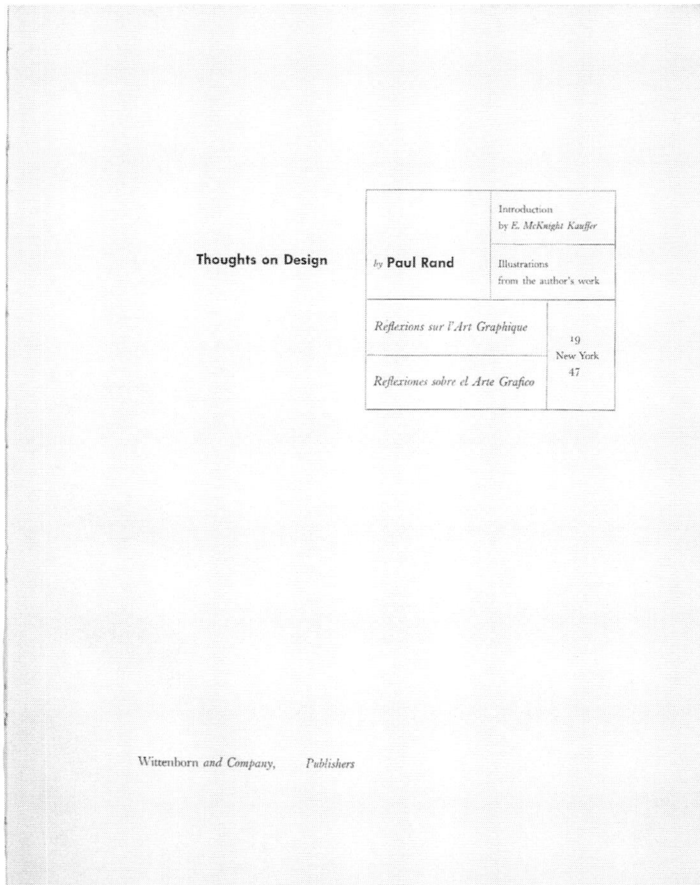
Thoughts on Design

by **Paul Rand**

Introduction
by E. McKnight Kauffer

Illustrations
from the author's work

Reflexions sur l'Art Graphique

Reflexiones sobre el Arte Grafico

19
New York
47

Wittenborn *and Company,* *Publishers*

Thoughts on Design continued

Rand was prolific, and an all-rounder in the same way that Hans Schleger (Zero) was in Britain. His work has much in common with that designer, combining a painterly approach, or imaginative graphics, with sensitive typography – even in advertising. *Thoughts on Design* shows one hundred examples from his first ten years in practice, displayed with a fine sense of the use of space, contrast and relationships, resulting in a sequence which is coherent yet varied. There is an awareness of the grid, but it is broken almost as much as it is held to.

The book which Rand illustrates here is – especially for American book design of the period – very daring in the way the text is positioned on the page.

The spread opposite shows Rand's ability to place illustrations and text, their positioning apparently decided purely by his sensitive eye. There are occasional hints at a grid – if you are searching for it. The top of the A does in fact follow a main grid line; the captions follow a secondary one. Folios provide a key spot against which captions can be aligned; images are anchored to them also, but their positions are adjusted to *visually* align. Such subtleties are often ignored by more systems-minded designers, who prefer to follow the grid out of the window, come what may.

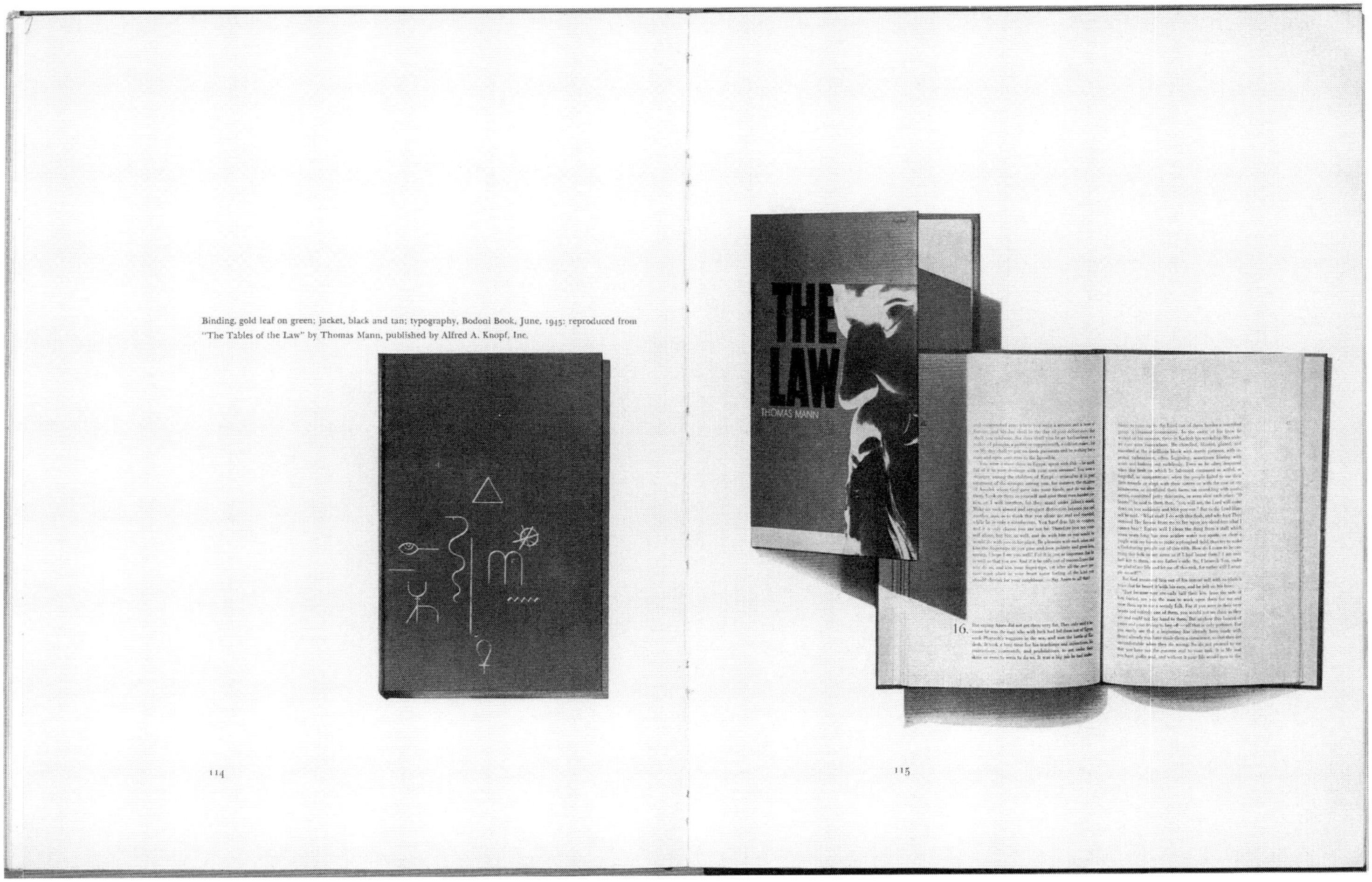
Binding, gold leaf on green; jacket, black and tan; typography, Bodoni Book, June, 1945; reproduced from "The Tables of the Law" by Thomas Mann, published by Alfred A. Knopf, Inc.

Paul Rand was one of the most notable graphic designers of the twentieth century. While *typographer* and *book designer* were well-established professions, it was only in the 1940s that the *graphic designer* superseded the advertising artist and that humble drudge the layout man, to become an amalgam of the two. But it was more than that. The job description included almost any graphic work, from posters to signage, packaging to postage stamps, railway livery to booklets and brochures. A new society demanded design be applied to areas the Bauhaus had hardly dared to dream of.

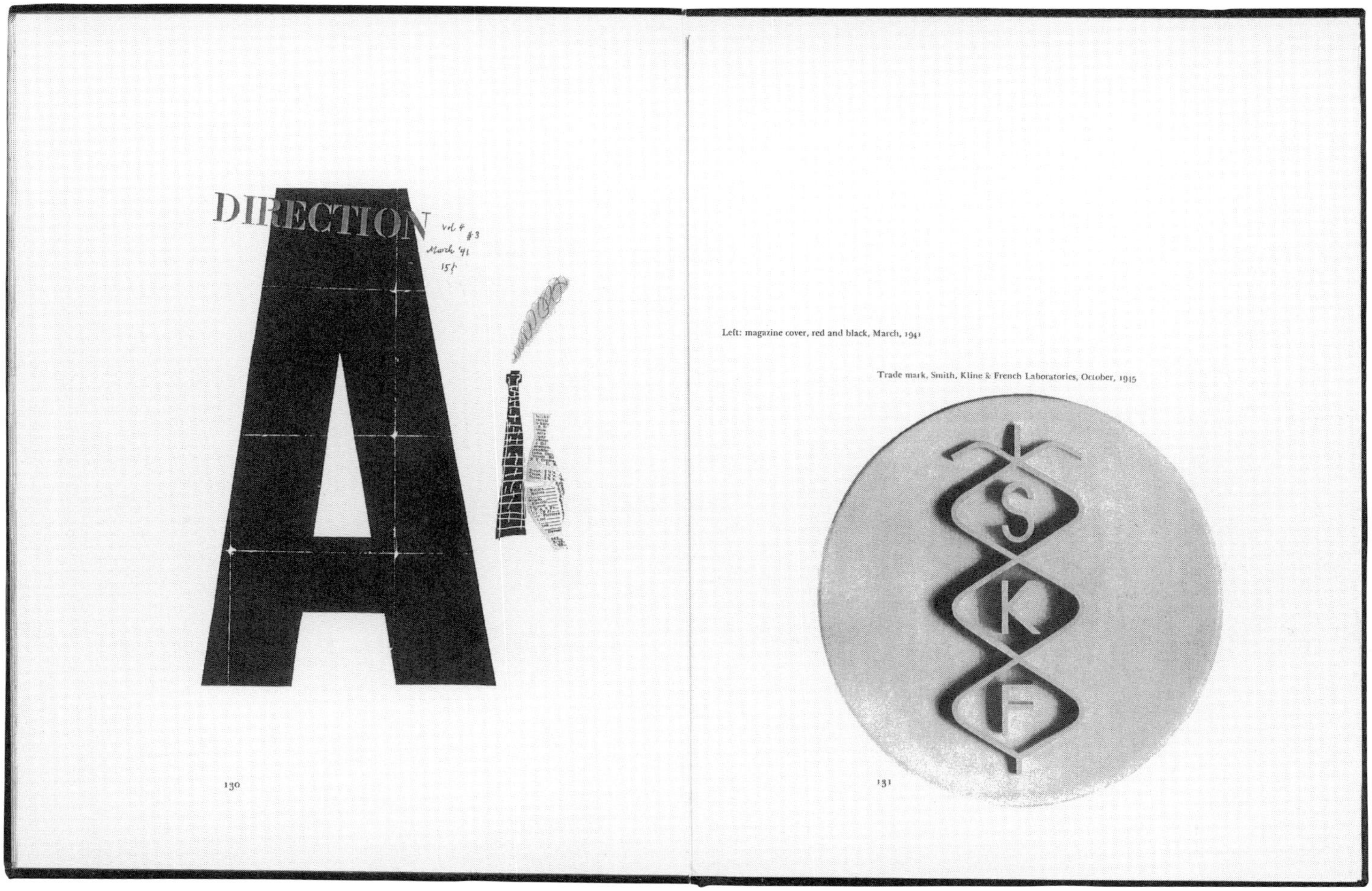

Paul Rand: *From Lascaux to Brooklyn*
Yale University Press, New Haven and London, 1996
Designed by Paul Rand
Illustrated at 50% actual size

At the end of his long career (he died the same year), Rand had lost none of his ability to handle type economically and imaginatively, nor his feeling for the placement of items on the page. New Typography had demanded, seventy years earlier, that unoccupied space be given as much consideration as the positioning of items in occupied areas. The freshness of this title spread demonstrates how valid that requirement can still be, and how skilfully Rand obeyed it.

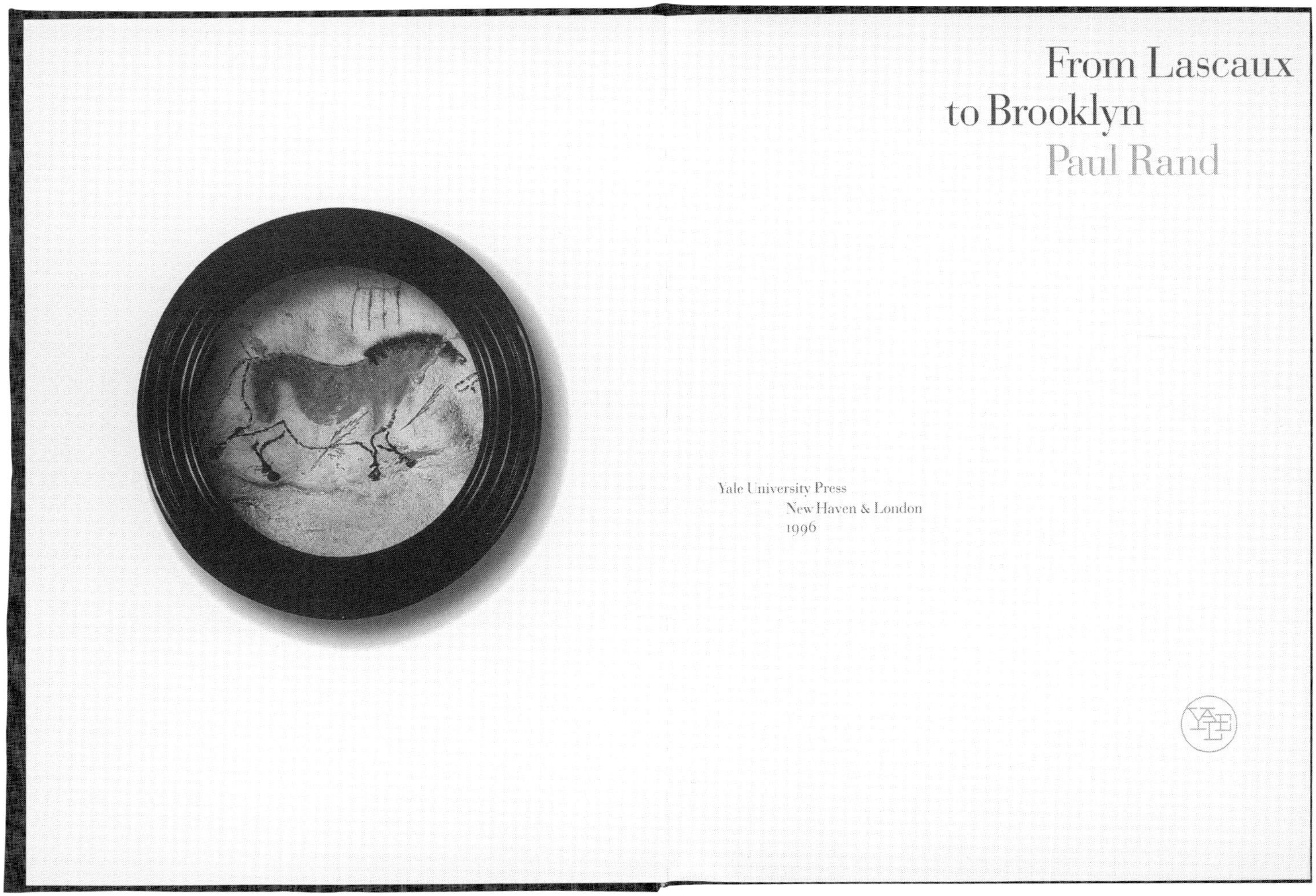

willem sandberg

The principles of the New Typography formulated by Tschichold in his two books had but limited effect before Nazism declared them degenerate and unacceptable. Only later, in the 1940s, did they become truly significant, affecting especially the course of Swiss and British design and printing. In both countries, not only were Tschichold's designs influential; his refining of typographic detailing brought a new clarity and cleanliness to the printed page.

Tschichold's unequalled design skills and sensitivity made him, despite his remarkable influence, a somewhat isolated figure. So is the Dutchman Willem Sandberg: effectively no predecessors, and no successors; although the printer-painter H N Werkman was an influence as were (less obviously) the Constructivists and Piet Zwart.

A *route touristique*, his painterly designs have the freedom and verve of Bauhaus work, but they were less geometric and mechanical, were tempered by a sensitivity in the use of space, and exhibited the more logical control of the New Typography. Five years older than Tschichold, he was largely a self-taught designer, his skill acquired during his pre-war involvement with the museum world. In the war he forged identity cards so good that even German experts were unable to distinguish real from false. ('The highest praise I have ever received for typographic work.') In time, so many – thousands – were made it was thought advisable to blow up the Record Office. This was done. Many of those involved were caught and executed, but Sandberg escaped and went into hiding with a new identity (and new identity card). He used this time as a fugitive making 'experimenta typographica', eighteen short manuscript books of various pensées and quotations, which were recreated in a printed form after the war.

The fine series of catalogues he designed from 1950 to 1960 for the Stedelijk Museum in Amsterdam, of which he was Director, built on those typographic experiments. Despite the end of the war, materials were still scarce. He exploited this by cultivating a rough 'imperfect' style. Torn paper shapes are in sympathy with the low-grade wrapping or packing papers he used. The natural colours of the papers (browns, beiges, greys) and their often hairy or oatmeal-like textures, were complemented by strong, simple, brightly coloured shapes. With long (strictly speaking, over-long) unjustified lines of text set in a grotesque – often in a very bold weight; confident use of space; freely arranged display matter in bold – and often expanded – typefaces (grotesques, egyptians, clarendons); all this gives these catalogues a unique and instantly recognisable character. The personal mix of painterly vision and strictly controlled typography is difficult to emulate. Unlike Swiss New Typography, his work is not based on a system. Unlike Tschichold, he was no propagandist for his own approach; but he shared with the German an innate feeling for the mise-en-page.

After the Stedelijk, Sandberg continued to work in the museum world. By 1964 he was advising for the Israel Museum in Jerusalem, and designing catalogues, posters and other material for numerous exhibitions elsewhere. His work could hardly be more different from the work being done at the same time in a Switzerland which had been untouched by war.

Willem Sandberg
Experimenta Typographica No 2
(*Gesundheit*)
Galerie der Spiegel, Cologne, 1969
Illustrated at 70% actual size

This is a translation into printed form of one of the manuscript books Sandberg created in hiding during the Occupation. While aware both of current concerns and the earlier work of artist-designers, he is entirely original. In these two spreads, New Typography principles are combined with the exuberance and wit found in Italian Futurist typography. Torn paper shapes marry well with the low-grade paper; his favourite rather expanded bold grotesque results in a characteristic horizontality.

The arrow on the recto opposite is composed of small 'a's.

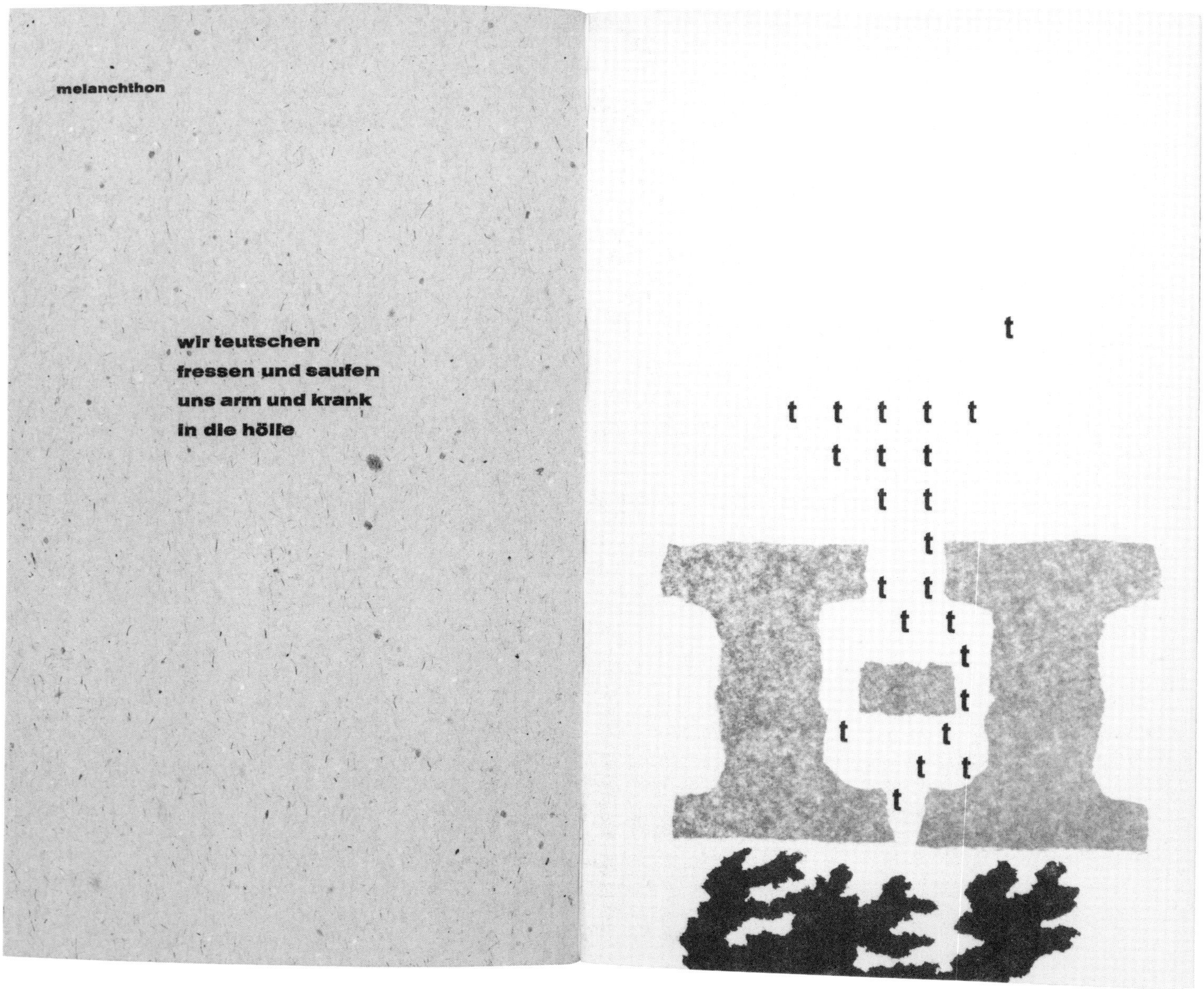

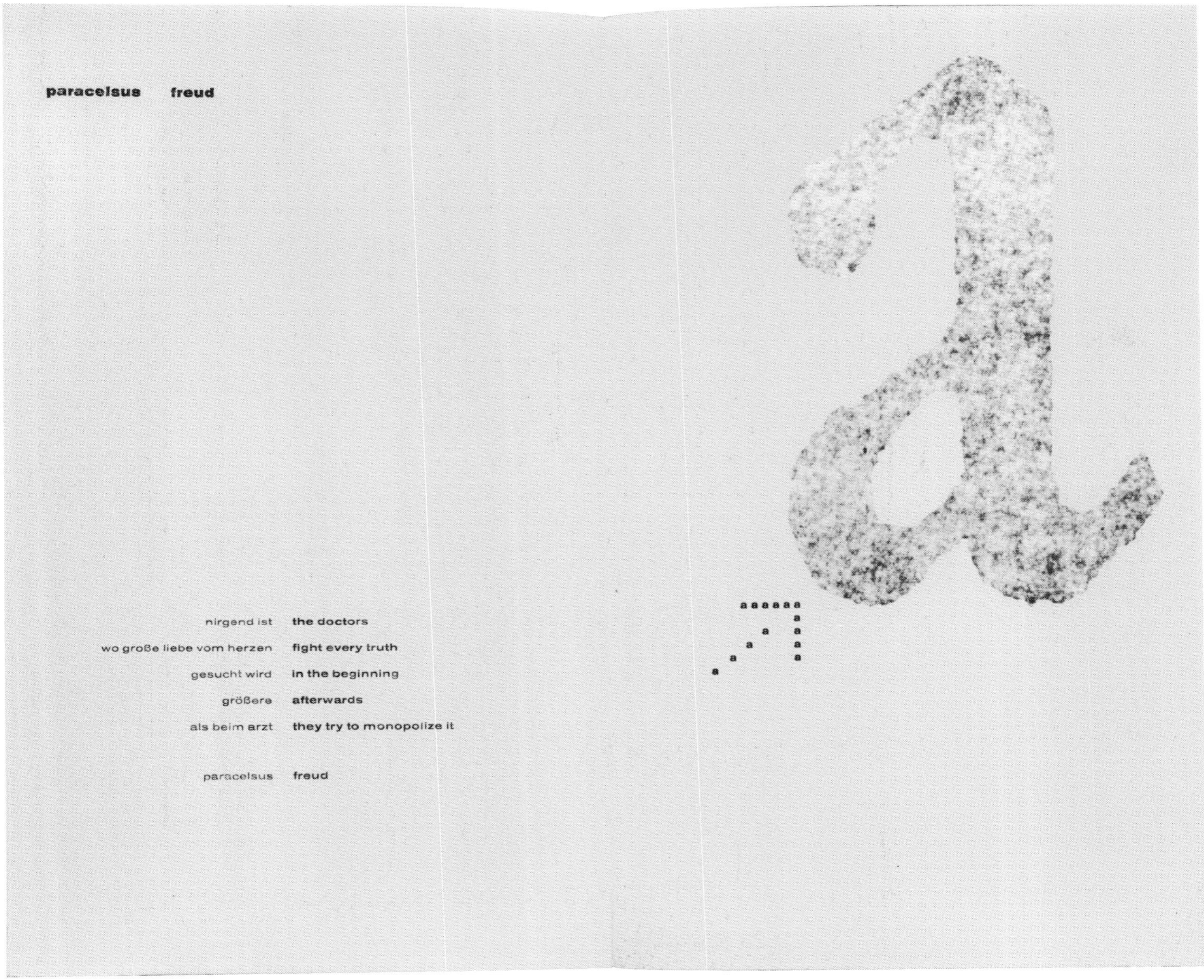

paracelsus **freud**

nirgend ist	**the doctors**
wo große liebe vom herzen	**fight every truth**
gesucht wird	**in the beginning**
größere	**afterwards**
als beim arzt	**they try to monopolize it**
paracelsus	**freud**

aaaaaa
a
a a
a a
a a
a

Experimenta Typographica No 2 continued

Like Herbert Bayer, Sandberg preferred not to use caps, although unlike Bayer he realised that they were desirable in continuous text. The recto on this spread again uses his 'trademark' expanded bold grotesque, and the pattern he has created floats quietly in the middle of the page. His sense of placing seemed unerring; yet he designed by eye, not geometry – the antithesis of de Stijl practice.

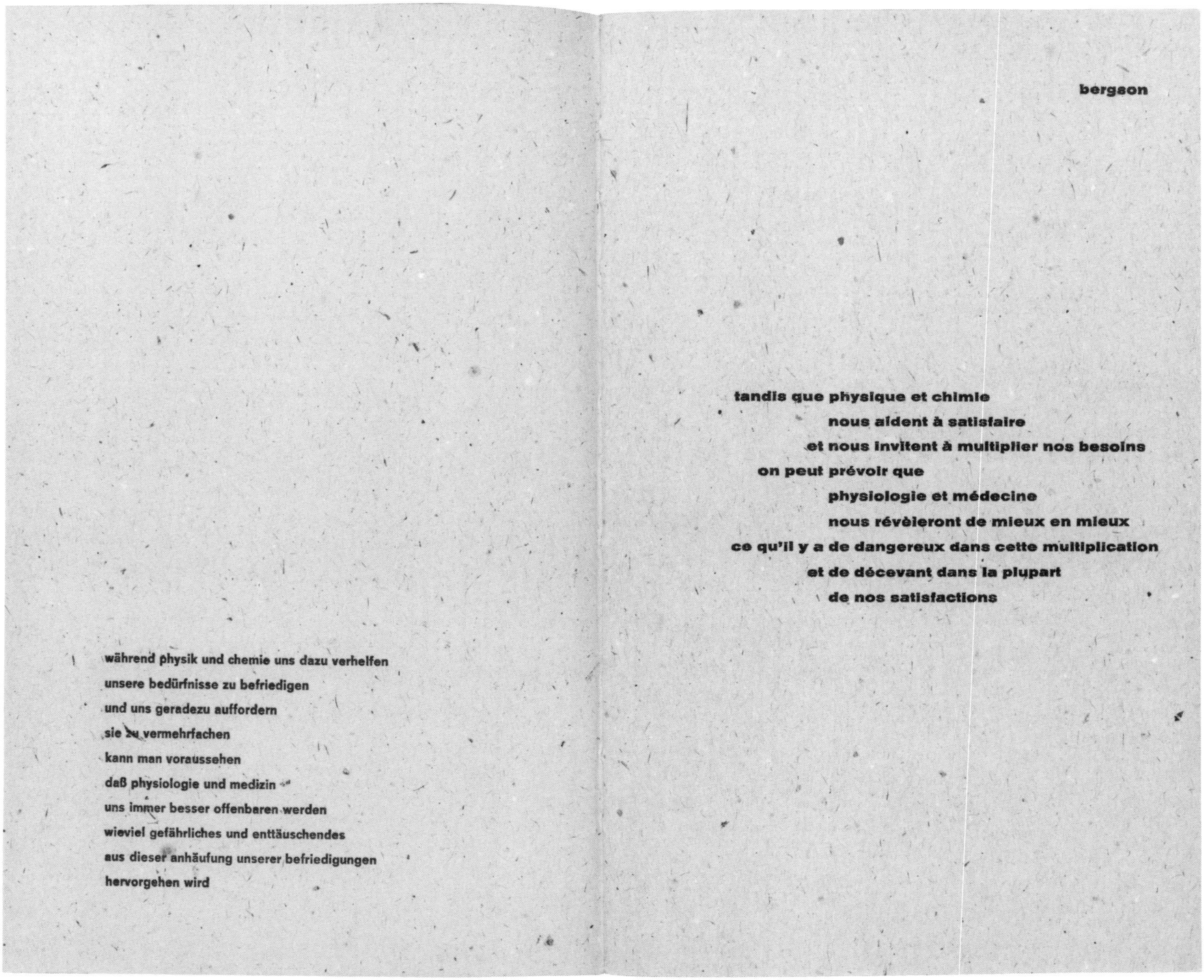

während physik und chemie uns dazu verhelfen
unsere bedürfnisse zu befriedigen
und uns geradezu auffordern
sie zu vermehrfachen
kann man voraussehen
daß physiologie und medizin
uns immer besser offenbaren werden
wieviel gefährliches und enttäuschendes
aus dieser anhäufung unserer befriedigungen
hervorgehen wird

bergson

tandis que physique et chimie
nous aident à satisfaire
et nous invitent à multiplier nos besoins
on peut prévoir que
physiologie et médecine
nous révèleront de mieux en mieux
ce qu'il y a de dangereux dans cette multiplication
et de décevant dans la plupart
de nos satisfactions

Willem Sandberg
Nu 2 (Quadrat-Print)
De Jong, Hilversum, 1969?
Designed by Willem Sandberg
Illustrated at 30% actual size

Quadrat-Prints were a series of experimental productions published by the Dutch printers de Jong. This cover design, on one of Sandberg's preferred rough-textured papers, shows his fascination with pattern created by bold types used abstractly. Whereas his preference was for small-size, if bold, heading types on text pages, such restraint was not always followed in his cover designs, where a painterly enjoyment of rich forms was given free rein. But in neither situation was he ever crude or 'Germanic' – to use the word in its vulgar sense, or as Tschichold might have used it when castigating Nazism.

Ben Nicholson
Catalogue, Stedelijk Museum
Amsterdam, 1954
Designed by Willem Sandberg
Illustrated at 59% actual size

This catalogue title page shows how original Sandberg's work could be. Few designers would arrange things with such risky simplicity. One line of type conveys three pieces of information, but they are carefully separated. The second line, seemingly unrelated to the first in any formal way, sits there in quiet confidence.

I suppose it is fatuous to attribute the characteristic horizontality of Sandberg's designs to the flat Dutch landscape.

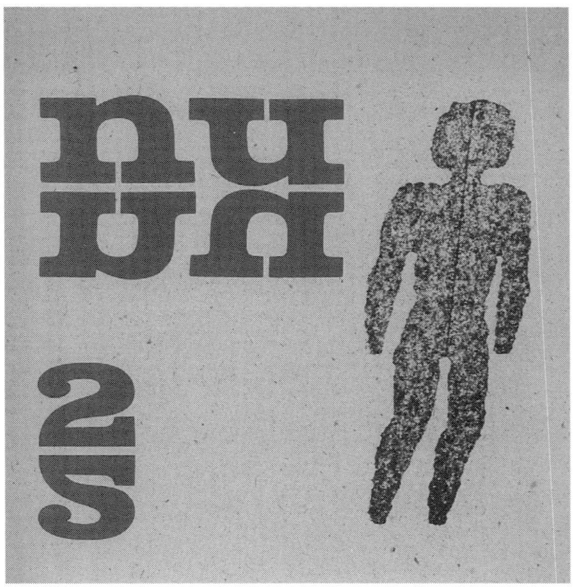

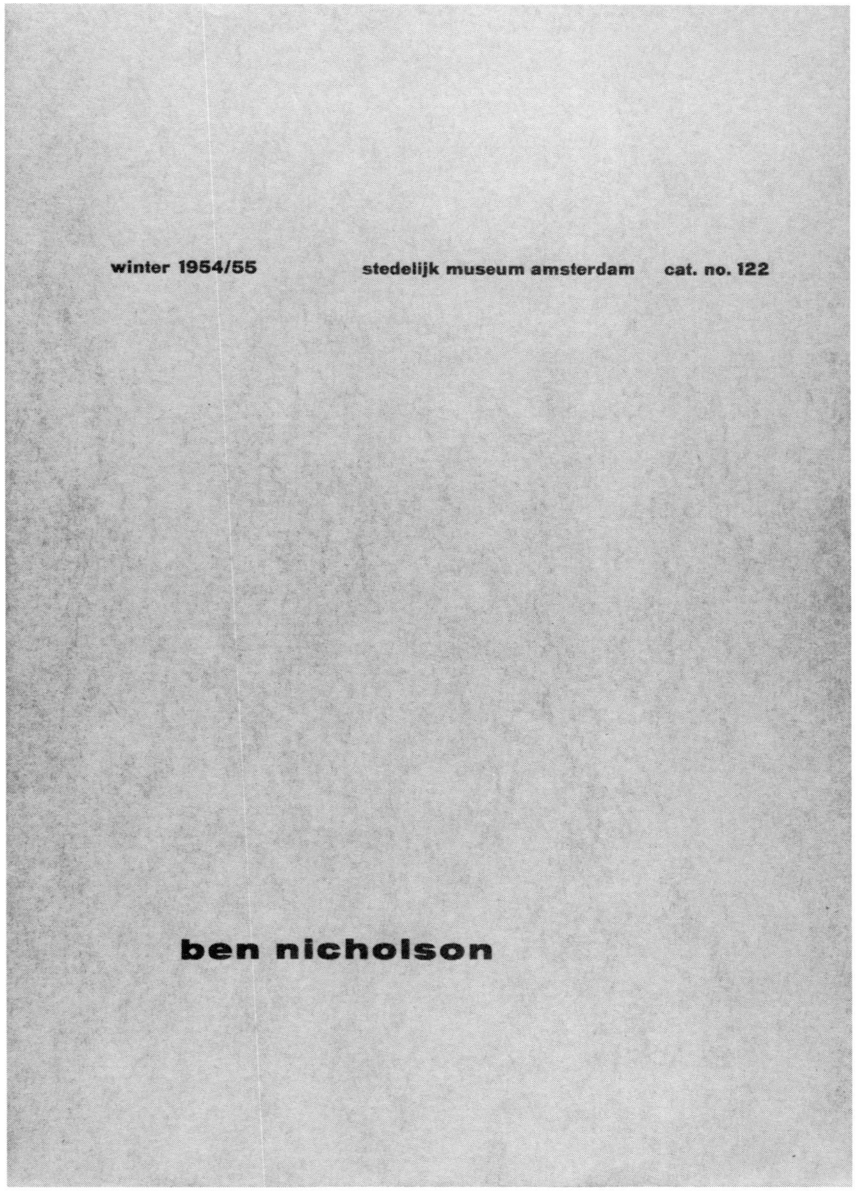

De Stijl
Catalogue, Stedelijk Museum
Amsterdam, 1951
Designed by Willem Sandberg
Illustrated at 51% actual size

More daring in his margins than Tschichold, the lines of bold type on tinted paper are, despite generous leading, a little too long for easy reading, although acceptable in the short texts of a catalogue. I often get the feeling that Sandberg thought rules were there to be broken. The bold heading is positioned just so.

Sandberg has wisely made no attempt to mimic de Stijl typography, not even by introducing allusive typefaces.

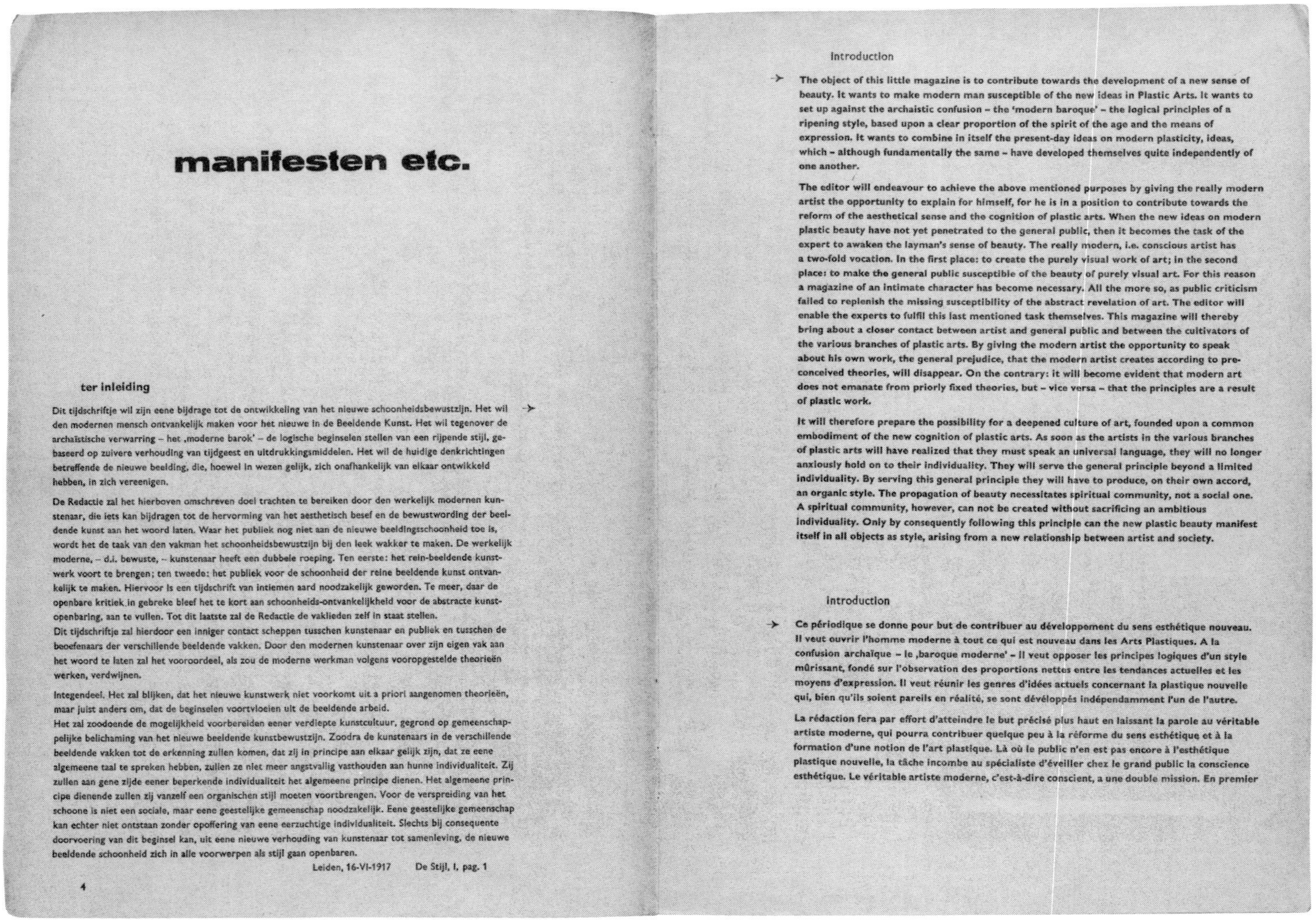

manifesten etc.

ter inleiding

Dit tijdschriftje wil zijn eene bijdrage tot de ontwikkeling van het nieuwe schoonheidsbewustzijn. Het wil den modernen mensch ontvankelijk maken voor het nieuwe in de Beeldende Kunst. Het wil tegenover de archaïstische verwarring – het ‚moderne barok' – de logische beginselen stellen van een rijpende stijl, gebaseerd op zuivere verhouding van tijdgeest en uitdrukkingsmiddelen. Het wil de huidige denkrichtingen betreffende de nieuwe beelding, die, hoewel in wezen gelijk, zich onafhankelijk van elkaar ontwikkeld hebben, in zich vereenigen.

De Redactie zal het hierboven omschreven doel trachten te bereiken door den werkelijk modernen kunstenaar, die iets kan bijdragen tot de hervorming van het aesthetisch besef en de bewustwording der beeldende kunst aan het woord laten. Waar het publiek nog niet aan de nieuwe beeldingsschoonheid toe is, wordt het de taak van den vakman het schoonheidsbewustzijn bij den leek wakker te maken. De werkelijk moderne, – d.i. bewuste, – kunstenaar heeft een dubbele roeping. Ten eerste: het rein-beeldende kunstwerk voort te brengen; ten tweede: het publiek voor de schoonheid der reine beeldende kunst ontvankelijk te maken. Hiervoor is een tijdschrift van intiemen aard noodzakelijk geworden. Te meer, daar de openbare kritiek in gebreke bleef het te kort aan schoonheids-ontvankelijkheid voor de abstracte kunstopenbaring, aan te vullen. Tot dit laatste zal de Redactie de vaklieden zelf in staat stellen.
Dit tijdschriftje zal hierdoor een inniger contact scheppen tusschen kunstenaar en publiek en tusschen de beoefenaars der verschillende beeldende vakken. Door den modernen kunstenaar over zijn eigen vak aan het woord te laten zal het vooroordeel, als zou de moderne werkman volgens vooropgestelde theorieën werken, verdwijnen.

Integendeel. Het zal blijken, dat het nieuwe kunstwerk niet voorkomt uit a priori aangenomen theorieën, maar juist anders om, dat de beginselen voortvloeien uit de beeldende arbeid.
Het zal zoodoende de mogelijkheid voorbereiden eener verdiepte kunstcultuur, gegrond op gemeenschappelijke belichaming van het nieuwe beeldende kunstbewustzijn. Zoodra de kunstenaars in de verschillende beeldende vakken tot de erkenning zullen komen, dat zij in principe aan elkaar gelijk zijn, dat ze eene algemeene taal te spreken hebben, zullen ze niet meer angstvallig vasthouden aan hunne individualiteit. Zij zullen aan gene zijde eener beperkende individualiteit het algemeene principe dienen. Het algemeene principe dienende zullen zij vanzelf een organischen stijl moeten voortbrengen. Voor de verspreiding van het schoone is niet een sociale, maar eene geestelijke gemeenschap noodzakelijk. Eene geestelijke gemeenschap kan echter niet ontstaan zonder opoffering van eene eerzuchtige individualiteit. Slechts bij consequente doorvoering van dit beginsel kan, uit eene nieuwe verhouding van kunstenaar tot samenleving, de nieuwe beeldende schoonheid zich in alle voorwerpen als stijl gaan openbaren.

Leiden, 16-VI-1917 De Stijl, I, pag. 1

4

Introduction

The object of this little magazine is to contribute towards the development of a new sense of beauty. It wants to make modern man susceptible of the new ideas in Plastic Arts. It wants to set up against the archaistic confusion – the 'modern baroque' – the logical principles of a ripening style, based upon a clear proportion of the spirit of the age and the means of expression. It wants to combine in itself the present-day ideas on modern plasticity, ideas, which – although fundamentally the same – have developed themselves quite independently of one another.

The editor will endeavour to achieve the above mentioned purposes by giving the really modern artist the opportunity to explain for himself, for he is in a position to contribute towards the reform of the aesthetical sense and the cognition of plastic arts. When the new ideas on modern plastic beauty have not yet penetrated to the general public, then it becomes the task of the expert to awaken the layman's sense of beauty. The really modern, i.e. conscious artist has a two-fold vocation. In the first place: to create the purely visual work of art; in the second place: to make the general public susceptible of the beauty of purely visual art. For this reason a magazine of an intimate character has become necessary. All the more so, as public criticism failed to replenish the missing susceptibility of the abstract revelation of art. The editor will enable the experts to fulfil this last mentioned task themselves. This magazine will thereby bring about a closer contact between artist and general public and between the cultivators of the various branches of plastic arts. By giving the modern artist the opportunity to speak about his own work, the general prejudice, that the modern artist creates according to preconceived theories, will disappear. On the contrary: it will become evident that modern art does not emanate from priorly fixed theories, but – vice versa – that the principles are a result of plastic work.

It will therefore prepare the possibility for a deepened culture of art, founded upon a common embodiment of the new cognition of plastic arts. As soon as the artists in the various branches of plastic arts will have realized that they must speak an universal language, they will no longer anxiously hold on to their individuality. They will serve the general principle beyond a limited individuality. By serving this general principle they will have to produce, on their own accord, an organic style. The propagation of beauty necessitates spiritual community, not a social one. A spiritual community, however, can not be created without sacrificing an ambitious individuality. Only by consequently following this principle can the new plastic beauty manifest itself in all objects as style, arising from a new relationship between artist and society.

introduction

Ce périodique se donne pour but de contribuer au développement du sens esthétique nouveau. Il veut ouvrir l'homme moderne à tout ce qui est nouveau dans les Arts Plastiques. A la confusion archaïque – le ‚baroque moderne' – il veut opposer les principes logiques d'un style mûrissant, fondé sur l'observation des proportions nettes entre les tendances actuelles et les moyens d'expression. Il veut réunir les genres d'idées actuels concernant la plastique nouvelle qui, bien qu'ils soient pareils en réalité, se sont dévéloppés indépendamment l'un de l'autre.

La rédaction fera par effort d'atteindre le but précisé plus haut en laissant la parole au véritable artiste moderne, qui pourra contribuer quelque peu à la réforme du sens esthétique et à la formation d'une notion de l'art plastique. Là où le public n'en est pas encore à l'esthétique plastique nouvelle, la tâche incombe au spécialiste d'éveiller chez le grand public la conscience esthétique. Le véritable artiste moderne, c'est-à-dire conscient, a une double mission. En premier

Jonge Schilders uit Uruguay
Catalogue, Stedelijk Museum Amsterdam, 1957
Designed by Willem Sandberg
Illustrated at 51% actual size

The italic bold grotesque gives movement to the whole spread; the absence of caps further speeds along the lines of type. Venues and dates are clearly set out, exploiting their pattern-making potential. Sandberg's uncanny feeling for space and balance, together with the consistent use of italic on the recto, unifies the seemingly unrelated groups of type. His approach to title page design is unusually delicate, despite his fondness for heavy, black types.

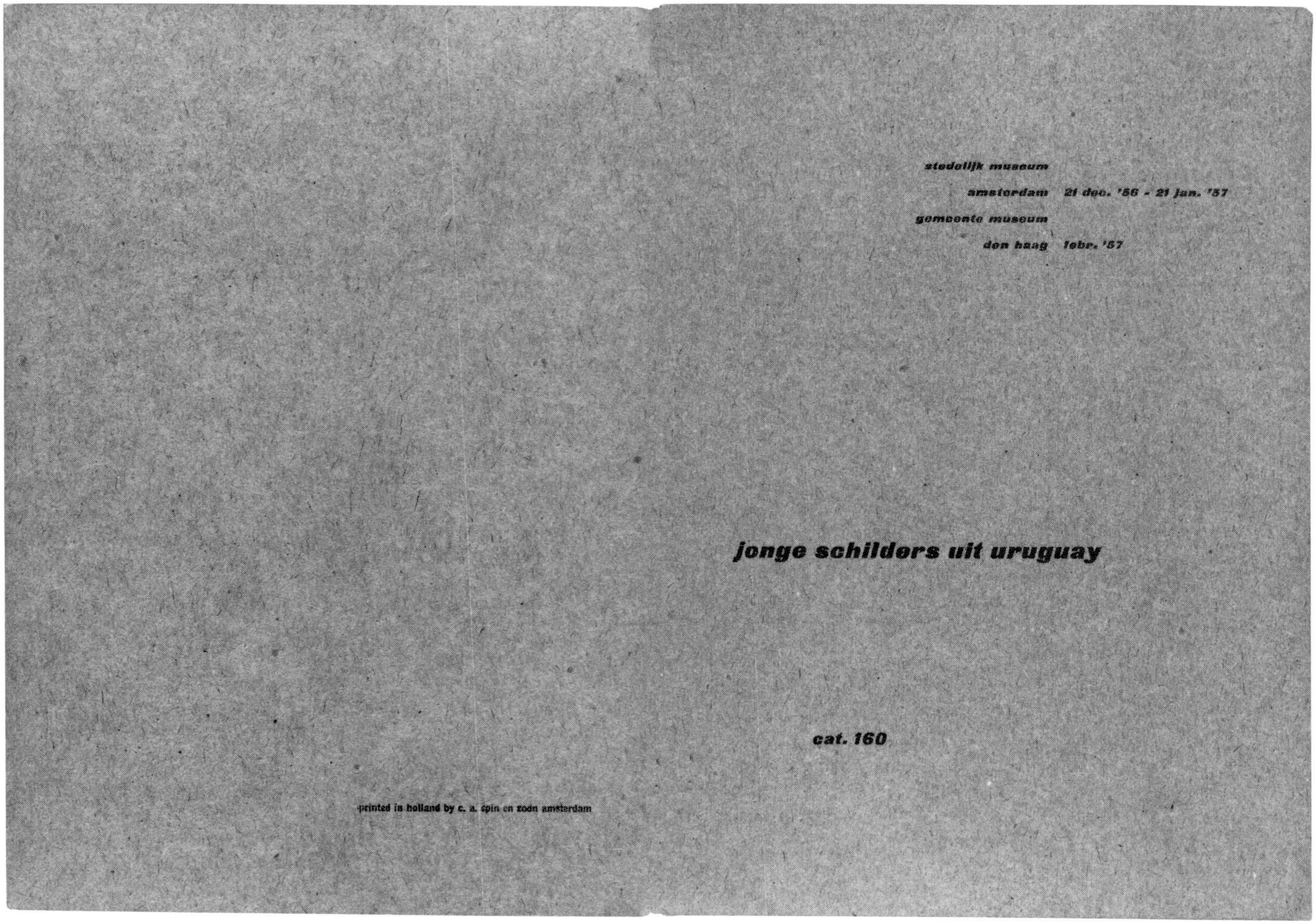

Jonge Schilders uit Uruguay continued

As with the de Stijl catalogue, the dark-toned paper necessitated the use of a bold grotesque text type, in this instance condensed. Such hindrances to readability, exacerbated by the long lines of text, never seemed of great concern to Sandberg.

There is little in the way of a grid; top margins are constant for text pages (including title page), and the details of the paintings echo the arrangement of the venues on that page, but follow their own requirements in detailing. Artist, title, medium and size, with short biographies of the artists, have been neatly and clearly organised in an entirely original way. There is nothing formulaic about Sandberg's catalogues.

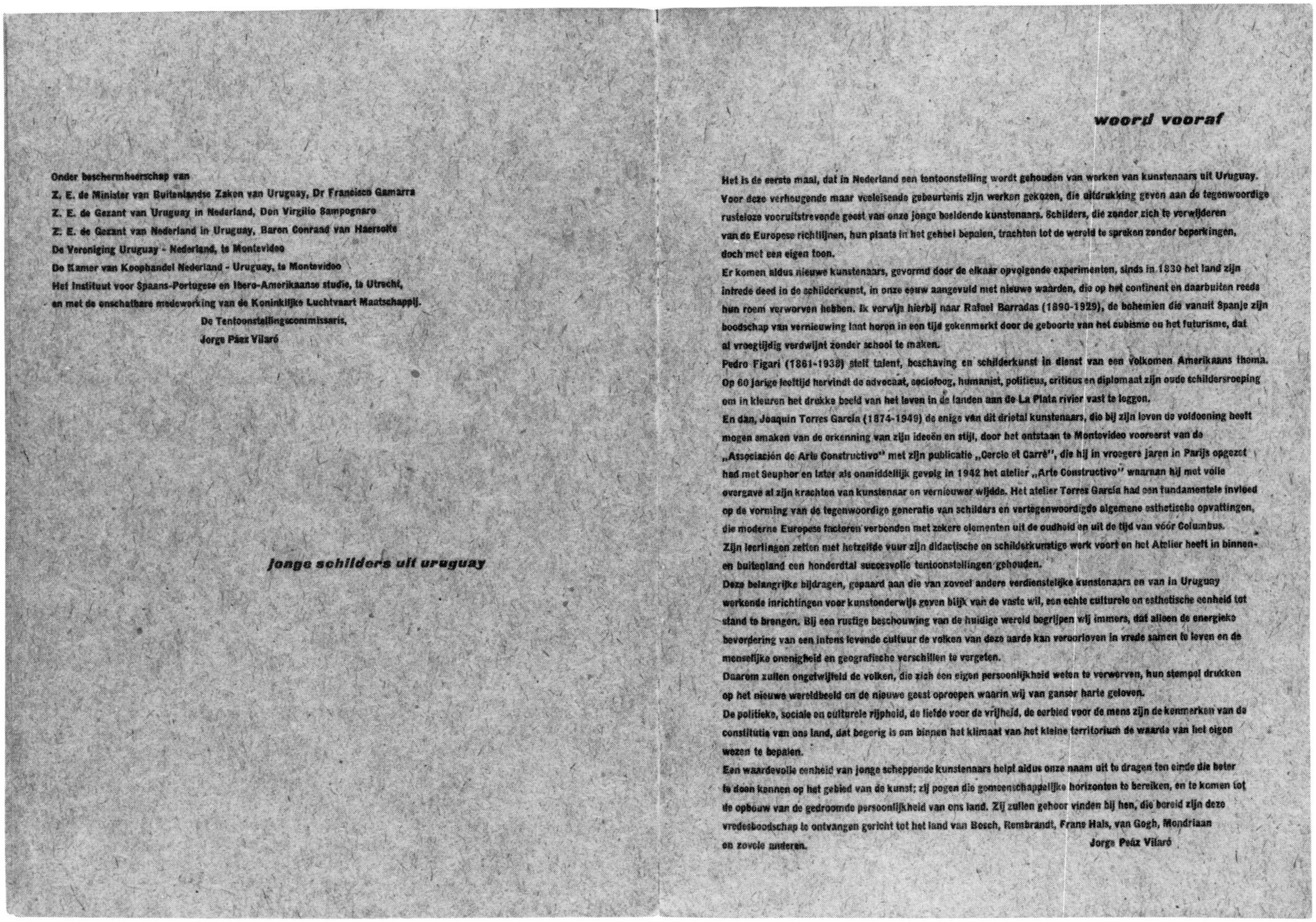

Onder beschermheerschap van
Z. E. de Minister van Buitenlandse Zaken van Uruguay, Dr Francisco Gamarra
Z. E. de Gezant van Uruguay in Nederland, Don Virgilio Sampognaro
Z. E. de Gezant van Nederland in Uruguay, Baron Conrand van Haersolte
De Vereniging Uruguay - Nederland, te Montevideo
De Kamer van Koophandel Nederland - Uruguay, te Montevideo
Het Instituut voor Spaans-Portugese en Ibero-Amerikaanse studie, te Utrecht,
en met de onschatbare medewerking van de Koninklijke Luchtvaart Maatschappij.

De Tentoonstellingscommissaris,
Jorge Páez Vilaró

jonge schilders uit uruguay

woord vooraf

Het is de eerste maal, dat in Nederland een tentoonstelling wordt gehouden van werken van kunstenaars uit Uruguay. Voor deze verheugende maar veeleisende gebeurtenis zijn werken gekozen, die uitdrukking geven aan de tegenwoordige rusteloze vooruitstrevende geest van onze jonge beeldende kunstenaars. Schilders, die zonder zich te verwijderen van de Europese richtlijnen, hun plants in het geheel bepalen, trachten tot de wereld te spreken zonder beperkingen, doch met een eigen toon.

Er komen aldus nieuwe kunstenaars, gevormd door de elkaar opvolgende experimenten, sinds in 1830 het land zijn intrede deed in de schilderkunst, in onze eeuw aangevuld met nieuwe waarden, die op het continent en daarbuiten reeds hun roem verworven hebben. Ik verwijs hierbij naar Rafael Barradas (1890-1929), de bohemien die vanuit Spanje zijn boodschap van vernieuwing laat horen in een tijd gekenmerkt door de geboorte van het cubisme en het futurisme, dat al vroegtijdig verdwijnt zonder school te maken.

Pedro Figari (1861-1938) stelt talent, beschaving en schilderkunst in dienst van een volkomen Amerikaans thema. Op 60 jarige leeftijd hervindt de advocaat, sociofoog, humanist, politicus, criticus en diplomaat zijn oude schildersroeping om in kleuren het drukke beeld van het leven in de landen aan de La Plata rivier vast te leggen.

En dan, Joaquin Torres García (1874-1949) de enige van dit drietal kunstenaars, die bij zijn leven de voldoening heeft mogen smaken van de erkenning van zijn ideeën en stijl, door het ontstaan te Montevideo vooreerst van de „Asociación de Arte Constructivo" met zijn publicatie „Cercle et Carré", die hij in vroegere jaren in Parijs opgezet had met Seuphor en later als onmiddellijk gevolg in 1942 het atelier „Arte Constructivo" waaraan hij met volle overgave al zijn krachten van kunstenaar en vernieuwer wijdde. Het atelier Torres García had een fundamentele invloed op de vorming van de tegenwoordige generatie van schilders en vertegenwoordigde algemene esthetische opvattingen, die moderne Europese factoren verbonden met zekere elementen uit de oudheid en uit de tijd van vóór Columbus.

Zijn leerlingen zetten met hetzelfde vuur zijn didactische en schilderkunstige werk voort en het Atelier heeft in binnen- en buitenland een honderdtal succesvolle tentoonstellingen gehouden.

Deze belangrijke bijdragen, gepaard aan die van zoveel andere verdienstelijke kunstenaars en van in Uruguay werkende inrichtingen voor kunstonderwijs geven blijk van de vaste wil, een echte culturele en esthetische eenheid tot stand te brengen. Bij een rustige beschouwing van de huidige wereld begrijpen wij immers, dat alleen de energieke bevordering van een intens levende cultuur de volken van deze aarde kan veroorloven in vrede samen te leven en de menselijke onenigheid en geografische verschillen te vergeten.

Daarom zullen ongetwijfeld de volken, die zich een eigen persoonlijkheid weten te verwerven, hun stempel drukken op het nieuwe wereldbeeld en de nieuwe geest oproepen waarin wij van ganser harte geloven.

De politieke, sociale en culturele rijpheid, de liefde voor de vrijheid, de eerbied voor de mens zijn de kenmerken van de constitutie van ons land, dat begerig is om binnen het klimaat van het kleine territorium de waarde van het eigen wezen te bepalen.

Een waardevolle eenheid van jonge scheppende kunstenaars helpt aldus onze naam uit te dragen ten einde die beter te doen kennen op het gebied van de kunst; zij pogen die gemeenschappelijke horizonten te bereiken, en te komen tot de opbouw van de gedroomde persoonlijkheid van ons land. Zij zullen gehoor vinden bij hen, die bereid zijn deze vredesboodschap te ontvangen gericht tot het land van Bosch, Rembrandt, Frans Hals, van Gogh, Mondriaan en zovele anderen.

Jorge Paéz Vilaró

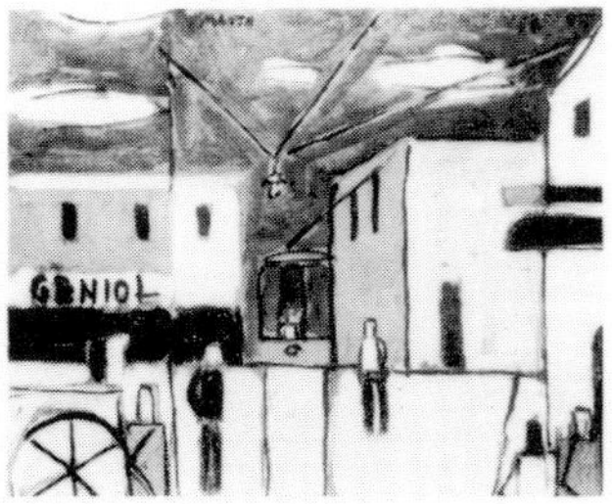

27

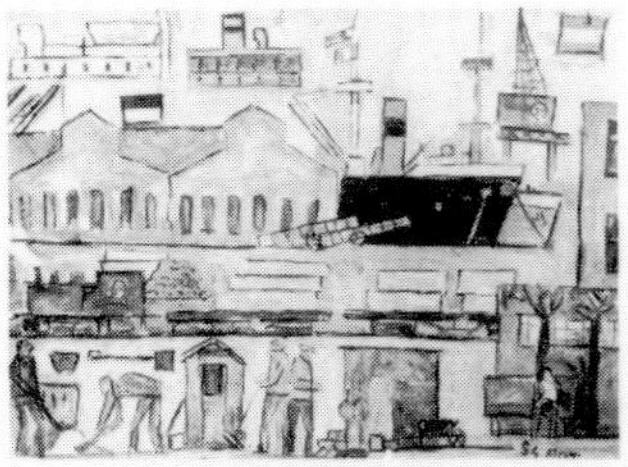

24

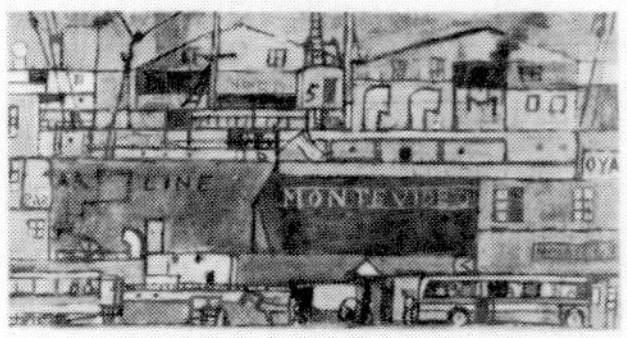

32

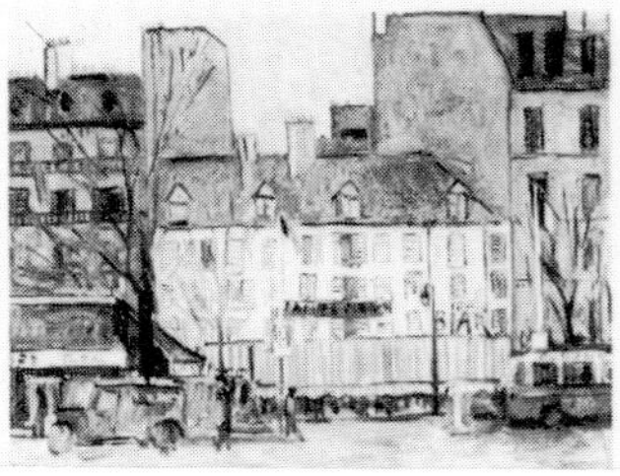

23

27 **Francisco Matto Vilaró**
24 **Uruquay Alpuy**
32 **Augusto Torres**
23 **Elsa Andrada de Torres**

catalogus

Aldama, Yamandú **1 Constructie, olie, 78×113**

Geboren 8 September 1931
Studeerde aan de School voor Toegepaste Kunsten en ging in 1955 over naar de School voor Schone Kunsten. Zijn leraren in de laatste tijd waren Pareja Piñeyro en Vincente Martín. Exposeerde in verschillende plaatselijke kunstzalen en in de Nationale Salon voor Schone Kunsten. Werd meermalen bekroond. Het Museum te San José bezit werken van hem.

Echave, José **2 Compositie, olie, 93×122**
3 Steltlopers, olie, 93×123
4 Treurende vrouwen, olie, 57×72

Geboren 27 November 1921
Autodidact. Exposeerde in de zalen te Montevideo van de Vrienden van de Kunst Vert Galant, en in de Panamerikaanse Unie te Washington in 1956. Zond in op de Biennale te Barcelona van 1956 en kreeg de prijs Nanco Ponseno de Puerto Rico. Talrijke decorschilderingen. Ontving de eerste prijs voor schilderkunst van de Nationale Salon voor Schone Kunsten in 1954 en de eerste prijs voor aquarellen van dezelfde Salon in 1953. Geeft op zijn atelier onderricht in het schilderen.

Espinola, Gomez Manuel **5 Bad, olie, 122×93**

Geboren 5 juli 1921
Autodidact. Exposeerde verscheidene malen bij de Vereniging van Kunstvrienden. Werd bekroond door de officiële salons. De stedelijke en nationale musea bezitten werken van hem.

García Reino, Oscar **6 Landschap, olie, 81×81**
7 Constructie, olie, 82×111
8 Compositie, olie, 114×87

Geboren 7 Februari 1910
Studeerde schilderkunst in de Kunstkring en later bij Prevosti en Torres García. Exposeerde in Buenos Aires, op de Biennales te Sao Paulo, Porto Alegre, Parijs en in verschillende zalen te Montevideo. Werd meermalen bekroond op de officiële salons. Er bevinden zich werken van hem in de stedelijke en nationale musea. De UNESCO heeft hem een beurs toegekend om zich in Brussel te specialiseren in gobelinkunst.

Willem Sandberg and H L C Jaffé
Kunst van Heden in het Stedelijk
Catalogue, Stedelijk Museum
Amsterdam, 1961
Designed by Willem Sandberg
Illustrated at 37% actual size

There is no evidence of a grid in either of these two spreads. Again the eye appears to be the final arbiter. The illustrations are positioned far more adeptly than in any of Max Bill's formalistic designs. Nothing aligns across, yet the pairs of pages are clearly organised as spreads. Sandberg's work in some ways appears more Italian than Dutch; but behind the freedom one senses a tight intellectual control, rather than the inherited visual literacy that Italians often seem to possess.

The plot of my story develops the idea that clarity and order can be achieved through logic, geometry and architectural structure. Sandberg's precision and elegance seem to have been achieved by quite other means. He replaces Max Bill's strivings for intellectual rigour with a personal, entirely visual, discipline, a sort of private geometry.

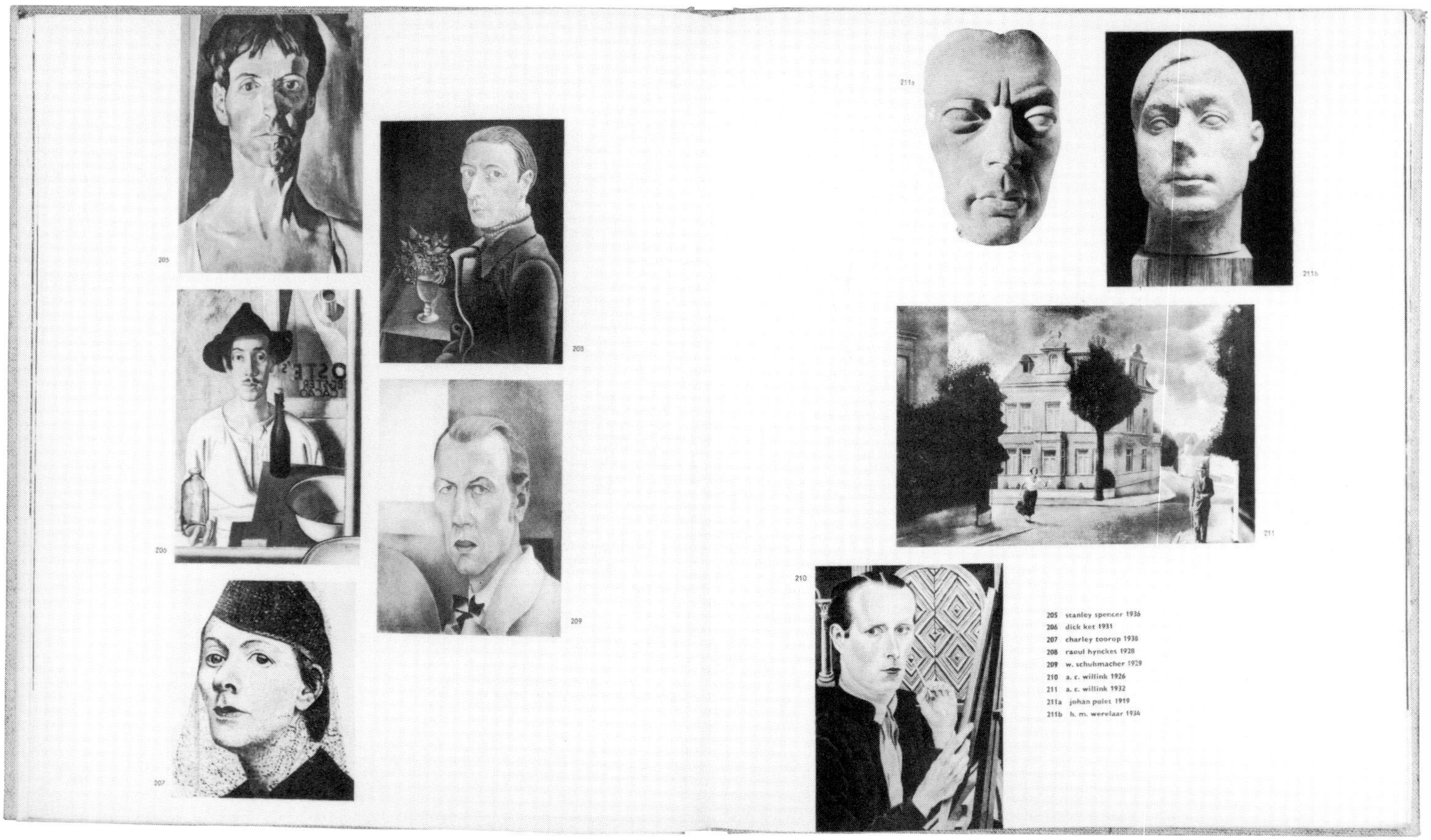

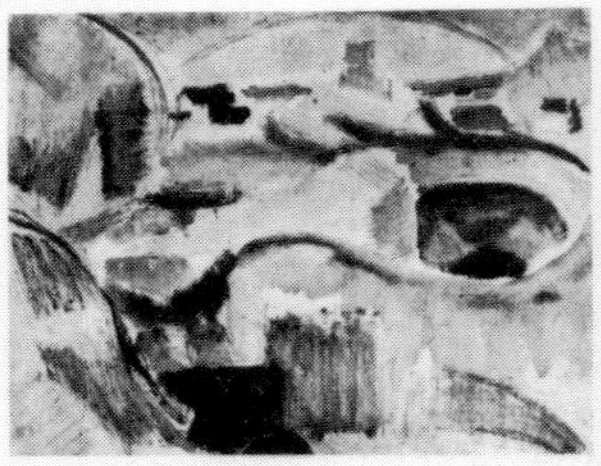

313

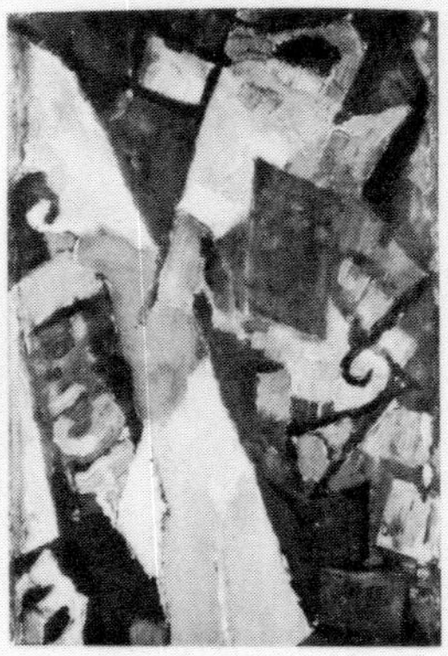

314

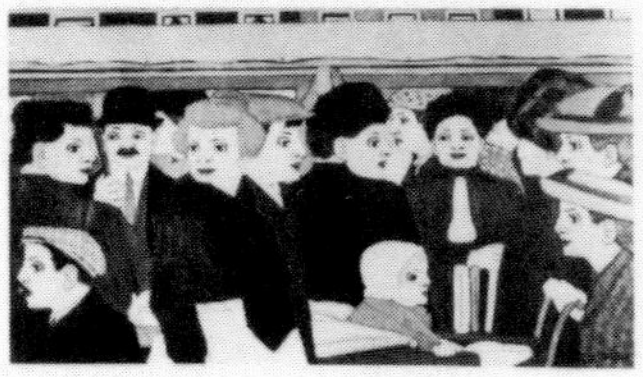

315

313 henri le fauconnier 1913
314 jan sluyters 1913
315 bart van der leck 1913
316 leo gestel 1913

316

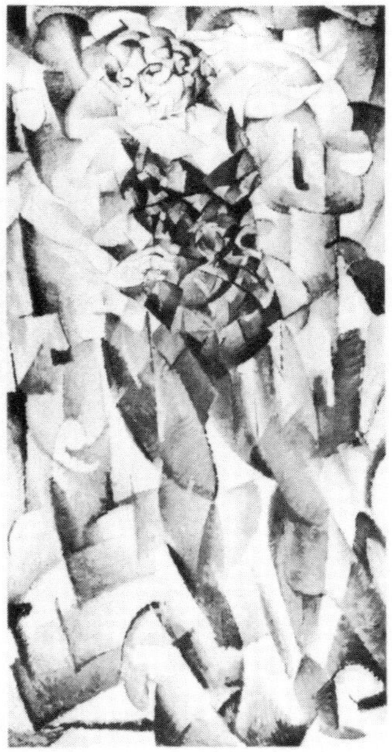

317 kees van dongen 1910 →

Kunst van Heden in het Stedelijk continued

Sandberg's secret geometry again governs the arrangement of the five elements here, for they appear related although there is no discernible formal structure apart from the markedly horizontal overall effect. Even the superficially wilful positioning of the Picasso head looks ordained. Sandberg needs no help from the grids and alignments which govern the work of more theoretical or conceptual designers. Such principles are key elements in Swiss design although, in the best of this, aesthetic decisions are also the final arbiter. But the Dutchman's seemingly intuitive approach makes a striking contrast, while remaining thoroughly modernist.

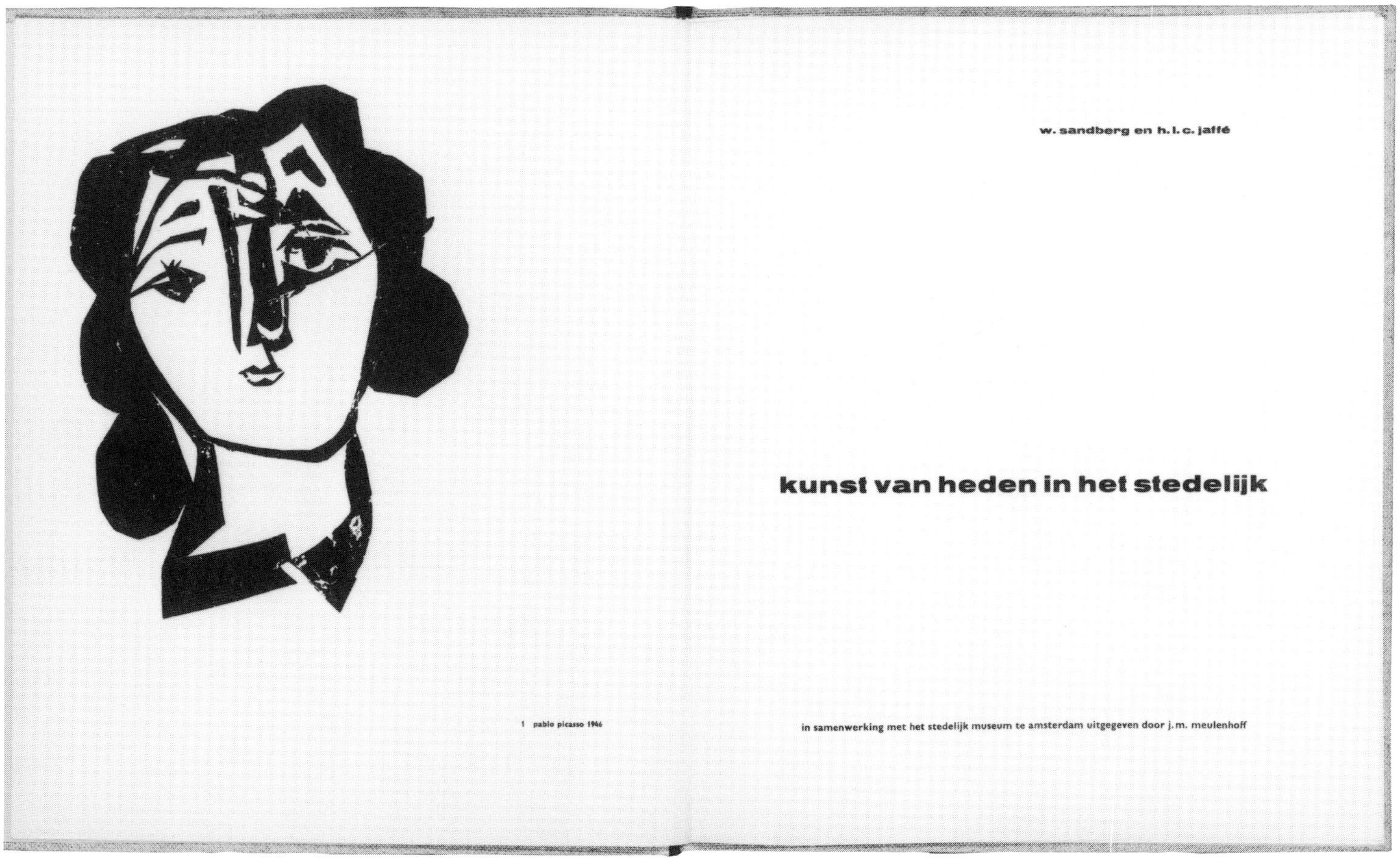

'Intolerant', 'absolute'; 'its military will to order and claim to sole domination correspond to those terrible components of the German character that unleashed the rule of Hitler'. These remarks, part of a tirade against Max Bill and his rationalised, machine-worshipping modernism, were made in 1945 by Jan Tschichold. Bill had claimed that the New Typography had been partly decorative in its use of rules, geometric shapes, large page numbers and so on; that his *new* New Typography was not only genuinely functional, but was in visual harmony with modern techniques and society. Tschichold attacked in further detail, rather disturbingly demolishing everything he had so fiercely believed in during the 1930s. The subject range of the Swiss style, he claimed, was limited to modern art and industrial literature (only partly true then, no longer true now); its refusal to indent paragraph openings was confusing (it was) as well as untraditional (one cannot imagine Bill being upset about that); it was often stylistically inappropriate (questionable); the reliance on asymmetrical pattern-making in general, and the grid in particular, was constricting, denying meaning to the text (surely the reverse is true). Tschichold, who had once praised the engineer, 'the designer of our epoch', now railed against the aesthetic fetish made of efficiency and machine production, which were social evils. We may have to accept them (he was no friend of the private presses) but we don't have to worship them. His reversion to classical formats – which use modern production methods just as much as asymmetric typography – was his way of solving the dilemma. Yet it was his experience in asymmetric design that enabled him to produce classical work which was more sensitive and far better than that of anyone else.

The creation of the Swiss New Typography is generally credited, perhaps not entirely correctly, to Max Bill. He clearly built upon much of Tschichold's work of the 1930s. The new ideas may also have benefited from the isolation resulting from Swiss neutrality during the war. But while Bill's display work, especially posters, includes appropriately simple 'architectural' typography, his books and catalogues are strangely awkward. There is an apparent indifference to aesthetic considerations, and one can understand Tschichold's dislike of his work. A purely functional design (or one claiming to be) is not automatically attractive; most designers would consider it important to make it so. Richard P Lohse, for instance, carefully manipulated the elements of his book *Neue Ausstellungsgestaltung* of 1953 (see pages 112-13) to achieve this.

Lohse was an altogether better typographer than Bill. Bill – trained as an architect, but also a painter, a sculptor, a teacher and a notably aggressive propagandist, some might say, self-promoter – had an architect's grand vision for the way modernist typography should advance in the modern mechanised world. But he lacked Tschichold's refinement, his concern for detail, and his understanding of how typography works.

In *Typographica 5* (1952) Bill wrote: 'There are few professional groups that accept as readily as typographers a safe and simple system of rules by which to work. The person who makes up these "recipes" and knows how to give them an authentic appearance will determine for some time the general trend of typography. But every proposition that is rigidly upheld is a potential obstacle to progress.' And: 'In no other branch of commercial art is the working medium so precise as in typography … It is the aim of every typographical artistic endeavour to lessen the incompatibility between the mathematically exact medium on the one hand and the haphazard shape of the text on the other. First and foremost the demands of language and legibility must be met. Only then can one afford any aesthetic consideration.'

The first part of that was seemingly a further shot in the petty warfare between Bill and Tschichold. Those 'recipes' were the points of style Tschichold had formulated for the New Typography, and he claimed that Bill had followed them faithfully in his own work. The 'rules' were: tight setting; fewest possible typefaces and styles; no letterspacing of lower case; emphasis achieved by means of italic or bold of the same face; lines in caps used only exceptionally, and then carefully letterspaced; the formation of groups, but not more than three. These 'rules', together with over a dozen later points of style, had been badly needed in both Germany and Switzerland (as well as post-war Britain); today, they are still generally recognised as good practice. Textual details only, they in no way inhibit the mode in which a designer works.

Neither of the antagonists seems to me, today, to have won that war, nor to have come out of it with dignity. What is certain is that, *then*, something more was needed than an architect's somewhat elementary contributions to the subject. It was mainly the demands of Swiss advertising that enriched the Swiss design system. Generally restrained and informative, rather than brash in its attempts at persuasion, or socially divisive in its aim to foment dissatisfaction with one's life, it was design-based, and thus easily adaptable. The result was 'Swiss design' as we now know it: taut, inventive and disciplined, with a sure-footed and refreshing use of space.

The 'hard-edge' system (never call it a style), as it developed, was (is) impersonal, objective, unadorned. It could be adapted for almost any type of print from posters to stationery. It was a boon for the publishers of the increasing numbers of heavily illustrated books which appeared from the 1950s onwards, for its structural grid solved the problem of relating those illustrations to their texts; a benefit which became even more important as the more flexible offset, which gave acceptable results for half-tones on most kinds of paper, replaced letterpress. It was particularly appropriate for books on architecture, art or design, where commentary and the commented-upon could be placed together. Separate plate sections inconveniently bundled away to the back of the book like an unimportant afterthought became a thing of the past.

Grotesques such as Akzidenz or Monotype series 215 were obligatory, and were used in a very restricted number of sizes and weights. Columns were generally narrow, giving flexibility, and leading minimal. Three columns in a square format were a favourite arrangement, happily coping with three languages. In later work, type was usually ranged left. Paragraph openings were not indented, although sometimes a line space was used – which is too large, and wastes a useful means of textual articulation.

The new Swiss typography related to the architecture of the period. The three-dimensional structure of exhibitions, and their two-dimensional information panels, were a seamless whole (notably not the case with earlier exhibitions such as the influential *Medaglia d'Oro* room, by Persico and Nizzoli, at the Italian Aeronautical show in 1934). In this area, Max Bill's simple 'architectural' typography was distinctly beneficial. Other designers, if not themselves architects also, worked with them on exhibitions, and an architectural bias was absorbed by a sort of osmosis. It seemed as if the Bauhaus dream of the 1920s – a drawing together of all design by means of compatible forms – was becoming a reality.

Most of the younger generation of designers trained at a design school, often Zurich or Basle. ('Swiss' design was not merely German-Swiss, it was largely Zurich-Swiss.) Architects had been useful influences – the two disciplines have much in common: a concern with horizontals and verticals; placing of interruptions on a rectangular plane; proportions and relationships. But post 1945, designers like Tschichold or Penguin's Hans Schmoller became increasingly concerned with refining typographic detailing. (Tschichold, at Penguin between 1947 and 1949 – preceding Schmoller – formulated the Penguin Composition Rules, the effect of which reverberated throughout the British printing industry.) Such detailing was not restricted to classical bookwork; it was incorporated into asymmetric design too. Herbert Spencer notably formulated, around 1950, a house style of fifty-four rules for Lund Humphries to use both in bookwork and in commercial printing.

As with architecture, modernist typography usually relied on a structural grid, and this became a key feature of the system. It is the means by which disparate elements – headings, text, illustrations, page numbers, captions, sometimes even notes – are knitted together in relation to each other; also the means by which a sequence of pages can be given unity within diversity. Tschichold seems to me to be completely wrong in claiming it was intolerant and constricting; although one must remember he made his criticisms in 1945, well before other designers started introducing greater sophistication to Bill's rather simplistic theories.

The Swiss magazine *Neue Grafik/New Graphic Design/Graphisme actuel*, published between 1958 and 1965, shows the system at its best. Designers such as Karl Gerstner, Richard P Lohse, J Müller-Brockmann, Hans Neuburg, Siegfried Odermatt, Emil Ruder, Rosemarie Tissi, Carlo Vivarelli, some young, some contemporaries of Max Bill, explored the system for its aesthetic potential, without loss of integrity or structure, and retaining a tension between text, pictures and space.

'The Control of Blank Space in Graphic Design' was the title of an article in *Neue Grafik*; 'The Typography of Order' by Emil Ruder appeared in the magazine *Graphis*. Swiss New Typography concisely defined.

Political events in 1930s Europe (except in Switzerland and the UK) encouraged, or forced, many designers, architects and artists to emigrate to America – sometimes, briefly, via England. This generation included many Bauhaus pioneers such as Moholy-Nagy and Herbert Bayer. Bauhaus graphic design was especially suited to advertising, which happily chimed with American interests.

The system that was developed in neutral Switzerland, intellectual and analytical, was less adaptable to more demonstrative American tastes or requirements; nor had Swiss designers generally need or desire to leave their country. Thus 'Swiss design' had less immediate influence on American work. The use of grotesques, sophisticated grids, the whole intellectual framework, made only a belated impact. Paul Rand, the most 'European' of the home-grown American pioneers, the most alert to the message of Tschichold's New Typography, was less enthusiastic about the more severe Swiss system.

Max Bill
Catalogue
Musée Rath, Geneva, 1972
Designed by Max Bill
Illustrated at 58% actual size

Bill had studied at the Bauhaus from 1927 to 1929; his subjects were metalwork, stage design, painting and architecture. Any typographic influence seems Bayer's rather than Joost Schmidt's, but he was most influenced by the New Typography, although he lacked Tschichold's finesse.

In this casual layout for his own 1972 exhibition catalogue, Bill has used the ghost of a grid, but it fails to hold the scattered and disparate elements together. Some radical visually based adjustment, or pattern-making, would be necessary before these two disjointed pages could become a coherent design. Bill often seems blind to the actual appearance of things, as opposed to some theoretical plan in his mind.

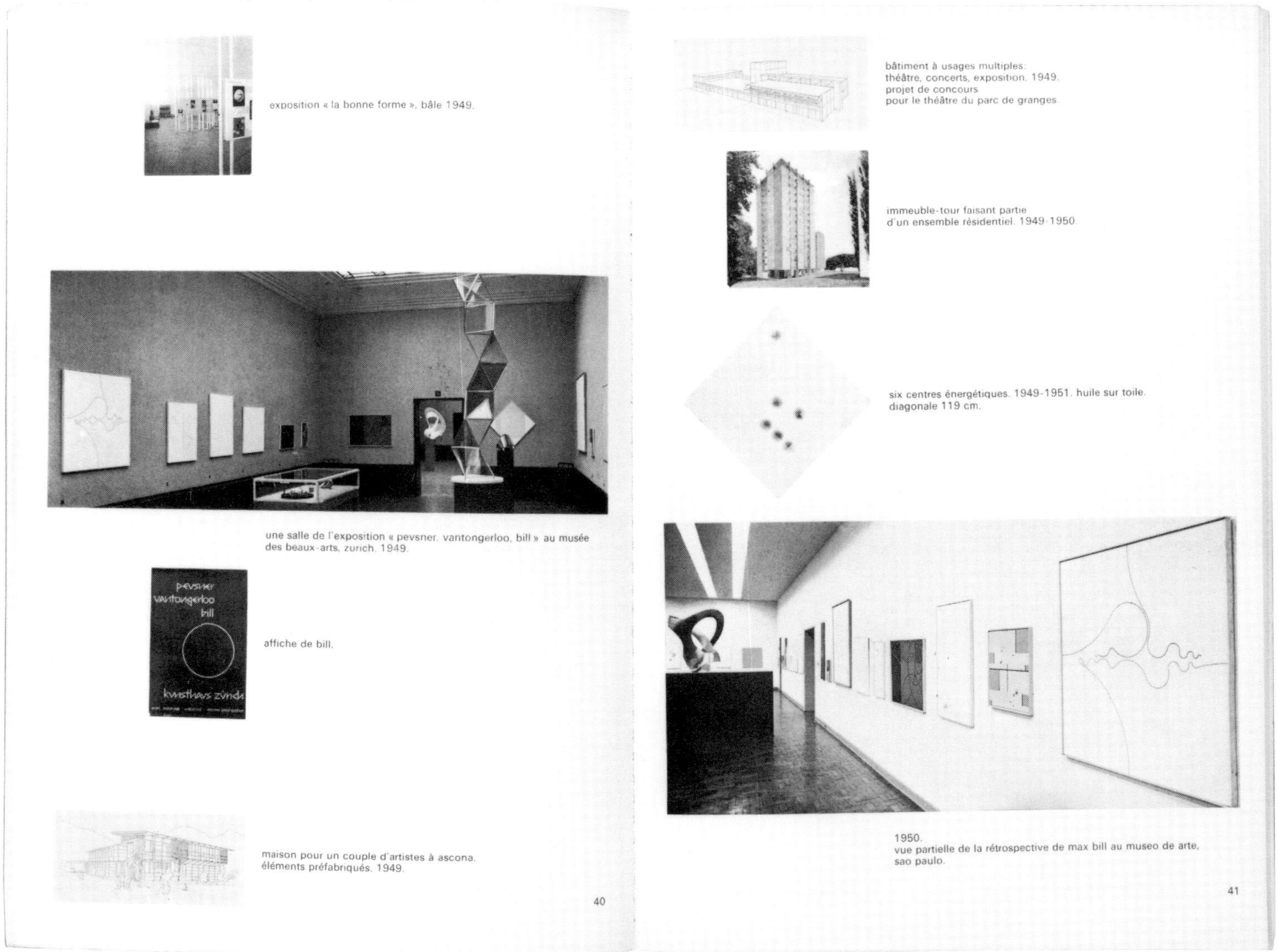

exposition « la bonne forme », bâle 1949.

une salle de l'exposition « pevsner, vantongerloo, bill » au musée des beaux-arts, zurich, 1949.

affiche de bill.

maison pour un couple d'artistes à ascona. éléments préfabriqués, 1949.

40

bâtiment à usages multiples: théâtre, concerts, exposition, 1949. projet de concours pour le théâtre du parc de granges.

immeuble-tour faisant partie d'un ensemble résidentiel, 1949-1950

six centres énergétiques, 1949-1951, huile sur toile. diagonale 119 cm.

1950. vue partielle de la rétrospective de max bill au museo de arte, sao paulo.

41

Joseph Albers etc
Catalogue
Kunsthaus, Zurich, 1956
Designed by Max Bill
Illustrated at 75% actual size

Using a grey, textured paper (but not low-grade, as Sandberg used), Bill has set the text in longish lines of bold grotesque. He uses no caps, which is a hurdle to readability, although in German their frequency is, admittedly, disrupting; he has here indented new paragraphs. The unjustified setting, as in Sandberg's catalogues, results in good, even wordspacing. The tight side margins of this small-format catalogue are not very imaginative, nor is the placing of the author's name.

The arrangement of the catalogue entries, using only positioning to distinguish between title, date, medium and dimensions, just about succeeds, even if the uniformity of typeface seems a little over-puritanical. Owners are given undue prominence. Such a desire for evenness of typographic colour and consistency, at the expense of clarifying content, is a little contrary to Bill's declarations on the subject.

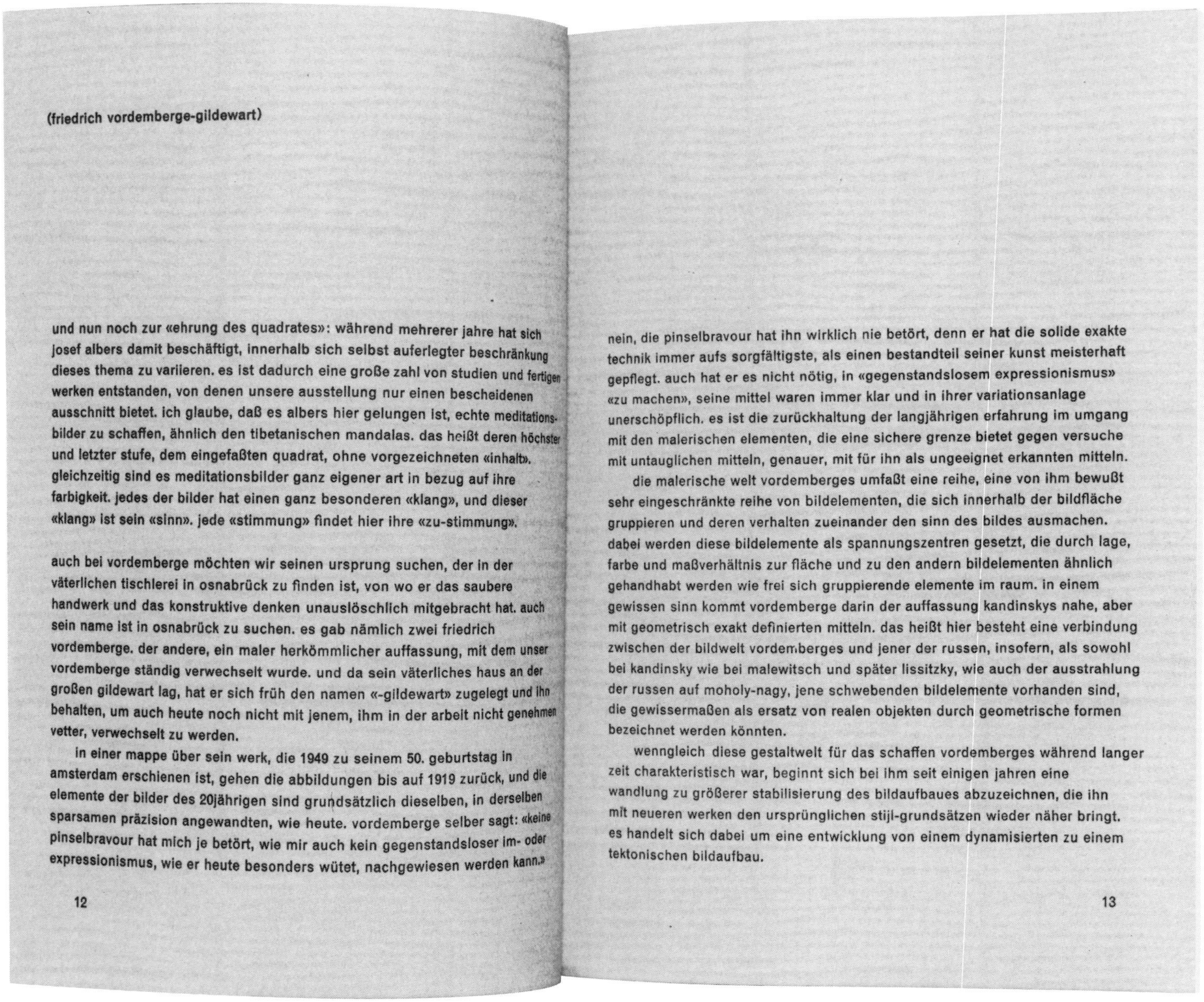
(friedrich vordemberge-gildewart)

und nun noch zur «ehrung des quadrates»: während mehrerer jahre hat sich josef albers damit beschäftigt, innerhalb sich selbst auferlegter beschränkung dieses thema zu variieren. es ist dadurch eine große zahl von studien und fertigen werken entstanden, von denen unsere ausstellung nur einen bescheidenen ausschnitt bietet. ich glaube, daß es albers hier gelungen ist, echte meditationsbilder zu schaffen, ähnlich den tibetanischen mandalas. das heißt deren höchster und letzter stufe, dem eingefaßten quadrat, ohne vorgezeichneten «inhalt». gleichzeitig sind es meditationsbilder ganz eigener art in bezug auf ihre farbigkeit. jedes der bilder hat einen ganz besonderen «klang», und dieser «klang» ist sein «sinn». jede «stimmung» findet hier ihre «zu-stimmung».

auch bei vordemberge möchten wir seinen ursprung suchen, der in der väterlichen tischlerei in osnabrück zu finden ist, von wo er das saubere handwerk und das konstruktive denken unauslöschlich mitgebracht hat. auch sein name ist in osnabrück zu suchen. es gab nämlich zwei friedrich vordemberge. der andere, ein maler herkömmlicher auffassung, mit dem unser vordemberge ständig verwechselt wurde. und da sein väterliches haus an der großen gildewart lag, hat er sich früh den namen «-gildewart» zugelegt und ihn behalten, um auch heute noch nicht mit jenem, ihm in der arbeit nicht genehmen vetter, verwechselt zu werden.

in einer mappe über sein werk, die 1949 zu seinem 50. geburtstag in amsterdam erschienen ist, gehen die abbildungen bis auf 1919 zurück, und die elemente der bilder des 20jährigen sind grundsätzlich dieselben, in derselben sparsamen präzision angewandten, wie heute. vordemberge selber sagt: «keine pinselbravour hat mich je betört, wie mir auch kein gegenstandsloser im- oder expressionismus, wie er heute besonders wütet, nachgewiesen werden kann.»

12

nein, die pinselbravour hat ihn wirklich nie betört, denn er hat die solide exakte technik immer aufs sorgfältigste, als einen bestandteil seiner kunst meisterhaft gepflegt. auch hat er es nicht nötig, in «gegenstandslosem expressionismus» «zu machen», seine mittel waren immer klar und in ihrer variationsanlage unerschöpflich. es ist die zurückhaltung der langjährigen erfahrung im umgang mit den malerischen elementen, die eine sichere grenze bietet gegen versuche mit untauglichen mitteln, genauer, mit für ihn als ungeeignet erkannten mitteln.

die malerische welt vordemberges umfaßt eine reihe, eine von ihm bewußt sehr eingeschränkte reihe von bildelementen, die sich innerhalb der bildfläche gruppieren und deren verhalten zueinander den sinn des bildes ausmachen. dabei werden diese bildelemente als spannungszentren gesetzt, die durch lage, farbe und maßverhältnis zur fläche und zu den andern bildelementen ähnlich gehandhabt werden wie frei sich gruppierende elemente im raum. in einem gewissen sinn kommt vordemberge darin der auffassung kandinskys nahe, aber mit geometrisch exakt definierten mitteln. das heißt hier besteht eine verbindung zwischen der bildwelt vordembergеs und jener der russen, insofern, als sowohl bei kandinsky wie bei malewitsch und später lissitzky, wie auch der ausstrahlung der russen auf moholy-nagy, jene schwebenden bildelemente vorhanden sind, die gewissermaßen als ersatz von realen objekten durch geometrische formen bezeichnet werden könnten.

wennglеich diese gestaltwelt für das schaffen vordemberges während langer zeit charakteristisch war, beginnt sich bei ihm seit einigen jahren eine wandlung zu größerer stabilisierung des bildaufbaues abzuzeichnen, die ihn mit neueren werken den ursprünglichen stijl-grundsätzen wieder näher bringt. es handelt sich dabei um eine entwicklung von einem dynamisierten zu einem tektonischen bildaufbau.

13

14 prefatio . 1942
litho . 60 x 48
15 seclusion . 1942
litho . 60 x 48
16 inscribed . 1944
linolschnitt . 32 x 40,5
17 adjusted . 1944
holzschnitt . 40,5 x 32
18 involute . 1944
linolschnitt . 40,5 x 32
19 fenced . 1944
linolschnitt . 40,5 x 32
20 two whites in two yellows . 1947–55
öl auf masonit . 40,5 x 81,5
21 beyond dawn . 1948–51
öl auf holz . 39 x 56
22 yellow dominant . 1948–52
öl auf holz . 45,5 x 68,5
23 tension between reds . 1948–52
öl auf holz . 45 x 69
24 blue front . 1948–55
öl auf masonit . 60,5 x 88
25 contented green . 1948–55
öl auf holz . 55,5 x 66,5
26 orange front . 1948–56
öl auf masonit . 60,5 x 88

27 in orange . 1955
öl auf masonit . 40,5 x 81,5
28 hommage to the square . green tension . 1951 privatbesitz zürich
öl auf masonit . 60 x 60
29 hommage to the square . la tehuana . 1951–56 (study)
50,5 x 50,5
30 hommage to the square . meditative . 1953
öl auf masonit . 81 x 81
31 hommage to the square . enclosed sound . 1953 (study)
öl auf holz . 45 x 45
32 hommage to the square . portal B . 1953
öl auf masonit . 91 x 91
33 hommage to the square . between two skies . 1954 privatbesitz zürich
öl auf masonit . 60 x 60
34 hommage to the square . assured . 1954
öl auf masonit . 81 x 81
35 hommage to the square . inward . 1954 (study)
öl auf masonit . 40 x 40
36 hommage to the square . completed . 1954 (study)
öl auf masonit . 40 x 40 privatbesitz zürich und ulm
37 hommage to the square . still remembered . 1954–56 (study)
öl auf masonit . 50,5 x 50,5
38 hommage to the square . out and in . 1955
öl auf masonit . 101 x 101
39 hommage to the square . bright hour . 1955 (study)
öl auf holz . 45 x 45

Joseph Albers etc
Catalogue
Kunsthaus, Zurich, 1956
Designed by Max Bill
Illustrated at 45% actual size

This title page, for the catalogue shown on pages 98-9, has a central spine running through the type. While hardly a startling idea, it binds the design together and logically splits the lines. The single type size and style further unifies the design; but the positioning of the groups lacks, for instance, Sandberg's adroit and individual sense of space.

Linus Birchler etc
Moderne Schweizer Architektur
Verlag Karl Werner, Basle, 1950?
Designed by Max Bill
Illustrated at 57% actual size

A spread from this work on Swiss architecture is shown on page 103. Like the Albers catalogue, its title page has a central spine, but the overall design is more subtle and more interesting. Its use of space and the feeling of movement in the lines of type show an aesthetic involvement so often lacking in Bill's work, yet its firm structure is created by exploiting and clarifying content.

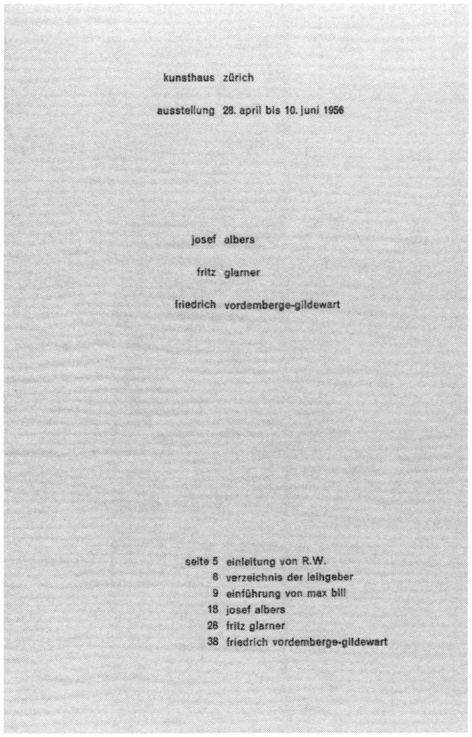
kunsthaus zürich
ausstellung 28. april bis 10. juni 1956

josef albers
fritz glarner
friedrich vordemberge-gildewart

seite 5 einleitung von R.W.
8 verzeichnis der leihgeber
9 einführung von max bill
18 josef albers
28 fritz glarner
38 friedrich vordemberge-gildewart

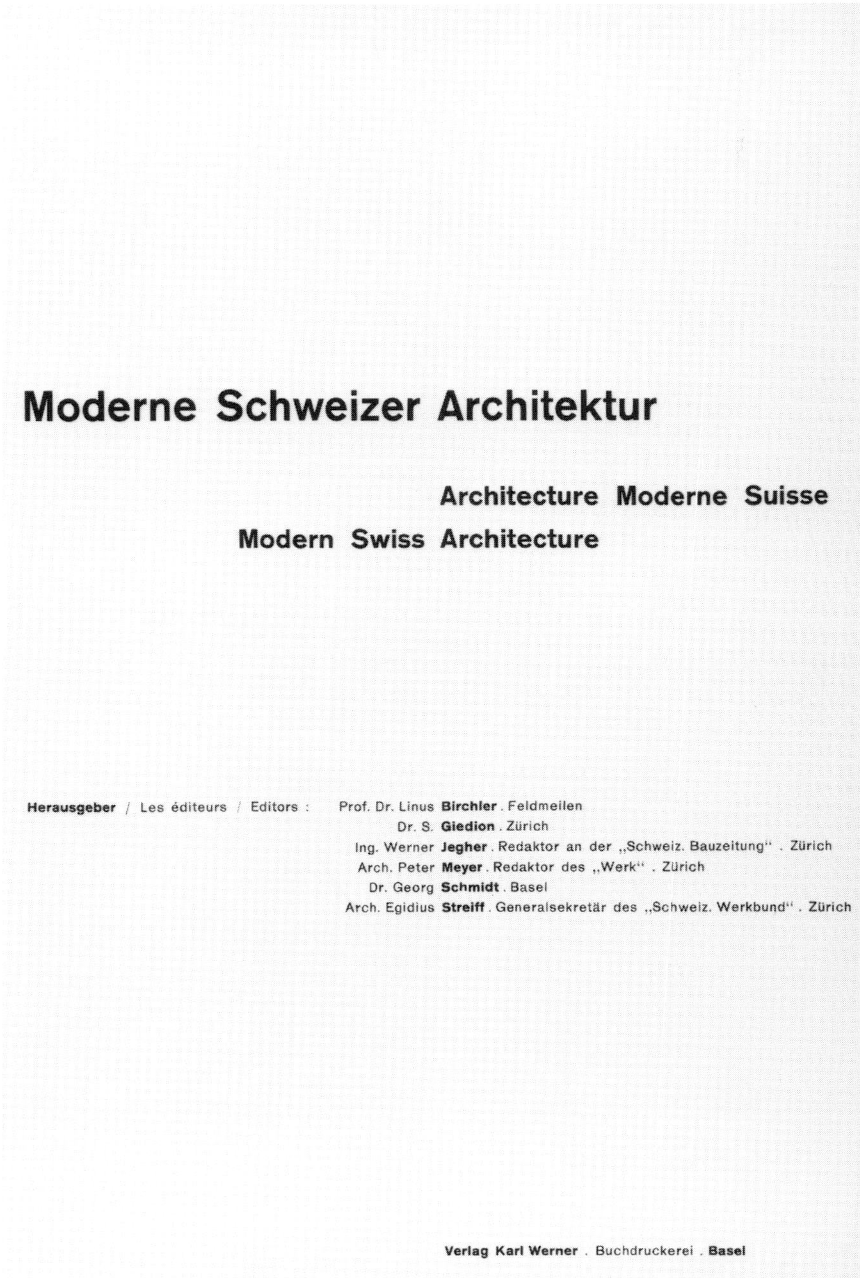
Moderne Schweizer Architektur

Architecture Moderne Suisse
Modern Swiss Architecture

Herausgeber / Les éditeurs / Editors : Prof. Dr. Linus **Birchler** . Feldmeilen
Dr. S. **Giedion** . Zürich
Ing. Werner **Jegher** . Redaktor an der „Schweiz. Bauzeitung" . Zürich
Arch. Peter **Meyer** . Redaktor des „Werk" . Zürich
Dr. Georg **Schmidt** . Basel
Arch. Egidius **Streiff** . Generalsekretär des „Schweiz. Werkbund" . Zürich

Verlag Karl Werner . Buchdruckerei . **Basel**

Le Corbusier: *Oeuvre Complète*
Les Editions d'Architecture
Erlenbach-Zurich, 1947 and 1953
Designed by Max Bill
Illustrated at 36% actual size

These spreads are from two volumes of the eight-volume *Complete Works*. Bill's design for them – a major series by any standard – hardly seems an adequate homage to the twentieth century's greatest architect. His handling of space and relationships is very uncertain: blank areas contribute nothing to the layout.

Publication spanned three decades, and Bill rightly made no attempt to keep the design completely consistent. The Bodoni of the 1947 volume (top) was replaced, in 1953, by a grotesque (bottom), although the three-column grid is retained. There is now a more positive relationship across the spread, but how banal it is! This is merely stage one of book design: getting the material onto the page, before allowing aesthetics to play its part.

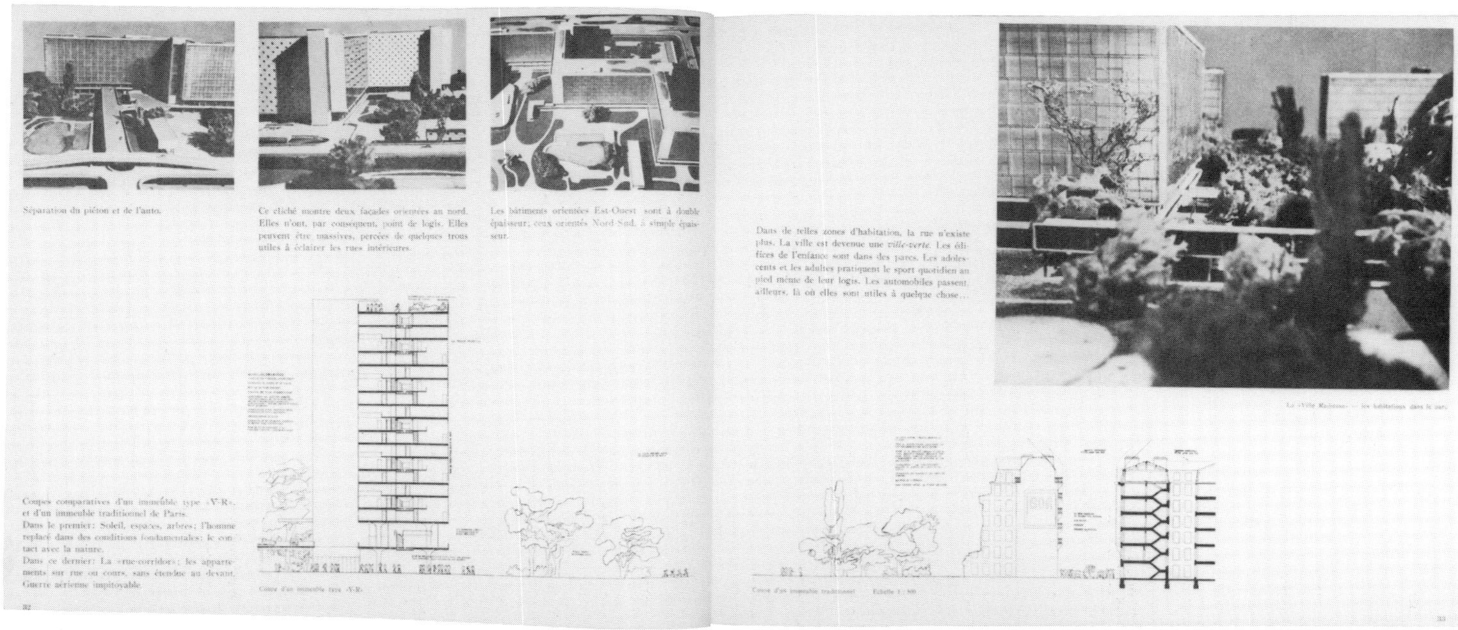

Séparation du piéton et de l'auto.

Ce cliché montre deux façades orientées au nord. Elles n'ont, par conséquent, point de logis. Elles peuvent être massives, percées de quelques trous utiles à éclairer les rues intérieures.

Les bâtiments orientées Est-Ouest sont à double épaisseur; ceux orientés Nord-Sud, à simple épaisseur.

Dans de telles zones d'habitation, la rue n'existe plus. La ville est devenue une *ville-verte*. Les édifices de l'enfance sont dans des parcs. Les adolescents et les adultes pratiquent le sport quotidien au pied même de leur logis. Les automobiles passent ailleurs, là où elles sont utiles à quelque chose...

Coupes comparatives d'un immeuble type «V-R», et d'un immeuble traditionnel de Paris.
Dans le premier: Soleil, espaces, arbres; l'homme replacé dans des conditions fondamentales: le contact avec la nature.
Dans ce dernier: La «rue-corridor»; les appartements sur rue ou cours, sans étendue au devant. Guerre aérienne impitoyable.

32

33

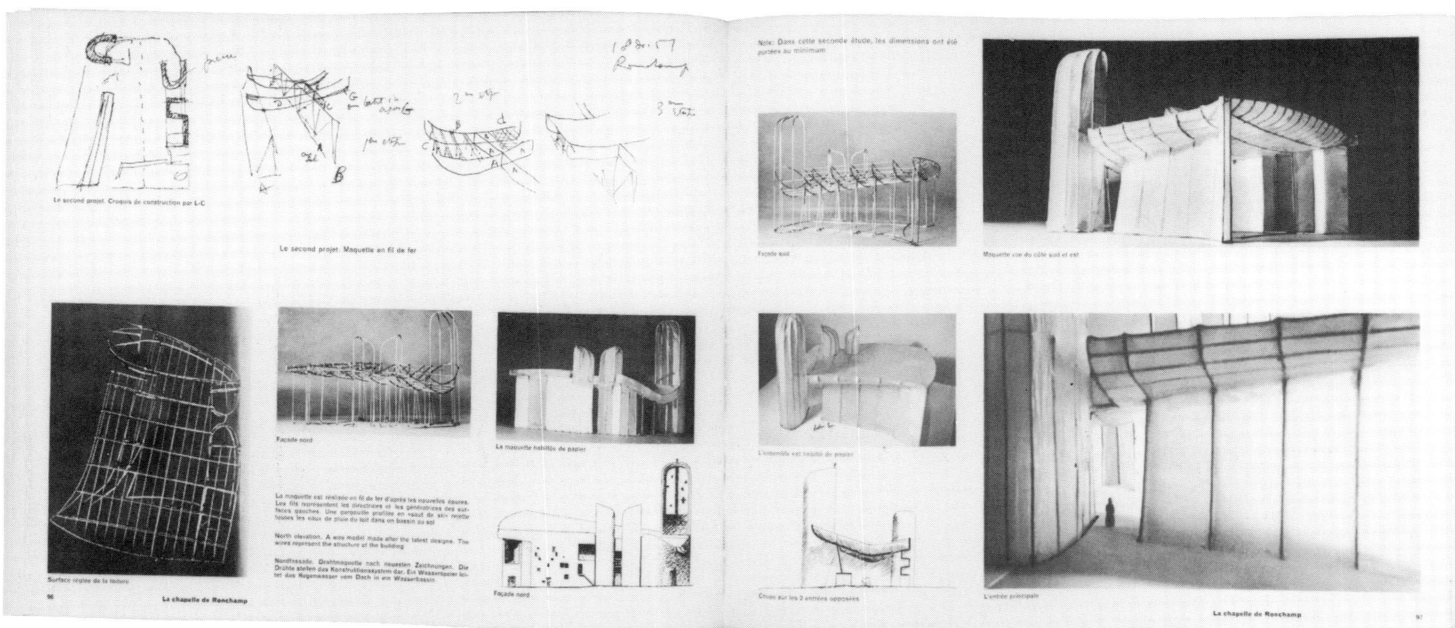

Le second projet. Croquis de construction par L-C

Le second projet. Maquette en fil de fer

Surface réglée de la toiture

Façade nord

La maquette habillée de papier

La maquette est réalisée en fil de fer d'après les nouvelles épures. Les fils représentent les directrices et les génératrices des surfaces gauches. Une gargouille profilée en «saut de ski» rejette toutes les eaux de pluie du toit dans un bassin au sol

North elevation. A wire model made after the latest designs. The wires represent the structure of the building

Nordfassade. Drahtmaquette nach neuesten Zeichnungen. Die Drähte stellen das Konstruktionssystem dar. Ein Wasserspeier leitet das Regenwasser vom Dach in ein Wasserbassin

Façade nord

96 La chapelle de Ronchamp

Note: Dans cette seconde étude, les dimensions ont été portées au minimum

Façade sud

Maquette vue du côté sud et est

L'ensemble est habillé de papier

Coupe sur les 2 entrées opposées

L'entrée principale

La chapelle de Ronchamp 97

Max Bill: *Robert Maillart*
Verlag für Architektur
Erlenbach-Zurich, 1949
Designed by Max Bill
Illustrated at 45% actual size

William Morris insisted that facing pages should be treated as one unit. Yet, fifty years on, Bill has achieved only a nebulous relationship – if that – between facing pages throughout this book. Simply aligning things at the top and (more or less) at the bottom is not enough. Rather than reflecting the elegance and precision of Maillart's bridges, some spreads seem deliberately ungainly. The mise-en-page of this one is better than most, but it is still spatially naive. Despite the economy of means – the use of only one type size, in two weights – the book, as an entity, is no typographic equivalent of Maillart's refined engineering, every part related to another, and to the whole.

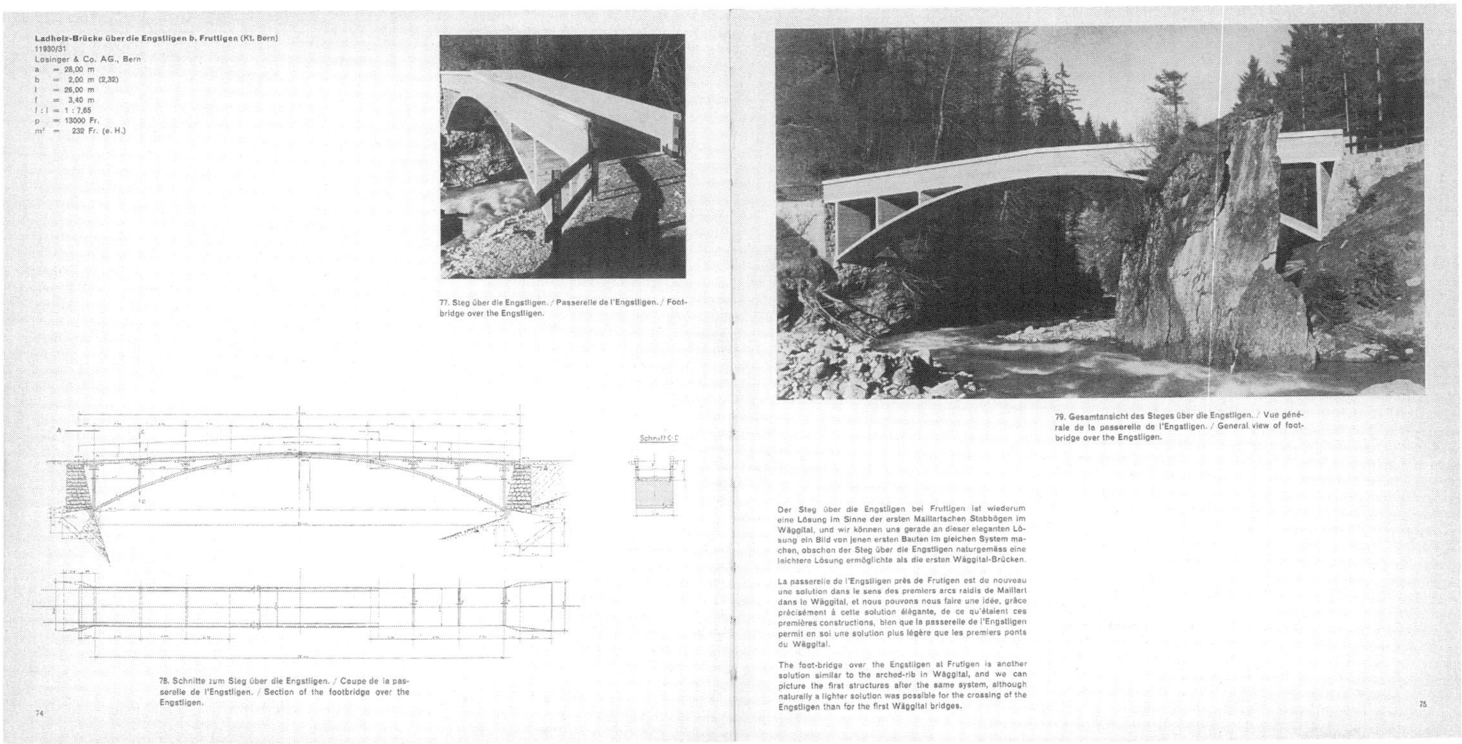
Ladholz-Brücke über die Engstligen b. Fruttigen (Kt. Bern)
11930/31
Losinger & Co. AG., Bern
a = 28,00 m
b = 2,00 m (2,32)
l = 26,00 m
f = 3,40 m
f : l = 1 : 7,65
p = 13000 Fr.
m² = 232 Fr. (e. H.)

77. Steg über die Engstligen. / Passerelle de l'Engstligen. / Footbridge over the Engstligen.

78. Schnitte zum Steg über die Engstligen. / Coupe de la passerelle de l'Engstligen. / Section of the footbridge over the Engstligen.

74

79. Gesamtansicht des Steges über die Engstligen. / Vue générale de la passerelle de l'Engstligen. / General view of footbridge over the Engstligen.

Der Steg über die Engstligen bei Fruttigen ist wiederum eine Lösung im Sinne der ersten Maillartschen Stabbögen im Wäggital, und wir können uns gerade an dieser eleganten Lösung ein Bild von jenen ersten Bauten im gleichen System machen, obschon der Steg über die Engstligen naturgemäss eine leichtere Lösung ermöglichte als die ersten Wäggital-Brücken.

La passerelle de l'Engstligen près de Frutigen est de nouveau une solution dans le sens des premiers arcs raidis de Maillart dans le Wäggital, et nous pouvons nous faire une idée, grâce précisément à cette solution élégante, de ce qu'étaient ces premières constructions, bien que la passerelle de l'Engstligen permit en soi une solution plus légère que les premiers ponts du Wäggital.

The foot-bridge over the Engstligen at Frutigen is another solution similar to the arched-rib in Wäggital, and we can picture the first structures after the same system, although naturally a lighter solution was possible for the crossing of the Engstligen than for the first Wäggital bridges.

75

Linus Birchler etc
Moderne Schweizer Architektur
Verlag Karl Werner, Basle, 1950?
Designed by Max Bill
Illustrated at 49% actual size

Although these pages are actually part of a set of loose sheets (bound up in this British Library example) the two are clearly intended as a pair; but there is little to link them visually. Nor do they reflect a key requirement of the new typography: that space and occupied areas, being of equal importance, should be given equal consideration. As so often in Bill's bookwork, spaces are merely haphazard holes. Would he design a building with such a cavalier disregard for blank areas? Well, the house illustrated is one of his own designs. So apparently not.

A pioneer exploiter of the grid, Bill favoured a very practical one giving two different column widths, seemingly based on a geometrical relationship. That principle is used here, in the book opposite, and in the next example.

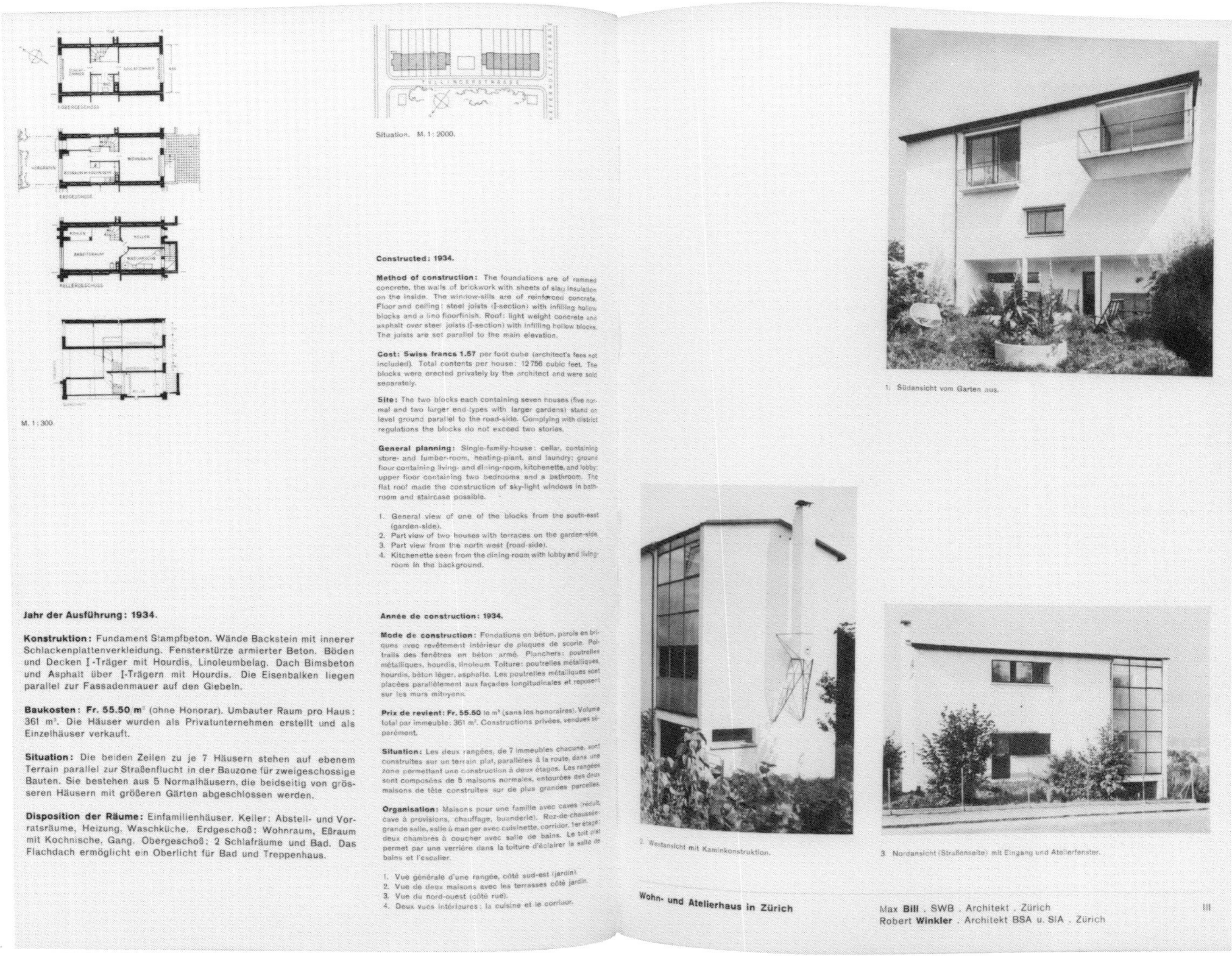

M. 1 : 300.

Situation. M. 1 : 2000.

Constructed: 1934.

Method of construction: The foundations are of rammed concrete, the walls of brickwork with sheets of slag insulation on the inside. The window-sills are of reinforced concrete. Floor and ceiling: steel joists (I-section) with infilling hollow blocks and a lino floorfinish. Roof: light weight concrete and asphalt over steel joists (I-section) with infilling hollow blocks. The joists are set parallel to the main elevation.

Cost: Swiss francs 1.57 per foot cube (architect's fees not included). Total contents per house: 12756 cubic feet. The blocks were erected privately by the architect and were sold separately.

Site: The two blocks each containing seven houses (five normal and two larger end-types with larger gardens) stand on level ground parallel to the road-side. Complying with district regulations the blocks do not exceed two stories.

General planning: Single-family-house: cellar, containing store- and lumber-room, heating-plant, and laundry; ground flour containing living- and dining-room, kitchenette, and lobby; upper floor containing two bedrooms and a bathroom. The flat roof made the construction of sky-light windows in bathroom and staircase possible.

1. General view of one of the blocks from the south-east (garden-side).
2. Part view of two houses with terraces on the garden-side.
3. Part view from the north west (road-side).
4. Kitchenette seen from the dining room with lobby and living-room in the background.

Jahr der Ausführung: 1934.

Konstruktion: Fundament Stampfbeton. Wände Backstein mit innerer Schlackenplattenverkleidung. Fensterstürze armierter Beton. Böden und Decken I-Träger mit Hourdis, Linoleumbelag. Dach Bimsbeton und Asphalt über I-Trägern mit Hourdis. Die Eisenbalken liegen parallel zur Fassadenmauer auf den Giebeln.

Baukosten: Fr. 55.50 m³ (ohne Honorar). Umbauter Raum pro Haus: 361 m³. Die Häuser wurden als Privatunternehmen erstellt und als Einzelhäuser verkauft.

Situation: Die beiden Zeilen zu je 7 Häusern stehen auf ebenem Terrain parallel zur Straßenflucht in der Bauzone für zweigeschossige Bauten. Sie bestehen aus 5 Normalhäusern, die beidseitig von grösseren Häusern mit größeren Gärten abgeschlossen werden.

Disposition der Räume: Einfamilienhäuser. Keller: Abstell- und Vorratsräume, Heizung, Waschküche. Erdgeschoß: Wohnraum, Eßraum mit Kochnische, Gang. Obergeschoß: 2 Schlafräume und Bad. Das Flachdach ermöglicht ein Oberlicht für Bad und Treppenhaus.

Année de construction: 1934.

Mode de construction: Fondations en béton, parois en briques avec revêtement intérieur de plaques de scorie. Poitrails des fenêtres en béton armé. Planchers: poutrelles métalliques, hourdis, linoleum. Toiture: poutrelles métalliques, hourdis, béton léger, asphalte. Les poutrelles métalliques sont placées parallèlement aux façades longitudinales et reposent sur les murs mitoyens.

Prix de revient: Fr. 55.50 le m³ (sans les honoraires). Volume total par immeuble: 361 m³. Constructions privées, vendues séparément.

Situation: Les deux rangées, de 7 immeubles chacune, sont construites sur un terrain plat, parallèles à la route, dans une zone permettant une construction à deux étages. Les rangées sont composées de 5 maisons normales, entourées des deux maisons de tête construites sur de plus grandes parcelles.

Organisation: Maisons pour une famille avec caves (réduit, cave à provisions, chauffage, buanderie). Rez-de-chaussée: grande salle, salle à manger avec cuisinette, corridor. 1er étage: deux chambres à coucher avec salle de bains. Le toit plat permet par une verrière dans la toiture d'éclairer la salle de bains et l'escalier.

1. Vue générale d'une rangée, côté sud-est (jardin).
2. Vue de deux maisons avec les terrasses côté jardin.
3. Vue du nord-ouest (côté rue).
4. Deux vues intérieures: la cuisine et le corridor.

1. Südansicht vom Garten aus.

2. Westansicht mit Kaminkonstruktion.

3. Nordansicht (Straßenseite) mit Eingang und Atelierfenster.

Wohn- und Atelierhaus in Zürich

Max **Bill** . SWB . Architekt . Zürich
Robert **Winkler** . Architekt BSA u. SIA . Zürich

III

Max Bill: *Form*
Verlag Karl Werner, Basle, 1952
Designed by Max Bill
Illustrated at 46% actual size

This book resembles a series of exhibition panels in its simplicity, and Bill seems more confident. All pictures align on a constant base. But there is insufficient space beneath them (in the rigidly held-to text column) to always cope with the three-language captions, so the first one often has to be separated from its companions and poked above the picture. This shows either a lack of foresight or an inflexible mind-set. Why not allow *two* text columns beneath the picture where necessary, and keep the captions together? And in the second spread, opposite, the captions on the left-hand page are curiously placed in relation both to the other captions and to the picture. Bill never seems to have heard the phrase 'The eye corrects the mind'.

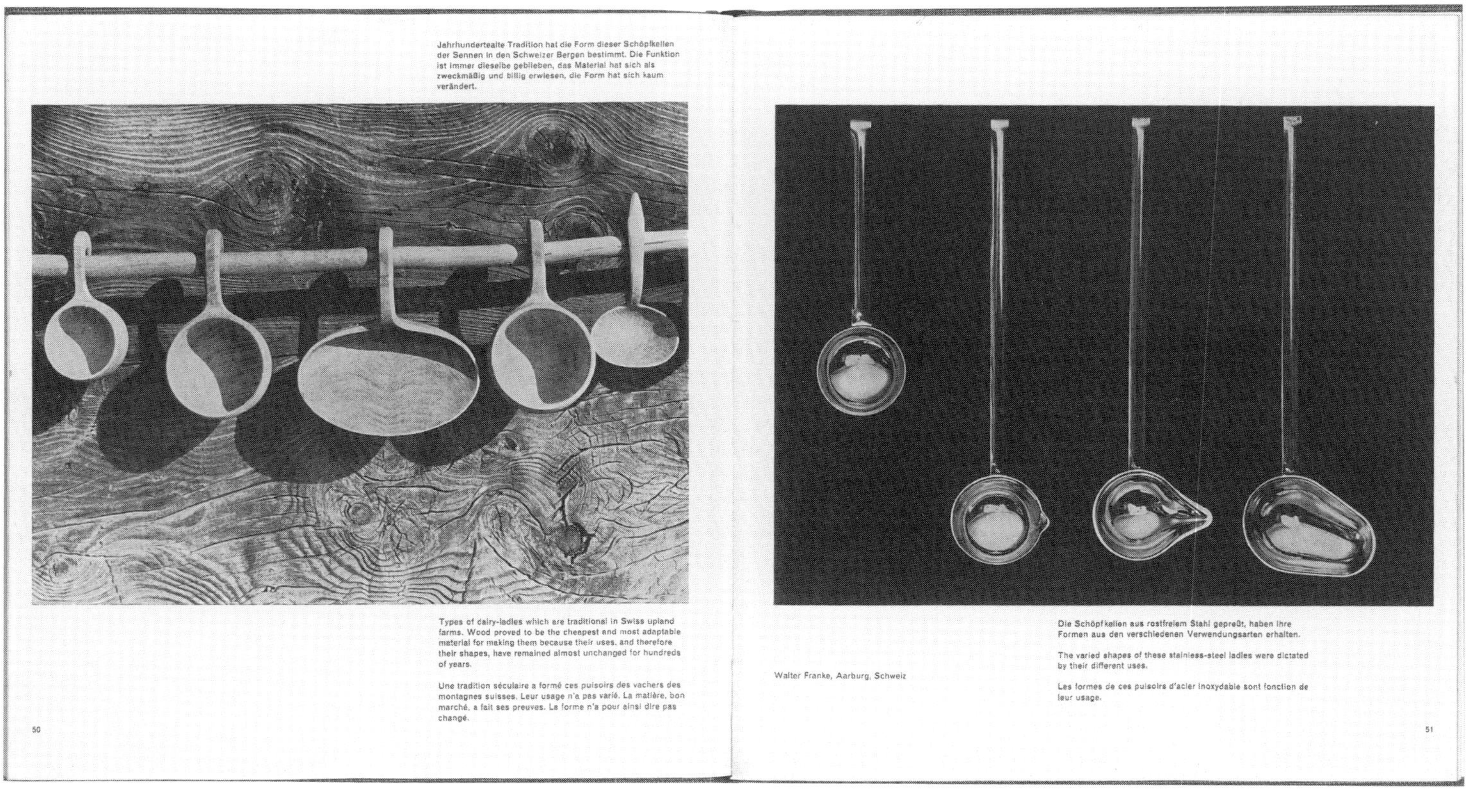
Jahrhundertealte Tradition hat die Form dieser Schöpfkellen der Sennen in den Schweizer Bergen bestimmt. Die Funktion ist immer dieselbe geblieben, das Material hat sich als zweckmäßig und billig erwiesen, die Form hat sich kaum verändert.

Types of dairy-ladles which are traditional in Swiss upland farms. Wood proved to be the cheapest and most adaptable material for making them because their uses, and therefore their shapes, have remained almost unchanged for hundreds of years.

Une tradition séculaire a formé ces puisoirs des vachers des montagnes suisses. Leur usage n'a pas varié. La matière, bon marché, a fait ses preuves. La forme n'a pour ainsi dire pas changé.

50

Walter Franke, Aarburg, Schweiz

Die Schöpfkellen aus rostfreiem Stahl gepreßt, haben ihre Formen aus den verschiedenen Verwendungsarten erhalten.

The varied shapes of these stainless-steel ladles were dictated by their different uses.

Les formes de ces puisoirs d'acier inoxydable sont fonction de leur usage.

51

I have found writing about Max Bill very difficult. He is so eminent, has been put on such a pedestal by people I respect. Yet, when I look at his actual work … Perhaps I am being too critical. But more thoroughly worked-out relationships, showing more subtlety and feeling for the placing of material within the page area, were being explored by Herbert Spencer at about the same time – as we shall see.

Bill's aggressively held ideas that typography should be rational, functional and in visual harmony with modern techniques and society, are eminently sane. His championing, while director of the Hochschule für Gestaltung at Ulm, of the artist-designer as opposed to the beliefs of the more scientifically inclined younger staff, was admirable. Yet while much of his three-dimensional and product design showed a concern for aesthetics as well as function, his typography, which is what concerns me, was often disappointingly disjointed and inflexible. He lacked the kind of aesthetic passion that could transform mere technical engineering into a Maillart bridge.

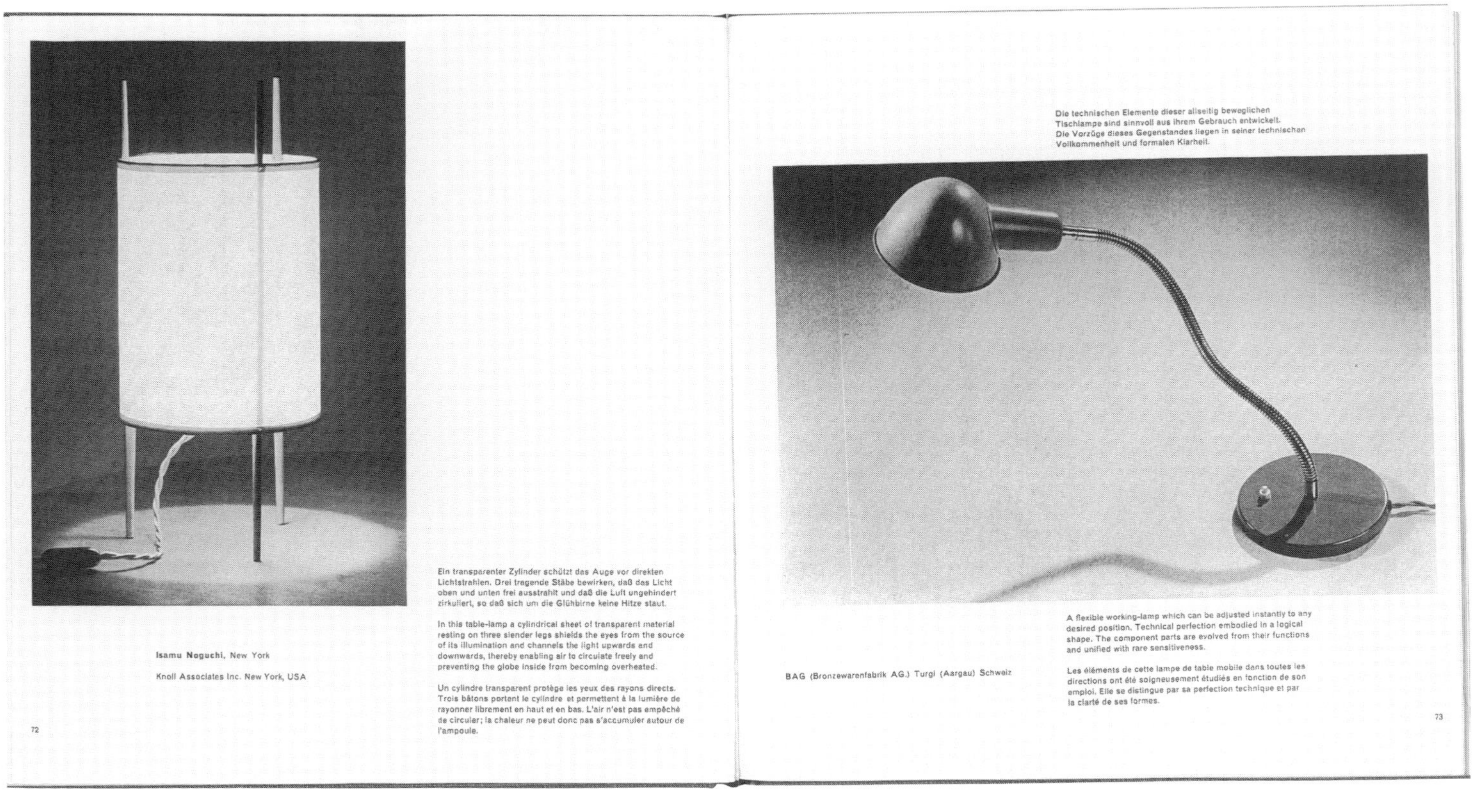

Ein transparenter Zylinder schützt das Auge vor direkten Lichtstrahlen. Drei tragende Stäbe bewirken, daß das Licht oben und unten frei ausstrahlt und daß die Luft ungehindert zirkuliert, so daß sich um die Glühbirne keine Hitze staut.

In this table-lamp a cylindrical sheet of transparent material resting on three slender legs shields the eyes from the source of its illumination and channels the light upwards and downwards, thereby enabling air to circulate freely and preventing the globe inside from becoming overheated.

Un cylindre transparent protège les yeux des rayons directs. Trois bâtons portent le cylindre et permettent à la lumière de rayonner librement en haut et en bas. L'air n'est pas empêché de circuler; la chaleur ne peut donc pas s'accumuler autour de l'ampoule.

Isamu Noguchi, New York

Knoll Associates Inc. New York, USA

72

Die technischen Elemente dieser allseitig beweglichen Tischlampe sind sinnvoll aus ihrem Gebrauch entwickelt. Die Vorzüge dieses Gegenstandes liegen in seiner technischen Vollkommenheit und formalen Klarheit.

A flexible working-lamp which can be adjusted instantly to any desired position. Technical perfection embodied in a logical shape. The component parts are evolved from their functions and unified with rare sensitiveness.

Les éléments de cette lampe de table mobile dans toutes les directions ont été soigneusement étudiés en fonction de son emploi. Elle se distingue par sa perfection technique et par la clarté de ses formes.

BAG (Bronzewarenfabrik AG.) Turgi (Aargau) Schweiz

73

Le Corbusier: *Oeuvre Complète 1934-38*
Les Editions d'Architecture
Erlenbach-Zurich, 1947
Designed by Max Bill
Illustrated at 43% actual size

This relatively early title page (for the book shown in the upper illustration on page 101) is set in Bodoni, apparently Bill's preferred type before grotesques superseded it. He was happier with such display work than with the more demanding problems of integrating text and illustrations. The wordspacing here is horribly wide; was this Bill's choice, or merely bad typesetting? But the overall design is neatly handled and well balanced, better than the title pages of later volumes in the series.

The unpleasantly tight outer margin does not seem to be the result of over-trimming during rebinding.

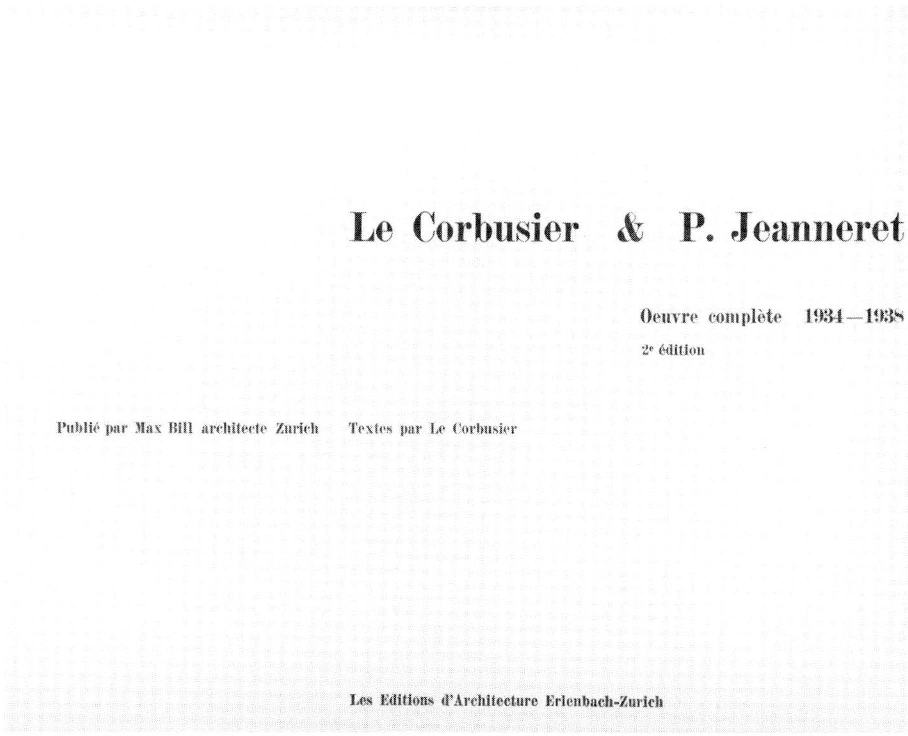

Le Corbusier & P. Jeanneret

Oeuvre complète 1934—1938

2e édition

Publié par Max Bill architecte Zurich Textes par Le Corbusier

Les Editions d'Architecture Erlenbach-Zurich

Richard P Lohse
Neue Ausstellungsgestaltung
Erlenbach-Zurich, 1953
Designed by Richard P Lohse
Illustrated at 43% actual size

Max Bill may have had a difficult author to deal with when designing the Le Corbusier books – two big egos battling it out. But the same awkwardnesses occur in his own books. Lohse, also designing his own material, handled it with skill. Spreads from this book are shown on pages 112-13. In its title page groups of Akzidenz Grotesque are precisely positioned, following the grid of the book. The design makes Bill's look very relaxed, even though that, too, follows its grid. Lohse's design cannot be said to usher in the new discipline, for he, at least, had been practising it for some years. But it brings a new feeling to these pages of mine.

I cannot admire the unnecessary breaking of Ex/hibitions. All five lines of that group would have been better ranged left.

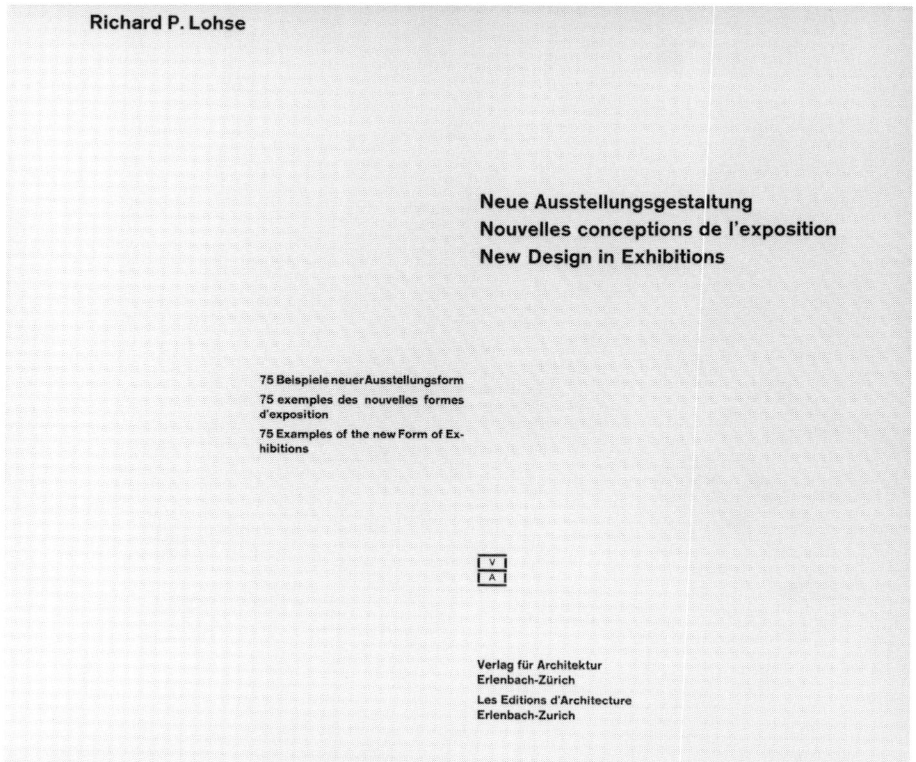

Richard P. Lohse

Neue Ausstellungsgestaltung
Nouvelles conceptions de l'exposition
New Design in Exhibitions

75 Beispiele neuer Ausstellungsform
75 exemples des nouvelles formes d'exposition
75 Examples of the new Form of Ex-hibitions

Verlag für Architektur
Erlenbach-Zürich
Les Editions d'Architecture
Erlenbach-Zurich

Neue Grafik/New Graphic Design/ Graphisme actuel
Cover design
Otto Walter, Olten, 1959
Designed by Carlo Vivarelli
Illustrated at 52% actual size

An informal group of Swiss designers evolved a new, flexible and sophisticated approach to the problems thrown up by the new requirements of the mid-twentieth century, and this magazine was, you might say, their house journal. Unlike Bill, they were not afraid to use large, bold type, although they continued to consider grotesques obligatory. Rather unexpectedly, they still justified text setting. The design structure was firmer than Bill's, more architectural; but function and aesthetics were equals, the latter no longer an afterthought – assuming Bill had considered them at all. Lohse's work, seen opposite and on pages 108-13, is an excellent illustration of the system in action; he was one of the magazine's four editors. In this cover design, the analysis of the text, its breaking down into groups, the use of space to help to define it, the use of only one size of type (except for the title): all this is characteristic.

An example of the design of this magazine can be seen on pages 66-7.

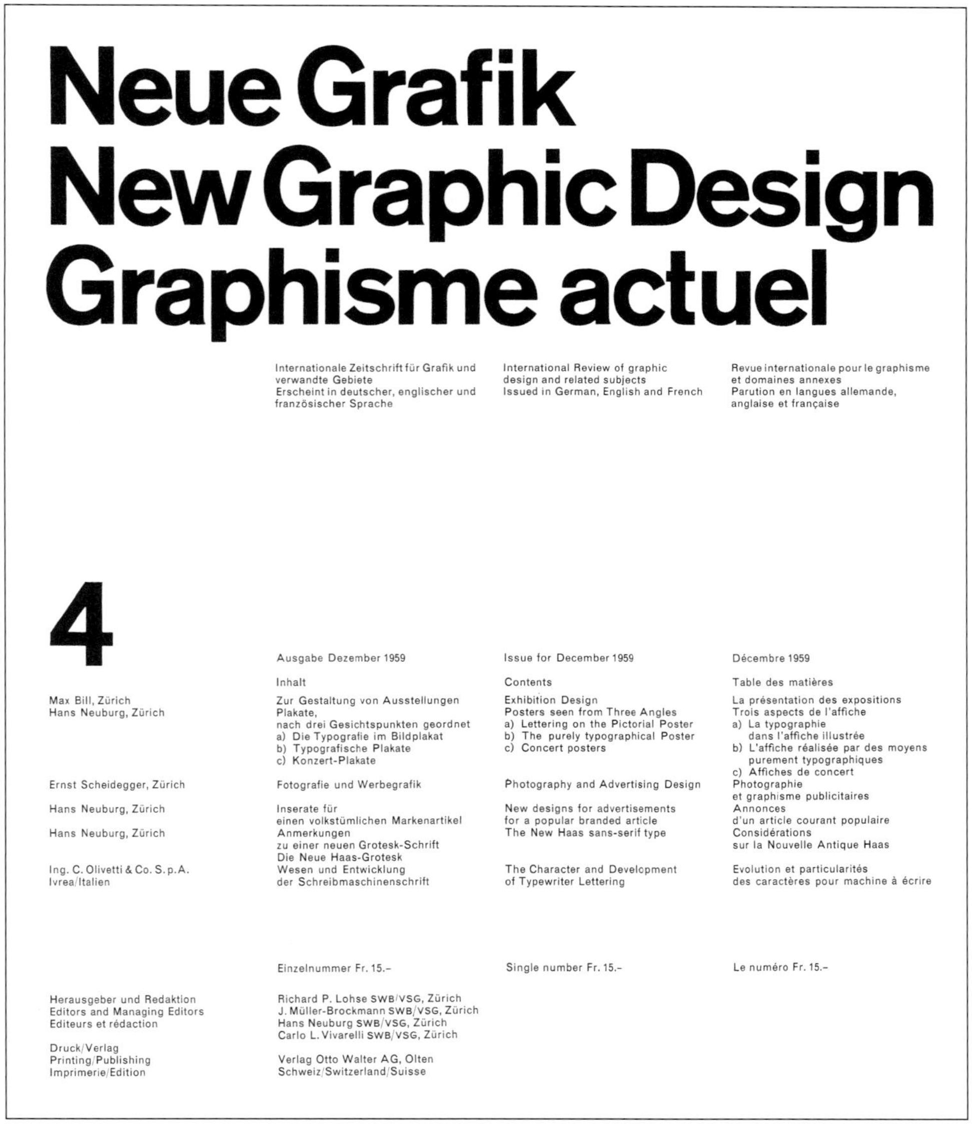

Neue Grafik
New Graphic Design
Graphisme actuel

Internationale Zeitschrift für Grafik und verwandte Gebiete
Erscheint in deutscher, englischer und französischer Sprache

International Review of graphic design and related subjects
Issued in German, English and French

Revue internationale pour le graphisme et domaines annexes
Parution en langues allemande, anglaise et française

4

	Ausgabe Dezember 1959	Issue for December 1959	Décembre 1959
	Inhalt	Contents	Table des matières
Max Bill, Zürich Hans Neuburg, Zürich	Zur Gestaltung von Ausstellungen Plakate, nach drei Gesichtspunkten geordnet a) Die Typografie im Bildplakat b) Typografische Plakate c) Konzert-Plakate	Exhibition Design Posters seen from Three Angles a) Lettering on the Pictorial Poster b) The purely typographical Poster c) Concert posters	La présentation des expositions Trois aspects de l'affiche a) La typographie dans l'affiche illustrée b) L'affiche réalisée par des moyens purement typographiques c) Affiches de concert
Ernst Scheidegger, Zürich	Fotografie und Werbegrafik	Photography and Advertising Design	Photographie et graphisme publicitaires
Hans Neuburg, Zürich	Inserate für einen volkstümlichen Markenartikel	New designs for advertisements for a popular branded article	Annonces d'un article courant populaire
Hans Neuburg, Zürich	Anmerkungen zu einer neuen Grotesk-Schrift Die Neue Haas-Grotesk	The New Haas sans-serif type	Considérations sur la Nouvelle Antique Haas
Ing. C. Olivetti & Co. S. p. A. Ivrea/Italien	Wesen und Entwicklung der Schreibmaschinenschrift	The Character and Development of Typewriter Lettering	Evolution et particularités des caractères pour machine à écrire
	Einzelnummer Fr. 15.–	Single number Fr. 15.–	Le numéro Fr. 15.–

Herausgeber und Redaktion
Editors and Managing Editors
Editeurs et rédaction

Richard P. Lohse SWB/VSG, Zürich
J. Müller-Brockmann SWB/VSG, Zürich
Hans Neuburg SWB/VSG, Zürich
Carlo L. Vivarelli SWB/VSG, Zürich

Druck/Verlag
Printing/Publishing
Imprimerie/Edition

Verlag Otto Walter AG, Olten
Schweiz/Switzerland/Suisse

C Giedion-Welcker: *Poètes à l'Ecart*
Verlag Benteli, 1946
Jacket designed by Richard P Lohse
Illustrated at 66% actual size

Lohse was designing in the 'Swiss manner' surprisingly early. Born in 1902, he was the exact contemporary of Tschichold, and six years older than Max Bill. He was far in advance of the younger man in his grasp of graphic design, and even in his choice of type. While Bill was still using Bodoni, Lohse used Akzidenz Grotesque; here it plays its essential role in this self-evidently 'hard-edge' design. Like Bill, Lohse was also an abstract painter, and the influence of his paintings of this time is reflected in this design of vertical bars and blocks of colour. The unusual arrangement shows a sure command of space. One feels only a Swiss designer would be so adventurous.

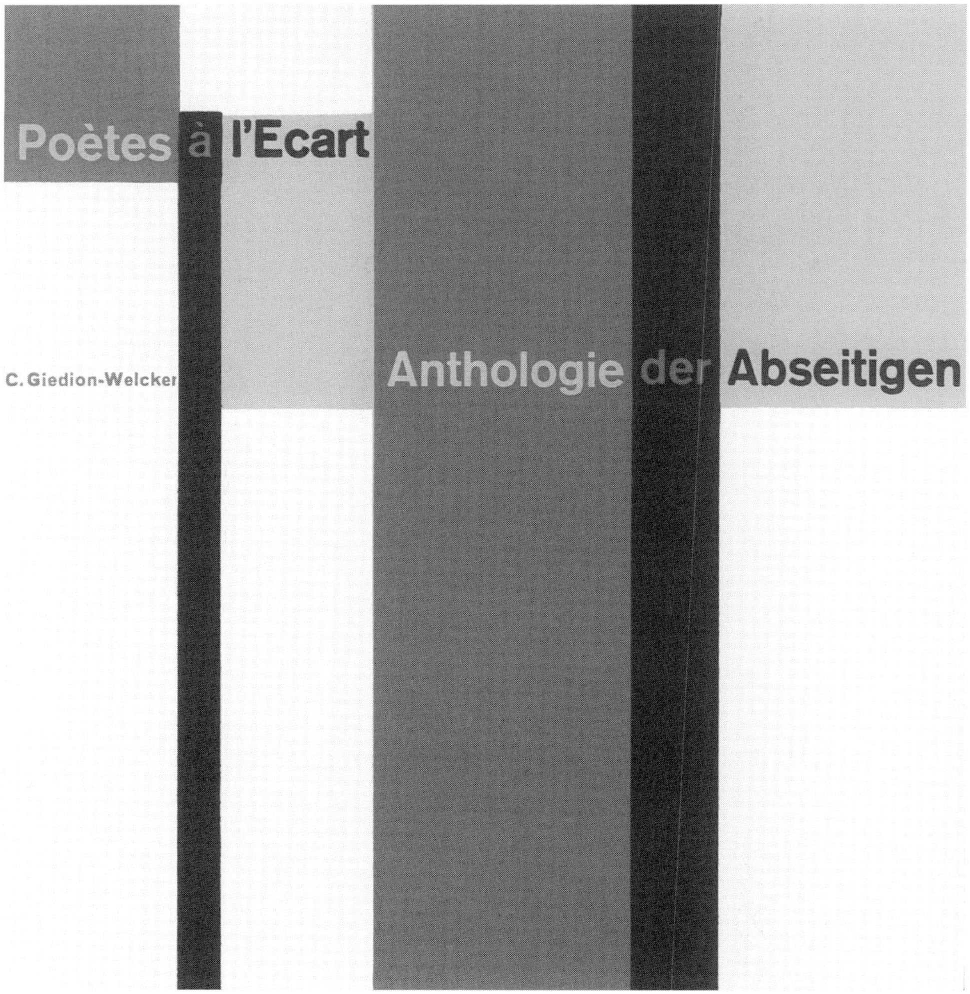

Poster
Designed by Richard P Lohse, 1950
Illustrated at 14% actual size

By 1950, Lohse had fully developed all the essentials of the Swiss New Typography. Type used vertically reflects Tschichold's earlier aims of creating a sense of urgency. While powerful and practical, it is also unashamedly pattern-making in intention. Horizontals and verticals are completely integrated. The pure, classic forms of Helvetica, here replacing Akzidenz, always give the Swiss system authority and presence. Derived from Akzidenz, basically it differs from that type of 1878 only in detail, although its overall appearance gives a different impression. It has some clarification of structure, and slightly flatter curves that allow tighter letter fit. The differences (especially the latter) result in a new confidence and strength, but lose some of the original subtlety.

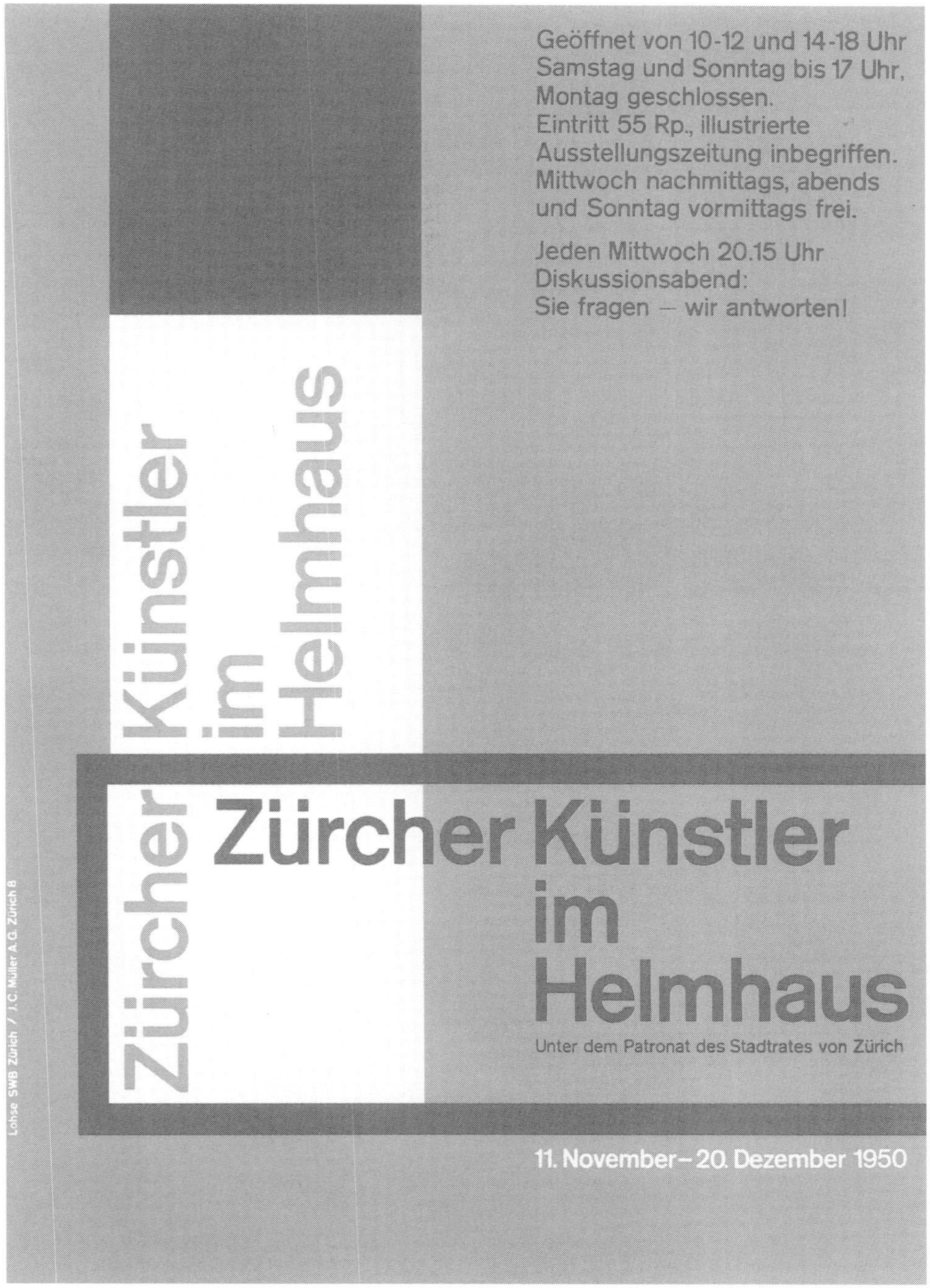

Magazine cover
Bauen & Wohnen
Style initiated 1949
Designed by Richard P Lohse
Illustrated at 28 and 56% actual size

For the cover design of each issue of this magazine, Lohse played variations on the unchanging three-column grid. The title finally settled down to one position, but it sometimes overprinted an illustration, and sometimes the text. The contents appeared on the cover, where a mixture of grotesques was used. The design was usually in two colours, but sometimes three. There might be a single large picture, or a mosaic of smaller ones; often, one picture overprinted another. Sometimes the grid sliced through a picture, as in issue 2/1952 here. Yet the basic identity was strong enough to survive all these variations.

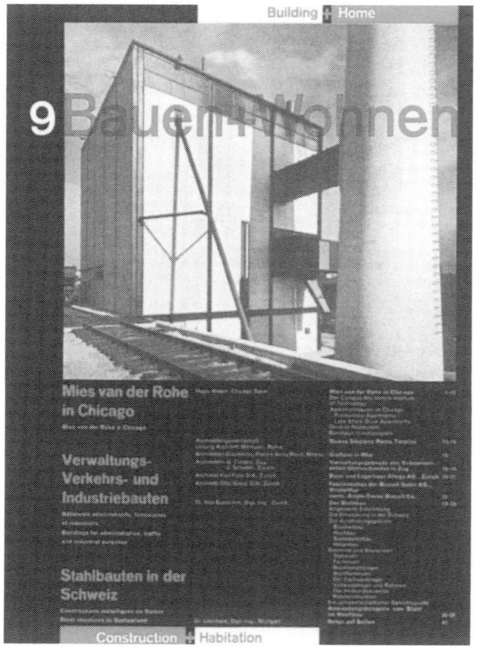

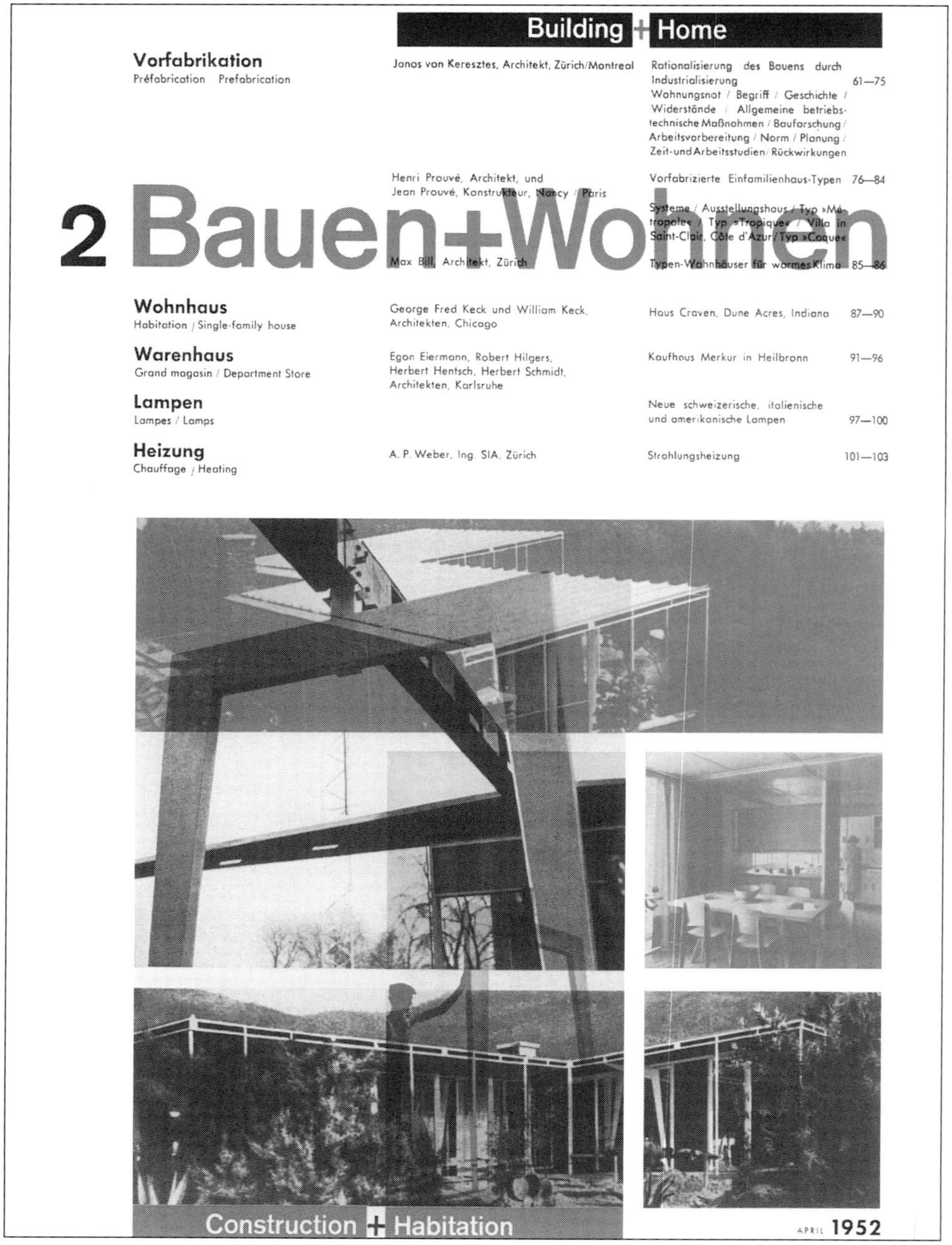

Richard P Lohse
Neue Ausstellungsgestaltung
Erlenbach-Zurich, 1953
Designed by Richard P Lohse
Illustrated at 68% actual size

This is the jacket for the book illustrated on the next two pages. Its design reflects the grid of the book. Type on the jacket is Akzidenz, although the text pages are set in Grotesque 215 and 216. Perhaps Lohse felt Akzidenz more satisfactory for display, while naturally using hot metal setting (Monotype) for text. The jacket was printed in black and yellow. In both jacket and book design, Lohse refines Bill's typographic dictats into an imaginative and flexible system; although I wonder how much influence Bill had on a designer clearly able to think for himself. Many Swiss designers, old and young, were working towards the same end at this time. It was something in the air. Moreover, Switzerland is a small country, and most of these designers were Zurich-based anyway. It was a group thing.

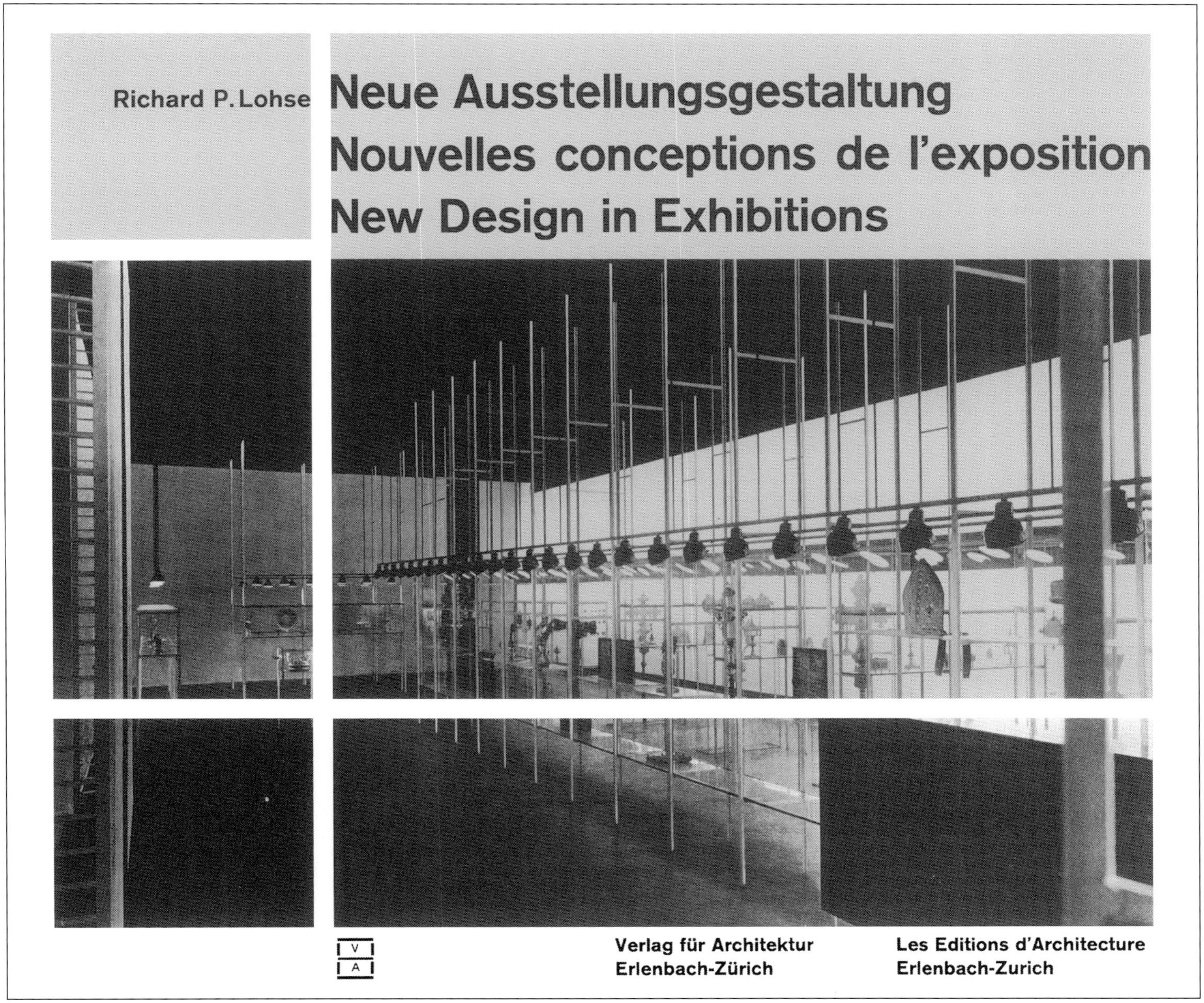

Richard P Lohse
Neue Ausstellungsgestaltung
Verlag für Architektur
Erlenbach-Zurich, 1953
Designed by Richard P Lohse
Illustrated at 35% actual size

In the same year (1953) as Bill's sixth Le Corbusier volume seen on page 101, Lohse designed this book with broadly the same format and comparable material. Here, aesthetics were as important to the designer as

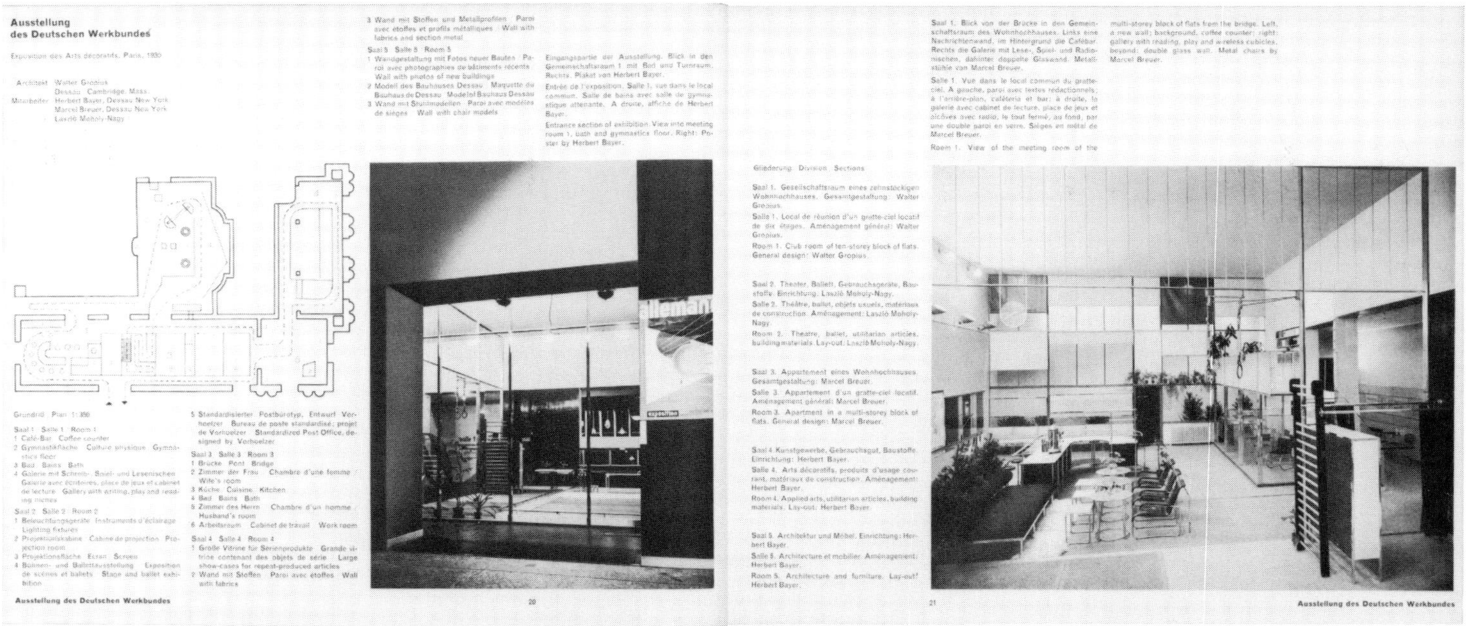

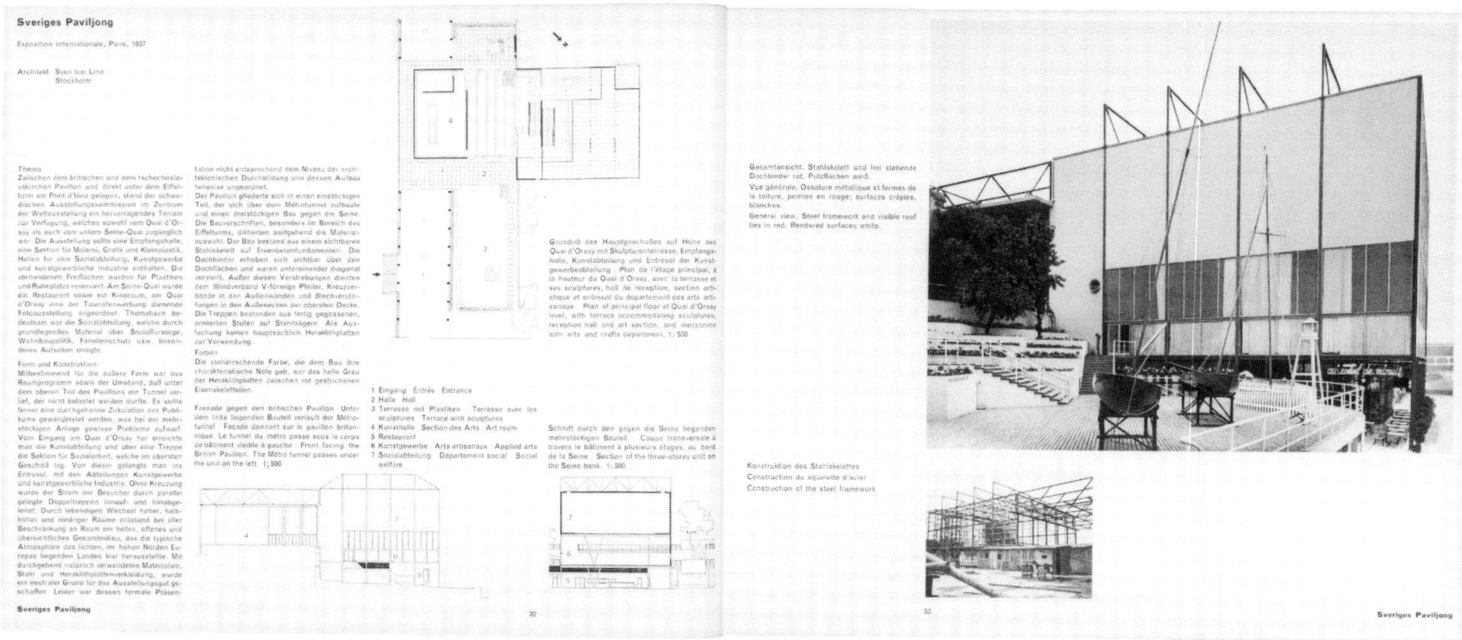

function. Minimal means were used: a four-column grid, with horizontal alignments obeying a horizontal grid; one type size, with bold running feet in the same size; and slightly larger bold headings. The text is in three languages. Type is justified, margins tight. Plans – always a problem – have been skilfully incorporated. The grid governs the design, but it is not a rigid dictatorship. The contents of every spread have been carefully and individually analysed; the design allows each particularity its true place. Yet the book overall is consistent and disciplined: variety within unity. This is Swiss *new* New Typography, successfully applied to bookwork.

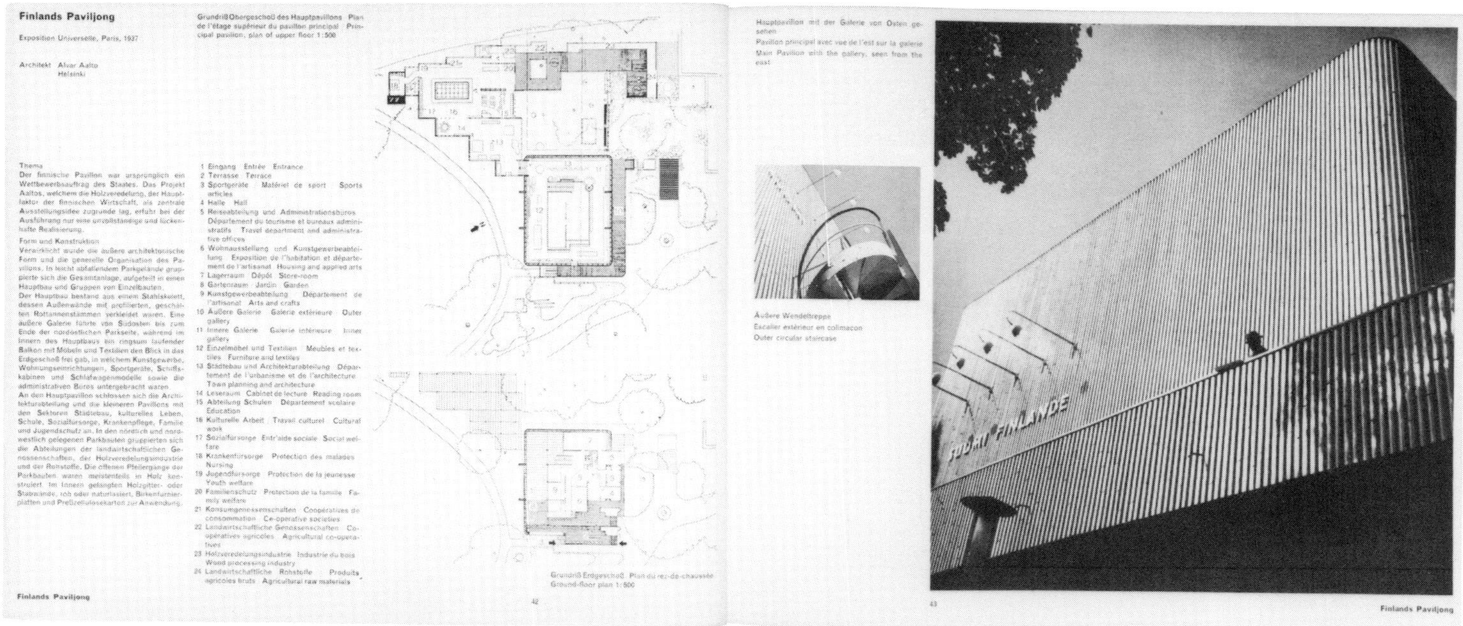
Finlands Paviljong

Exposition Universelle, Paris, 1937

Architekt Alvar Aalto, Helsinki

Finlands Paviljong

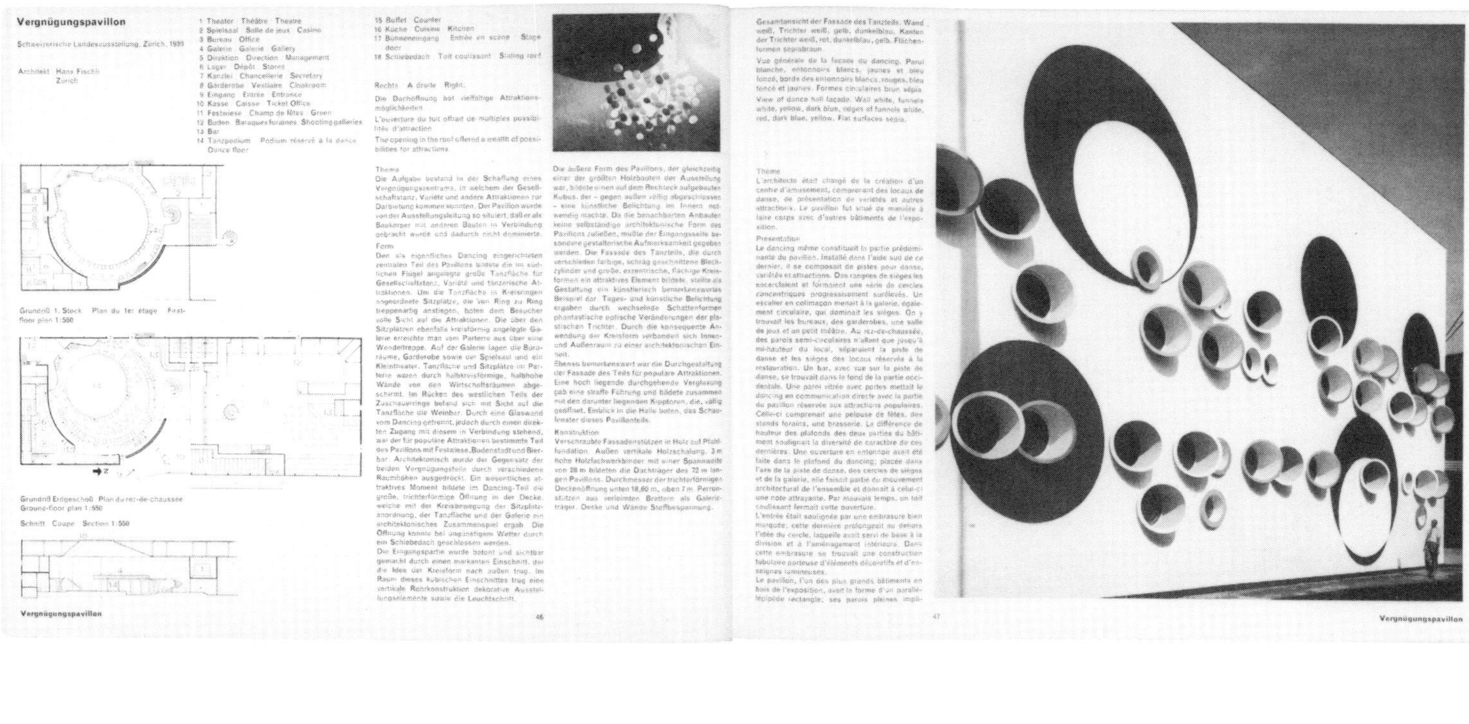
Vergnügungspavillon

Architekt Hans Fischli, Zürich

Vergnügungspavillon

Karl Gerstner: *Designing Programmes*
Alec Tiranti, London, 1964
Designed by Karl Gerstner
Illustrated at 54% actual size

For the younger generation of designers such as Karl Gerstner (born 1930) the disciplined system espoused by Lohse and his contemporaries needed further intellectual stiffening. This was to be no mere background theory, but an essential part of the aesthetic programme. Gerstner's book attempts to formulate their ideas.

The first spread here shows a 'space-wall-picture': patterns on a corrugated four-plane base, the appearance of which changes when the spectator moves from left to right. Viewpoints are shown on the line diagram, resulting images from each viewpoint are shown below it. While remote from book design or even typography, such analytical exercises are indicative of the free-ranging minds of these serious designers.

The more immediately relevant second spread shows how the use of a logotype can be controlled by enlarging it upwards, or to the left, following the mathematically derived grid.

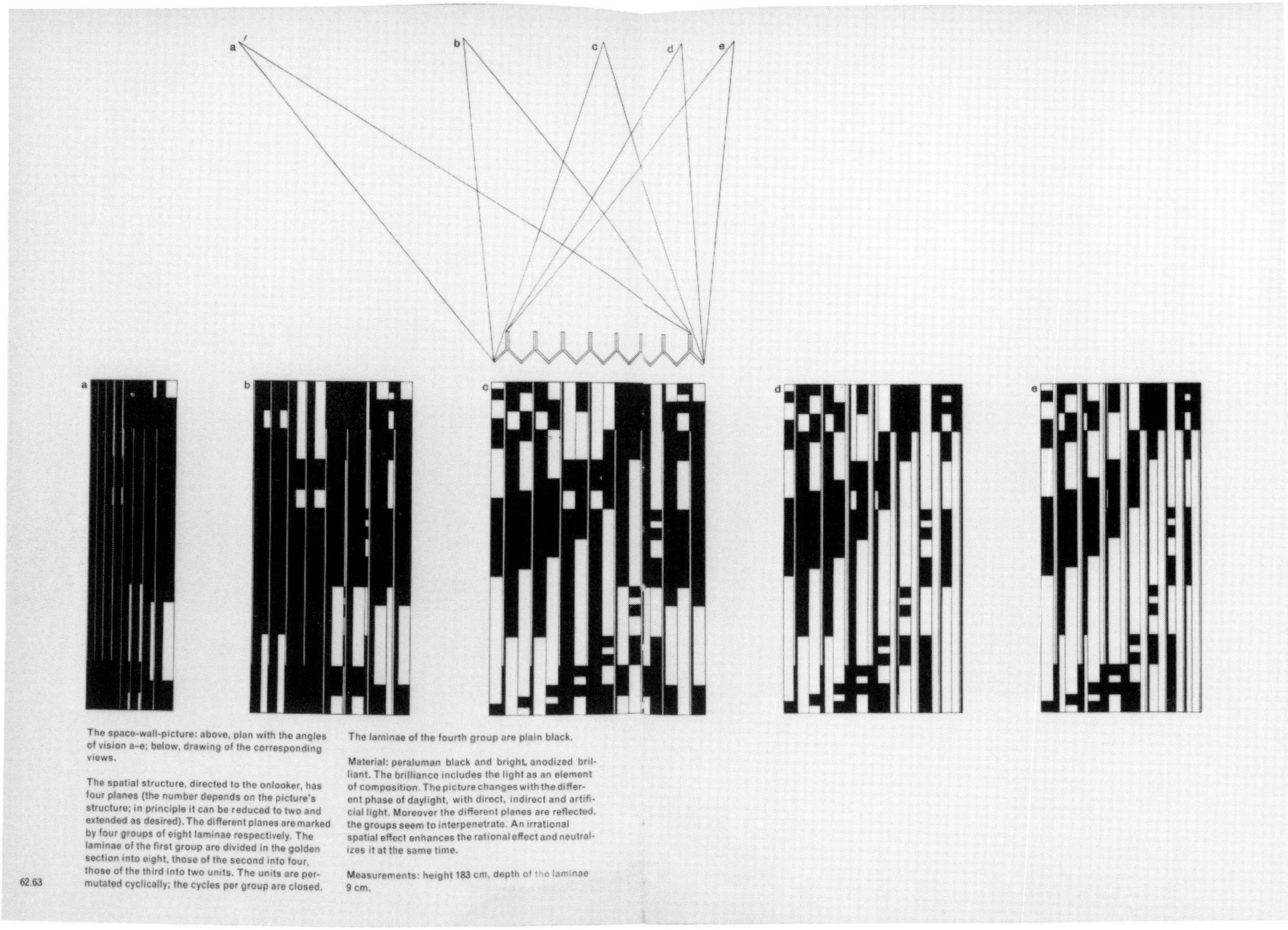

Illustrations on the right show the system applied to five different formats.

Despite the apparent confidence of their work, the need for conceptual reassurance was perhaps a sign of insecurity in this still young profession. Such intellectual games provided gravitas and bottom. Yet, if often over-theoretical, this younger generation of Swiss designers never forgot aesthetics. The viewer could, and probably did, remain ignorant of the agonising behind what he actually saw. It is quite possible that, buried beneath the apparent simplicity and dead-pan appearance of this book, there is a system of gratuitously complex mathematical interrelationships. We are talking here not of the golden section and other similar *geometric* devices based on the proportions of the page (although these continue to play their part in book design) but of their numerical and notational equivalent, utilising multiples derived from a unit of typographic measurement.

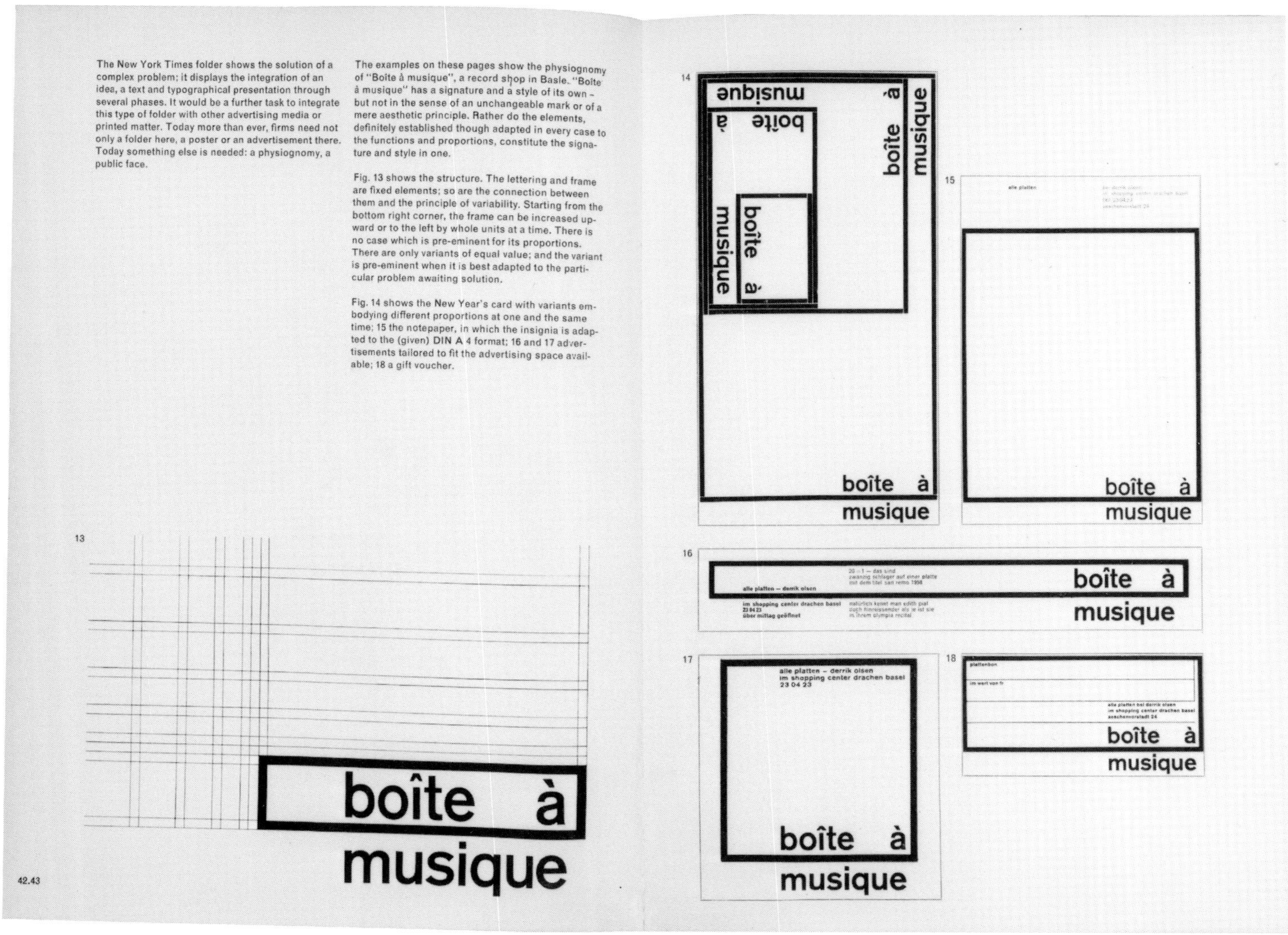
The New York Times folder shows the solution of a complex problem; it displays the integration of an idea, a text and typographical presentation through several phases. It would be a further task to integrate this type of folder with other advertising media or printed matter. Today more than ever, firms need not only a folder here, a poster or an advertisement there. Today something else is needed: a physiognomy, a public face.

The examples on these pages show the physiognomy of "Boîte à musique", a record shop in Basle. "Boîte à musique" has a signature and a style of its own – but not in the sense of an unchangeable mark or of a mere aesthetic principle. Rather do the elements, definitely established though adapted in every case to the functions and proportions, constitute the signature and style in one.

Fig. 13 shows the structure. The lettering and frame are fixed elements; so are the connection between them and the principle of variability. Starting from the bottom right corner, the frame can be increased upward or to the left by whole units at a time. There is no case which is pre-eminent for its proportions. There are only variants of equal value; and the variant is pre-eminent when it is best adapted to the particular problem awaiting solution.

Fig. 14 shows the New Year's card with variants embodying different proportions at one and the same time; 15 the notepaper, in which the insignia is adapted to the (given) DIN A 4 format; 16 and 17 advertisements tailored to fit the advertising space available; 18 a gift voucher.

Charles-Albert Reichen
A History of Astronomy
Leisure Arts, London, 1965
Designed by Erik Nitsche
Illustrated at 56% actual size

The series *The New Illustrated Library of Science and Invention*, to which this book and the next belong, was originated in Switzerland by Editions Rencontre in 1962. Erik Nitsche, the designer and producer, was born in Switzerland, but had worked in America since 1934. Yet he had clearly kept in touch with what was going on in his native country, for these at bottom are Swiss books. Maintaining the rigour of the Swiss grid, the effect is somewhat softened both by the use of a modern face, and the lavish illustrations, the majority of which are not only old engravings or prints, but are also free shapes. Their full potential has been exploited, and played off against the strict typography. The copyright/contents spread here is especially effective. Headings (such as 'contents' here) are hair-raisingly close to the top edge.

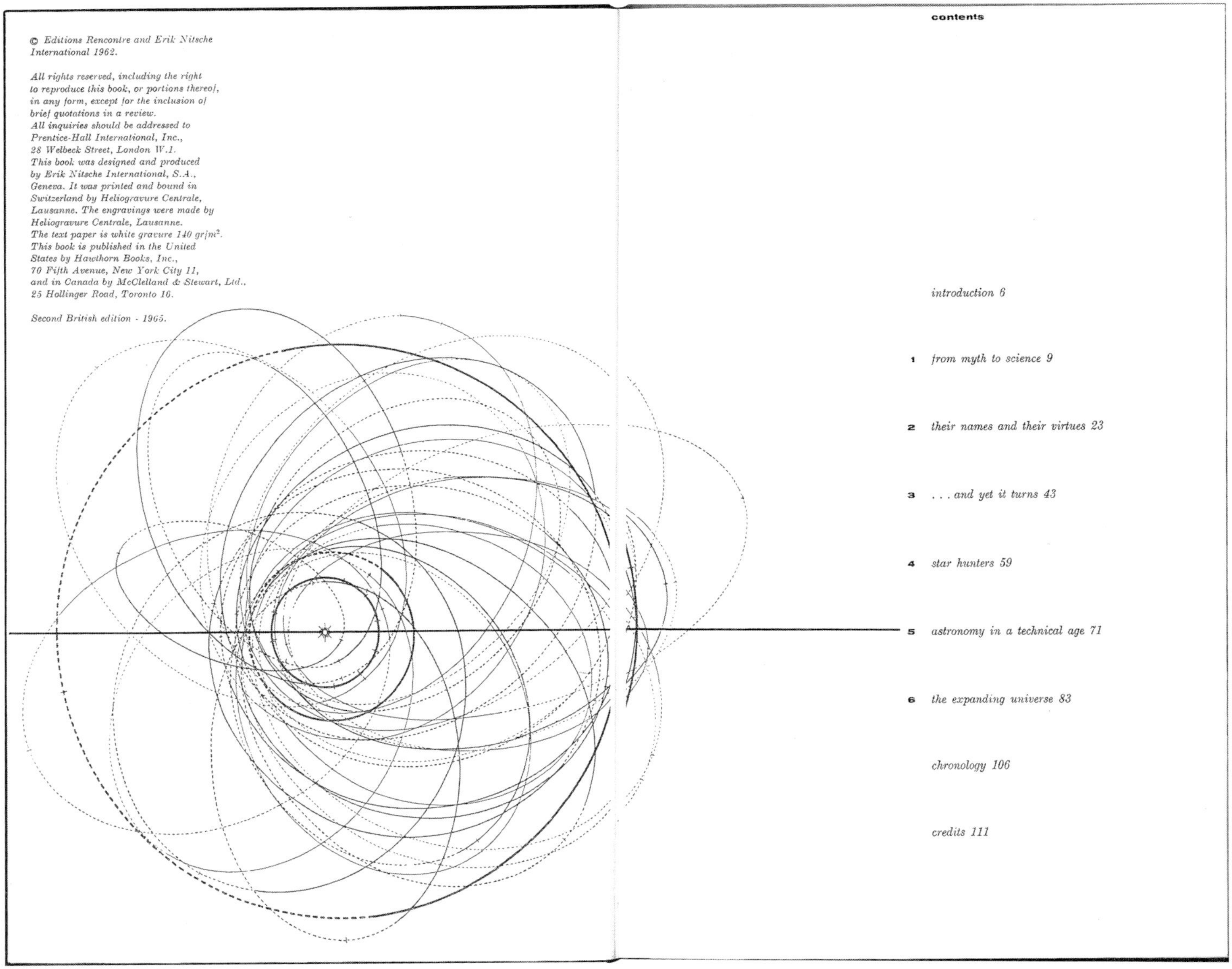

© Editions Rencontre and Erik Nitsche International 1962.

All rights reserved, including the right to reproduce this book, or portions thereof, in any form, except for the inclusion of brief quotations in a review. All inquiries should be addressed to Prentice-Hall International, Inc., 28 Welbeck Street, London W.1. This book was designed and produced by Erik Nitsche International, S.A., Geneva. It was printed and bound in Switzerland by Heliogravure Centrale, Lausanne. The engravings were made by Heliogravure Centrale, Lausanne. The text paper is white gravure 140 gr/m². This book is published in the United States by Hawthorn Books, Inc., 70 Fifth Avenue, New York City 11, and in Canada by McClelland & Stewart, Ltd., 25 Hollinger Road, Toronto 16.

Second British edition - 1965.

contents

102

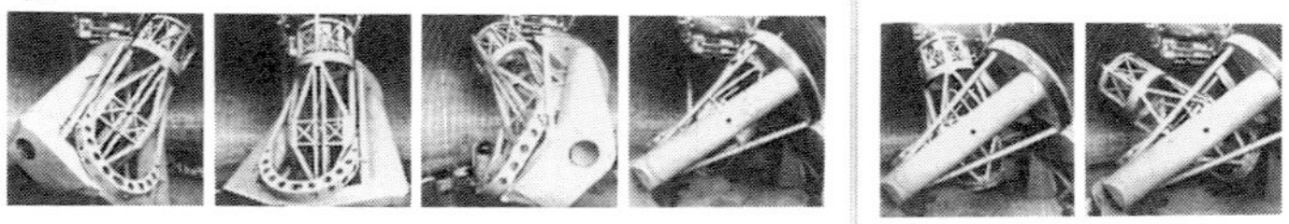

40-inch Yerkes refractor, dating back to 1897, remains unequalled for its clarity of definition. The 100-inch reflector on Mount Wilson, of 1917, and the great 200-inch Hale telescope established on Mount Palomar in 1948-50, with its companion, the wide-angle 48-inch Schmidt, have revolutionized astronomical observations. Then there is the Mount Hamilton Observatory of 1938 and Texas's McDonald Observatory of 1939.

What has been discovered in the last half century with the aid of these powerful new instruments? No less than a whole new universe, of unimaginable size, which seems to be arranged in a hierarchy of units of increasing complexity. The radius of this universe is perhaps ten billion light years, though no one can say for certain because the ideas and findings of modern astronomy are in constant flux. The fundamental unit is the star, like our sun. The stars are often arranged in clusters (for groups or families of celestial objects seem characteristic of the new universe—and there is some evidence that all the stars may have been formed in clusters). The stars in turn, of different types and ages, are embedded in enormous galaxies of widely varying forms and sizes, and finally the galaxies themselves are gathered in clusters of just a few to many thousands, sometimes measuring as much as ten million light years across, all moving as a unit. In the arms of the galaxies and in the space between them are varying concentrations of cosmic dust and gas that assume increasing importance today, for from these concentrations, under the influence of gravitational attraction, the stars, planets and galaxies seem to have been formed.

The process of birth is not yet too well defined, but there is now an accepted cycle for the evolution of the stars, which are divided by astronomers into a number of types and classes according to their age and the material from which they were formed. The young stars, found usually in the dusty arms of the galaxies, are hot, blue and brilliant: the older stars, found at the center of spiral galaxies, in elliptical galaxies, or in globular star clusters are far less brilliant and are reddish in color, the more massive ones becoming huge red giants. There are many stages in between. All stars, however, spend most of their lives as thermonuclear furnaces, converting hydrogen into helium and radiating energy in the process. As the hydrogen fuel is used up the helium core grows heavier and hotter, making the star unstable, while deep within its interior additional thermonuclear processes convert the helium into heavier elements. Eventually the star swells, then collapses upon itself, turning into a dense, dead white dwarf and eventually, as it cools, into an invisible black dwarf. A number of stars (the novae and dwarf novae) flare up periodically as they age into an intense, brief brilliance, while a much smaller number, the supernovae, disintegrate in one immense explosion with a flash that is a good hundred million times brighter than that of our sun, spewing out in their death agonies the heavy elements in their interiors to enrich the cosmic dust and gas out of which new stars will be made. Only three supernovae explosions have been recorded in our own galaxy: the first in 1054 (its remains form the Crab Nebula), and two more in 1572, and 1604.

102 Six views showing various east-west and north-south positions of the huge 200-inch Hale telescope at Mount Palomar.
103 Cross-section of the older Mount Wilson observatory, also in California. In existence since 1904, Mount Wilson was set up under George Hale to study the sun. In 1917 the giant 100-inch telescope was completed, and with this telescope Edwin Hubble made his sensational investigation of the extra-galactic nebulae, including the theory of the recession of the galaxies. In 1948 the 6 million dollar, 200-inch Hale telescope took over.

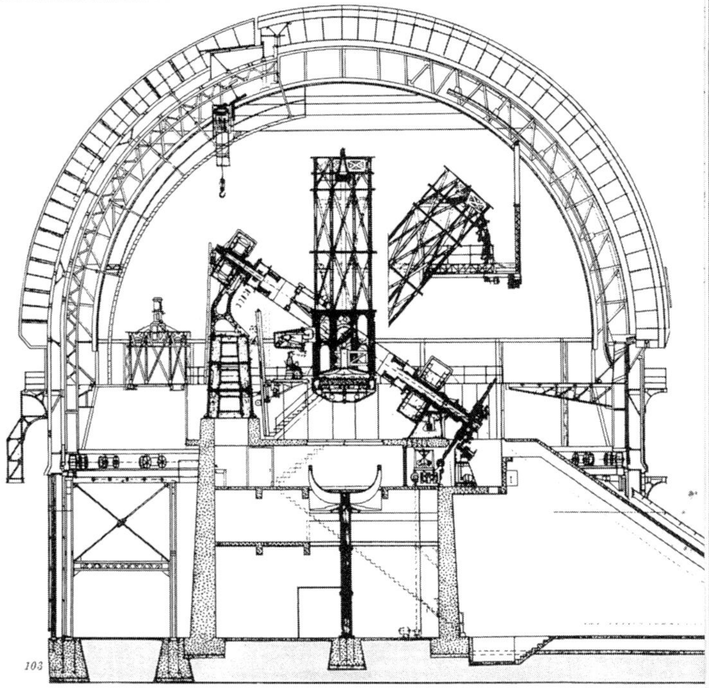

103

Maurice Fabre
A History of Land Transportation
Leisure Arts, London, 1964
Designed by Erik Nitsche
Illustrated at 56% actual size

Another volume from the same series as the previous example, this follows an identical pattern. The spread opposite shows a device used throughout the series – the massing together of a 'parade' of illustrations. The treatment is particularly appropriate here. Collecting all the compatible material for this witty and deceptively simple spread must have been a daunting task. To have got them all tonally consistent is yet more of an achievement.

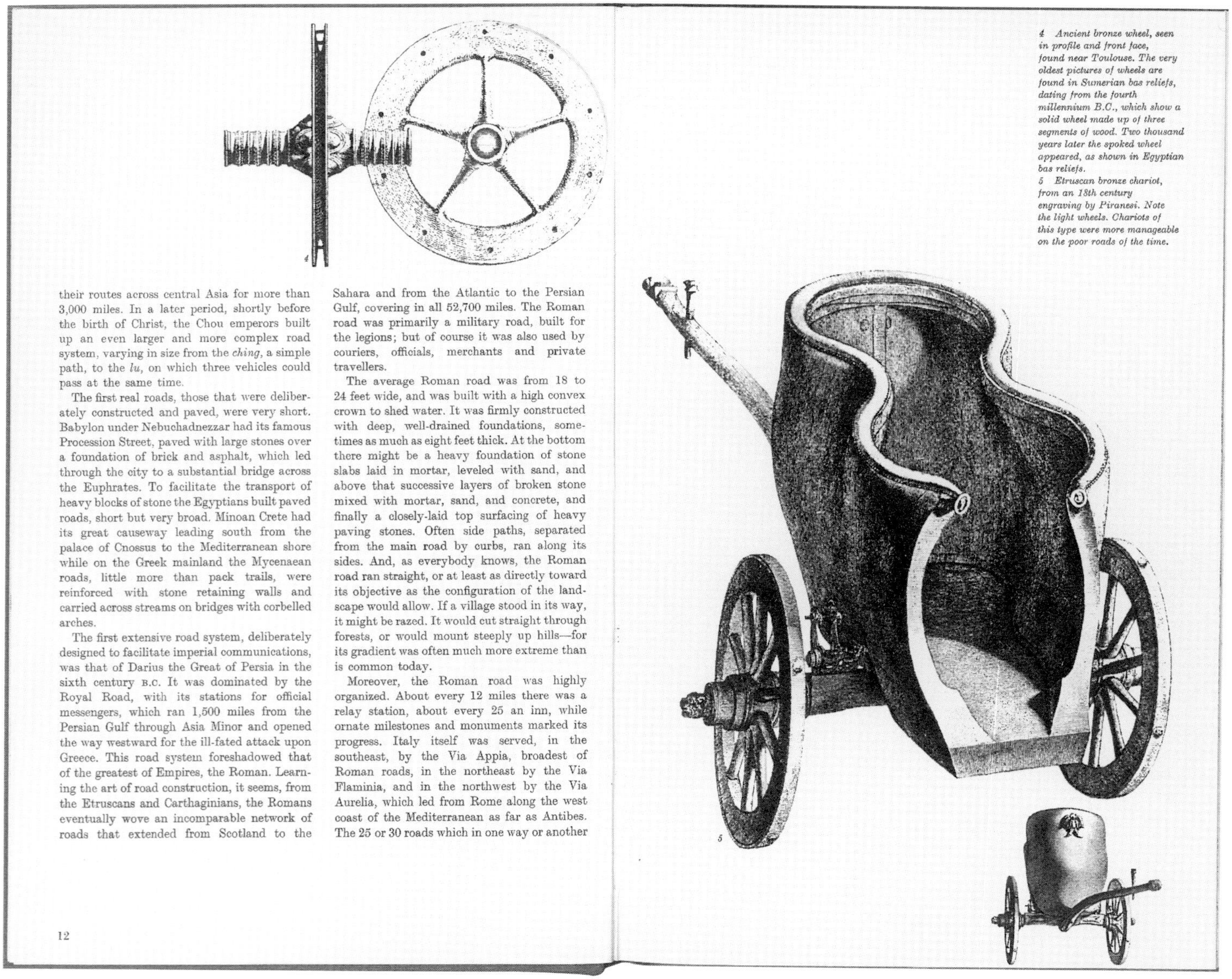

their routes across central Asia for more than 3,000 miles. In a later period, shortly before the birth of Christ, the Chou emperors built up an even larger and more complex road system, varying in size from the *ching*, a simple path, to the *lu*, on which three vehicles could pass at the same time.

The first real roads, those that were deliberately constructed and paved, were very short. Babylon under Nebuchadnezzar had its famous Procession Street, paved with large stones over a foundation of brick and asphalt, which led through the city to a substantial bridge across the Euphrates. To facilitate the transport of heavy blocks of stone the Egyptians built paved roads, short but very broad. Minoan Crete had its great causeway leading south from the palace of Cnossus to the Mediterranean shore while on the Greek mainland the Mycenaean roads, little more than pack trails, were reinforced with stone retaining walls and carried across streams on bridges with corbelled arches.

The first extensive road system, deliberately designed to facilitate imperial communications, was that of Darius the Great of Persia in the sixth century B.C. It was dominated by the Royal Road, with its stations for official messengers, which ran 1,500 miles from the Persian Gulf through Asia Minor and opened the way westward for the ill-fated attack upon Greece. This road system foreshadowed that of the greatest of Empires, the Roman. Learning the art of road construction, it seems, from the Etruscans and Carthaginians, the Romans eventually wove an incomparable network of roads that extended from Scotland to the Sahara and from the Atlantic to the Persian Gulf, covering in all 52,700 miles. The Roman road was primarily a military road, built for the legions; but of course it was also used by couriers, officials, merchants and private travellers.

The average Roman road was from 18 to 24 feet wide, and was built with a high convex crown to shed water. It was firmly constructed with deep, well-drained foundations, sometimes as much as eight feet thick. At the bottom there might be a heavy foundation of stone slabs laid in mortar, leveled with sand, and above that successive layers of broken stone mixed with mortar, sand, and concrete, and finally a closely-laid top surfacing of heavy paving stones. Often side paths, separated from the main road by curbs, ran along its sides. And, as everybody knows, the Roman road ran straight, or at least as directly toward its objective as the configuration of the landscape would allow. If a village stood in its way, it might be razed. It would cut straight through forests, or would mount steeply up hills—for its gradient was often much more extreme than is common today.

Moreover, the Roman road was highly organized. About every 12 miles there was a relay station, about every 25 an inn, while ornate milestones and monuments marked its progress. Italy itself was served, in the southeast, by the Via Appia, broadest of Roman roads, in the northeast by the Via Flaminia, and in the northwest by the Via Aurelia, which led from Rome along the west coast of the Mediterranean as far as Antibes. The 25 or 30 roads which in one way or another

12

4 Ancient bronze wheel, seen in profile and front face, found near Toulouse. The very oldest pictures of wheels are found in Sumerian bas reliefs, dating from the fourth millennium B.C., which show a solid wheel made up of three segments of wood. Two thousand years later the spoked wheel appeared, as shown in Egyptian bas reliefs.
5 Etruscan bronze chariot, from an 18th century engraving by Piranesi. Note the light wheels. Chariots of this type were more manageable on the poor roads of the time.

Daimler and son in their first car, 1886 (123); 1889 Daimler car (124); von Loon's 1895 car (125); Karl Benz in his 1887 car (127).

Daimler taxi, Berlin 1898 (128); Stoewer's first car, 1899 (129); 1903 sports car "Italia" (126 and 130); a 1906 Peugeot (131).

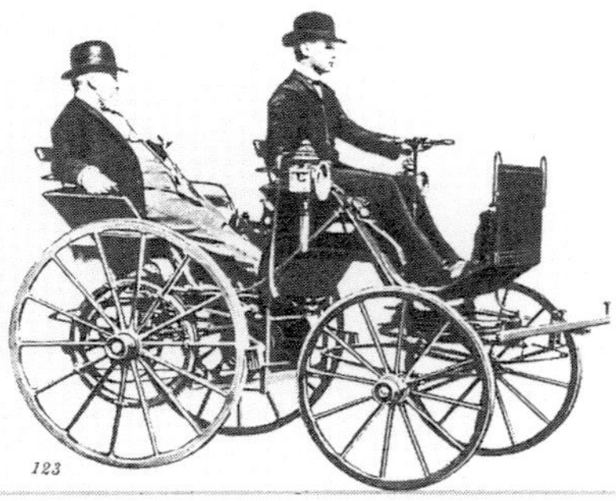

123

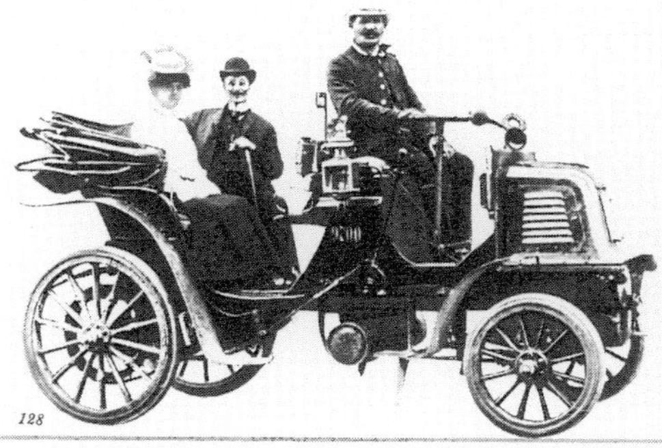

128

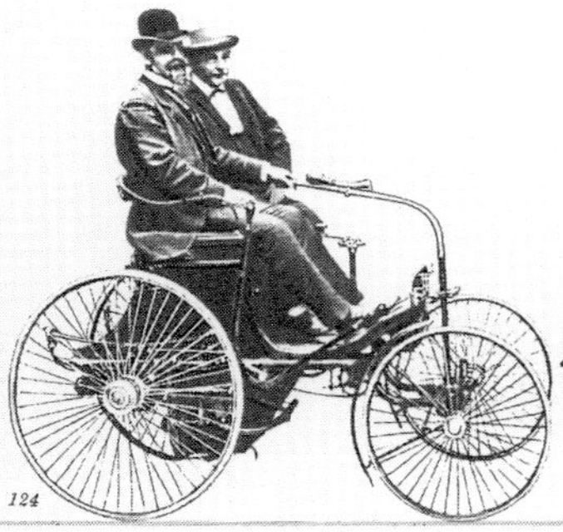

124

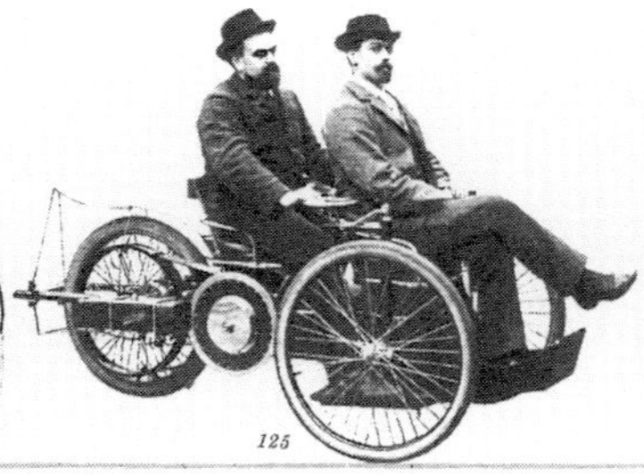

125

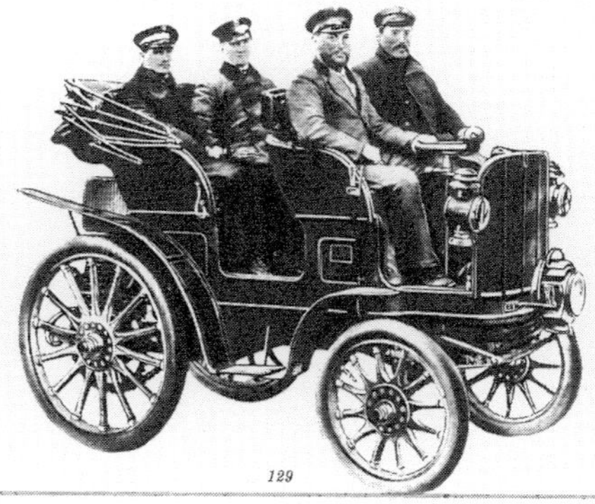

129

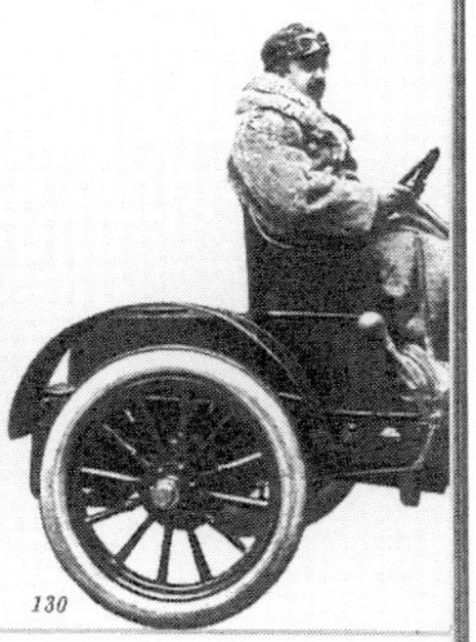

130

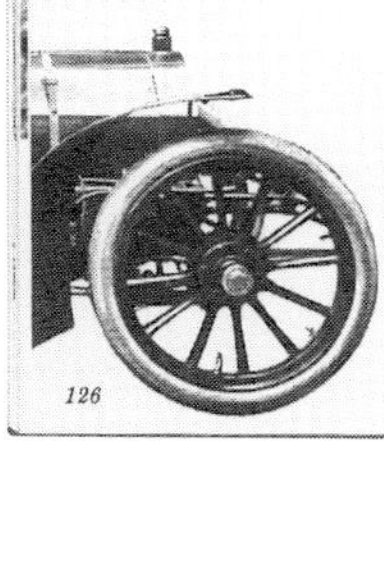

126

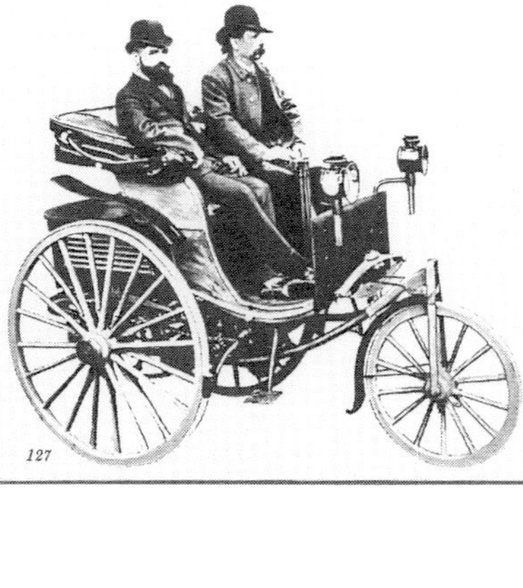

127

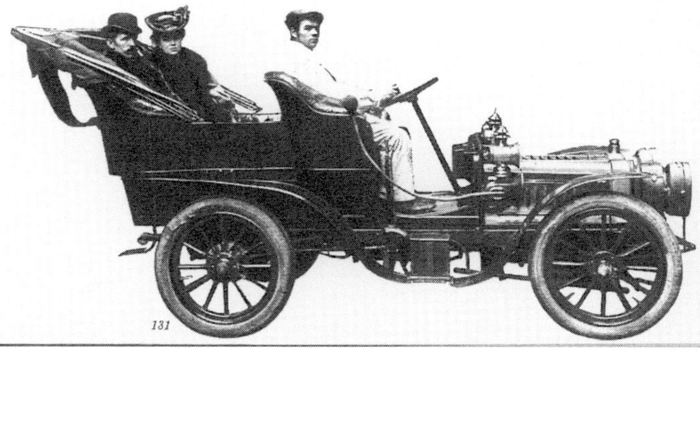

131

Paul Klee Notebooks Volume 2
The Nature of Nature
Edited by Jürg Spiller
Lund Humphries, London, 1973
Illustrated at 46% actual size

This is the English version of the original Swiss edition published by Schwabe Verlag, Basel, 1970. It is inconceivable that such diverse material, running to 450 pages of Volume 2 alone, could have been handled in such an orderly manner without the developments made by earlier Swiss designers. The problem is similar to that which Moholy-Nagy attempted to solve in his *Vision in Motion* (see pages 54-5) – to insert illustrations in the correct place within the text. But here the problem is more difficult: the illustrations are notes and sketches, and do not merely accompany or illustrate the text, they are part of the text. No designer is named. Presumably the editor created the layout himself, on a given three-column grid, with a horizontal grid line one-third down the page. But the English edition must have required considerable replanning. Who by? The translator, Heinz Norden? It is a remarkable achievement. The use of only two sizes of a single type (Grotesque 215, with its bold 216) adds to the control and clarity. Anything more would confuse. The counter-productive effect of trying too hard, demonstrated by the four type styles in *Vision in Motion*, has been avoided.

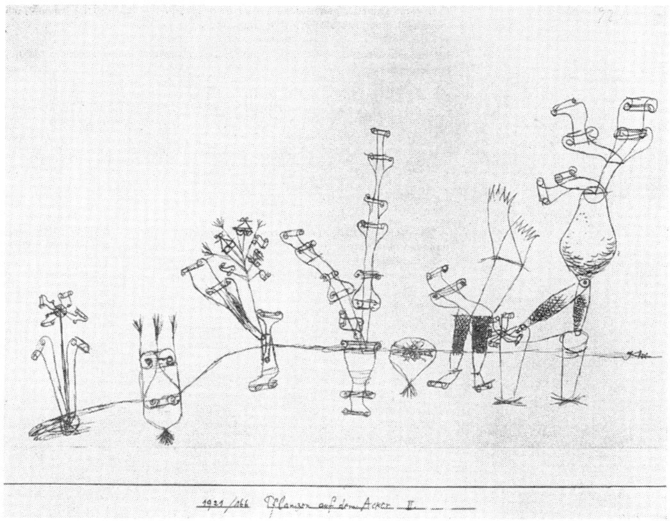

1921/166: *Plants in the field II.*
Seven growths in a row side by side.
Pen-and-ink. 26·6 × 14·6.

Diary entry, 1906/772:
'I am lovingly caring for the pear saplings brought from Italy and have actually transplanted one vigorous branch. This form of growing also constitutes a pretty experiment in capillary action.'

52

A particle, in other words, must be shaped in such a way as to lend itself to movement and conduction. For particles have no separate existence, merely serving in support of larger functions. They mediate – they are the middle links that receive and transmit.
A particle subserves some higher process that is capable of further development. It is a building-brick in a higher order which it transmits in several directions, over into three dimensions.

In the matter of plants: On one occasion, for example, I managed to root a slip in the following manner:

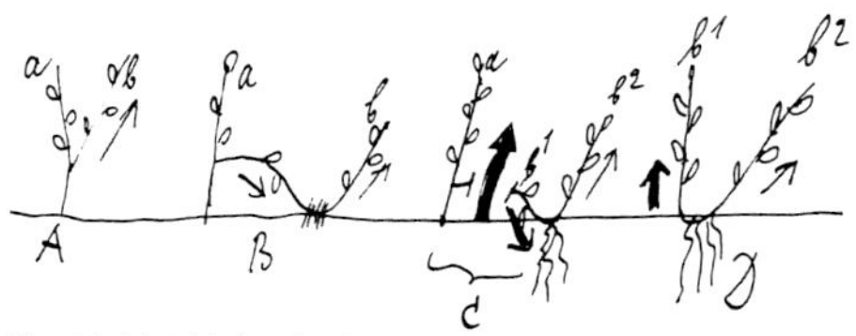

The original plant A had two branches, a and b. When it had reached stage B, I bent branch b down into the soil, where I secured it in the middle. After a lapse of time sufficient for rooting, I cut branch b close to branch a (Stage C), thus gaining a separate new plant with the branches b1 and b2. At Stage D, these two branches are shown having grown further, b2 in the original direction, b1 in the one opposite. I conclude that the appropriate structures must adapt themselves to these two directions, so that the sap may flow both up and down.

53

One- and two-dimensional square movement on a pictorial base. 39/115.
Movement: two-dimensional and double-directed progressions. Extension and contraction. 17/104a.
Measure and weight and their movement:
Expansion–imponsion, rarefaction–condensation. 42/2.
Movement of the square from normal to abnormal. 17/48.
Motion sequence (genetic) from within to without. Series of squares represented spatially. 17/69.
Augmentation modes: shift, rotation, reflection. An example of complementary reversal. 60/71.

Approach, essence, semblance.
Essence contrasted with semblance.
Dynamic forces. Concepts: dynamic form–limiting form.
Interior–exterior. 8/7.

Representation by essence and by appearance.

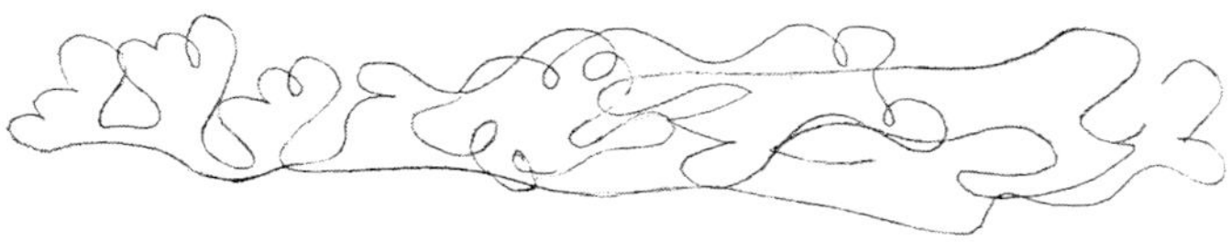

Drawing from the Theory of form and figuration. 9/61a.

114

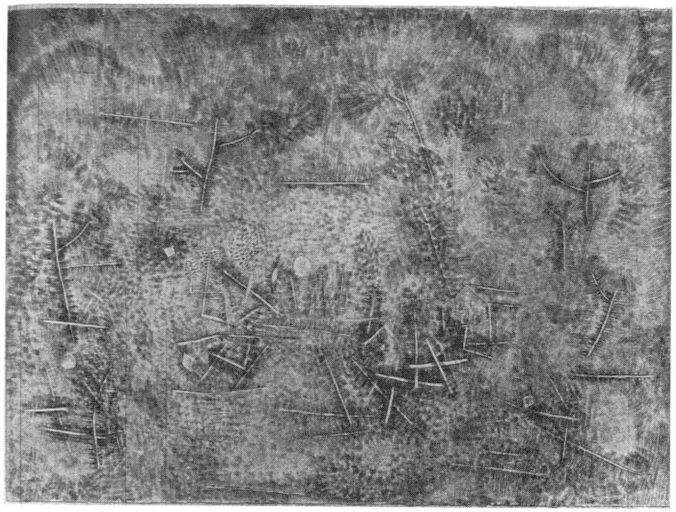

1926/B 8: *Forest clearing.*
Watercolour. 36·7 × 51·2.

115

The Nature of Nature continued

The spaces within the text, which are necessary to allow the illustrations to be placed correctly, are strangely unworrying. The switching to three columns, even for the main text, is also self-explanatory and therefore understandable and acceptable even when they go off-grid, as in the fourth spread, in order to relate to and range with the illustration beneath. Captions may be placed above or below the illustrations of the paintings (themselves sometimes aligned on the top, sometimes on the grid line one-third down) – whichever suits the overall pattern of the spread. Throughout, the arrangement of the text has been the primary consideration, but the overall mise-en-page – pure aesthetics – has played an important part in adjusting the final positioning.

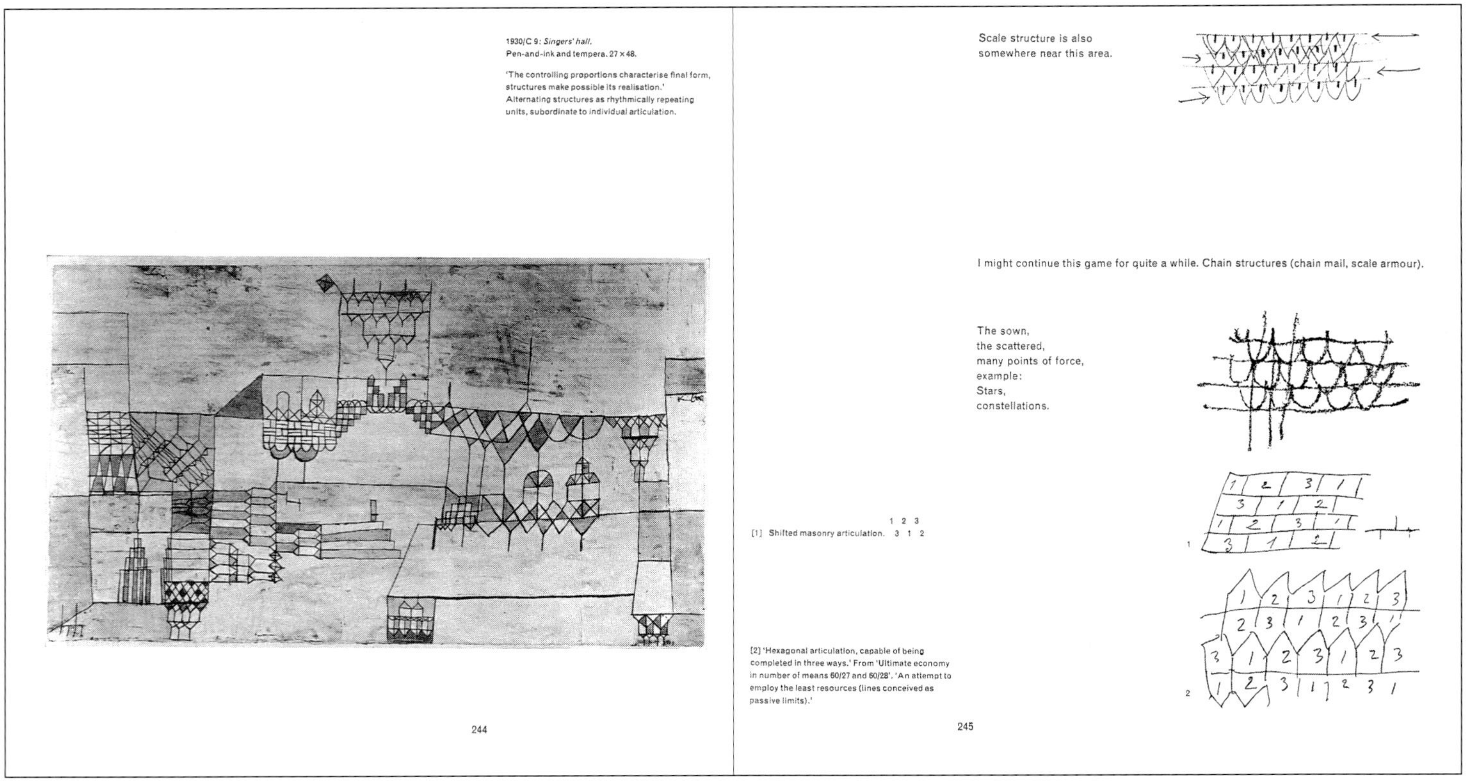

1930/C 9: *Singers' hall.*
Pen-and-ink and tempera. 27 × 48.

'The controlling proportions characterise final form, structures make possible its realisation.' Alternating structures as rhythmically repeating units, subordinate to individual articulation.

244

Scale structure is also somewhere near this area.

I might continue this game for quite a while. Chain structures (chain mail, scale armour).

The sown,
the scattered,
many points of force,
example:
Stars,
constellations.

1 2 3
[1] Shifted masonry articulation. 3 1 2

[2] 'Hexagonal articulation, capable of being completed in three ways.' From 'Ultimate economy in number of means 60/27 and 60/28'. 'An attempt to employ the least resources (lines conceived as passive limits).'

245

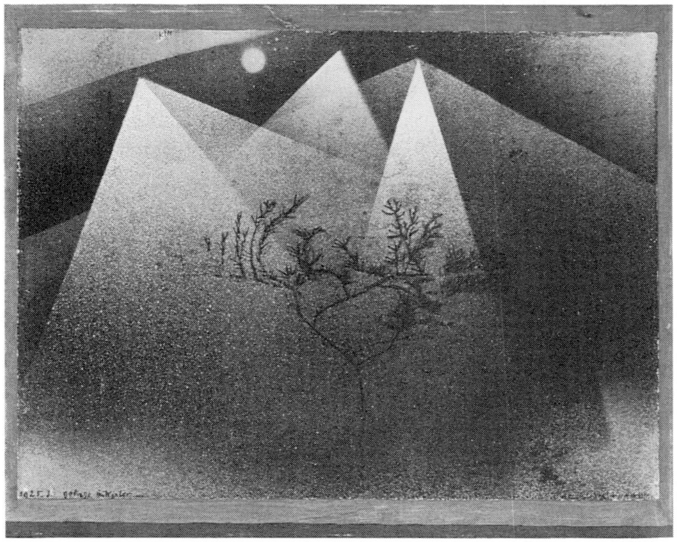

1925/3: *Mountains in winter.*
Watercolour with air brush. 28 × 37.

390

White peak

Deep fall
Normal grey base
Action commences

Black peak
Figuration example 60/45.

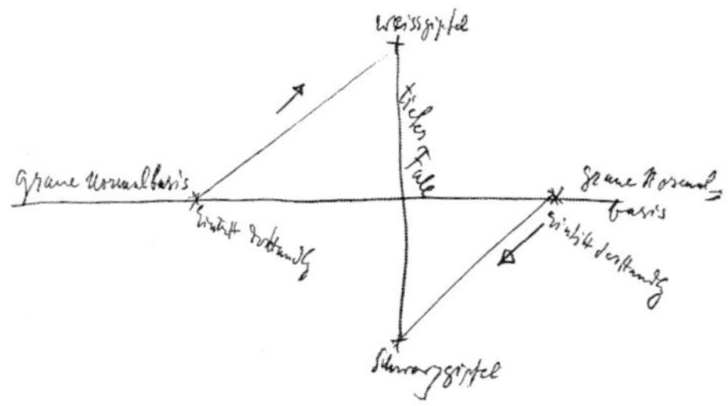

A. Wide range,
the black low and white high
visibly intervening in the action.
This wide swing of the pendulum
from black to white
lends force to the action.

Within a wide range, the dramatic character moves in steps from remote control by the poles

all the way to open struggle, the sharp clash of extremes.

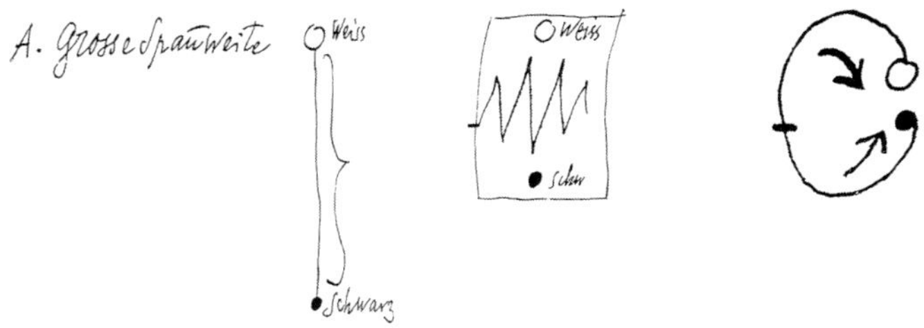

391

the british new typography

Four years after Tschichold's argument with Max Bill, the New Typography, and the *new* New Typography, were making their belated impact on the British scene at the Central School of Arts & Crafts in London. The two designers responsible were both young. Anthony Froshaug was born in 1920, Herbert Spencer in 1924. Already a name in the typographic world by 1949, Spencer began teaching, well, hardly the *new* generation; effectively, the *same* generation.

Froshaug was a designer of small-scale work – stationery, simple exhibition catalogues, leaflets, which he printed himself. His sensitive layouts, elegant and rational, were strongly influenced by Tschichold's early work. He normally restricted his type to two weights of Gill – roman and bold – and used them in a limited number of small sizes. His book design for *The Wanderer (Le Grand Meaulnes)*, Paul Elek, 1947, was set in Bodoni. He was an inspired teacher, a formative influence who taught students to think clearly and logically. He later taught at Ulm, where he designed the *Quarterly Review* in impeccable minimalist style.

Very different, and perhaps in the long term more widely influential, was Herbert Spencer. His analysis of a problem would result in an uncomplicated answer: practical, functional, straightforward. It sounds dull, which it sometimes was, but, at its best, an apparently simple design concealed sensitive organisation. He was one of the first British designers (if not *the* first) to design books using a grid (the biennial *Designers in Britain*). They were remarkably different from Swiss work: the effect was more relaxed, but the pattern-making in these mainly pictorial books was very carefully planned. The large numbers of books he designed for Lund Humphries from 1950 to 1975 were some of the most elegant and professional illustrated books produced in this country. He died as I was writing this book.

The Central School tradition continued long after Froshaug and Spencer had left. Their students often became part-time teachers in other schools, spreading the gospel; many went on to become the big guns of British typographic design. Lacking the innate flair of the Italians or the Swiss, British designers seemed to find the sanity and logic of the new typography congenial. Their work did its job very effectively, and reflected the zeitgeist of post-war Britain, with its social reforms, planning, and hope for the future.

There was no looking back. Book packagers bustled in, well aware of the commercial advantages of ensuring professionalism in every aspect of bookmaking, including design. In a world still peopled by The Gentlemen, they were The Players. The books created were usually well illustrated. This new demand – and the British were (still are) often rather good at publishing, especially for the growing international market – ensured the continuance of the grid tradition, even if the results were sometimes no more than practical and efficient.

Some British books of the 1960s and 1970s were less than that: as grey in their design as in their printing (these were the depressing years of the early general use of offset and film-setting). The original Swiss ruthlessness had become watered-down in the English way. Yet a few design groups, often comprised, in whole or in part, of ex-Central School students, were producing Swiss-influenced work of exceptional quality in fields other than bookmaking. Ken Briggs's work for the National Theatre, The Worshipful Company of Goldsmiths, or the Burrell Collection was particularly notable in its powerful combination of genuine Swiss rigour tempered by dramatic photographs or period illustrations, colour, and (often) imaginative choice of typeface. Other design groups such as Pentagram also effectively adopted – or adapted – Swiss principles. Some attempts were made to evade the constrictions of the grid, but generally it was too friendly a refuge from nerve-racking adventures in free design for it to be foregone.

The remarkable improvements in printing standards since the 1990s seem to have encouraged publishers of art and architecture books (especially) to become more adventurous. These works, heavily illustrated, often in colour throughout, are finely produced in every way. Exhibition catalogues, too, have advanced from the earlier eight-page, poorly-printed affair with a few miserably reproduced half-tones. Marketing ploy this fresh professionalism may be, but the resulting books and catalogues are very desirable objects. Reacting to the new opportunities offered, designers picked up the principles of grid-dependent design (which had degenerated into a tired formula), dusted them off and seriously re-examined ways of using the grid, asymmetry and space without ignoring practicalities, sane use of type, or readers' requirements.

Invitation card
Designed by Anthony Froshaug, 1949
Illustrated actual size

A lot of the work of the late 1940s looks dated; but the unforced modernism of this Froshaug design, in which an analytical intellect exploits a sensitive feeling for space, stands up well to scrutiny today. The sense of the text, carefully modulated, is allowed to dictate layout. Designs like this, clearly indebted to Tschichold, were characteristic of Central School typography, and formed the basis of much subsequent British work, although many of its subtleties were lost over time. A pity, for despite its pared-down elements there is nothing banal about it; quite the reverse. To arrive at such deceptive simplicity is hard work. Perhaps a chaotic private life (which Froshaug had) is counteracted by creating calm and controlled designs like this.

Froshaug mannerisms such as laterally centred full points derived from Tschichold may not have survived long; but the varied, finely considered vertical spacing of lines; the economy with which the sense of the first line is clarified; the startling single word in black letter set amongst all that Gill; the positioning of the design within the overall space, with unequal margins all round; even the rather un-modernist use of a line of letterspaced caps: all this is the work of a master. Today's designers – book designers included – could learn a lot from a careful study of this unpretentious little invitation card.

Rudolf Steiner Hall *Licensee F W Goodman* 33 Park Road London N W I

Goethe Bicentenary Presentation / 7pm 25 & 26 April 1949

ELEONORE SCHJELDERUP

in her original dramatic rendering in German of Goethe's **Faust**
First appearance in England after successful tour of Western Germany where Press commented: an astonishing achievement . the multitude of characters come to life through El. Schjelderup's great artistry . an arresting personality . in the front rank of German artists

Advance enquiries HAMpstead 36 09
Box Office open 10-1 daily from Monday 18 April PADdington 99 67

Designers in Britain 4
Edited and designed by Herbert Spencer
Society of Industrial Artists
with Alan Wingate, London, 1954
Illustrated at 43% actual size

Although Herbert Spencer would quickly dismiss the idea that art played any part in design, articles in his magazine *Typographica* reveal a serious interest in the 'arty' pioneers. Much of his own work simply required commonsense thinking (after all, he wrote the book *Design in Business Printing*, which stressed practical needs, not aesthetics). Yet despite his calm, undemonstrative and rather enigmatic personality, when the opportunity arose, as in *Designers in Britain*, his feel for the mise-en-page equalled, even surpassed, that of the best Swiss design. Not for him Max Bill's favourite device of aligning the material on top and (more or less) bottom margins, letting the space between muddle along as best it may. Spencer did the opposite: he created a strong picture pattern which would relate to the outer margins without necessarily meeting them. Simple, balanced, clear and sane, his designs left no loose ends to flap around, unrelated to other parts, or the whole.

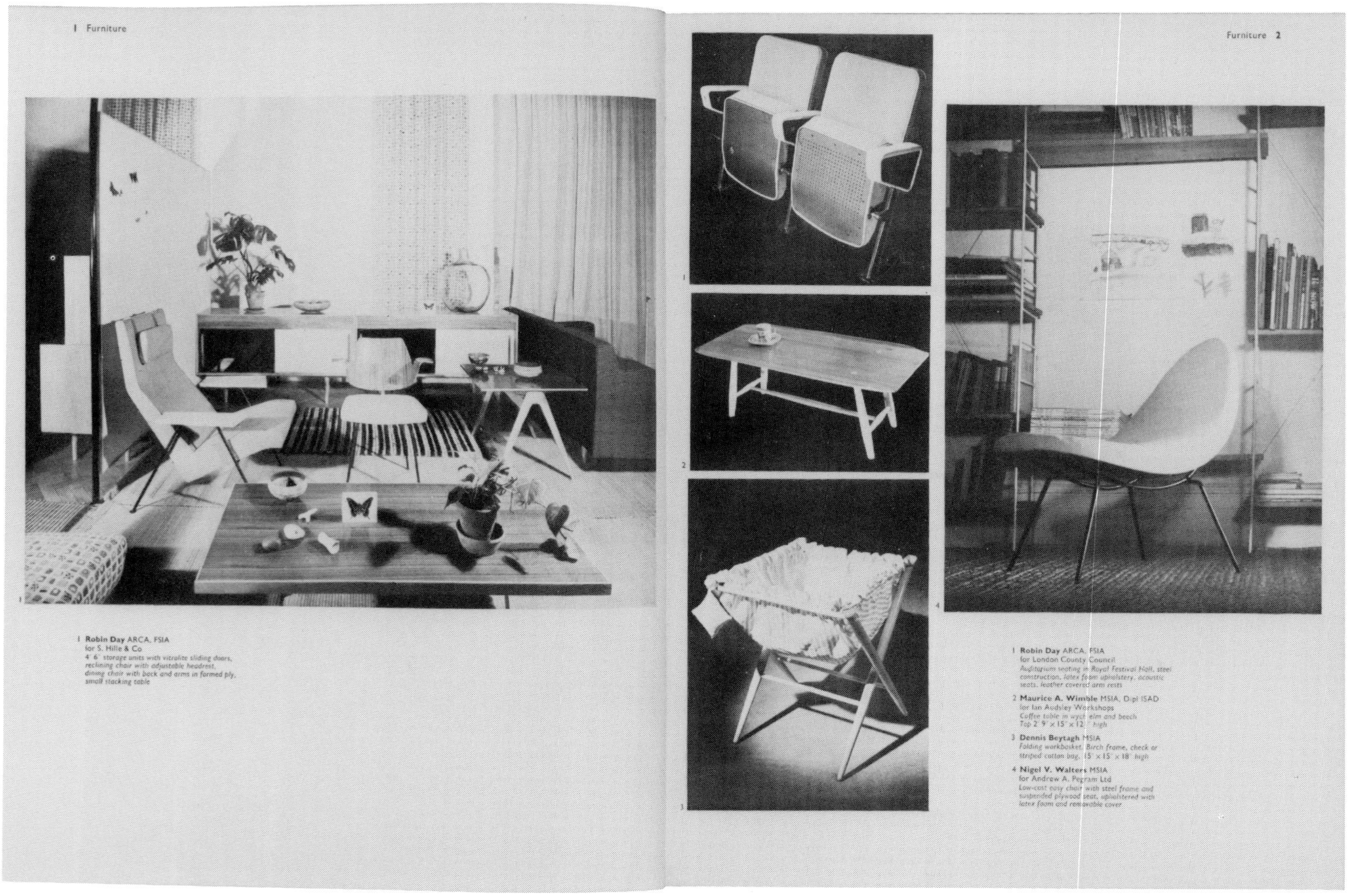

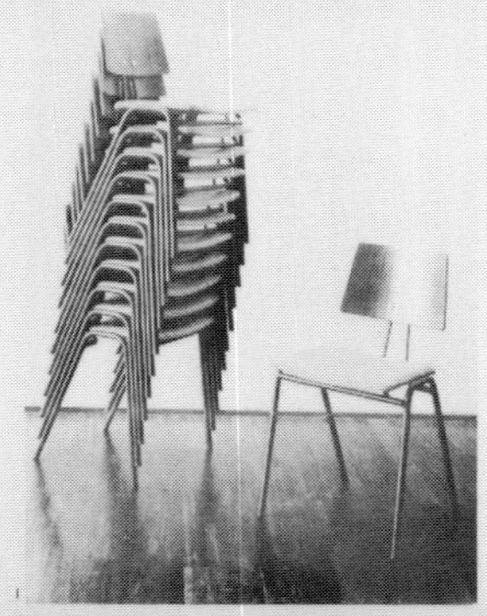
1

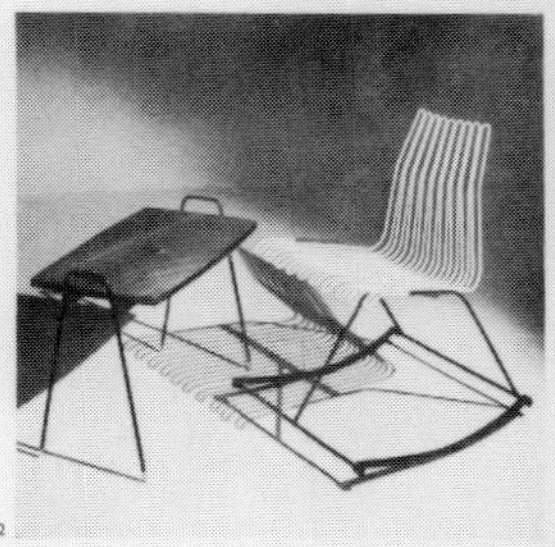
2

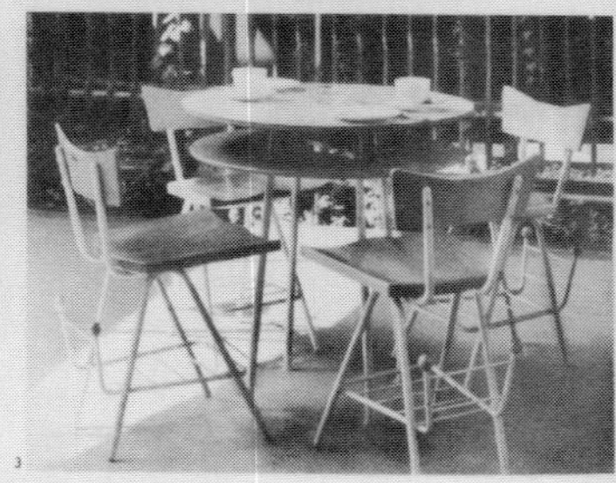
3

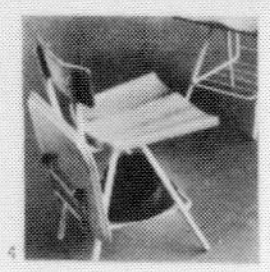
4

1 **Robin Day** ARCA, FSIA
for Kingfisher Ltd
Stacking chair: steel frame, ply back, padded seat

2 **Ernest Race** FSIA
for Time-Life International
Manufactured by Ernest Race Ltd
Nesting rocking chair in enamelled steel rod. Nesting coffee table: enamelled steel rod with turned brass feet, top of oiled teak

3, 4 **Neville Ward** B Arch, ARIBA, FSIA and **Frank Austin** FSIA of Ward & Austin
for Charles Hagenbach Ltd
Restaurant furniture

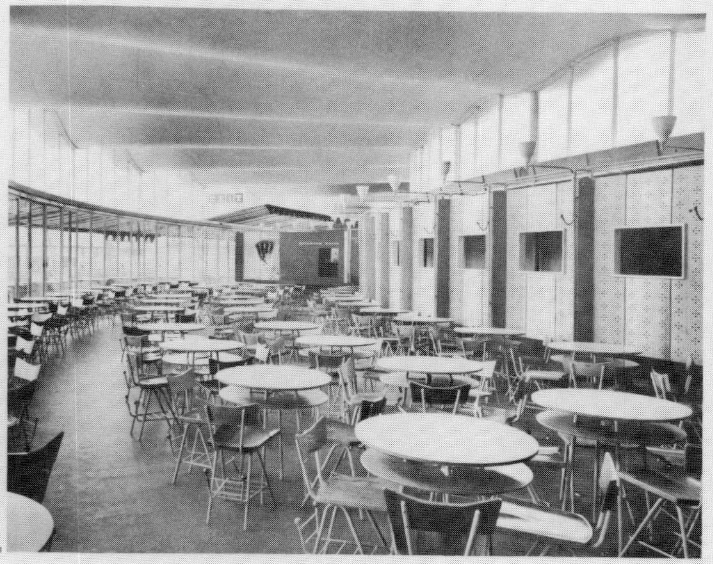
1

1 **Neville Ward** B Arch, ARIBA, FSIA
Frank Austin FSIA and
Mary Ward B Arch, ARIBA
for Festival of Britain
Interior Thameside restaurant

Designers in Britain continued

This was designed in 1953, the same year as Lohse's book on exhibition design (see pages 112-13) and the second Le Corbusier volume I show (see page 101). It could never be taken for Swiss work. While employing the same principle of a grid, Spencer effectively re-invented it. Flexible, playing permutations on two widths of columns, his version was more sophisticated than the form the Swiss were then using, while avoiding the obsessive complexity of some of their later grids. Space and structure were just as important, but these pages are almost organic in their sense of movement, and less hard-edged. Even the spread of illustrations, with its awkward mix of rectangles and free shapes, is given a formal pattern. Captions, clearly organised, are set in only one size of Gill, in bold, roman and italic (Tschichold would have approved). The grid was shown on the endpapers. Spencer was a pioneer in exploiting so comprehensively its use in book design. Produced only four years after he and Froshaug started their seminal teaching at the Central, this book has all the freshness of a spring morning, the dew still on the grass ... It was to be a few years before the stale air of consumerism started to haze this vision of a new design for a new society.

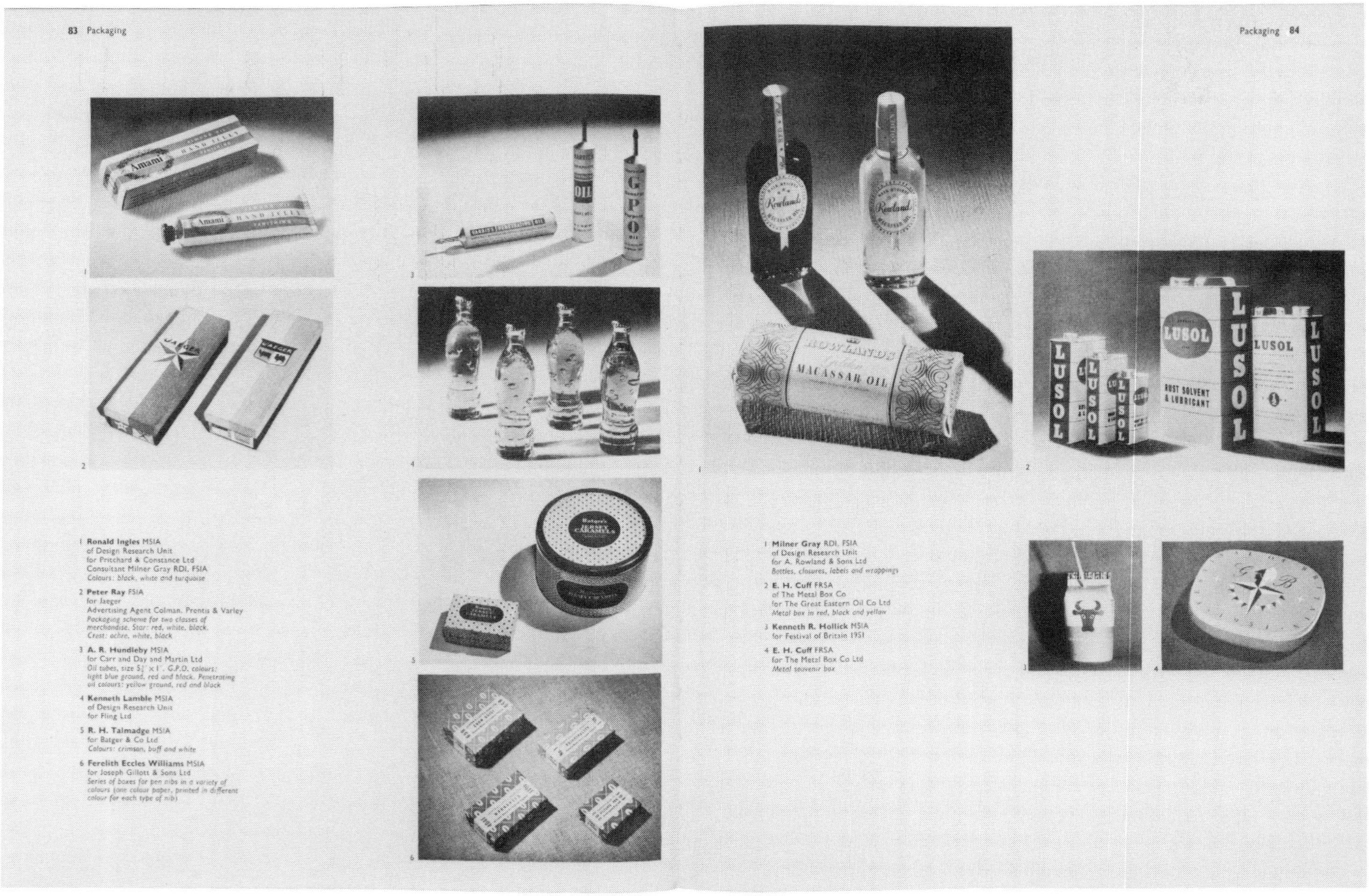

83 Packaging

1 **Ronald Ingles** MSIA
of Design Research Unit
for Pritchard & Constance Ltd
Consultant Milner Gray RDI, FSIA
Colours: black, white and turquoise

2 **Peter Ray** FSIA
for Jaeger
Advertising Agent Colman, Prentis & Varley
Packaging scheme for two classes of merchandise. Star: red, white, black. Crest: ochre, white, black

3 **A. R. Hundleby** MSIA
for Carr and Day and Martin Ltd
Oil tubes, size 5¼" × 1". G.P.O. colours: light blue ground, red and black. Penetrating oil colours: yellow ground, red and black

4 **Kenneth Lamble** MSIA
of Design Research Unit
for Fling Ltd

5 **R. H. Talmadge** MSIA
for Batger & Co Ltd
Colours: crimson, buff and white

6 **Ferelith Eccles Williams** MSIA
for Joseph Gillott & Sons Ltd
Series of boxes for pen nibs in a variety of colours (one colour paper, printed in different colour for each type of nib)

Packaging **84**

1 **Milner Gray** RDI, FSIA
of Design Research Unit
for A. Rowland & Sons Ltd
Bottles, closures, labels and wrappings

2 **E. H. Cuff** FRSA
of The Metal Box Co
for The Great Eastern Oil Co Ltd
Metal box in red, black and yellow

3 **Kenneth R. Hollick** MSIA
for Festival of Britain 1951

4 **E. H. Cuff** FRSA
for The Metal Box Co Ltd
Metal souvenir box

As an apprentice designer in the few weeks before being transformed into 22912933 Signalman Bartram at Catterick's infamous Le Cateau lines, I worked on this volume.

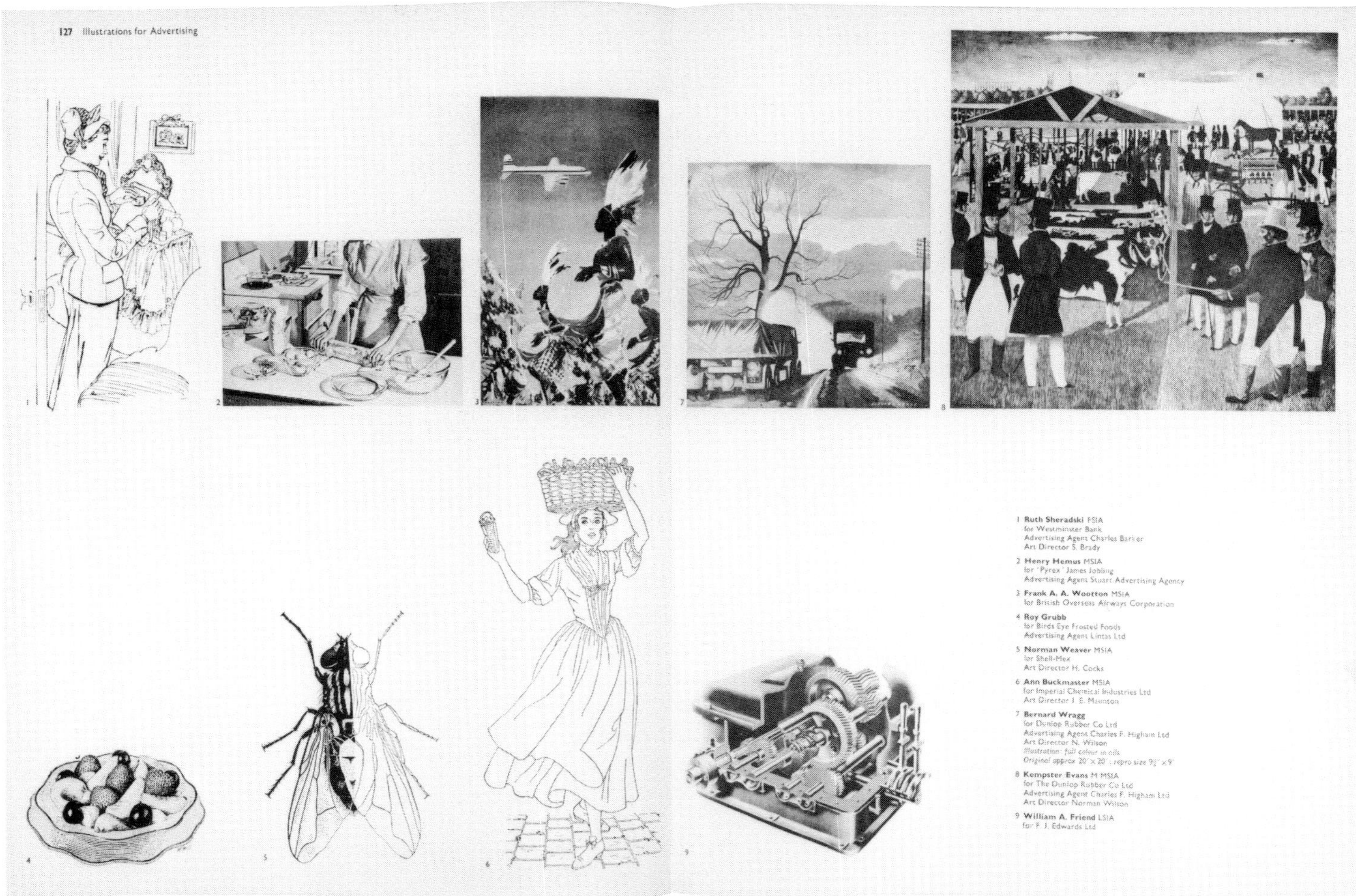

127 Illustrations for Advertising

1 **Ruth Sheradski** FSIA
for Westminster Bank
Advertising Agent Charles Barker
Art Director S. Brady

2 **Henry Hemus** MSIA
for 'Pyrex' James Jobling
Advertising Agent Stuart Advertising Agency

3 **Frank A. A. Wootton** MSIA
for British Overseas Airways Corporation

4 **Roy Grubb**
for Birds Eye Frosted Foods
Advertising Agent Lintas Ltd

5 **Norman Weaver** MSIA
for Shell-Mex
Art Director H. Cocks

6 **Ann Buckmaster** MSIA
for Imperial Chemical Industries Ltd
Art Director J. E. Maunton

7 **Bernard Wragg**
for Dunlop Rubber Co Ltd
Advertising Agent Charles F. Higham Ltd
Art Director N. Wilson
Illustration: full colour in oils
Original approx 20″ × 20″; repro size 9½″ × 9″

8 **Kempster Evans** M MSIA
for The Dunlop Rubber Co Ltd
Advertising Agent Charles F. Higham Ltd
Art Director Norman Wilson

9 **William A. Friend** LSIA
for F. J. Edwards Ltd

Designers in Britain continued

It is not merely the use of Gill which places the *Designers in Britain* title page in the early 1950s; its clean and simple design is characteristic of the period, and particularly characteristic of Spencer's style at the time. That simplicity is more difficult to arrive at successfully than it looks. My publisher said the design looked like one of mine. If only. But I am not ashamed that, nearly fifty years later, he made the connection.

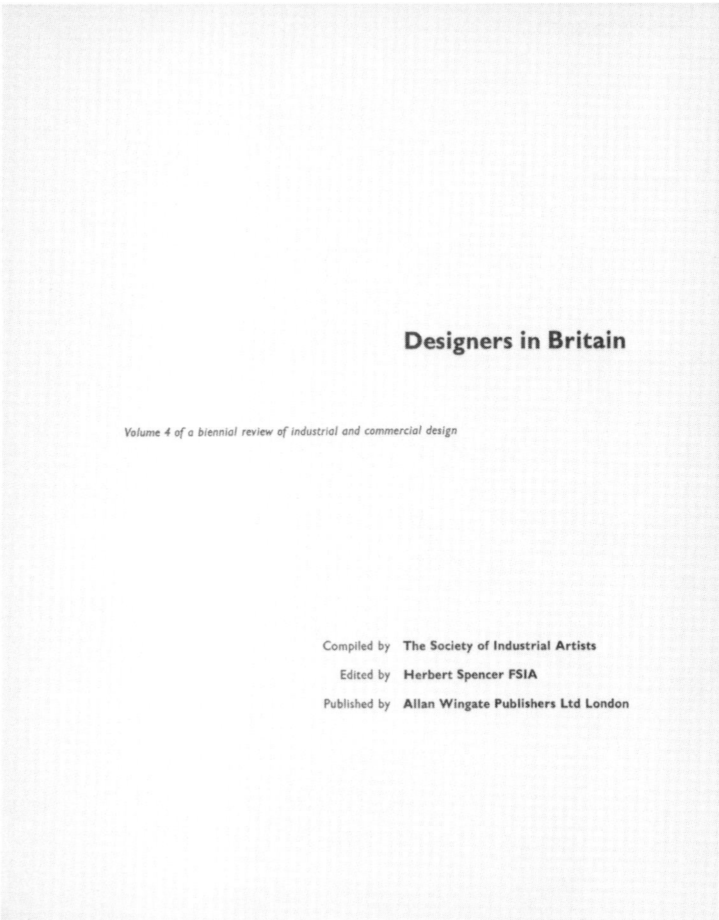

Designers in Britain

Volume 4 of a biennial review of industrial and commercial design

Compiled by **The Society of Industrial Artists**
Edited by **Herbert Spencer FSIA**
Published by **Allan Wingate Publishers Ltd London**

John B Hilling: *Cardiff and the Valleys*
Lund Humphries, London, 1973
Designed by Herbert Spencer
and Christine Charlton
Illustrated at 44% actual size

Emphasised by the use of fashionable Helvetica (replacing Gill), a more direct influence of Swiss New Typography is apparent in this powerful 1973 design; yet it is not aped slavishly. Helvetica seemed to encourage games with alignment, as with the i and the h here. This alignment is continued down the page, and it also follows the main grid line of the text pages. But Spencer never allowed such carefully worked-out consistency to dominate, or to result in a sterile formula.

The author's name, set here in the tight spacing normally used for Helvetica, should have been given a little attention.

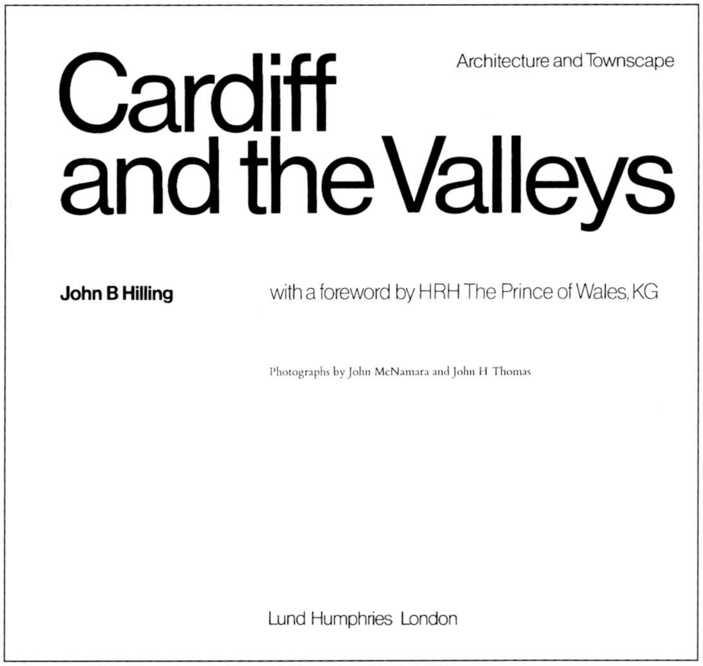

Architecture and Townscape

Cardiff
and the Valleys

John B Hilling

with a foreword by HRH The Prince of Wales, KG

Photographs by John McNamara and John H Thomas

Lund Humphries London

Georg Germann: *Gothic Revival*
Lund Humphries, London, 1972
Designed by Herbert Spencer
and Christine Charlton
Illustrated at 44% actual size

No dogmatic theorist in the Bill mould, Spencer was never wholly committed to using sanserifs or grotesques. Here, where such types would clearly have been inappropriate, the text is in Old Style No 2. The grid devised not only allows for lengthy marginal notes, but also for figure references (in bold). Type is ranged left – Spencer always seemed more partial to this than Swiss designers, and I can only agree with his preference. If it is not carefully done, it can result in a very ragged right-hand edge; but the benefit of even wordspacing outweighs this, and type certainly looks better this way. If word breaks are acceptable, then undue variation in line length can be avoided, although some typographers are dogmatic in their claim that one of the main advantages of unjustified setting is that words are *not* broken. Myself, I think it often advisable in narrow measures, but less important in wider ones, as in this example.

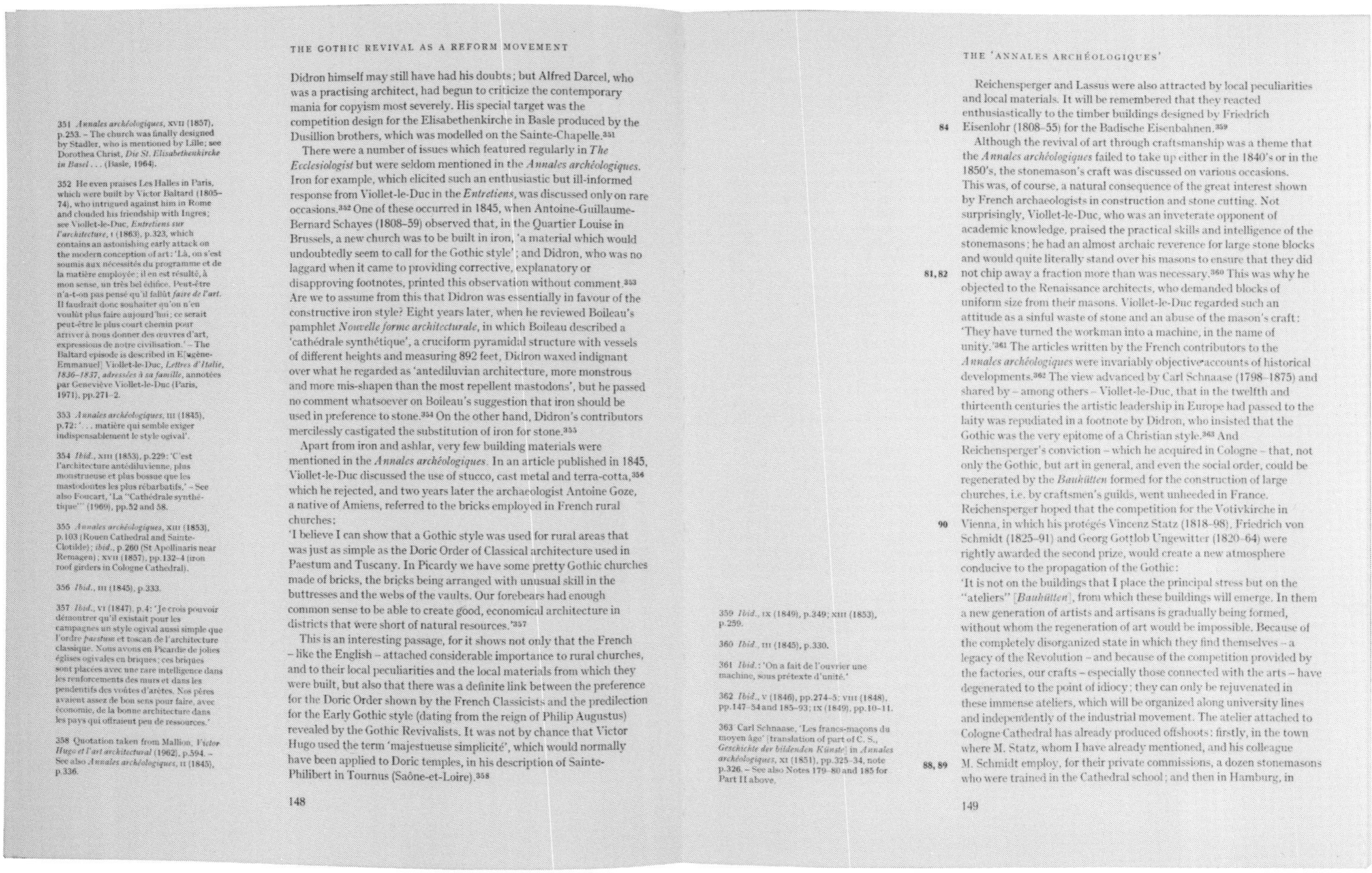
THE GOTHIC REVIVAL AS A REFORM MOVEMENT

351 *Annales archéologiques*, XVII (1857), p.253. – The church was finally designed by Stadler, who is mentioned by Lille; see Dorothea Christ, *Die St. Elisabethenkirche in Basel* ... (Basle, 1964).

352 He even praises Les Halles in Paris, which were built by Victor Baltard (1805–74), who intrigued against him in Rome and clouded his friendship with Ingres; see Viollet-le-Duc, *Entretiens sur l'architecture*, I (1863), p.323, which contains an astonishing early attack on the modern conception of art: 'Là, on s'est soumis aux nécessités du programme et de la matière employée; il en est résulté, à mon sense, un très bel édifice. Peut-être n'a-t-on pas pensé qu'il fallût *faire de l'art*. Il faudrait donc souhaiter qu'on n'en voulût plus faire aujourd'hui; ce serait peut-être le plus court chemin pour arriver à nous donner des œuvres d'art, expressions de notre civilisation.' – The Baltard episode is described in E[ugène-Emmanuel] Viollet-le-Duc, *Lettres d'Italie, 1836–1837, adressées à sa famille*, annotées par Geneviève Viollet-le-Duc (Paris, 1971), pp.271–2.

353 *Annales archéologiques*, III (1845), p.72: '... matière qui semble exiger indispensablement le style ogival'.

354 *Ibid.*, XIII (1853), p.229: 'C'est l'architecture antédiluvienne, plus monstrueuse et plus bossue que les mastodontes les plus rébarbatifs.' – See also Foucart, 'La "Cathédrale synthétique"' (1969), pp.52 and 58.

355 *Annales archéologiques*, XIII (1853), p.103 (Rouen Cathedral and Sainte-Clotilde); *ibid.*, p.260 (St Apollinaris near Remagen); XVII (1857), pp.132–4 (iron roof girders in Cologne Cathedral).

356 *Ibid.*, III (1845), p.333.

357 *Ibid.*, VI (1847), p.4: 'Je crois pouvoir démontrer qu'il existait pour les campagnes un style ogival aussi simple que l'ordre *paestum* et toscan de l'architecture classique. Nous avons en Picardie de jolies églises ogivales en briques; ces briques sont placées avec une rare intelligence dans les renforcements des murs et dans les pendentifs des voûtes d'arêtes. Nos pères avaient assez de bon sens pour faire, avec économie, de la bonne architecture dans les pays qui offraient peu de ressources.'

358 Quotation taken from Mallion, *Victor Hugo et l'art architectural* (1962), p.594. – See also *Annales archéologiques*, II (1845), p.336.

Didron himself may still have had his doubts; but Alfred Darcel, who was a practising architect, had begun to criticize the contemporary mania for copyism most severely. His special target was the competition design for the Elisabethenkirche in Basle produced by the Dusillion brothers, which was modelled on the Sainte-Chapelle.[351]

There were a number of issues which featured regularly in *The Ecclesiologist* but were seldom mentioned in the *Annales archéologiques*. Iron for example, which elicited such an enthusiastic but ill-informed response from Viollet-le-Duc in the *Entretiens*, was discussed only on rare occasions.[352] One of these occurred in 1845, when Antoine-Guillaume-Bernard Schayes (1808–59) observed that, in the Quartier Louise in Brussels, a new church was to be built in iron, 'a material which would undoubtedly seem to call for the Gothic style'; and Didron, who was no laggard when it came to providing corrective, explanatory or disapproving footnotes, printed this observation without comment.[353] Are we to assume from this that Didron was essentially in favour of the constructive iron style? Eight years later, when he reviewed Boileau's pamphlet *Nouvelle forme architecturale*, in which Boileau described a 'cathédrale synthétique', a cruciform pyramidal structure with vessels of different heights and measuring 892 feet, Didron waxed indignant over what he regarded as 'antediluvian architecture, more monstrous and more mis-shapen than the most repellent mastodons', but he passed no comment whatsoever on Boileau's suggestion that iron should be used in preference to stone.[354] On the other hand, Didron's contributors mercilessly castigated the substitution of iron for stone.[355]

Apart from iron and ashlar, very few building materials were mentioned in the *Annales archéologiques*. In an article published in 1845, Viollet-le-Duc discussed the use of stucco, cast metal and terra-cotta,[356] which he rejected, and two years later the archaeologist Antoine Goze, a native of Amiens, referred to the bricks employed in French rural churches:

'I believe I can show that a Gothic style was used for rural areas that was just as simple as the Doric Order of Classical architecture used in Paestum and Tuscany. In Picardy we have some pretty Gothic churches made of bricks, the bricks being arranged with unusual skill in the buttresses and the webs of the vaults. Our forebears had enough common sense to be able to create good, economical architecture in districts that were short of natural resources.'[357]

This is an interesting passage, for it shows not only that the French – like the English – attached considerable importance to rural churches, and to their local peculiarities and the local materials from which they were built, but also that there was a definite link between the preference for the Doric Order shown by the French Classicists and the predilection for the Early Gothic style (dating from the reign of Philip Augustus) revealed by the Gothic Revivalists. It was not by chance that Victor Hugo used the term 'majestueuse simplicité', which would normally have been applied to Doric temples, in his description of Sainte-Philibert in Tournus (Saône-et-Loire).[358]

148

359 *Ibid.*, IX (1849), p.349; XIII (1853), p.259.

360 *Ibid.*, III (1845), p.330.

361 *Ibid.*: 'On a fait de l'ouvrier une machine, sous prétexte d'unité.'

362 *Ibid.*, V (1846), pp.274–5; VIII (1848), pp.147–54 and 185–93; IX (1849), pp.10–11.

363 Carl Schnaase, 'Les francs-maçons du moyen âge' [translation of part of C. S., *Geschichte der bildenden Künste*] in *Annales archéologiques*, XI (1851), pp.325–34, note p.326. – See also Notes 179–80 and 185 for Part II above.

THE 'ANNALES ARCHÉOLOGIQUES'

Reichensperger and Lassus were also attracted by local peculiarities and local materials. It will be remembered that they reacted enthusiastically to the timber buildings designed by Friedrich
84 Eisenlohr (1808–55) for the Badische Eisenbahnen.[359]

Although the revival of art through craftsmanship was a theme that the *Annales archéologiques* failed to take up either in the 1840's or in the 1850's, the stonemason's craft was discussed on various occasions. This was, of course, a natural consequence of the great interest shown by French archaeologists in construction and stone cutting. Not surprisingly, Viollet-le-Duc, who was an inveterate opponent of academic knowledge, praised the practical skills and intelligence of the stonemasons; he had an almost archaic reverence for large stone blocks and would quite literally stand over his masons to ensure that they did
81, 82 not chip away a fraction more than was necessary.[360] This was why he objected to the Renaissance architects, who demanded blocks of uniform size from their masons. Viollet-le-Duc regarded such an attitude as a sinful waste of stone and an abuse of the mason's craft: 'They have turned the workman into a machine, in the name of unity.'[361] The articles written by the French contributors to the *Annales archéologiques* were invariably objective accounts of historical developments.[362] The view advanced by Carl Schnaase (1798–1875) and shared by – among others – Viollet-le-Duc, that in the twelfth and thirteenth centuries the artistic leadership in Europe had passed to the laity was repudiated in a footnote by Didron, who insisted that the Gothic was the very epitome of a Christian style.[363] And Reichensperger's conviction – which he acquired in Cologne – that, not only the Gothic, but art in general, and even the social order, could be regenerated by the *Bauhütten* formed for the construction of large churches, i.e. by craftsmen's guilds, went unheeded in France. Reichensperger hoped that the competition for the Votivkirche in
90 Vienna, in which his protégés Vincenz Statz (1818–98), Friedrich von Schmidt (1825–91) and Georg Gottlob Ungewitter (1820–64) were rightly awarded the second prize, would create a new atmosphere conducive to the propagation of the Gothic:

'It is not on the buildings that I place the principal stress but on the "ateliers" [*Bauhütten*], from which these buildings will emerge. In them a new generation of artists and artisans is gradually being formed, without whom the regeneration of art would be impossible. Because of the completely disorganized state in which they find themselves – a legacy of the Revolution – and because of the competition provided by the factories, our crafts – especially those connected with the arts – have degenerated to the point of idiocy; they can only be rejuvenated in these immense ateliers, which will be organized along university lines and independently of the industrial movement. The atelier attached to Cologne Cathedral has already produced offshoots: firstly, in the town where M. Statz, whom I have already mentioned, and his colleague
88, 89 M. Schmidt employ, for their private commissions, a dozen stonemasons who were trained in the Cathedral school; and then in Hamburg, in

149

The book was divided into text pages (on cartridge) and an illustration section (on art paper) – an old-fashioned practice by today's standards. The first spread here follows the grid, but in the second one, opposite, the pictures are half-page width. The picture pattern and relationship to caption is carefully organised, but the running head, always subservient to the notional grid, can sometimes look unanchored to anything on the actual page. Order and simplicity are the guiding principles, resulting in pleasing spatial patterns. In book design, less fuss is clearer communication. This is not wasted space, it is productive space.

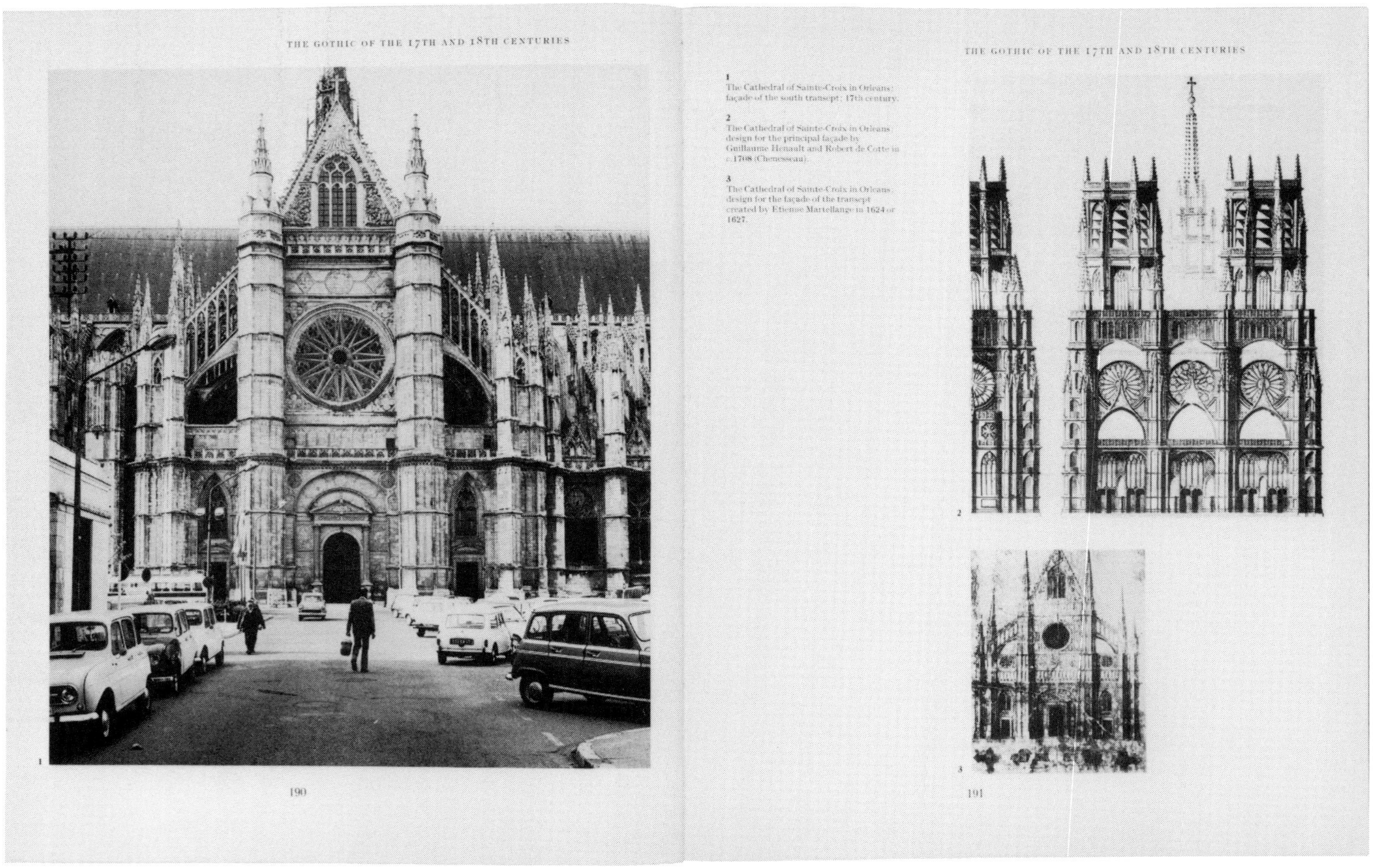
THE GOTHIC OF THE 17TH AND 18TH CENTURIES

1

190

THE GOTHIC OF THE 17TH AND 18TH CENTURIES

1
The Cathedral of Sainte-Croix in Orleans: façade of the south transept: 17th century.

2
The Cathedral of Sainte-Croix in Orleans: design for the principal façade by Guillaume Henault and Robert de Cotte in c.1708 (Chenesseau).

3
The Cathedral of Sainte-Croix in Orleans: design for the façade of the transept created by Etienne Martellange in 1624 or 1627.

2

3

191

7
Human Figure with Geometrically Determined Proportions; reproduction taken from the Cesariano edition of Vitruvius (Como, 1521).

8
Milan Cathedral: section (Cesariano, 1521).

9
Milan Cathedral: section (Cesariano, 1521).

10
Monastery Chapel of Batalha: section (Murphy, 1792–5: R.I.B.A.).

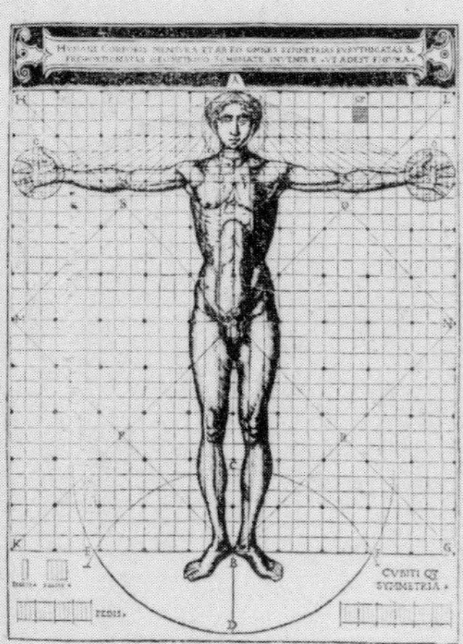

7

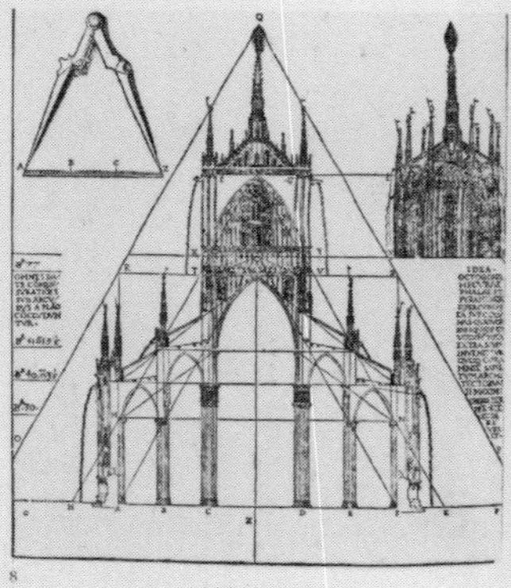

8

THE GOTHIC OF THE 17TH AND 18TH CENTURIES

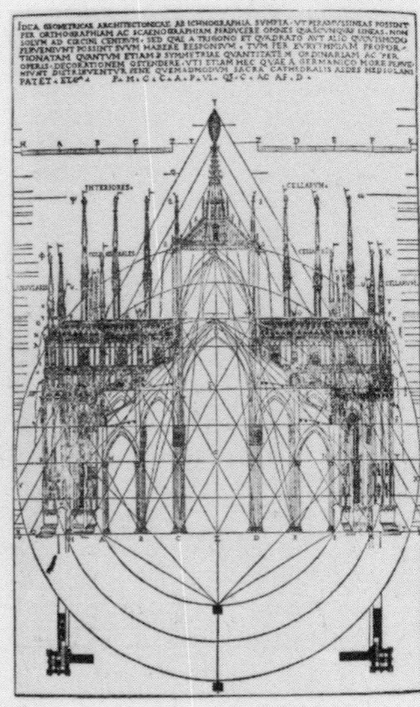

9

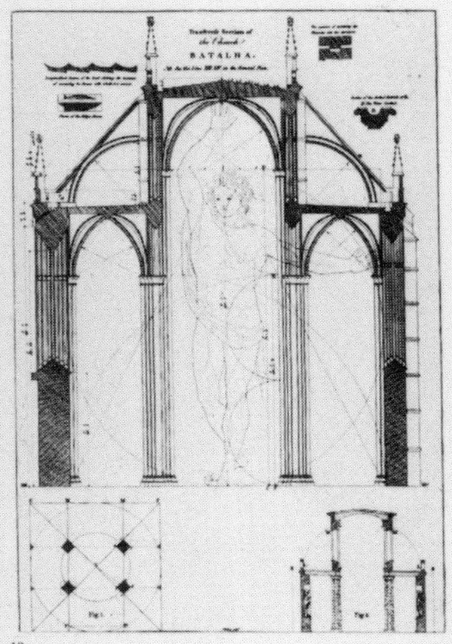

10

Jackson Pollock
Catalogue, Marlborough Fine Art
London, 1961
Designed by Herbert Spencer
Illustrated at 49% actual size

By 1961, Grotesque series 215 (with bold 216) had replaced Gill as the modernist designer's sanserif of choice; it was itself to be superseded by Univers. Characteristically, for the previous book on the Gothic Revival, Spencer felt *any* sanserif was inappropriate.

Spencer's designs (at their best) have a refinement lacking in his B-list contemporaries. The strong pattern-making and sensitively exploited space can be noted instantly; the subtleties of the 'near view' – typographic detailing such as choice of type size and leading, and spatial organisation of information, are less immediately obvious but equally vital, both improving the overall look and also in aiding the reader. Against this careful work, many catalogues of the time, by respected designers, seem a little off-hand, even crude.

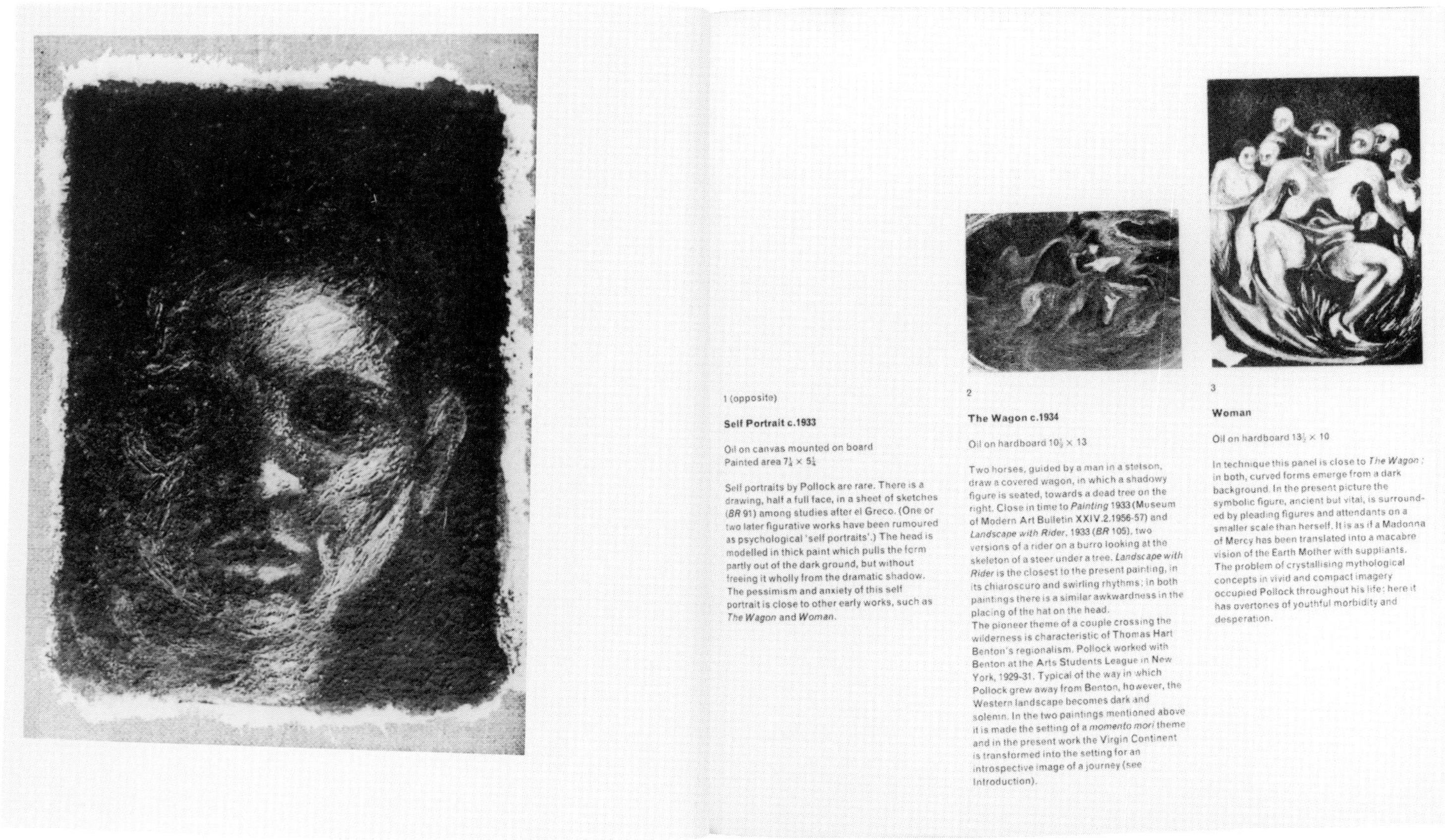

1 (opposite)

Self Portrait c.1933

Oil on canvas mounted on board
Painted area $7\frac{1}{4} \times 5\frac{1}{4}$

Self portraits by Pollock are rare. There is a drawing, half a full face, in a sheet of sketches (*BR* 91) among studies after el Greco. (One or two later figurative works have been rumoured as psychological 'self portraits'.) The head is modelled in thick paint which pulls the form partly out of the dark ground, but without freeing it wholly from the dramatic shadow. The pessimism and anxiety of this self portrait is close to other early works, such as *The Wagon* and *Woman*.

2

The Wagon c.1934

Oil on hardboard $10\frac{1}{2} \times 13$

Two horses, guided by a man in a stetson, draw a covered wagon, in which a shadowy figure is seated, towards a dead tree on the right. Close in time to *Painting* 1933 (Museum of Modern Art Bulletin XXIV.2.1956-57) and *Landscape with Rider*, 1933 (*BR* 105), two versions of a rider on a burro looking at the skeleton of a steer under a tree. *Landscape with Rider* is the closest to the present painting, in its chiaroscuro and swirling rhythms; in both paintings there is a similar awkwardness in the placing of the hat on the head.
The pioneer theme of a couple crossing the wilderness is characteristic of Thomas Hart Benton's regionalism. Pollock worked with Benton at the Arts Students League in New York, 1929-31. Typical of the way in which Pollock grew away from Benton, however, the Western landscape becomes dark and solemn. In the two paintings mentioned above it is made the setting of a *momento mori* theme and in the present work the Virgin Continent is transformed into the setting for an introspective image of a journey (see Introduction).

3

Woman

Oil on hardboard $13\frac{1}{2} \times 10$

In technique this panel is close to *The Wagon*; in both, curved forms emerge from a dark background. In the present picture the symbolic figure, ancient but vital, is surrounded by pleading figures and attendants on a smaller scale than herself. It is as if a Madonna of Mercy has been translated into a macabre vision of the Earth Mother with suppliants. The problem of crystallising mythological concepts in vivid and compact imagery occupied Pollock throughout his life; here it has overtones of youthful morbidity and desperation.

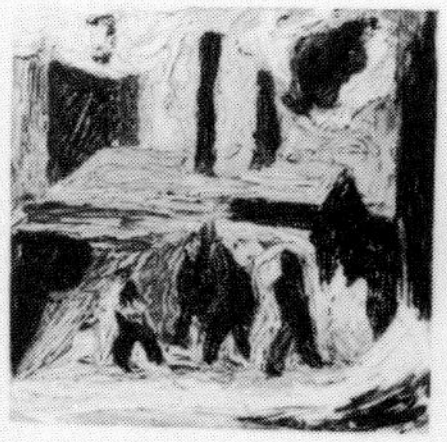

4

Landscape with figures

Oil on canvas on hardboard
$7\frac{1}{2} \times 8$ (sight measurements)

Possibly an industrial scene, though the thickness of the paint obscures specific detail. The simplified forms of the foreground figures may be connected with the undulating forms in No.5.

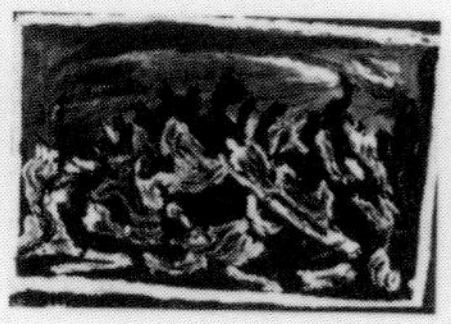

5

Untitled Painting c.1936

Oil on board $10\frac{7}{8} \times 16\frac{7}{8}$
Exhibited:
Sidney Janis Gallery 1958
Reproduced:
Janis 1958 4
O'Hara 3
BR 106

At the time this painting was done (Lee Krasner estimates c.1936) it may not have seemed too far from Pollock's contemporary work. It could have been interpreted as a subjective marine (like *Seascape*, *BR* 104) or as a pseudo-Dantesque scene (*The Flame*, *BR* 103). With hindsight, however, the facture of this painting seems prophetic. Although there is a lingering pyramidal composition, Pollock shows himself able to establish forms wholly by means of paint. It is applied with a fat medium, so that the paint finds its own level, and, here and there, slight paint trails have been dropped. The paint, which is generally sluggish in the earlier paintings, takes on a mobility and sensuality that Pollock was to extend for the rest of his painting life. The painted area is irregularly filled; presumably cut from a larger board.

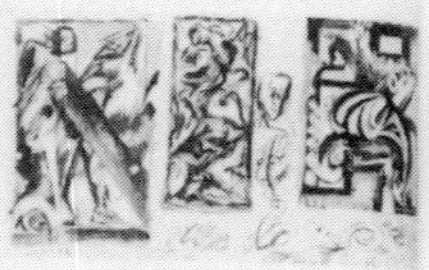

6

Drawing c.1935

Ink and gouache on paper.
$10\frac{3}{4} \times 19\frac{1}{2}$ (sight measurements)

Three drawings, contained by bounding lines with sketches in the margins. The subject at left may be *Christ Carrying the Cross*. The central scene is not readable as a specific subject, but neither is it non-figurative. The implication of a dramatic figure or figures anticipates later black paintings, such as No.21, 1951 (repro *Parsons* 1951). The scene on the right is a cubist-type interior. The knotted rattlesnakes in the margins, as well as the profile with a feathered bonnet, recall Pollock's interest in American Indian art. The mixture of motives on this single sheet is characteristic of Pollock's wide ranging and feverish imagination.

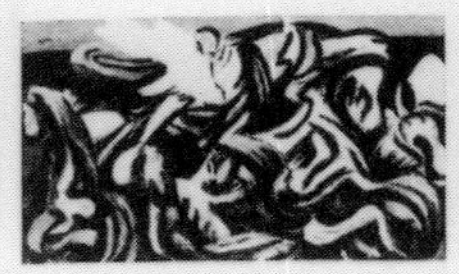

7

'Panel' G c.1936
Oil on hardboard $4\frac{1}{2} \times 7\frac{3}{4}$

Of the same piece or make of hardboard as Nos.8, 9, and 10, though not originally mounted with 8 and 9.
The central figure is in the traditional pose of a rider breaking in a horse, one arm stretched behind him holding his hat. The movement of the scene is expressed by staccato curves. Though more highly abstracted than Thomas Hart Benton, the basic idea of celebrating mid-Western subjects probably comes from Benton who 'translated the flame-like distortions of Tintoretto and el Greco into a simplified modern idiom which served admirably to express the romantic dynamism with which he viewed American life' (John I. H. Baur, *Revolution and Tradition in American Art*, Harvard University Press, 1951, p40).

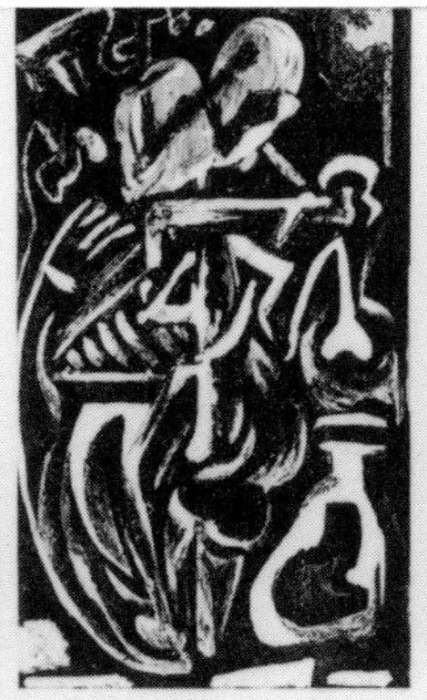

8

'Panel' A c.1936

Oil on hardboard $7\frac{3}{4} \times 4\frac{7}{8}$ (sight measurements)
Exhibited:
Sidney Janis Gallery 1958
Reproduced:
Janis 1958 3 (as first on left of a group of four paintings described as a panel, though, in fact, on hardboard).
Arts. William Rubin. *Notes on Masson and Pollock*. 34. 2. 1959 (as one of a group).
BR 108 (as one of a group).

One of a series of paintings originally done on a single piece of hardboard. On several occasions Pollock painted runs of pictures on one board or canvas (see Nos. 53 and 57). Subject problematic. Lee Krasner Pollock considers it might be a 'male and female' subject. My reading tends towards a simplified figure bent over a desk or apparatus. Given Pollock's romantic interests an alchemist (?) may be intended or an image of research (?) influenced by the themes of Mexican murals. At any rate, the painting seems provocative of meanings, rather than purely non-figurative.

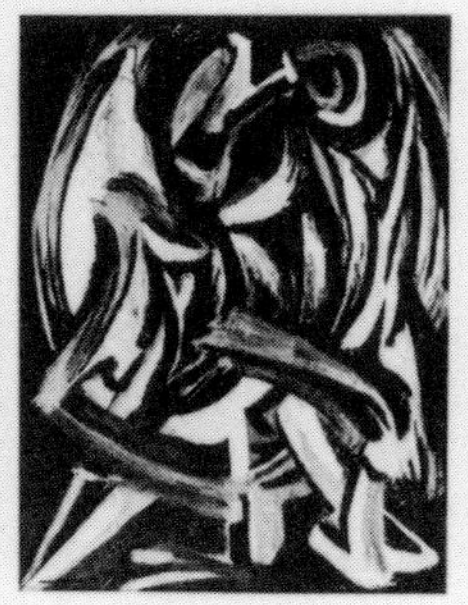

9

'Panel' B c.1936

Oil on hardboard $7\frac{1}{2} \times 5\frac{1}{2}$
Exhibited:
Sidney Janis Gallery 1958
Reproduced:
Janis 1958 3 (as second from left of a group of four paintings).
Arts. 34. 2. 1959 (as one of a group).
BR 108 (as one of a group).

Jackson Pollock continued

This catalogue was unusually extensive for a private gallery at the time. Each painting was given a substantial critical commentary. While many spreads had works ranged on a baseline, this was not rigidly held to if the material demanded a different layout, although the three-column grid was always respected. For every spread the page pattern was thoughtfully considered, even if the final solution was slightly unexpected, as in the spread opposite. Visual surprises like this are part of the modernist repertoire; and if the occasion allowed, as with Jackson Pollock, Spencer was never one for the kind of auto-pilot solution that the B-list designers knocked off, using the grid not as a springboard, but as a sofa.

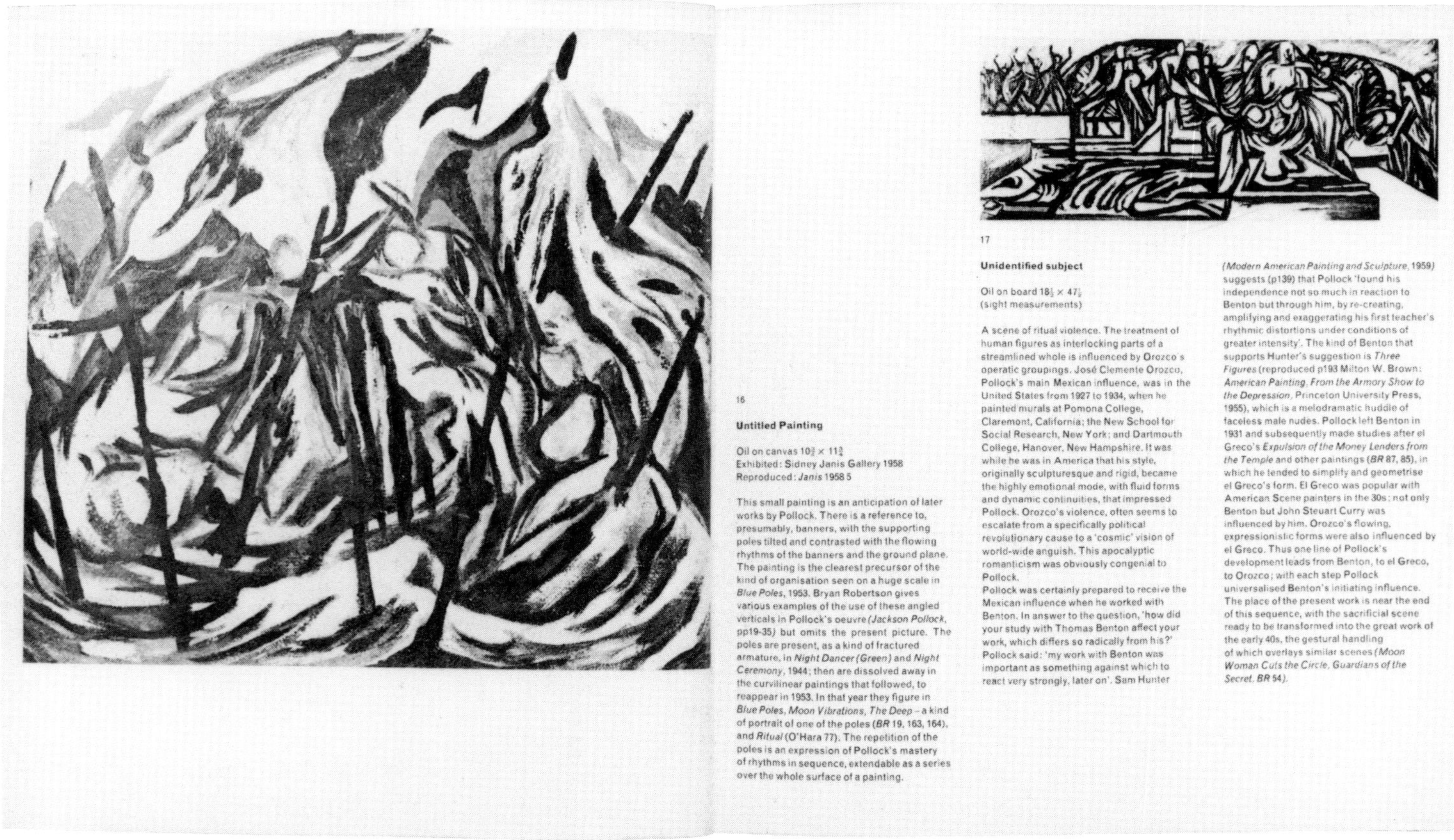

16

Untitled Painting

Oil on canvas 10¾ × 11¾
Exhibited: Sidney Janis Gallery 1958
Reproduced: *Janis* 1958 5

This small painting is an anticipation of later works by Pollock. There is a reference to, presumably, banners, with the supporting poles tilted and contrasted with the flowing rhythms of the banners and the ground plane. The painting is the clearest precursor of the kind of organisation seen on a huge scale in *Blue Poles*, 1953. Bryan Robertson gives various examples of the use of these angled verticals in Pollock's oeuvre *(Jackson Pollock*, pp19-35*)* but omits the present picture. The poles are present, as a kind of fractured armature, in *Night Dancer (Green)* and *Night Ceremony*, 1944; then are dissolved away in the curvilinear paintings that followed, to reappear in 1953. In that year they figure in *Blue Poles*, *Moon Vibrations*, *The Deep* – a kind of portrait of one of the poles (*BR* 19, 163, 164), and *Ritual* (O'Hara 77). The repetition of the poles is an expression of Pollock's mastery of rhythms in sequence, extendable as a series over the whole surface of a painting.

17

Unidentified subject

Oil on board 18½ × 47½
(sight measurements)

A scene of ritual violence. The treatment of human figures as interlocking parts of a streamlined whole is influenced by Orozco's operatic groupings. José Clemente Orozco, Pollock's main Mexican influence, was in the United States from 1927 to 1934, when he painted murals at Pomona College, Claremont, California; the New School for Social Research, New York; and Dartmouth College, Hanover, New Hampshire. It was while he was in America that his style, originally sculpturesque and rigid, became the highly emotional mode, with fluid forms and dynamic continuities, that impressed Pollock. Orozco's violence, often seems to escalate from a specifically political revolutionary cause to a 'cosmic' vision of world-wide anguish. This apocalyptic romanticism was obviously congenial to Pollock.
Pollock was certainly prepared to receive the Mexican influence when he worked with Benton. In answer to the question, 'how did your study with Thomas Benton affect your work, which differs so radically from his?' Pollock said: 'my work with Benton was important as something against which to react very strongly, later on'. Sam Hunter *(Modern American Painting and Sculpture*, 1959*)* suggests (p139) that Pollock 'found his independence not so much in reaction to Benton but through him, by re-creating, amplifying and exaggerating his first teacher's rhythmic distortions under conditions of greater intensity'. The kind of Benton that supports Hunter's suggestion is *Three Figures* (reproduced p193 Milton W. Brown: *American Painting, From the Armory Show to the Depression*, Princeton University Press, 1955), which is a melodramatic huddle of faceless male nudes. Pollock left Benton in 1931 and subsequently made studies after el Greco's *Expulsion of the Money Lenders from the Temple* and other paintings (*BR* 87, 85), in which he tended to simplify and geometrise el Greco's form. El Greco was popular with American Scene painters in the 30s: not only Benton but John Steuart Curry was influenced by him. Orozco's flowing, expressionistic forms were also influenced by el Greco. Thus one line of Pollock's development leads from Benton, to el Greco, to Orozco; with each step Pollock universalised Benton's initiating influence. The place of the present work is near the end of this sequence, with the sacrificial scene ready to be transformed into the great work of the early 40s, the gestural handling of which overlays similar scenes *(Moon Woman Cuts the Circle, Guardians of the Secret, BR* 54*)*.

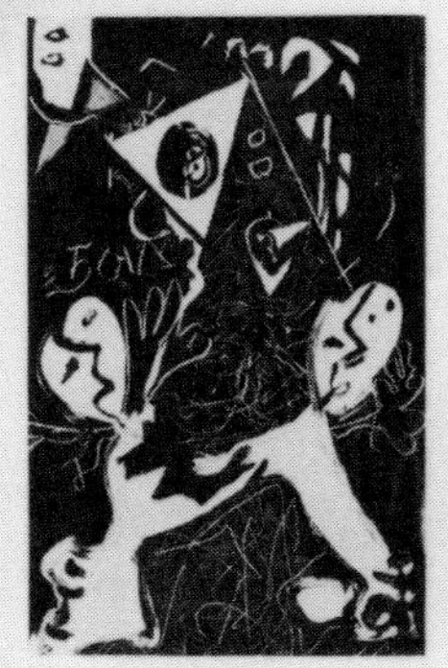

45

Painting 1944

Oil on canvas 23 × 15

Sgraffito, found in occasional early Pollocks, such as No.25 in the present exhibition, is dominant in this painting; a scratched line fills in between bare canvas and summary painted areas. A Cubist device lingers in this informal work, the triangular head, but it has become less a metaphor of the head's structure, than a schematic form like a primitive mask.

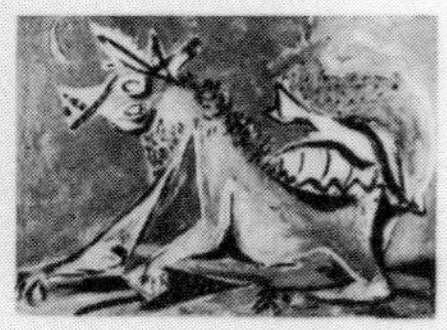

46

Horse

Oil on canvas 15¾ × 22

The horse, which Pollock used in the 30s in a mid-Western context, reappears in the 40s, though stylistically and thematically changed. The white horse in the tenth scene of Picasso's *The Dream and Lie of Franco* and drawings of the horse in *Guernica* have intervened.

47 (right)

The Child Proceeds 1946

Oil on canvas 43 × 22
S Jackson Pollock
Inscribed on stretcher: Jackson Pollock 1.4
Exhibited:
Art of this Century 1946
Sidney Janis Gallery 1958
Reproduced:
Janis 1958, 16

A pair of sexually contrasted figures, another statement of the figures in *Male and Female* and *Two* (*BR* 125).

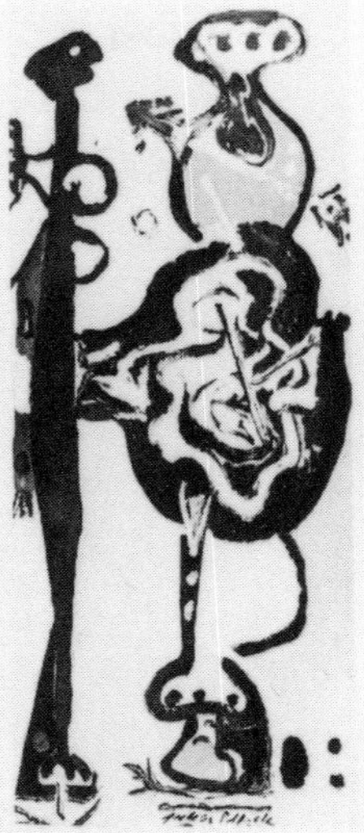

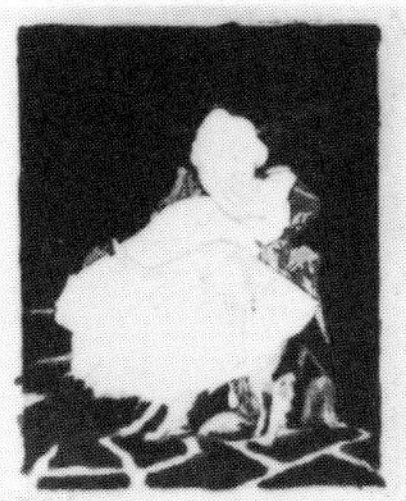

48

The Debutante

Duco and ink on paper 13½ × 11½

On a page from a magazine Pollock has laid and folded the skin from a can of paint. A dog and an umbrella are visible on the printed page, most of which has been inked out. Still readable of the original advertisement are 'Aquatogs sold at better stores everywhere' and a footnote, from which the title is taken, 'Debutante and Misses coats in Seal Skin Satin'. The magazine, dated April 28, 1946, had obviously been in the studio for some time and used casually to deposit the skimmed paint on, and its potential as an image suddenly recognised.

NOTE

Duco is the trade name of an American commercial paint. It is used here to cover the use of enamel or lacquer in Pollock's work. Harold Rosenberg records (*The Search for Jackson Pollock*, Art News, 59, 10, 1961) that the Mexican muralist Siqueiros lectured at the Artists' Union in the 30s on the use of Duco and was known locally as "Il Duco".

Painting and Sculpture of a Decade 1954-64
Calouste Gulbenkian Foundation
with the Tate Gallery, London, 1964
Designed by Edward Wright and Robin Fior
Illustrated at 52% actual size

For Edward Wright, lettering and typography were exercises in image making. As an artist-designer following in the tradition of those whose work Herbert Spencer showed in *Typographica* or in the book *Pioneers of Modern Typography*, he was equally at home creating a large-scale mural abstracted from letterforms, small-scale plaques of sculptured lettering, or display typography. Born in Liverpool of Ecuadorian parents, his work had an unEnglish power and intensity belying his slight build and quiet, worried manner – a contrast to Robin Fior's more exuberant personality. Fior was especially notable for the radical propaganda he designed for CND, the Committee of 100, and the Labour Party. How effectively the

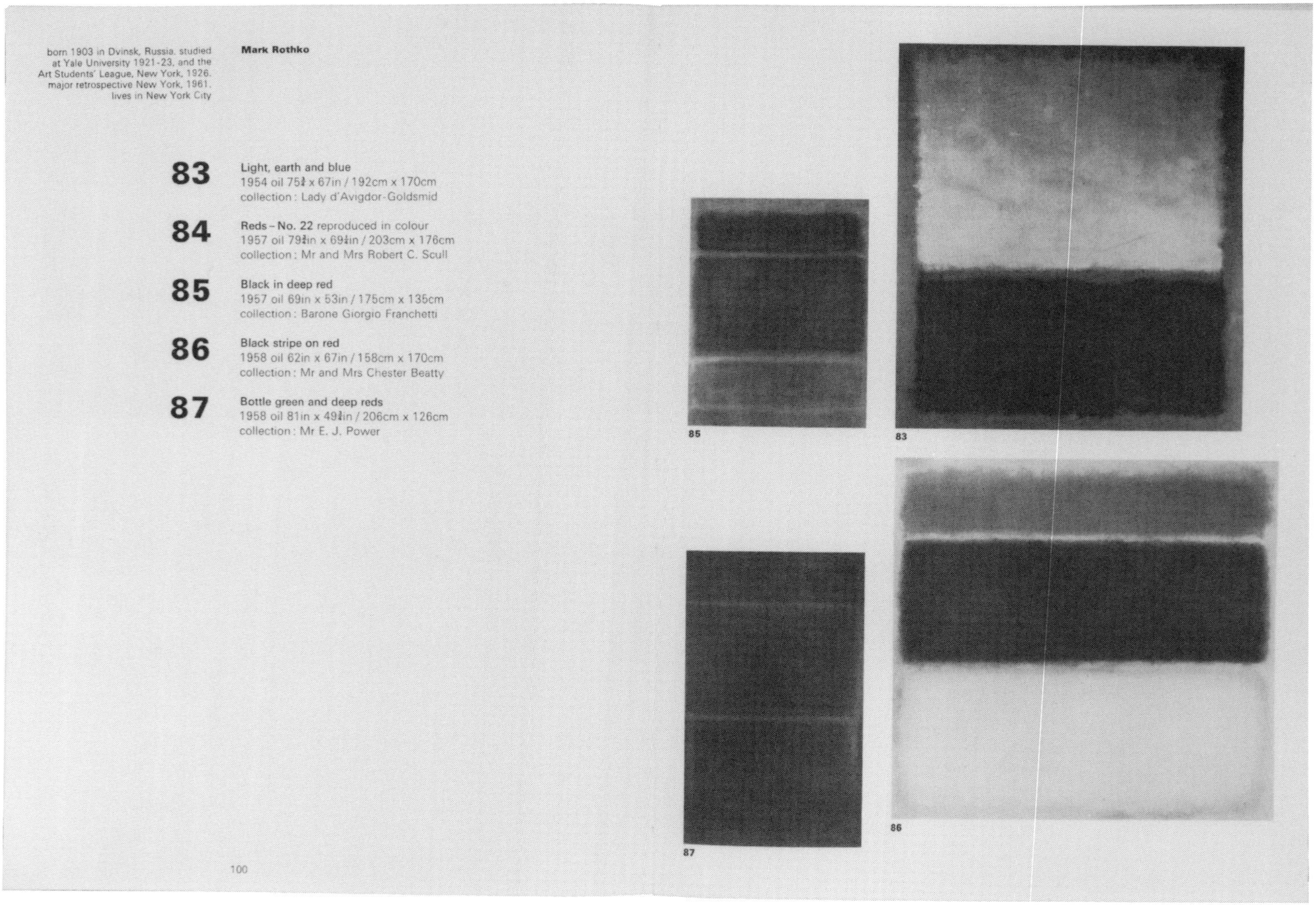
born 1903 in Dvinsk, Russia. studied at Yale University 1921-23, and the Art Students' League, New York, 1926. major retrospective New York, 1961. lives in New York City

Mark Rothko

83 **Light, earth and blue**
1954 oil 75¾ x 67in / 192cm x 170cm
collection : Lady d'Avigdor-Goldsmid

84 **Reds – No. 22** reproduced in colour
1957 oil 79¾in x 69¼in / 203cm x 176cm
collection : Mr and Mrs Robert C. Scull

85 **Black in deep red**
1957 oil 69in x 53in / 175cm x 135cm
collection : Barone Giorgio Franchetti

86 **Black stripe on red**
1958 oil 62in x 67in / 158cm x 170cm
collection : Mr and Mrs Chester Beatty

87 **Bottle green and deep reds**
1958 oil 81in x 49¾in / 206cm x 126cm
collection : Mr E. J. Power

85

83

87

86

100

individuality of their work could be combined is seen in this catalogue.

A grid was probably chosen not merely for practical reasons, but also on aesthetic, even ideological grounds. Being then the sharp end of design, its use conveyed an appropriate image for the material. The bold handling of space almost aggressively emphasises the modernity of the works; the strong numbers, functionally useful, contribute to this. They are perhaps also a reference to the Bauhaus love of large numerals and page numbers. The total effect is very cutting edge, reflecting the paintings and sculpture shown; but practical considerations have been exploited to achieve this.

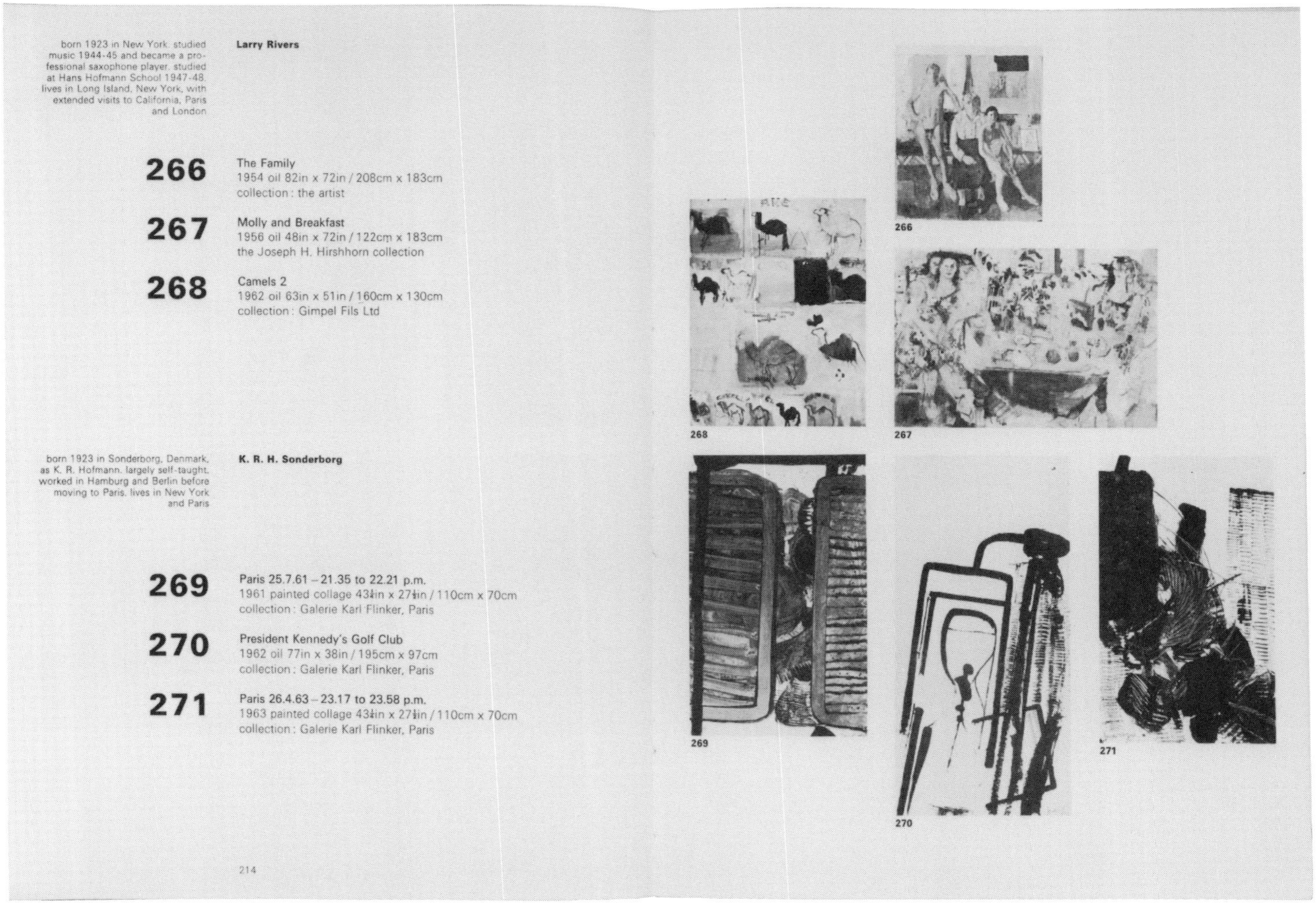
born 1923 in New York. studied music 1944-45 and became a professional saxophone player. studied at Hans Hofmann School 1947-48. lives in Long Island, New York, with extended visits to California, Paris and London

Larry Rivers

266 The Family
1954 oil 82in x 72in / 208cm x 183cm
collection: the artist

267 Molly and Breakfast
1956 oil 48in x 72in / 122cm x 183cm
the Joseph H. Hirshhorn collection

268 Camels 2
1962 oil 63in x 51in / 160cm x 130cm
collection: Gimpel Fils Ltd

born 1923 in Sonderborg, Denmark, as K. R. Hofmann. largely self-taught. worked in Hamburg and Berlin before moving to Paris. lives in New York and Paris

K. R. H. Sonderborg

269 Paris 25.7.61 – 21.35 to 22.21 p.m.
1961 painted collage 43¼in x 27½in / 110cm x 70cm
collection: Galerie Karl Flinker, Paris

270 President Kennedy's Golf Club
1962 oil 77in x 38in / 195cm x 97cm
collection: Galerie Karl Flinker, Paris

271 Paris 26.4.63 – 23.17 to 23.58 p.m.
1963 painted collage 43¼in x 27½in / 110cm x 70cm
collection: Galerie Karl Flinker, Paris

214

266 267 268 269 270 271

O S Nock: *Railways Then and Now*
Paul Elek, London, 1975
Designed by Harold and Adina Bartram
Illustrated at 43% actual size

Paul Elek was one of many central Europeans who have played a significant part in British publishing since the Second World War. Their books covered most categories from short-run novels to large, well-illustrated popular works. There is a tale here yet to be told.

Paul Elek's list ranged from reprints of classics illustrated by some of the most notable British artists of the time (the late 1940s) – Keith Vaughan, John Minton, Edward Burra, Anthony Gross, William Scott – to books such as this, profusely illustrated with prints and photographs. The 1960s onwards saw the publication of many 'coffee-table books' as they were sniffily termed, their lavish illustrations kept apart by a meagre text. This book, superior to those productions, provides a succinct history of railways throughout the world. Its serious intent is matched by the careful design, governed by a simple practical grid, with spreads engineered as coherent units. Since most of the illustrations were photo-

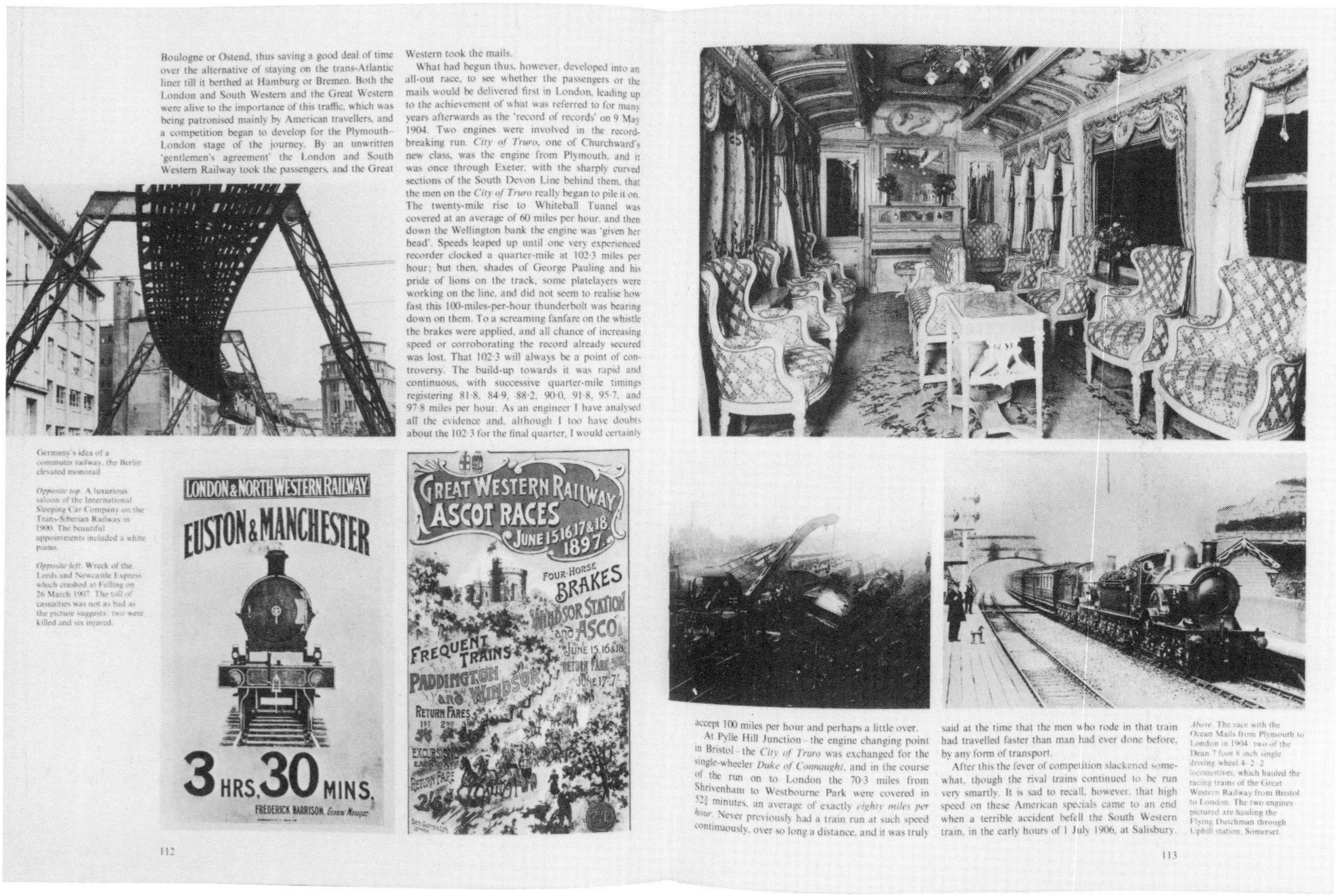

Boulogne or Ostend, thus saving a good deal of time over the alternative of staying on the trans-Atlantic liner till it berthed at Hamburg or Bremen. Both the London and South Western and the Great Western were alive to the importance of this traffic, which was being patronised mainly by American travellers, and a competition began to develop for the Plymouth–London stage of the journey. By an unwritten 'gentlemen's agreement' the London and South Western Railway took the passengers, and the Great Western took the mails.

What had begun thus, however, developed into an all-out race, to see whether the passengers or the mails would be delivered first in London, leading up to the achievement of what was referred to for many years afterwards as the 'record of records' on 9 May 1904. Two engines were involved in the record-breaking run. *City of Truro*, one of Churchward's new class, was the engine from Plymouth, and it was once through Exeter, with the sharply curved sections of the South Devon Line behind them, that the men on the *City of Truro* really began to pile it on. The twenty-mile rise to Whiteball Tunnel was covered at an average of 60 miles per hour, and then down the Wellington bank the engine was 'given her head'. Speeds leaped up until one very experienced recorder clocked a quarter-mile at 102·3 miles per hour; but then, shades of George Pauling and his pride of lions on the track, some platelayers were working on the line, and did not seem to realise how fast this 100-miles-per-hour thunderbolt was bearing down on them. To a screaming fanfare on the whistle the brakes were applied, and all chance of increasing speed or corroborating the record already secured was lost. That 102·3 will always be a point of controversy. The build-up towards it was rapid and continuous, with successive quarter-mile timings registering 81·8, 84·9, 88·2, 90·0, 91·8, 95·7, and 97·8 miles per hour. As an engineer I have analysed all the evidence and, although I too have doubts about the 102·3 for the final quarter, I would certainly accept 100 miles per hour and perhaps a little over.

At Pylle Hill Junction – the engine changing point in Bristol – the *City of Truro* was exchanged for the single-wheeler *Duke of Connaught*, and in the course of the run on to London the 70·3 miles from Shrivenham to Westbourne Park were covered in 52¾ minutes, an average of exactly *eighty miles per hour*. Never previously had a train run at such speed continuously, over so long a distance, and it was truly said at the time that the men who rode in that train had travelled faster than man had ever done before, by any form of transport.

After this the fever of competition slackened somewhat, though the rival trains continued to be run very smartly. It is sad to recall, however, that high speed on these American specials came to an end when a terrible accident befell the South Western train, in the early hours of 1 July 1906, at Salisbury.

Germany's idea of a commuter railway, the Berlin elevated monorail

Opposite top. A luxurious saloon of the International Sleeping Car Company on the Trans-Siberian Railway in 1900. The beautiful appointments included a white piano.

Opposite left. Wreck of the Leeds and Newcastle Express which crashed at Felling on 26 March 1907. The toll of casualties was not as bad as the picture suggests: two were killed and six injured.

Above. The race with the Ocean Mails from Plymouth to London in 1904: two of the Dean 7 foot 8 inch single driving wheel 4–2–2 locomotives, which hauled the racing trains of the Great Western Railway from Bristol to London. The two engines pictured are hauling the Flying Dutchman through Uphill station, Somerset.

112

113

graphs, some trimming was permissible to tighten up the layout. Possibly one of the last books to be printed with all the richness and depth of photogravure, it is a far cry from the greyly printed and casually designed productions frequently found at this time. Here, a grid allowed variety in the page pattern while maintaining the order demanded. Twenty-five years later, the basic grid seen here is still found to be viable, even if space is used more generously than in this tightly packed design.

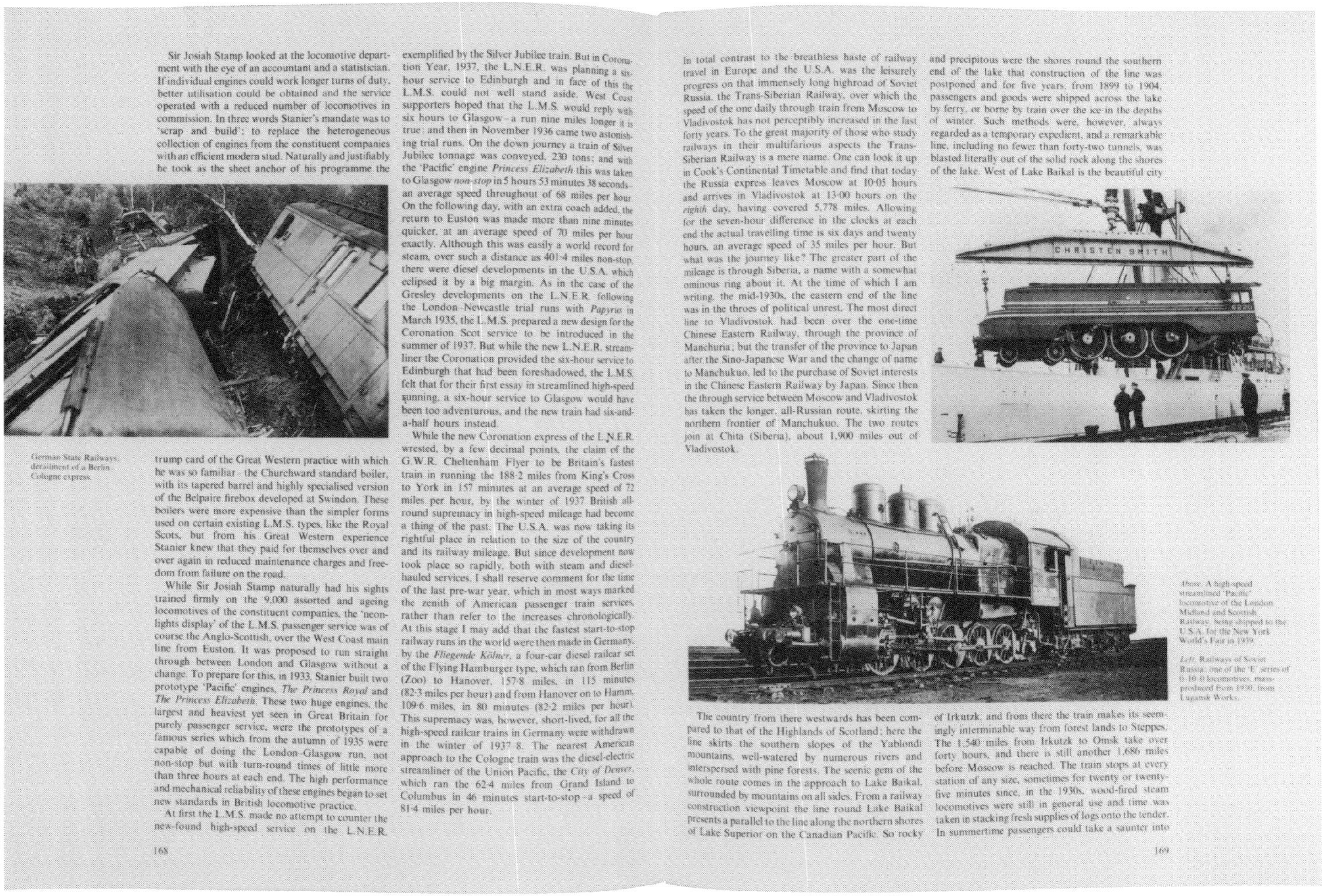
Sir Josiah Stamp looked at the locomotive department with the eye of an accountant and a statistician. If individual engines could work longer turns of duty, better utilisation could be obtained and the service operated with a reduced number of locomotives in commission. In three words Stanier's mandate was to 'scrap and build': to replace the heterogeneous collection of engines from the constituent companies with an efficient modern stud. Naturally and justifiably he took as the sheet anchor of his programme the trump card of the Great Western practice with which he was so familiar – the Churchward standard boiler, with its tapered barrel and highly specialised version of the Belpaire firebox developed at Swindon. These boilers were more expensive than the simpler forms used on certain existing L.M.S. types, like the Royal Scots, but from his Great Western experience Stanier knew that they paid for themselves over and over again in reduced maintenance charges and freedom from failure on the road.

While Sir Josiah Stamp naturally had his sights trained firmly on the 9,000 assorted and ageing locomotives of the constituent companies, the 'neon-lights display' of the L.M.S. passenger service was of course the Anglo-Scottish, over the West Coast main line from Euston. It was proposed to run straight through between London and Glasgow without a change. To prepare for this, in 1933, Stanier built two prototype 'Pacific' engines, *The Princess Royal* and *The Princess Elizabeth*. These two huge engines, the largest and heaviest yet seen in Great Britain for purely passenger service, were the prototypes of a famous series which from the autumn of 1935 were capable of doing the London–Glasgow run, not non-stop but with turn-round times of little more than three hours at each end. The high performance and mechanical reliability of these engines began to set new standards in British locomotive practice.

At first the L.M.S. made no attempt to counter the new-found high-speed service on the L.N.E.R. exemplified by the Silver Jubilee train. But in Coronation Year, 1937, the L.N.E.R. was planning a six-hour service to Edinburgh and in face of this the L.M.S. could not well stand aside. West Coast supporters hoped that the L.M.S. would reply with six hours to Glasgow – a run nine miles longer it is true; and then in November 1936 came two astonishing trial runs. On the down journey a train of Silver Jubilee tonnage was conveyed, 230 tons; and with the 'Pacific' engine *Princess Elizabeth* this was taken to Glasgow *non-stop* in 5 hours 53 minutes 38 seconds – an average speed throughout of 68 miles per hour. On the following day, with an extra coach added, the return to Euston was made more than nine minutes quicker, at an average speed of 70 miles per hour exactly. Although this was easily a world record for steam, over such a distance as 401·4 miles non-stop, there were diesel developments in the U.S.A. which eclipsed it by a big margin. As in the case of the Gresley developments on the L.N.E.R. following the London–Newcastle trial runs with *Papyrus* in March 1935, the L.M.S. prepared a new design for the Coronation Scot service to be introduced in the summer of 1937. But while the new L.N.E.R. streamliner the Coronation provided the six-hour service to Edinburgh that had been foreshadowed, the L.M.S. felt that for their first essay in streamlined high-speed running, a six-hour service to Glasgow would have been too adventurous, and the new train had six-and-a-half hours instead.

While the new Coronation express of the L.N.E.R. wrested, by a few decimal points, the claim of the G.W.R. Cheltenham Flyer to be Britain's fastest train in running the 188·2 miles from King's Cross to York in 157 minutes at an average speed of 72 miles per hour, by the winter of 1937 British all-round supremacy in high-speed mileage had become a thing of the past. The U.S.A. was now taking its rightful place in relation to the size of the country and its railway mileage. But since development now took place so rapidly, both with steam and diesel-hauled services, I shall reserve comment for the time of the last pre-war year, which in most ways marked the zenith of American passenger train services, rather than refer to the increases chronologically. At this stage I may add that the fastest start-to-stop railway runs in the world were then made in Germany, by the *Fliegende Kölner*, a four-car diesel railcar set of the Flying Hamburger type, which ran from Berlin (Zoo) to Hanover, 157·8 miles, in 115 minutes (82·3 miles per hour) and from Hanover on to Hamm, 109·6 miles, in 80 minutes (82·2 miles per hour). This supremacy was, however, short-lived, for all the high-speed railcar trains in Germany were withdrawn in the winter of 1937–8. The nearest American approach to the Cologne train was the diesel-electric streamliner of the Union Pacific, the *City of Denver*, which ran the 62·4 miles from Grand Island to Columbus in 46 minutes start-to-stop – a speed of 81·4 miles per hour.

German State Railways: derailment of a Berlin–Cologne express.

168

In total contrast to the breathless haste of railway travel in Europe and the U.S.A. was the leisurely progress on that immensely long highroad of Soviet Russia, the Trans-Siberian Railway, over which the speed of the one daily through train from Moscow to Vladivostok has not perceptibly increased in the last forty years. To the great majority of those who study railways in their multifarious aspects the Trans-Siberian Railway is a mere name. One can look it up in Cook's Continental Timetable and find that today the Russia express leaves Moscow at 10·05 hours and arrives in Vladivostok at 13·00 hours on the *eighth* day, having covered 5,778 miles. Allowing for the seven-hour difference in the clocks at each end the actual travelling time is six days and twenty hours, an average speed of 35 miles per hour. But what was the journey like? The greater part of the mileage is through Siberia, a name with a somewhat ominous ring about it. At the time of which I am writing, the mid-1930s, the eastern end of the line was in the throes of political unrest. The most direct line to Vladivostok had been over the one-time Chinese Eastern Railway, through the province of Manchuria; but the transfer of the province to Japan after the Sino-Japanese War and the change of name to Manchukuo, led to the purchase of Soviet interests in the Chinese Eastern Railway by Japan. Since then the through service between Moscow and Vladivostok has taken the longer, all-Russian route, skirting the northern frontier of Manchukuo. The two routes join at Chita (Siberia), about 1,900 miles out of Vladivostok.

The country from there westwards has been compared to that of the Highlands of Scotland; here the line skirts the southern slopes of the Yablondi mountains, well-watered by numerous rivers and interspersed with pine forests. The scenic gem of the whole route comes in the approach to Lake Baikal, surrounded by mountains on all sides. From a railway construction viewpoint the line round Lake Baikal presents a parallel to the line along the northern shores of Lake Superior on the Canadian Pacific. So rocky and precipitous were the shores round the southern end of the lake that construction of the line was postponed and for five years, from 1899 to 1904, passengers and goods were shipped across the lake by ferry, or borne by train over the ice in the depths of winter. Such methods were, however, always regarded as a temporary expedient, and a remarkable line, including no fewer than forty-two tunnels, was blasted literally out of the solid rock along the shores of the lake. West of Lake Baikal is the beautiful city of Irkutzk, and from there the train makes its seemingly interminable way from forest lands to Steppes. The 1,540 miles from Irkutzk to Omsk take over forty hours, and there is still another 1,686 miles before Moscow is reached. The train stops at every station of any size, sometimes for twenty or twenty-five minutes since, in the 1930s, wood-fired steam locomotives were still in general use and time was taken in stacking fresh supplies of logs onto the tender. In summertime passengers could take a saunter into

Above. A high-speed streamlined 'Pacific' locomotive of the London Midland and Scottish Railway, being shipped to the U.S.A. for the New York World's Fair in 1939.

Left. Railways of Soviet Russia: one of the 'E' series of 0-10-0 locomotives, mass-produced from 1930, from Lugansk Works.

169

David Munrow
Instruments of the Middle Ages and Renaissance
Oxford University Press, 1976
Designed by Alan Bartram
Illustrated at 34% actual size

David Munrow, a key figure in the early music revival, was a virtuoso performer reputed to be able to play any musical instrument that could be blown. His enthusiasm for his subject made him a notable broadcaster and illuminates this book, in which descriptions of period instruments and their development are enriched by over two hundred illustrations garnered from a wide range of sources. The design attempted to integrate the diverse material while reflecting the personality of this exuberant and erudite musician. Scholarship, information and entertainment went hand-in-hand.

The boxed set of records by Munrow's Early Music Consort included a copy of this book; hence its large, square and untraditional format. This allowed a design of four text columns. No attempt was made to create a period atmosphere; and despite Tschichold's later belief that the Swiss grid system was suitable only for books on modern art or industrial literature, no classical approach

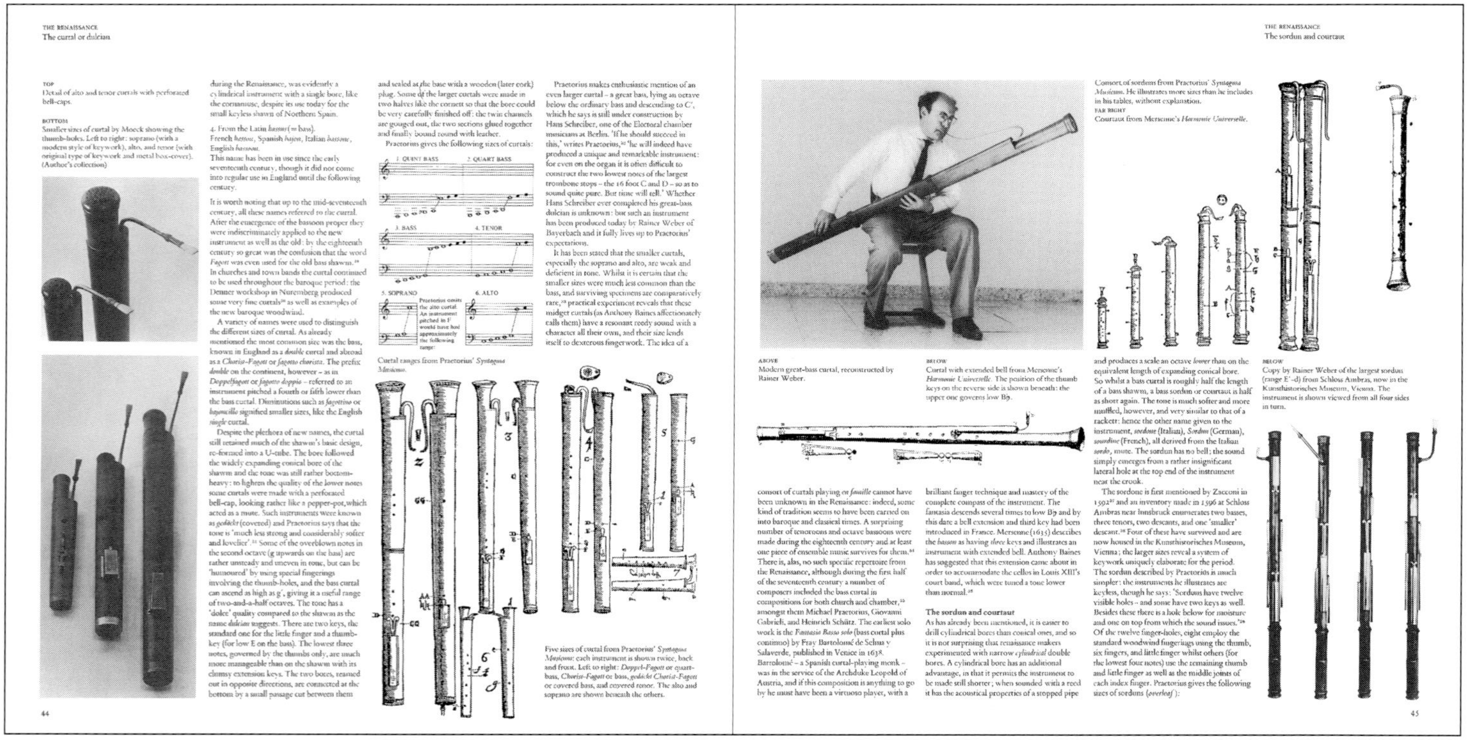

could have coped with the complexity of the material found here. The grid governed, ordered and integrated the page. Additionally, horizontal alignments were created wherever possible. Although the very different subject and the packed-in overall appearance disguises this, the bones of Lohse's design for *Neue Austellungsgestaltung* (pages 112-13) can be found in the skeleton of this design.

The only nod to tradition is the type – Bembo; yet even this is set unjustified, making the pages look less solid, and the Swiss belief in minimal changes in size or style is held to, although captions might have been more clearly differentiated from the text by a more obvious size change. Running heads, so often merely decorative, here list the instruments described on the page. The specially taken and imaginatively lit and organised photographs of instruments – their use demonstrated by Munrow himself or by members of his Consort – were by Godfrey Macdomnic.

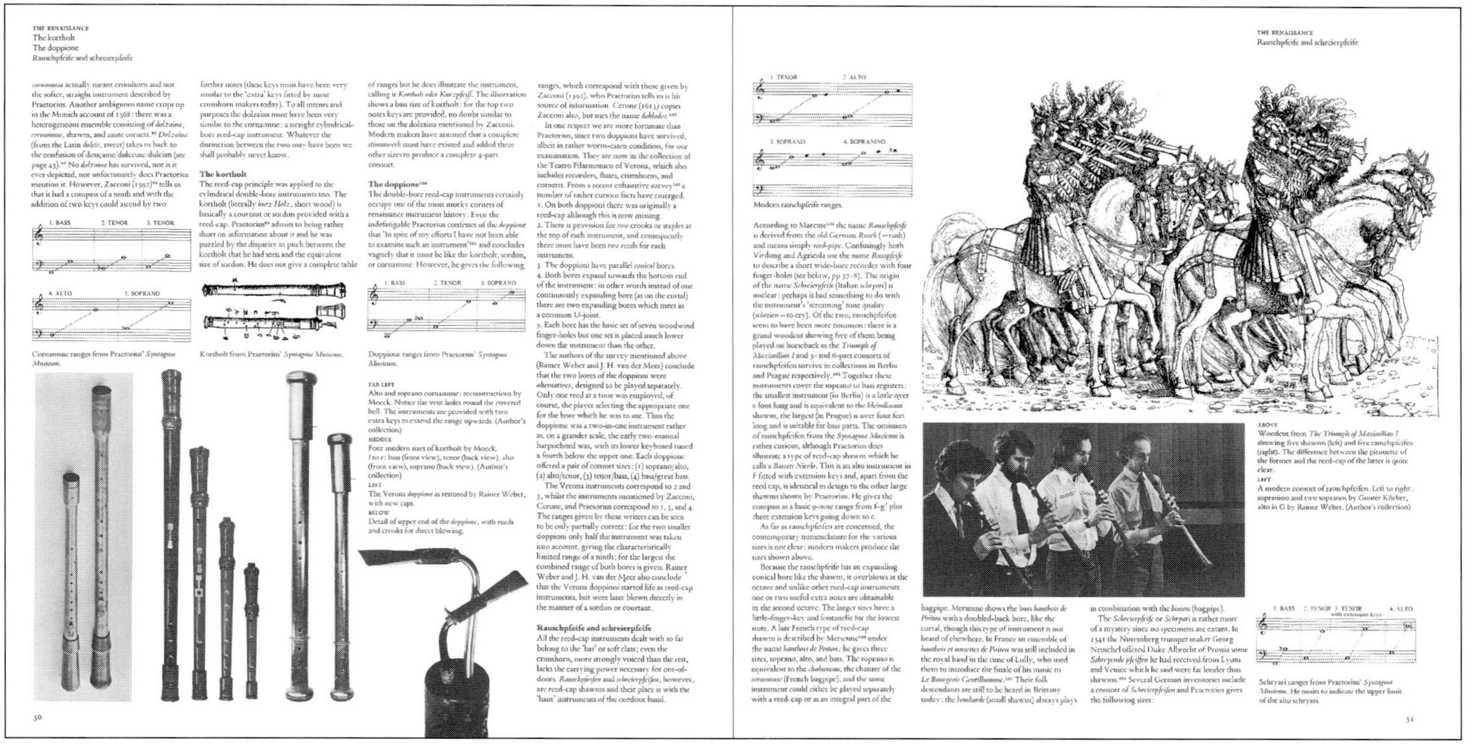

Instruments of the Middle Ages and Renaissance
continued

The successful design of a book of this complexity, especially one so personal, requires rapport between author and designer. The author's inscription in my copy – 'apologies for having been so stubborn' – suggests more conflict than was in fact the case.

David Munrow died, aged thirty-four, a week or so after publication.

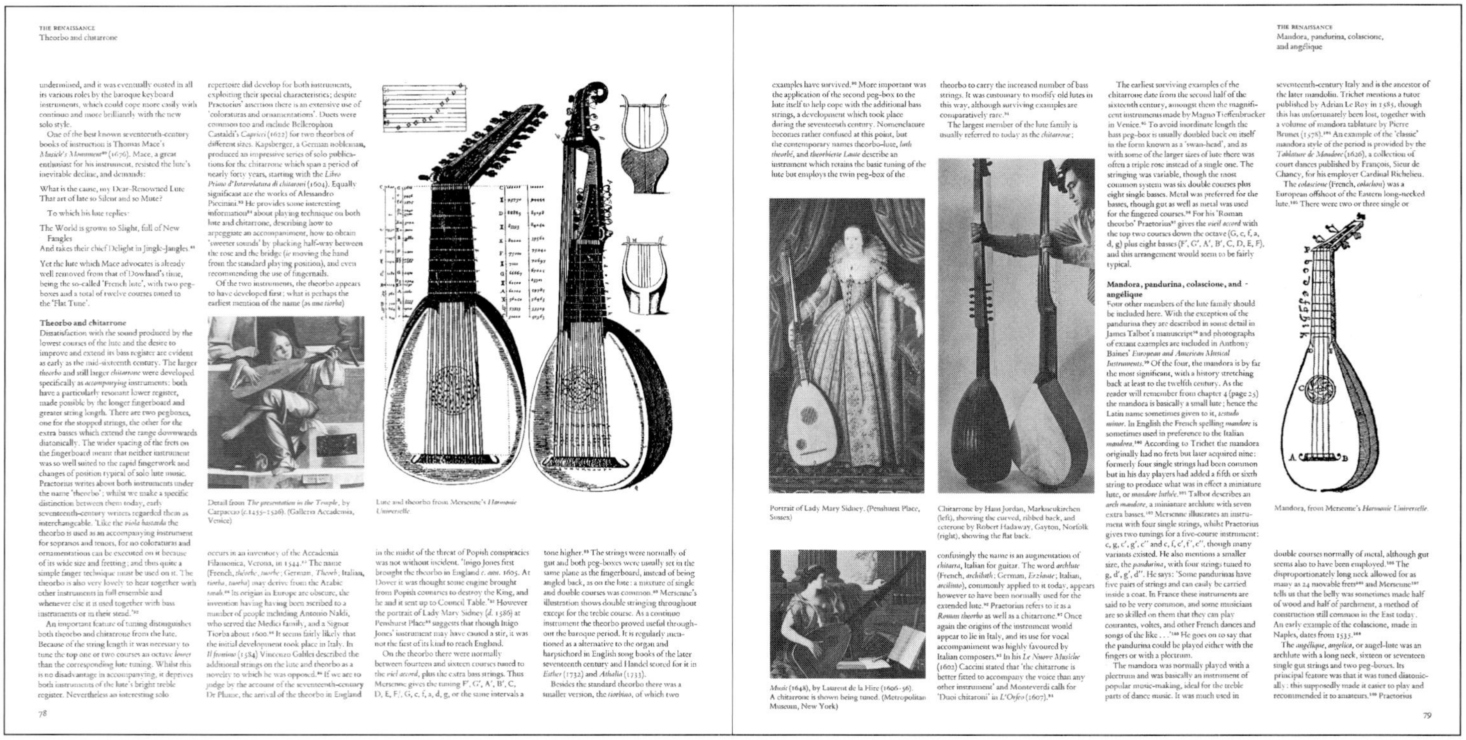

Henry Moore Complete Drawings Volume 3: 1940–49
Edited by Ann Garrould
The Henry Moore Foundation
with Lund Humphries, London, 2001
Designed by Alan Bartram
Illustrated at 40% actual size

Grids have been used ever since Gutenberg started printing; their use has become more sophisticated largely because of the design structures that illustrated books require. Although recent technology allows variable type measures to be achieved easily, practicalities and consideration for the reader militate against this for most books, especially those of more than minimal text.

This catalogue raisonné is one volume of seven, each illustrating well over one thousand drawings, with a production period spread over nine years. So here the grid was again a practical and aesthetic necessity, aiding both designer and printer. It had to be flexible enough to cope with the varied material. One of nine columns was devised, allowing four widths of illustrations. A constant width of type column, enabling the information to be presented consistently, was clearly desirable, although it could be shunted around the page as necessary – so long as it respected the grid.

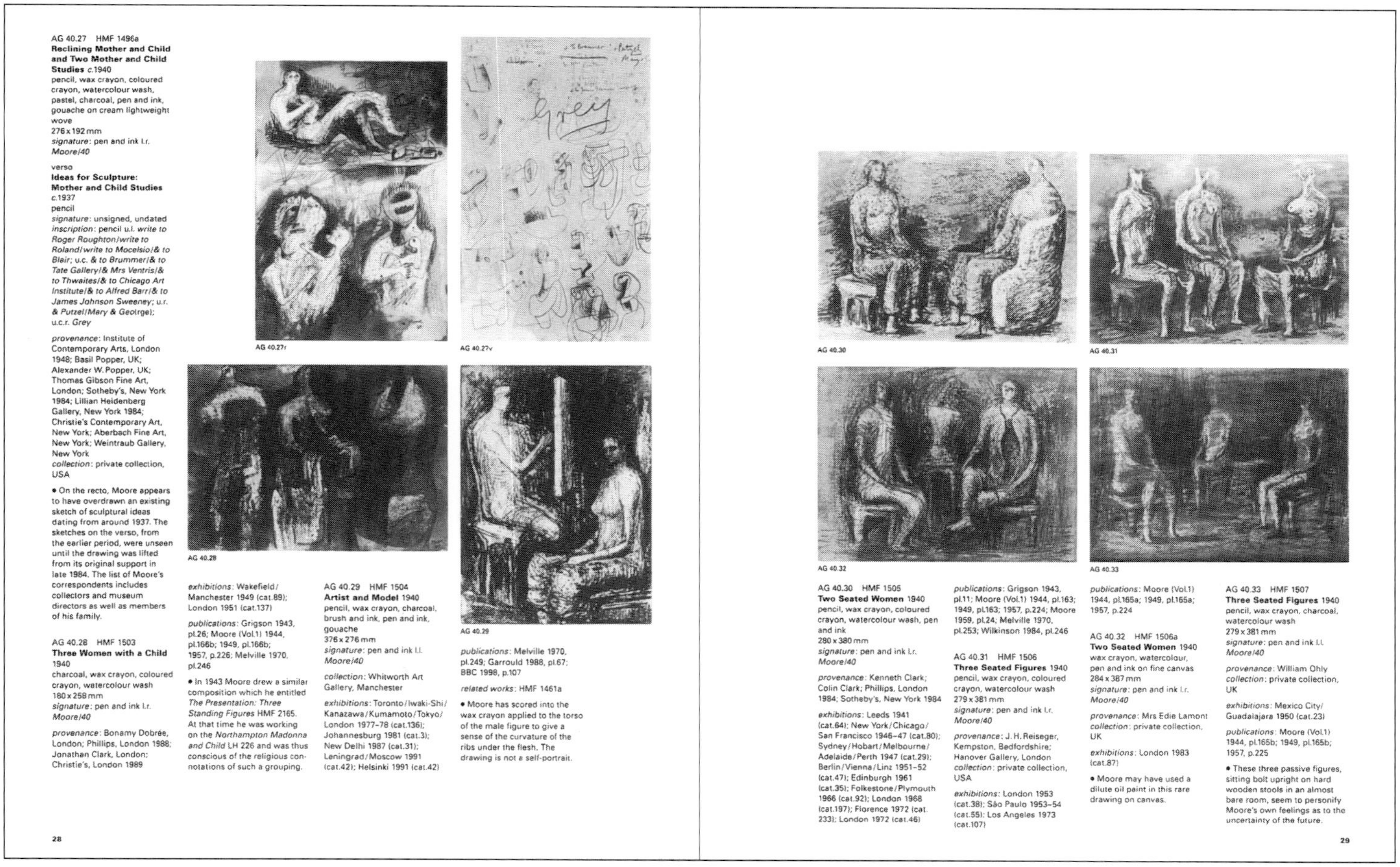

AG 40.27 HMF 1496a
Reclining Mother and Child and Two Mother and Child Studies *c.*1940
pencil, wax crayon, coloured crayon, watercolour wash, pastel, charcoal, pen and ink, gouache on cream lightweight wove
276 x 192 mm
signature: pen and ink l.r. *Moore/40*

verso
Ideas for Sculpture: Mother and Child Studies *c.*1937
pencil
signature: unsigned, undated
inscription: pencil u.l. *write to Roger Roughton/write to Roland/write to Mocelsio/& to Blair;* u.c. *& to Brummer/& to Tate Gallery/& Mrs Ventris/& to Thwaites/& to Chicago Art Institute/& to Alfred Barr/& to James Johnson Sweeney;* u.r. *& Putzel(Mary & Geo(rge);* u.c.r. *Grey*

provenance: Institute of Contemporary Arts, London 1948; Basil Popper, UK; Alexander W. Popper, UK; Thomas Gibson Fine Art, London; Sotheby's, New York 1984; Lillian Heidenberg Gallery, New York 1984; Christie's Contemporary Art, New York; Aberbach Fine Art, New York; Weintraub Gallery, New York
collection: private collection, USA

• On the recto, Moore appears to have overdrawn an existing sketch of sculptural ideas dating from around 1937. The sketches on the verso, from the earlier period, were unseen until the drawing was lifted from its original support in late 1984. The list of Moore's correspondents includes collectors and museum directors as well as members of his family.

AG 40.27r

AG 40.27v

AG 40.28

AG 40.28 HMF 1503
Three Women with a Child 1940
charcoal, wax crayon, coloured crayon, watercolour wash
180 x 258 mm
signature: pen and ink l.r. *Moore/40*

provenance: Bonamy Dobrée, London; Phillips, London 1988; Jonathan Clark, London; Christie's, London 1989

exhibitions: Wakefield/Manchester 1949 (cat.89); London 1951 (cat.137)

publications: Grigson 1943, pl.26; Moore (Vol.1) 1944, pl.166b; 1949, pl.166b; 1957, p.226; Melville 1970, pl.246

• In 1943 Moore drew a similar composition which he entitled *The Presentation: Three Standing Figures* HMF 2165. At that time he was working on the *Northampton Madonna and Child* LH 226 and was thus conscious of the religious connotations of such a grouping.

AG 40.29 HMF 1504
Artist and Model 1940
pencil, wax crayon, charcoal, brush and ink, pen and ink, gouache
376 x 276 mm
signature: pen and ink l.l. *Moore/40*

collection: Whitworth Art Gallery, Manchester

exhibitions: Toronto/Iwaki-Shi/Kanazawa/Kumamoto/Tokyo/London 1977–78 (cat.136); Johannesburg 1981 (cat.3); New Delhi 1987 (cat.31); Leningrad/Moscow 1991 (cat.42); Helsinki 1991 (cat.42)

AG 40.29

publications: Melville 1970, pl.249; Garrould 1988, pl.67; BBC 1998, p.107

related works: HMF 1461a

• Moore has scored into the wax crayon applied to the torso of the male figure to give a sense of the curvature of the ribs under the flesh. The drawing is not a self-portrait.

28

AG 40.30

AG 40.31

AG 40.32

AG 40.33

AG 40.30 HMF 1505
Two Seated Women 1940
pencil, wax crayon, coloured crayon, watercolour wash, pen and ink
280 x 380 mm
signature: pen and ink l.r. *Moore/40*

provenance: Kenneth Clark; Colin Clark; Phillips, London 1984; Sotheby's, New York 1984

exhibitions: Leeds 1941 (cat.64); New York/Chicago/San Francisco 1946–47 (cat.80); Sydney/Hobart/Melbourne/Adelaide/Perth 1947 (cat.29); Berlin/Vienna/Linz 1951–52 (cat.47); Edinburgh 1961 (cat.35); Folkestone/Plymouth 1966 (cat.92); London 1968 (cat.197); Florence 1972 (cat.233); London 1972 (cat.46)

publications: Grigson 1943, pl.11; Moore (Vol.1) 1944, pl.163; 1949, pl.163; 1957, p.224; Moore 1959, pl.24; Melville 1970, pl.253; Wilkinson 1984, pl.246

AG 40.31 HMF 1506
Three Seated Figures 1940
pencil, wax crayon, coloured crayon, watercolour wash
279 x 381 mm
signature: pen and ink l.r. *Moore/40*

provenance: J. H. Reiseger, Kempston, Bedfordshire; Hanover Gallery, London
collection: private collection, USA

exhibitions: London 1953 (cat.38); São Paulo 1953–54 (cat.55); Los Angeles 1973 (cat.107)

publications: Moore (Vol.1) 1944, pl.165a; 1949, pl.165a; 1957, p.224

AG 40.32 HMF 1506a
Two Seated Women 1940
wax crayon, watercolour, pen and ink on fine canvas
284 x 387 mm
signature: pen and ink l.r. *Moore/40*

provenance: Mrs Edie Lamont
collection: private collection, UK

exhibitions: London 1983 (cat.87)

• Moore may have used a dilute oil paint in this rare drawing on canvas.

AG 40.33 HMF 1507
Three Seated Figures 1940
pencil, wax crayon, charcoal, watercolour wash
279 x 381 mm
signature: pen and ink l.l. *Moore/40*

provenance: William Ohly
collection: private collection, UK

exhibitions: Mexico City/Guadalajara 1950 (cat.23)

publications: Moore (Vol.1) 1944, pl.165b; 1949, pl.165b; 1957, p.225

• These three passive figures, sitting bolt upright on hard wooden stools in an almost bare room, seem to personify Moore's own feelings as to the uncertainty of the future.

29

Henry Moore Complete Drawings continued

Alignments across the spread were contrived wherever possible, to produce an orderly layout, although no picture could be trimmed, as all sheet edges had to be shown. Any consequent irregularities of depth, therefore, had to be accepted. Only occasionally did illustrations creep off the vertical grid. Some effort was made to vary page arrangements and avoid monotony; the use of space and asymmetry were the essential means of achieving this.

Although a grotesque typeface was chosen as being the most suitable solution to the problems presented by this particular text, classic serif types look entirely at home in modernist bookmaking, as several of my examples show; including this book you are reading.

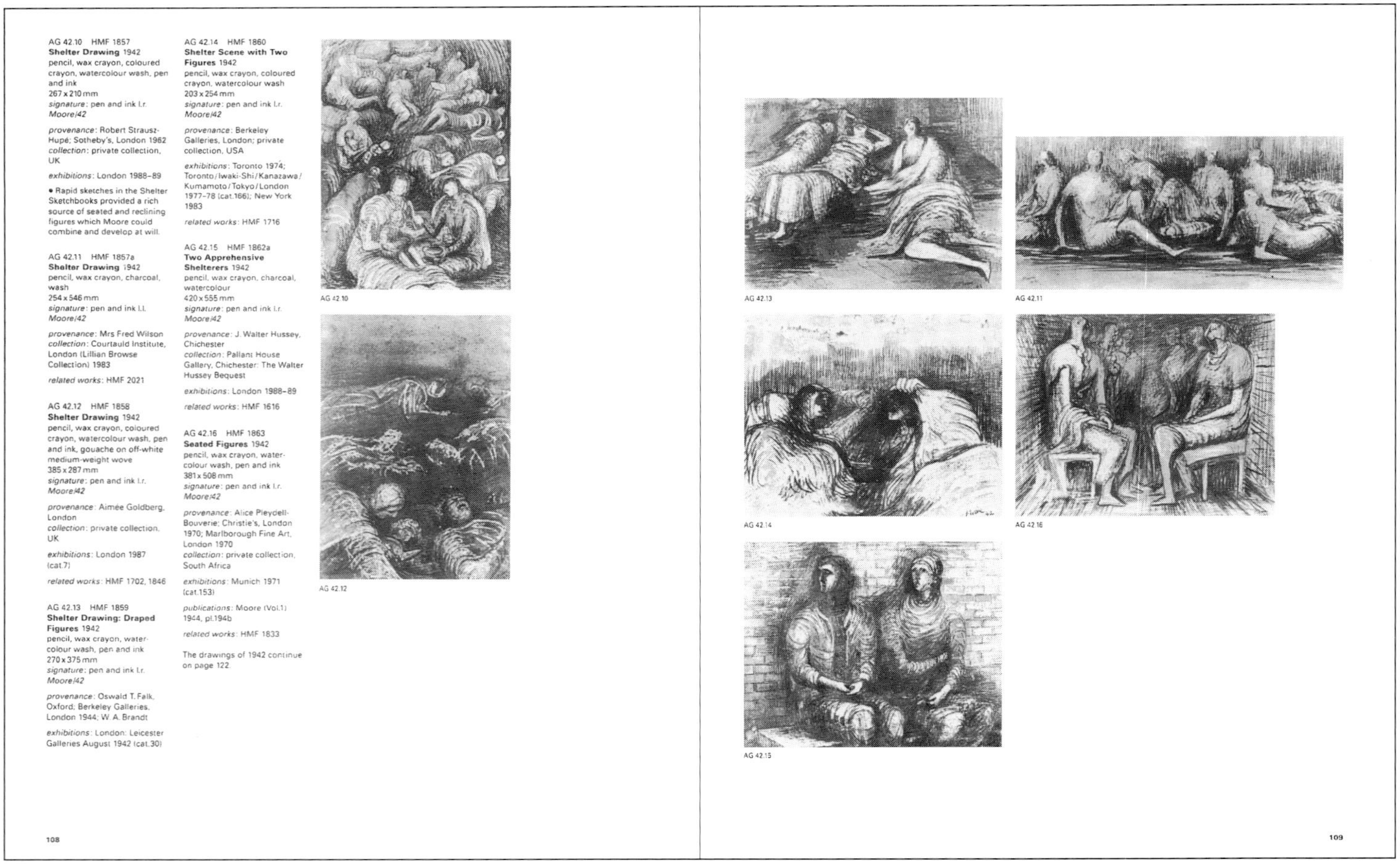

AG 42.10 HMF 1857
Shelter Drawing 1942
pencil, wax crayon, coloured crayon, watercolour wash, pen and ink
267 x 210 mm
signature: pen and ink l.r. *Moore/42*

provenance: Robert Strausz-Hupé; Sotheby's, London 1962
collection: private collection, UK

exhibitions: London 1988–89

• Rapid sketches in the Shelter Sketchbooks provided a rich source of seated and reclining figures which Moore could combine and develop at will.

AG 42.11 HMF 1857a
Shelter Drawing 1942
pencil, wax crayon, charcoal, wash
254 x 546 mm
signature: pen and ink l.l. *Moore/42*

provenance: Mrs Fred Wilson
collection: Courtauld Institute, London (Lillian Browse Collection) 1983

related works: HMF 2021

AG 42.12 HMF 1858
Shelter Drawing 1942
pencil, wax crayon, coloured crayon, watercolour wash, pen and ink, gouache on off-white medium-weight wove
385 x 287 mm
signature: pen and ink l.r. *Moore/42*

provenance: Aimée Goldberg, London
collection: private collection, UK

exhibitions: London 1987 (cat.7)

related works: HMF 1702, 1846

AG 42.13 HMF 1859
Shelter Drawing: Draped Figures 1942
pencil, wax crayon, watercolour wash, pen and ink
270 x 375 mm
signature: pen and ink l.r. *Moore/42*

provenance: Oswald T. Falk, Oxford; Berkeley Galleries, London 1944; W. A. Brandt

exhibitions: London: Leicester Galleries August 1942 (cat.30)

AG 42.14 HMF 1860
Shelter Scene with Two Figures 1942
pencil, wax crayon, coloured crayon, watercolour wash
203 x 254 mm
signature: pen and ink l.r. *Moore/42*

provenance: Berkeley Galleries, London; private collection, USA

exhibitions: Toronto 1974; Toronto/Iwaki-Shi/Kanazawa/Kumamoto/Tokyo/London 1977–78 (cat.166); New York 1983

related works: HMF 1716

AG 42.15 HMF 1862a
Two Apprehensive Shelterers 1942
pencil, wax crayon, charcoal, watercolour
420 x 555 mm
signature: pen and ink l.r. *Moore/42*

provenance: J. Walter Hussey, Chichester
collection: Pallant House Gallery, Chichester: The Walter Hussey Bequest

exhibitions: London 1988–89

related works: HMF 1616

AG 42.16 HMF 1863
Seated Figures 1942
pencil, wax crayon, watercolour wash, pen and ink
381 x 508 mm
signature: pen and ink l.r. *Moore/42*

provenance: Alice Pleydell-Bouverie; Christie's, London 1970; Marlborough Fine Art, London 1970
collection: private collection, South Africa

exhibitions: Munich 1971 (cat.153)

publications: Moore (Vol.1) 1944, pl.194b

related works: HMF 1833

The drawings of 1942 continue on page 122.

AG 42.10 AG 42.12 AG 42.13 AG 42.11 AG 42.14 AG 42.16 AG 42.15

108 109

When the final two volumes of this catalogue raisonné appeared in autumn 2003, I asked someone from the Henry Moore Foundation if the project would have been conceived in book form today, or merely put on the internet. 'Oh, the internet, certainly.' Yet books are more convenient in many ways, and enable an easier comparison of illustrations.

The nine years taken to complete this project have seen major changes in printing technology and methodology. Postscript was just replacing existing typesetting systems, so we had to choose a type – Univers – likely to be available in this form. My preferred choice would have been the unPostscripted Video, or the very similar Imago, Postscripted later. But I designed all seven volumes using old-fashioned paste-ups with printed grid sheets, cut-up galleys and trimmed photocopies of illustration proofs. I believe that, with such a mass of material, sometimes subject to last-minute changes as continuing research threw up new items or additional information, this is the easiest, quickest and clearest way.

We were lucky in that the whole team remained intact throughout, and not only at the Foundation, which was responsible for assembling the material. The editor (the sculptor's niece), the typesetter, printer, co-publisher, designer and, not least, the overall coordinator who kept the whole cumbersome vehicle moving, were all able to stay with the project. The sharp-eyed will notice that the paper used for volumes 5 and 6 – the first to be produced, as the material for these later years was more accessible – is slightly less white than in the other volumes: perhaps the only visible consequence of the extended production time.

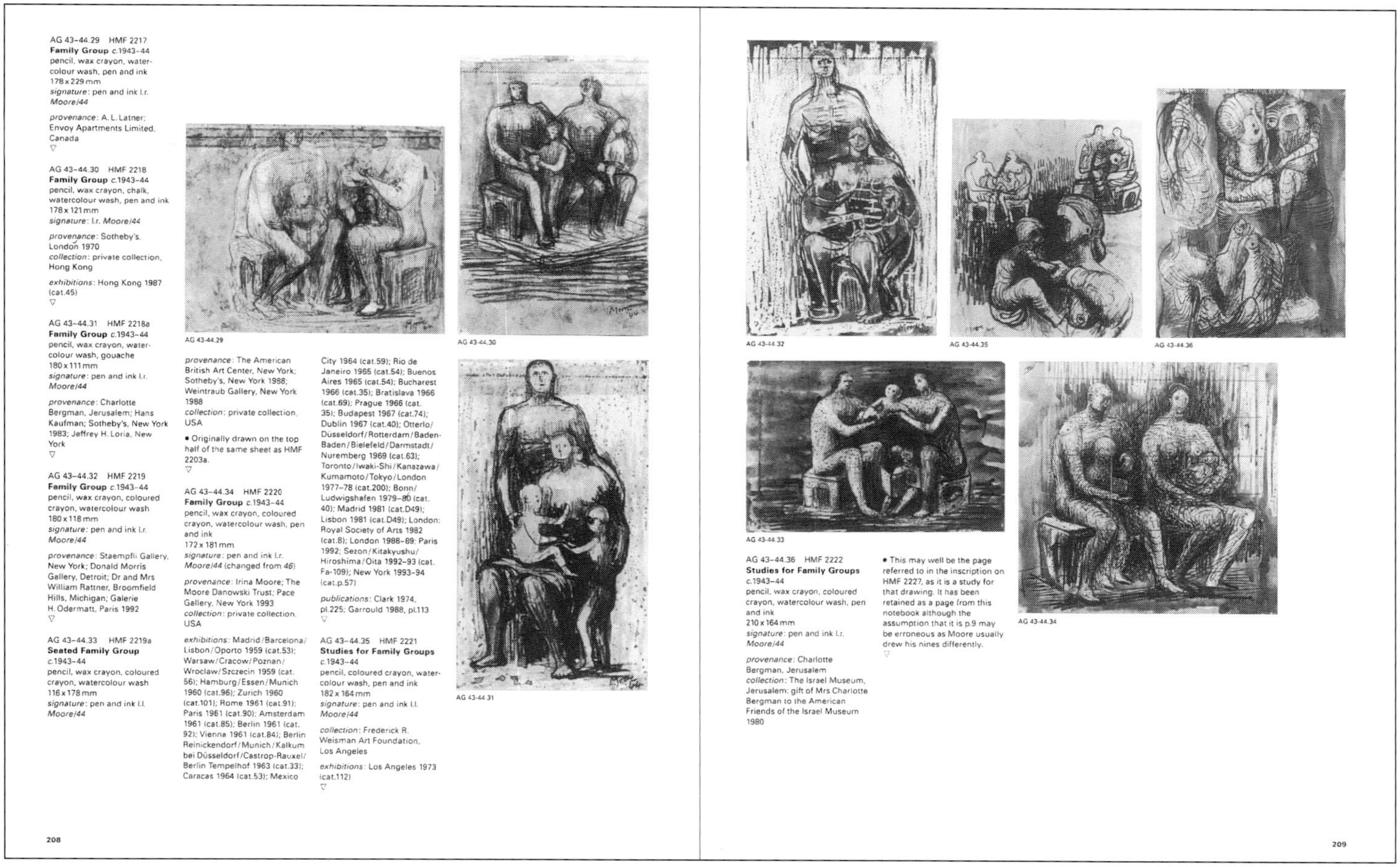
AG 43–44.29 HMF 2217
Family Group *c.*1943–44
pencil, wax crayon, watercolour wash, pen and ink
178 x 229 mm
signature: pen and ink l.r. *Moore/44*
provenance: A. L. Latner; Envoy Apartments Limited, Canada
▽

AG 43–44.30 HMF 2218
Family Group *c.*1943–44
pencil, wax crayon, chalk, watercolour wash, pen and ink
178 x 121 mm
signature: l.r. *Moore/44*
provenance: Sotheby's, London 1970
collection: private collection, Hong Kong
exhibitions: Hong Kong 1987 (cat.45)
▽

AG 43–44.31 HMF 2218a
Family Group *c.*1943–44
pencil, wax crayon, watercolour wash, gouache
180 x 111 mm
signature: pen and ink l.r. *Moore/44*
provenance: Charlotte Bergman, Jerusalem; Hans Kaufman; Sotheby's, New York 1983; Jeffrey H. Loria, New York
▽

AG 43–44.32 HMF 2219
Family Group *c.*1943–44
pencil, wax crayon, coloured crayon, watercolour wash
180 x 118 mm
signature: pen and ink l.r. *Moore/44*
provenance: Staempfli Gallery, New York; Donald Morris Gallery, Detroit; Dr and Mrs William Rattner, Broomfield Hills, Michigan; Galerie H. Odermatt, Paris 1992
▽

AG 43–44.33 HMF 2219a
Seated Family Group *c.*1943–44
pencil, wax crayon, coloured crayon, watercolour wash
116 x 178 mm
signature: pen and ink l.l. *Moore/44*

AG 43-44.29

provenance: The American British Art Center, New York; Sotheby's, New York 1988; Weintraub Gallery, New York 1988
collection: private collection, USA
• Originally drawn on the top half of the same sheet as HMF 2203a.
▽

AG 43–44.34 HMF 2220
Family Group *c.*1943–44
pencil, wax crayon, coloured crayon, watercolour wash, pen and ink
172 x 181 mm
signature: pen and ink l.r. *Moore/44* (changed from *46*)
provenance: Irina Moore; The Moore Danowski Trust; Pace Gallery, New York 1993
collection: private collection, USA
exhibitions: Madrid/Barcelona/Lisbon/Oporto 1959 (cat.53); Warsaw/Cracow/Poznan/Wroclaw/Szczecin 1959 (cat.56); Hamburg/Essen/Munich 1960 (cat.96); Zurich 1960 (cat.101); Rome 1961 (cat.91); Paris 1961 (cat.90); Amsterdam 1961 (cat.85); Berlin 1961 (cat.92); Vienna 1961 (cat.84); Berlin Reinickendorf/Munich/Kalkum bei Düsseldorf/Castrop-Rauxel/Berlin Tempelhof 1963 (cat.33); Caracas 1964 (cat.53); Mexico City 1964 (cat.59); Rio de Janeiro 1965 (cat.54); Buenos Aires 1965 (cat.54); Bucharest 1966 (cat.35); Bratislava 1966 (cat.69); Prague 1966 (cat.35); Budapest 1967 (cat.74); Dublin 1967 (cat.40); Otterlo/Düsseldorf/Rotterdam/Baden-Baden/Bielefeld/Darmstadt/Nuremberg 1969 (cat.63); Toronto/Iwaki-Shi/Kanazawa/Kumamoto/Tokyo/London 1977–78 (cat.200); Bonn/Ludwigshafen 1979–80 (cat.40); Madrid 1981 (cat.D49); Lisbon 1981 (cat.D49); London: Royal Society of Arts 1982 (cat.8); London 1988–89; Paris 1992; Sezon/Kitakyushu/Hiroshima/Oita 1992–93 (cat.Fa-109); New York 1993–94 (cat.p.57)
publications: Clark 1974, pl.225; Garrould 1988, pl.113
▽

AG 43–44.35 HMF 2221
Studies for Family Groups *c.*1943–44
pencil, coloured crayon, watercolour wash, pen and ink
182 x 164 mm
signature: pen and ink l.l. *Moore/44*
collection: Frederick R. Weisman Art Foundation, Los Angeles
exhibitions: Los Angeles 1973 (cat.112)
▽

AG 43-44.30

AG 43-44.31

208

AG 43-44.32 AG 43-44.35 AG 43-44.36

AG 43-44.33

AG 43–44.36 HMF 2222
Studies for Family Groups *c.*1943–44
pencil, wax crayon, coloured crayon, watercolour wash, pen and ink
210 x 164 mm
signature: pen and ink l.r. *Moore/44*
provenance: Charlotte Bergman, Jerusalem
collection: The Israel Museum, Jerusalem: gift of Mrs Charlotte Bergman to the American Friends of the Israel Museum 1980
• This may well be the page referred to in the inscription on HMF 2227, as it is a study for that drawing. It has been retained as a page from this notebook although the assumption that it is p.9 may be erroneous as Moore usually drew his nines differently.
▽

AG 43-44.34

209

Pat Schleger
Zero: Hans Schleger – A Life of Design
Lund Humphries, London, 2001
Designed by Pat Schleger with Virginia Foden
Illustrated at 47% actual size

Hans Schleger ('Zero') was one of the small band of pioneering pre-war 'British' designers. He was of German origin, as was F H K Henrion. Jan Le Witt and George Him were Polish. Barnett Freedman was the son of Russian Jews. Misha Black was born in Azerbaydzhan, Russia. Abram Games and Tom Eckersley were English. Of them all, Schleger had most typographic flair, clearly deriving from a full understanding of Tschichold's New Typography. Versatile and creative, his work covered a wide range of categories; but as far as I am aware, he designed no books.

This book was compiled and designed by his widow, who had worked with him for twenty-five years. Using his favourite Walbaum (with Univers), it reflects his combination of freedom and control, his feeling for space and sensitive

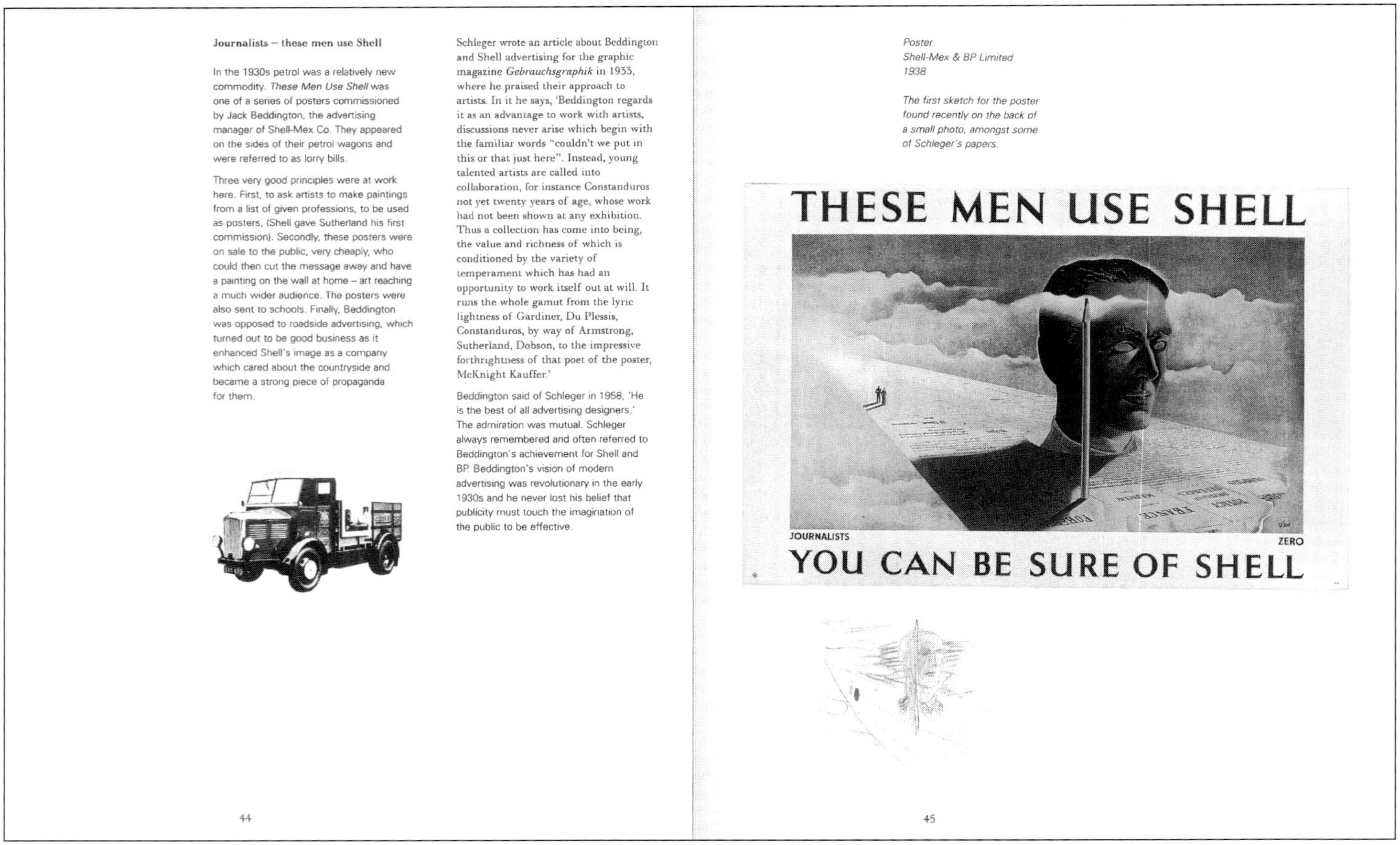

Journalists – these men use Shell

In the 1930s petrol was a relatively new commodity. *These Men Use Shell* was one of a series of posters commissioned by Jack Beddington, the advertising manager of Shell-Mex Co. They appeared on the sides of their petrol wagons and were referred to as lorry bills.

Three very good principles were at work here. First, to ask artists to make paintings from a list of given professions, to be used as posters, (Shell gave Sutherland his first commission). Secondly, these posters were on sale to the public, very cheaply, who could then cut the message away and have a painting on the wall at home – art reaching a much wider audience. The posters were also sent to schools. Finally, Beddington was opposed to roadside advertising, which turned out to be good business as it enhanced Shell's image as a company which cared about the countryside and became a strong piece of propaganda for them.

Schleger wrote an article about Beddington and Shell advertising for the graphic magazine *Gebrauchsgraphik* in 1933, where he praised their approach to artists. In it he says, 'Beddington regards it as an advantage to work with artists, discussions never arise which begin with the familiar words "couldn't we put in this or that just here". Instead, young talented artists are called into collaboration, for instance Constanduros not yet twenty years of age, whose work had not been shown at any exhibition. Thus a collection has come into being, the value and richness of which is conditioned by the variety of temperament which has had an opportunity to work itself out at will. It runs the whole gamut from the lyric lightness of Gardiner, Du Plessis, Constanduros, by way of Armstrong, Sutherland, Dobson, to the impressive forthrightness of that poet of the poster, McKnight Kauffer.'

Beddington said of Schleger in 1958, 'He is the best of all advertising designers.' The admiration was mutual. Schleger always remembered and often referred to Beddington's achievement for Shell and BP. Beddington's vision of modern advertising was revolutionary in the early 1930s and he never lost his belief that publicity must touch the imagination of the public to be effective.

44

Poster
Shell-Mex & BP Limited
1938

The first sketch for the poster found recently on the back of a small photo, amongst some of Schleger's papers.

45

typography. A grid is held to more firmly – or more obviously, especially for the captions – than in Paul Rand's *Thoughts on Design* (see pages 79-81), but the same skill in floating free shapes on the page is seen in both books, and neither are concerned to show the margins of the original. The design integrates Zero's open-minded painterly eye with Swiss structures.

There can be no question that, while the best illustrated book design and production today is remarkable for its professionalism and concern for detail, the wider field of graphic design entirely lacks the wit, creative imagination and painterly vision shown by Hans Schleger and his contemporaries. We – designers and the general public – are all impoverished by this.

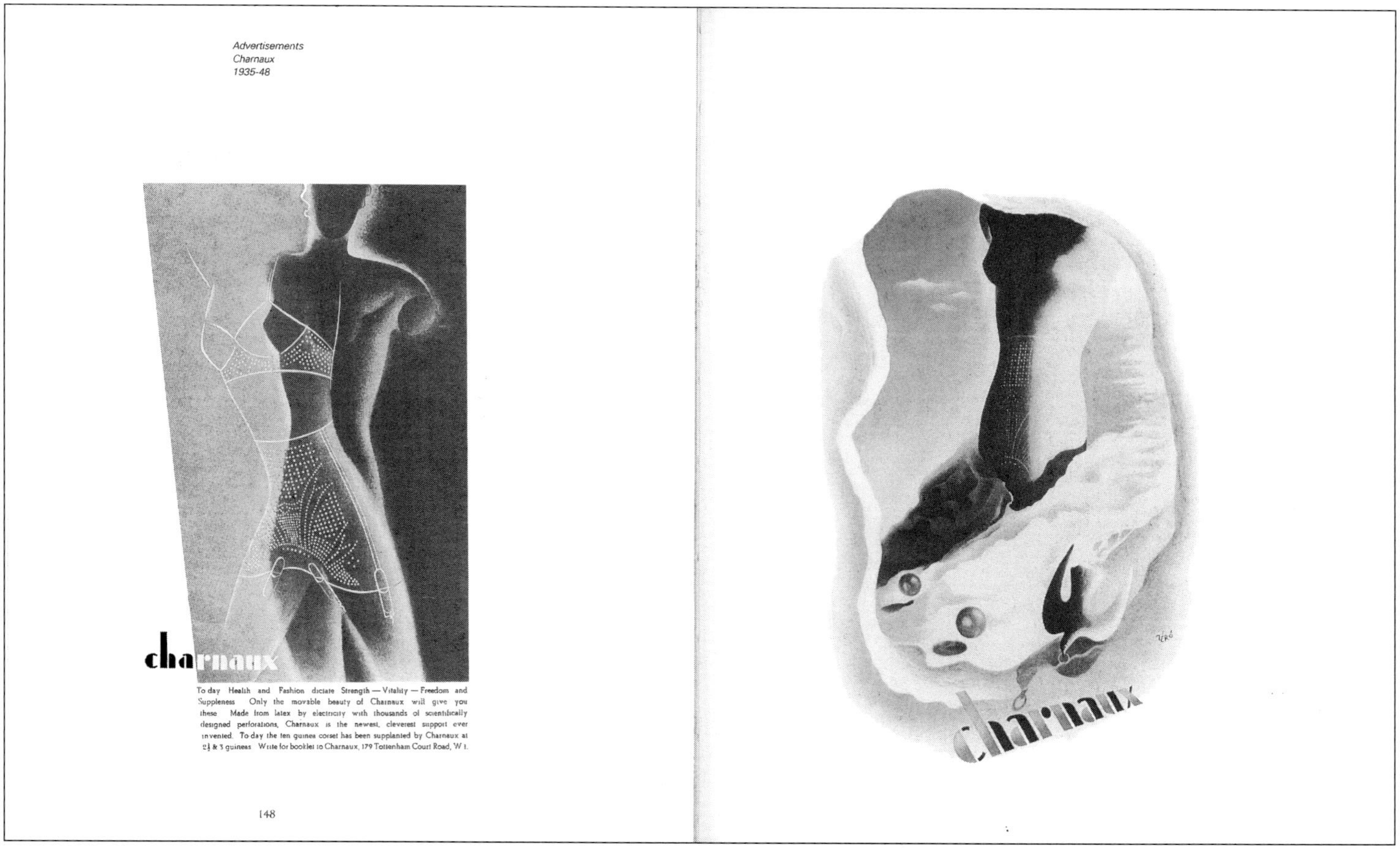
Advertisements
Charnaux
1935-48

148

John Soane Architect
Master of Space and Light
Edited by Margaret Richardson
and MaryAnne Stevens
Royal Academy of Arts, London, 1999
Designed by Esterson Lakersteen
Illustrated at 40% actual size

The major advances in printing technology in the last decade of the twentieth century have resulted in books fully in harmony with the spirit of modernism, as both Bill and early Tschichold demanded. They reflect in every way the efficiency of machine production, with their unprecedented quality of illustration reproduction, whether black-and-white

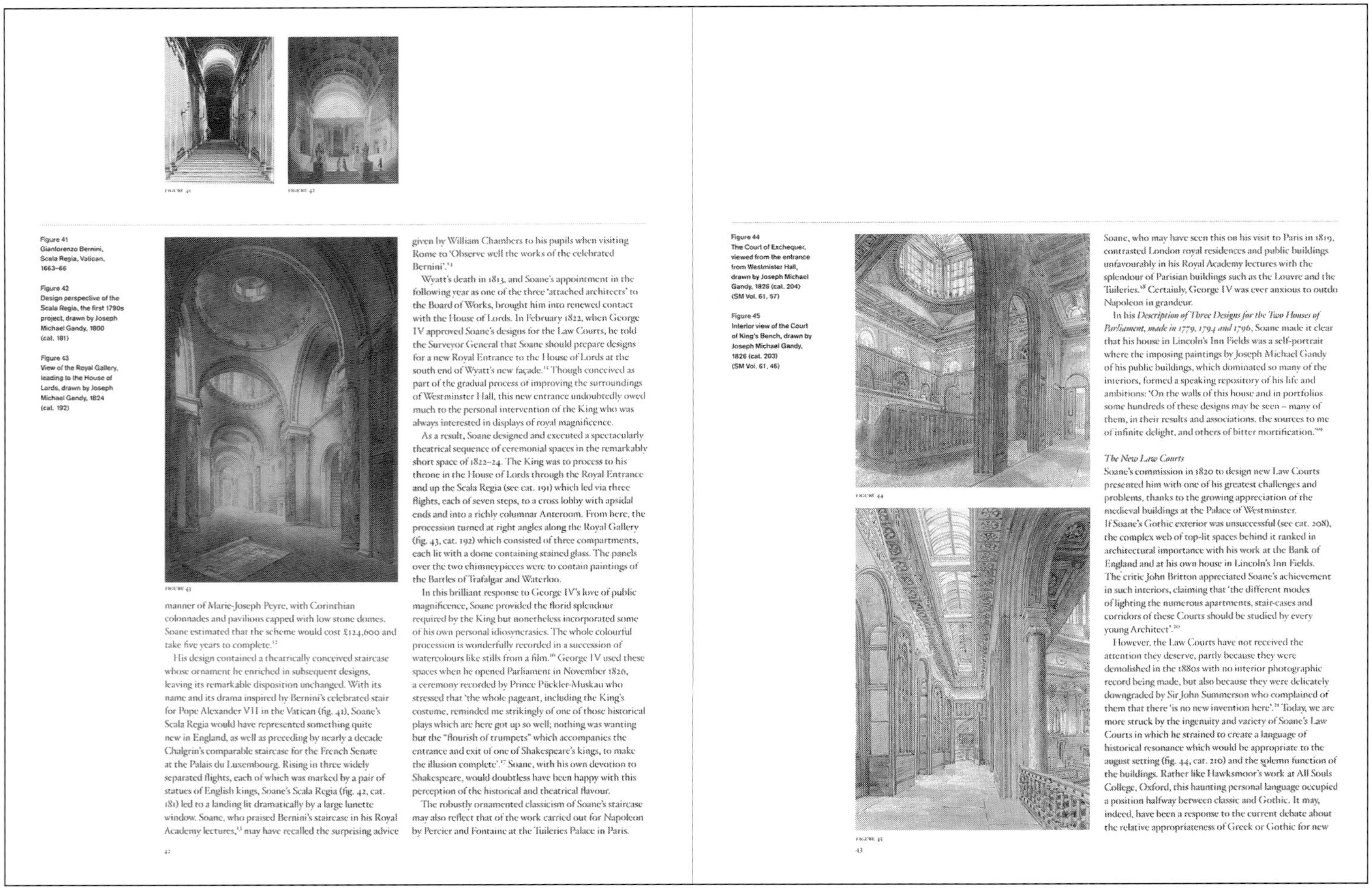

Figure 41
Gianlorenzo Bernini, Scala Regia, Vatican, 1663–66

Figure 42
Design perspective of the Scala Regia, the first 1790s project, drawn by Joseph Michael Gandy, 1800 (cat. 181)

Figure 43
View of the Royal Gallery, leading to the House of Lords, drawn by Joseph Michael Gandy, 1824 (cat. 192)

manner of Marie-Joseph Peyre, with Corinthian colonnades and pavilions capped with low stone domes. Soane estimated that the scheme would cost £124,600 and take five years to complete.[12]

His design contained a theatrically conceived staircase whose ornament he enriched in subsequent designs, leaving its remarkable disposition unchanged. With its name and its drama inspired by Bernini's celebrated stair for Pope Alexander VII in the Vatican (fig. 41), Soane's Scala Regia would have represented something quite new in England, as well as preceding by nearly a decade Chalgrin's comparable staircase for the French Senate at the Palais du Luxembourg. Rising in three widely separated flights, each of which was marked by a pair of statues of English kings, Soane's Scala Regia (fig. 42, cat. 181) led to a landing lit dramatically by a large lunette window. Soane, who praised Bernini's staircase in his Royal Academy lectures,[13] may have recalled the surprising advice given by William Chambers to his pupils when visiting Rome to 'Observe well the works of the celebrated Bernini'.[14]

Wyatt's death in 1813, and Soane's appointment in the following year as one of the three 'attached architects' to the Board of Works, brought him into renewed contact with the House of Lords. In February 1822, when George IV approved Soane's designs for the Law Courts, he told the Surveyor General that Soane should prepare designs for a new Royal Entrance to the House of Lords at the south end of Wyatt's new façade.[15] Though conceived as part of the gradual process of improving the surroundings of Westminster Hall, this new entrance undoubtedly owed much to the personal intervention of the King who was always interested in displays of royal magnificence.

As a result, Soane designed and executed a spectacularly theatrical sequence of ceremonial spaces in the remarkably short space of 1822–24. The King was to process to his throne in the House of Lords through the Royal Entrance and up the Scala Regia (see cat. 191) which led via three flights, each of seven steps, to a cross lobby with apsidal ends and into a richly columnar Anteroom. From here, the procession turned at right angles along the Royal Gallery (fig. 43, cat. 192) which consisted of three compartments, each lit with a dome containing stained glass. The panels over the two chimneypieces were to contain paintings of the Battles of Trafalgar and Waterloo.

In this brilliant response to George IV's love of public magnificence, Soane provided the florid splendour required by the King but nonetheless incorporated some of his own personal idiosyncrasies. The whole colourful procession is wonderfully recorded in a succession of watercolours like stills from a film.[16] George IV used these spaces when he opened Parliament in November 1826, a ceremony recorded by Prince Pückler-Muskau who stressed that 'the whole pageant, including the King's costume, reminded me strikingly of one of those historical plays which are here got up so well; nothing was wanting but the "flourish of trumpets" which accompanies the entrance and exit of one of Shakespeare's kings, to make the illusion complete'.[17] Soane, with his own devotion to Shakespeare, would doubtless have been happy with this perception of the historical and theatrical flavour.

The robustly ornamented classicism of Soane's staircase may also reflect that of the work carried out for Napoleon by Percier and Fontaine at the Tuileries Palace in Paris.

42

Figure 44
The Court of Exchequer, viewed from the entrance from Westmister Hall, drawn by Joseph Michael Gandy, 1826 (cat. 204) (SM Vol. 61, 57)

Figure 45
Interior view of the Court of King's Bench, drawn by Joseph Michael Gandy, 1826 (cat. 203) (SM Vol. 61, 46)

Soane, who may have seen this on his visit to Paris in 1819, contrasted London royal residences and public buildings unfavourably in his Royal Academy lectures with the splendour of Parisian buildings such as the Louvre and the Tuileries.[18] Certainly, George IV was ever anxious to outdo Napoleon in grandeur.

In his *Description of Three Designs for the Two Houses of Parliament, made in 1779, 1794 and 1796*, Soane made it clear that his house in Lincoln's Inn Fields was a self-portrait where the imposing paintings by Joseph Michael Gandy of his public buildings, which dominated so many of the interiors, formed a speaking repository of his life and ambitions: 'On the walls of this house and in portfolios some hundreds of these designs may be seen – many of them, in their results and associations, the sources to me of infinite delight, and others of bitter mortification.'[19]

The New Law Courts

Soane's commission in 1820 to design new Law Courts presented him with one of his greatest challenges and problems, thanks to the growing appreciation of the medieval buildings at the Palace of Westminster.
If Soane's Gothic exterior was unsuccessful (see cat. 208), the complex web of top-lit spaces behind it ranked in architectural importance with his work at the Bank of England and at his own house in Lincoln's Inn Fields.
The critic John Britton appreciated Soane's achievement in such interiors, claiming that 'the different modes of lighting the numerous apartments, stair-cases and corridors of these Courts should be studied by every young Architect'.[20]

However, the Law Courts have not received the attention they deserve, partly because they were demolished in the 1880s with no interior photographic record being made, but also because they were delicately downgraded by Sir John Summerson who complained of them that there 'is no new invention here'.[21] Today, we are more struck by the ingenuity and variety of Soane's Law Courts in which he strained to create a language of historical resonance which would be appropriate to the august setting (fig. 44, cat. 210) and the solemn function of the buildings. Rather like Hawksmoor's work at All Souls College, Oxford, this haunting personal language occupied a position halfway between classic and Gothic. It may, indeed, have been a response to the current debate about the relative appropriateness of Greek or Gothic for new

43

or colour. Yet the best are created with Tschichold-like sensitivity, displaying none of the ruthless dogma that Bill expounded, and that was so unhappily evident in his work. In this book, the overall spatial control is in a different and more accomplished form than that found in earlier modernist works.

While the practical benefits of grids are always a consideration, the previous examples show them used for other reasons too: for mainly aesthetic effect; as a production device intrinsic to the nature of the book; and as a way of keeping a grip on a large quantity of diverse material. The grid of this Soane book has yet another job to do: it holds together spreads where, reflecting the subtitle, space and asymmetry are used with unusual daring. The five-column grid effectively relates introductory texts, catalogue entries, and a mass of varied illustrations – plans, drawings, watercolours, prints, photographs (including several of models). Consequently, despite its dramatic visual and spatial variations between spreads, this 300-page book is all-of-a-piece.

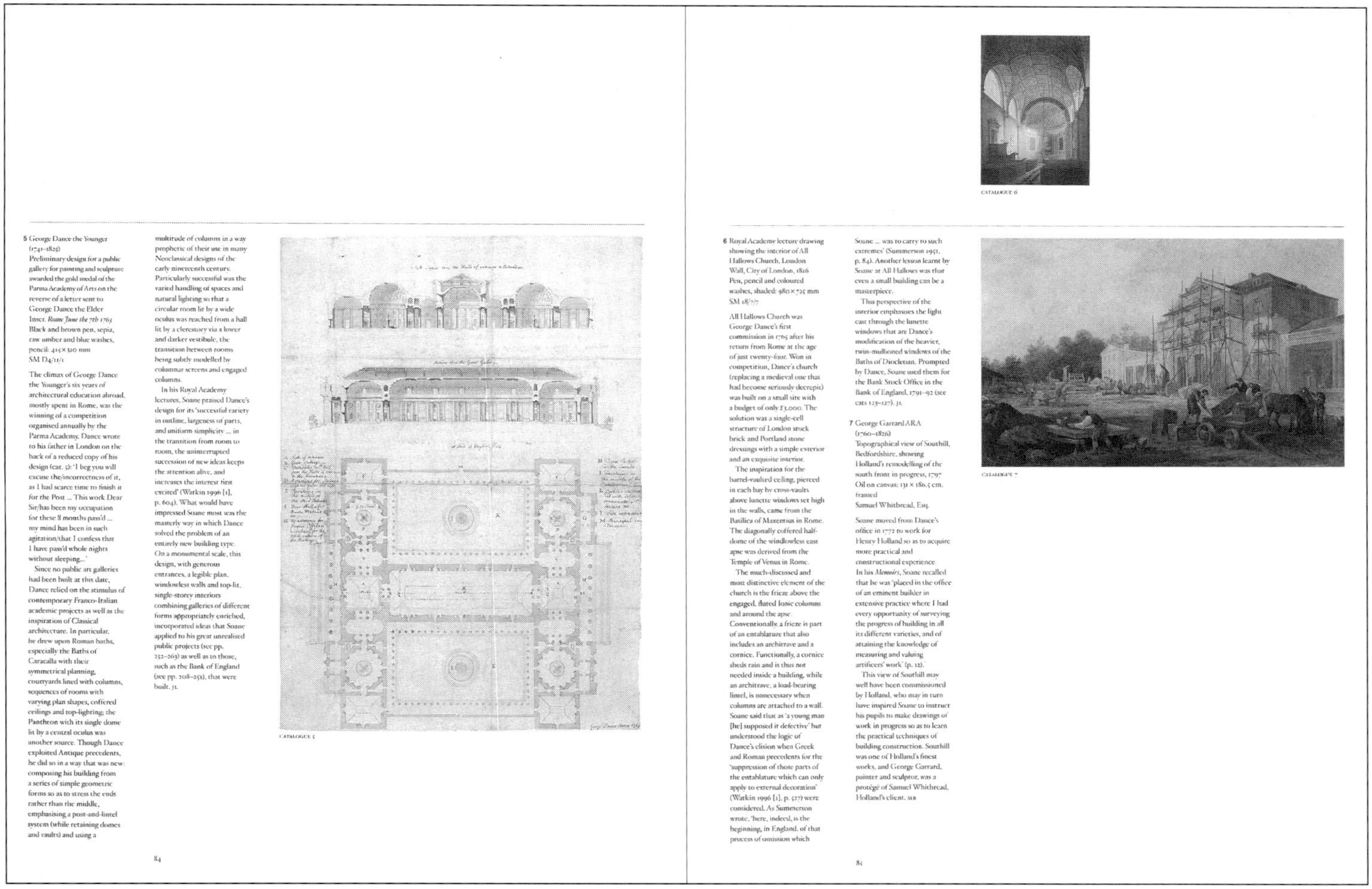

5 George Dance the Younger (1741–1825)
Preliminary design for a public gallery for painting and sculpture awarded the gold medal of the Parma Academy of Arts on the reverse of a letter sent to George Dance the Elder
Inscr. *Rome June the 7th 1763*
Black and brown pen, sepia, raw umber and blue washes, pencil: 415 × 310 mm
SM D4/11/1

The climax of George Dance the Younger's six years of architectural education abroad, mostly spent in Rome, was the winning of a competition organised annually by the Parma Academy. Dance wrote to his father in London on the back of a reduced copy of his design (cat. 5): 'I beg you will excuse the/incorrectness of it, as I had scarce time to finish it for the Post ... This work Dear Sir/has been my occupation for these 8 months pass'd ... my mind has been in such agitation/that I confess that I have pass'd whole nights without sleeping...'

Since no public art galleries had been built at this date, Dance relied on the stimulus of contemporary Franco-Italian academic projects as well as the inspiration of Classical architecture. In particular, he drew upon Roman baths, especially the Baths of Caracalla with their symmetrical planning, courtyards lined with columns, sequences of rooms with varying plan shapes, coffered ceilings and top-lighting; the Pantheon with its single dome lit by a central oculus was another source. Though Dance exploited Antique precedents, he did so in a way that was new: composing his building from a series of simple geometric forms so as to stress the ends rather than the middle, emphasising a post-and-lintel system (while retaining domes and vaults) and using a multitude of columns in a way prophetic of their use in many Neoclassical designs of the early nineteenth century. Particularly successful was the varied handling of spaces and natural lighting so that a circular room lit by a wide oculus was reached from a hall lit by a clerestory via a lower and darker vestibule, the transition between rooms being subtly modelled by columnar screens and engaged columns.

In his Royal Academy lectures, Soane praised Dance's design for its 'successful variety in outline, largeness of parts, and uniform simplicity ... in the transition from room to room, the uninterrupted succession of new ideas keeps the attention alive, and increases the interest first excited' (Watkin 1996 [1], p. 604). What would have impressed Soane most was the masterly way in which Dance solved the problem of an entirely new building type. On a monumental scale, this design, with generous entrances, a legible plan, windowless walls and top-lit, single-storey interiors combining galleries of different forms appropriately enriched, incorporated ideas that Soane applied to his great unrealised public projects (see pp. 252–263) as well as to those, such as the Bank of England (see pp. 208–251), that were built. JL

CATALOGUE 5

84

CATALOGUE 6

6 Royal Academy lecture drawing showing the interior of All Hallows Church, London Wall, City of London, 1816
Pen, pencil and coloured washes, shaded: 980 × 725 mm
SM 18/7/7

All Hallows Church was George Dance's first commission in 1765 after his return from Rome at the age of just twenty-four. Won in competition, Dance's church (replacing a medieval one that had become seriously decrepit) was built on a small site with a budget of only £3,000. The solution was a single-cell structure of London stock brick and Portland stone dressings with a simple exterior and an exquisite interior.

The inspiration for the barrel-vaulted ceiling, pierced in each bay by cross-vaults above lunette windows set high in the walls, came from the Basilica of Maxentius in Rome. The diagonally coffered half-dome of the windowless east apse was derived from the Temple of Venus in Rome.

The much-discussed and most distinctive element of the church is the frieze above the engaged, fluted Ionic columns and around the apse. Conventionally, a frieze is part of an entablature that also includes an architrave and a cornice. Functionally, a cornice sheds rain and is thus not needed inside a building, while an architrave, a load-bearing lintel, is unnecessary when columns are attached to a wall. Soane said that as 'a young man [he] supposed it defective' but understood the logic of Dance's elision when Greek and Roman precedents for the 'suppression of those parts of the entablature which can only apply to external decoration' (Watkin 1996 [1], p. 527) were considered. As Summerson wrote, 'here, indeed, is the beginning, in England, of that process of omission which Soane ... was to carry to such extremes' (Summerson 1951, p. 84). Another lesson learnt by Soane at All Hallows was that even a small building can be a masterpiece.

This perspective of the interior emphasises the light cast through the lunette windows that are Dance's modification of the heavier, twin-mullioned windows of the Baths of Diocletian. Prompted by Dance, Soane used them for the Bank Stock Office in the Bank of England, 1791–92 (see cats 123–127). JL

7 George Garrard ARA (1760–1826)
Topographical view of Southill, Bedfordshire, showing Holland's remodelling of the south front in progress, 1797
Oil on canvas: 131 × 186.5 cm, framed
Samuel Whitbread, Esq.

Soane moved from Dance's office in 1772 to work for Henry Holland so as to acquire more practical and constructional experience. In his *Memoirs*, Soane recalled that he was 'placed in the office of an eminent builder in extensive practice where I had every opportunity of surveying the progress of building in all its different varieties, and of attaining the knowledge of measuring and valuing artificers' work' (p. 12).

This view of Southill may well have been commissioned by Holland, who may in turn have inspired Soane to instruct his pupils to make drawings of work in progress so as to learn the practical techniques of building construction. Southill was one of Holland's finest works, and George Garrard, painter and sculptor, was a protégé of Samuel Whitbread, Holland's client. MR

CATALOGUE 7

85

John Soane Architect continued

Once the basic structure had been planned, with a large top margin – usually delineated by a rule – the general scheme was to place small illustrations, some plans, section headings and endnotes in this area. A neat way of handling such itsy-bitsy material, this also helps to contribute to the book's visual unity.

Swiss New Typography was its remote ancestor – it is difficult to believe this book would look the way it does without that work done almost fifty years previously – but it demonstrates how it can be reinvented to create quite different effects. Here is modernism, alive and well.

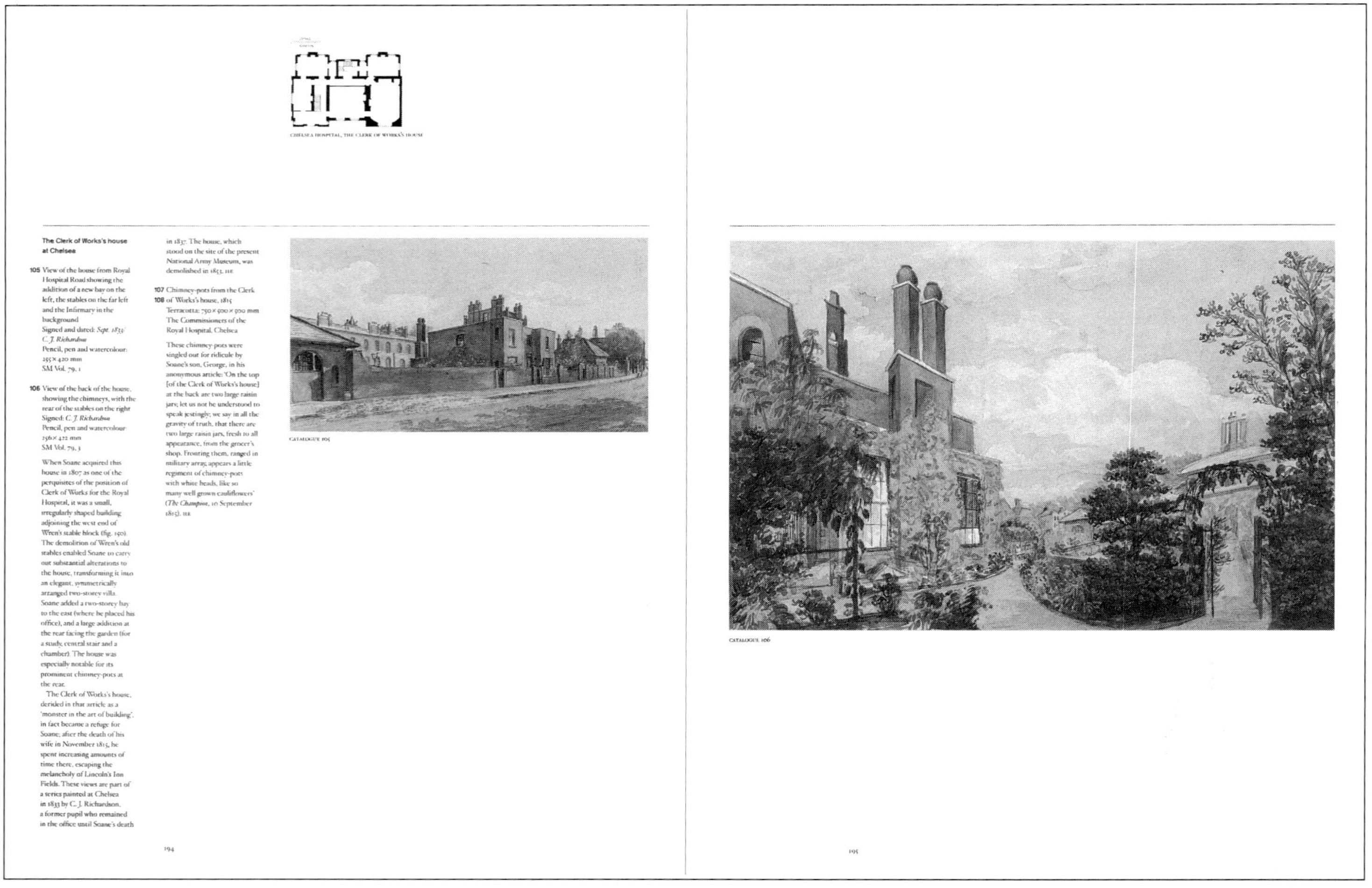

CHELSEA HOSPITAL, THE CLERK OF WORKS'S HOUSE

The Clerk of Works's house at Chelsea

105 View of the house from Royal Hospital Road showing the addition of a new bay on the left, the stables on the far left and the Infirmary in the background
Signed and dated: *Sept. 1833/ C. J. Richardson*
Pencil, pen and watercolour: 255 × 420 mm
SM Vol. 79, 1

106 View of the back of the house, showing the chimneys, with the rear of the stables on the right
Signed: *C. J. Richardson*
Pencil, pen and watercolour: 256 × 422 mm
SM Vol. 79, 3

When Soane acquired this house in 1807 as one of the perquisites of the position of Clerk of Works for the Royal Hospital, it was a small, irregularly shaped building adjoining the west end of Wren's stable block (fig. 150). The demolition of Wren's old stables enabled Soane to carry out substantial alterations to the house, transforming it into an elegant, symmetrically arranged two-storey villa. Soane added a two-storey bay to the east (where he placed his office), and a large addition at the rear facing the garden (for a study, central stair and a chamber). The house was especially notable for its prominent chimney-pots at the rear.

The Clerk of Works's house, derided in that article as a 'monster in the art of building', in fact became a refuge for Soane; after the death of his wife in November 1815, he spent increasing amounts of time there, escaping the melancholy of Lincoln's Inn Fields. These views are part of a series painted at Chelsea in 1833 by C. J. Richardson, a former pupil who remained in the office until Soane's death in 1837. The house, which stood on the site of the present National Army Museum, was demolished in 1853. 118

107 Chimney-pots from the Clerk
108 of Works's house, 1815
Terracotta: 750 × 500 × 500 mm
The Commissioners of the Royal Hospital, Chelsea

These chimney-pots were singled out for ridicule by Soane's son, George, in his anonymous article: 'On the top [of the Clerk of Works's house] at the back are two large raisin jars; let us not be understood to speak jestingly; we say in all the gravity of truth, that there are two large raisin jars, fresh to all appearance, from the grocer's shop. Fronting them, ranged in military array, appears a little regiment of chimney-pots with white heads, like so many well grown cauliflowers' (*The Champion*, 10 September 1815). 118

CATALOGUE 105

CATALOGUE 106

194

195

Tyringham, Buckinghamshire,
for William Praed, 1792–1800

51 Joseph Parkins, model-maker
Model of the house,
c. 1793–94
Mahogany: 305 × 533 × 482 mm
SM X236

This is a fine example of a 'client' model made before the design for the tribune or inner hall was finalised. It was made from design drawings supplied by Soane and divides horizontally into three layers to show the interiors.

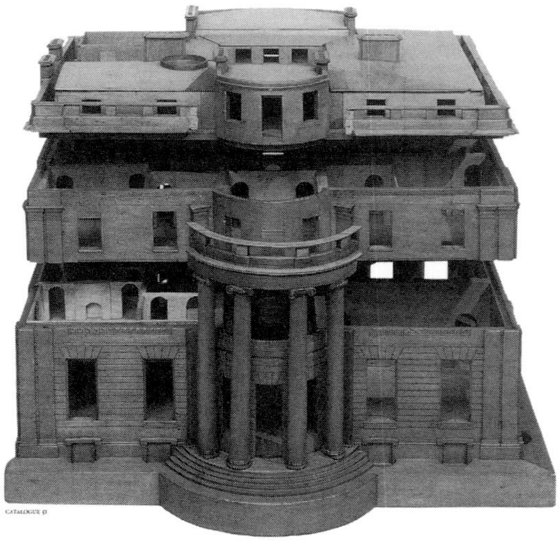

CATALOGUE 51

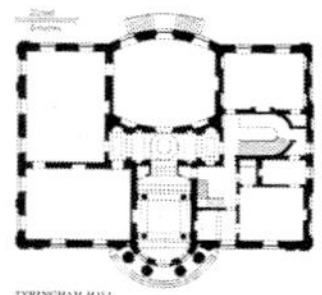

TYRINGHAM HALL

52 Design perspective of the interior of the hall, with inset plans of the hall and chamber floor, drawn by Joseph Michael Gandy, February 1798
Inset: *to shew the manner of lighting the Tribune and the end of the Hall*
Pen and watercolour:
845 × 560 mm
SM 13/5/5

53 Topographical sketch made on the spot, of the garden side of the house, showing the offices, bridge and gateway, drawn by Joseph Michael Gandy, July 1798
Dated: *ab 2 pm July 98*
Pencil, pen and watercolour:
246 × 481 mm
SM Vol. 60, 121

54 Perspective view of the garden side of the house, drawn by Joseph Michael Gandy, August 1798
Dated: *August 24th 1798*
Pen and watercolour:
626 × 948 mm
SM 13/5/1

55 Perspective view of the entrance façade, with the offices on the right, drawn by Joseph Michael Gandy, August 1798
Pen and watercolour:
625 × 949 mm
SM 13/5/3

Gandy worked up this presentation view from sketches between 27 July and 7 August, and entitled it 'Sunset'.

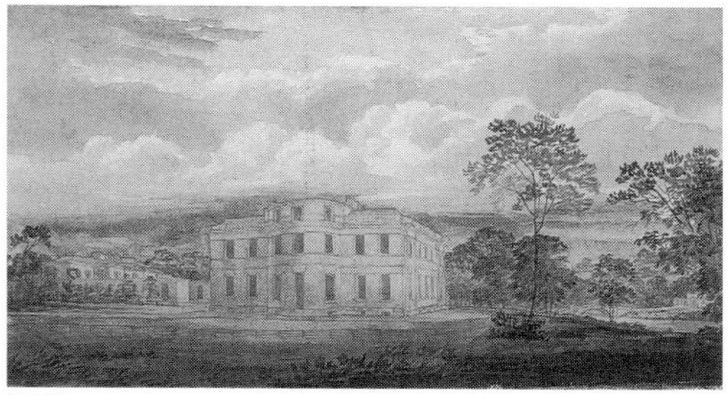

CATALOGUE 53

conclusion

Any artefact, regardless of how 'functionally', 'structurally' or 'logically' conceived, will retain some aspects of the personality of its creator. So the design system that the Swiss devised is, almost inevitably, interpreted differently by individual designers. Sixty years later it is still being retranslated, just as Greek or Latin classics are constantly being newly 'Englished' to make them acceptable to readers living in a different age. And although the Swiss hard-edge idea appeared to become a formula when unimaginatively used, it is not intrinsically incapable of development. Nothing, even functionally expressed, can ever be reduced unequivocally to forms eternally accepted as inevitable.

Hard-edge design, which I prefer to call the Swiss New Typography, has also been called the International Style. But although its principles were enthusiastically taken up in many countries outside Switzerland – the grid, the type, the alignments, the horizontals and verticals, the use of space – only Swiss designers, and German-Swiss at that, had a true flair for creating the unexpected or dramatic mise-en-page which still respected the grid structure. The Müller-Brockmanns, the Gerstners, the Odermatts: the skill with which these designers, and a host of others, manipulated the system, whether for posters, brochures, books, stationery, packaging, has never been approached by designers in other countries. It seems the fully fledged style, in all its rigour and daring, was not exportable, and it defeated all attempts to mimic it. To call it the International Style is plainly not just misleading, but wrong. Yet its influence cannot be denied; and while it appears to have been initially less sympathetically received in America, in Britain at least its essence is still a powerful force in the design of the modern book.

In this volume I have referred to modern architecture and its concern with space, structure and function. Perhaps, by relating it to architecture, I am trying to make book design seem more significant and more important than it is. Book designers cannot change society in the way modern movement architects hoped to; and even *their* contributions to the built environment since the Bauhaus have been depressing, far from the brave new world dreams of the 1920s and 1945. Despite individual architectural successes, mere islands amongst the dross, the vision of making towns and cities beautiful, as a strategy for reducing conflicts within society and (now) different ethnic groups, has not been fulfilled. We sometimes persuade ourselves we can eventually create a perfect world but, paraphrasing Stoppard's Herzen again, there is something wrong with the picture. For there is no such place, that's why it's called utopia. So to worry about the appearance of such micro items as books seems hardly worthwhile. Nonetheless, well-designed and well-produced books can play their part, no matter how small, in the enhancement of our lives.

Neither architecture nor book design is art in pure form, for both need to provide answers to utilitarian or functional requirements as well as being visually pleasing. In both, the form should relate to the function. Both provide a space/time experience, the progression through a well-designed building being echoed in the sequence of pages in a book. Parts should relate to each other, and to the whole. The early twentieth-century Dutch architect H P Berlage coined the phrase 'unity in diversity', which was appropriated by de Stijl. It is hardly original, being essentially a principle of Western art for two thousand years, even if less overtly and less concisely expressed. The centre of Rome consists of buildings from Roman times to the present day. Nothing conforms in direction, angle, height, colour, alignment of windows or cornice; often not in material; yet, except for the environmental catastrophe of the Vittorio Emanuele II monument, all is unified. Paint and plaster is usually 'distressed' by time and weather – further diversity within unity. It would be difficult to emulate such an extreme example, created over centuries, in a single lifetime today. (Although Alan Fletcher's book *The Art of Looking Sideways*, Phaidon, 2001, has a very good try.)

Variety within an overall unity is often achieved, in both disciplines, with the help of some form of grid, module or mathematical relationship, although this is generally more apparent in bookwork. And while printability and readability must always be major concerns, the book designer shares with the architect the problem of resolving certain dichotomies. Analysis/intuition, order/informality, intellect/emotion; such oppositions are, in book design, joined by other potential conflicts: aesthetics against communication, simplicity against dullness, liveliness and surprise against confusion and distraction. No designer has a check list of these, ticking them off as work proceeds; but they are part of any designer's baggage, and decisions about them, conscious or not (often simply resolved by the designer's personality), will play a significant part in the final design.

Pages could be devoted to discussing the pros and cons of each of those concepts. Or the whole rigmarole could be reduced, as far as the reader is affected, to a banality. Unlike the Swiss or the Germans, the British are not a tidy nation. A look at our towns, with their litter, graffiti, chewing gum on pavements, stickers on almost any vertical surface, crude road marking, environmentally destructive shop fascias, careless signposting – to name a few examples – suggests we are possibly the most visually thoughtless people in Europe. Yet neat and tidy, which sounds so unexciting, so bourgeois, are virtues in book design, and they are the distinguishing characteristics of the best British books. Of the many approaches to the subject, I have chosen to concentrate on the one which reflects the architectural sense of order and clarity initiated by the 1940s and 1950s Swiss designers. The books we have just seen in my final sequence were influenced by that innovative Swiss work, although they show it can be adapted and developed to suit a different age and different tastes. And, just as Gropius said of the Bauhaus, it will remain alive, 'so long as it does not congeal into a static form, so long as it seeks the essence of life in continual change'.

Reader, it is for you to continue the story. As an example …

… a more imaginative way of structuring parts of this book
would have been along the lines taken on the next two pages. →
Easily achieved today
on an AppleMac
but you need an inventive and open mind
visual skill
and a highly developed sense
of what is and what is not
advantageous.
Not advisable for a lengthy book
perhaps
– or not before
a careful conditioning process of the reading public –
it is a development of Stefan Themerson's earlier ideas on internal
vertical
justification
the germ of which might be found in
Mallarmé's
Le Coup de dés
with which this book
opens.

A spread from
Stefan Themerson: 'Kurt Schwitters on a time-chart'
Typographica 16
Lund Humphries, London, 1967
Illustrated at 86% actual size

1910 1920

("Les Mots en Liberté")

2000 shrapnels exploding, dazzling white handkerchiefs full of gold srrrrrr TUMB TUMB 2000 grenades extended
grabbing crashingly very black hair Zang———srrrrr
TUMB ZANG TUMB TUUMB the orchestra of noises of war
blotted out under a note of silence held in the high
sky by gilded spheric balloons which watch the shooting.

He seems to be treating language not as a means of communication,
not as an instrument for thinking,
not even as an expression of emotions,
but *as behaviour.*

This, to some extent, is perhaps true also with other writing-experiments of the time. And it is fascinating to notice that to study language as behaviour becomes the subject of what is going to be called neuro-linguistics, psycho-linguistics. One of their hypotheses suggests that:

(Anatol Rapaport,
ETC, Autumn 1958)
(Sapir & Whorf, *idem*)

The ideas, perceptions, and metaphysics of the whole culture is determined (or at least strongly influenced) by the language structure peculiar to it;
in other words: **our language does our thinking for us.**

Therefore: If you want to better us by changing our perceptions,
attitudes,
behaviour,
try to change our linguistic habits,
our syntax, vocabulary, & style.

This is what the futurists and dadaists were trying to do in the twenties,

This is what the dictators and other politicans were trying to do in the thirties,

This is what in the forties writers decided is no business of literature,

And this is what the omnipresent admen (political, industrial, commercial) are trying to do today.

All this does not mean that Marinetti was the source and origin of the movement. He was a seismograph among other seismographs.

The same forces which made him praise **the power of the Machine,**
made the future *Bauhaus* **accept courageously the machine as an instrument worthy of Artists.**

The same forces which made him praise **A Racing Motor-car, its frame adorned with great pipes, like snakes with explosive breath . . .**

(for amusement's sake confer: S. I. Hayakawa: 'Sexual Symbolism of the American Automobile'; ☛ or, if you prefer: Freud's 'Interpretation of Dreams').

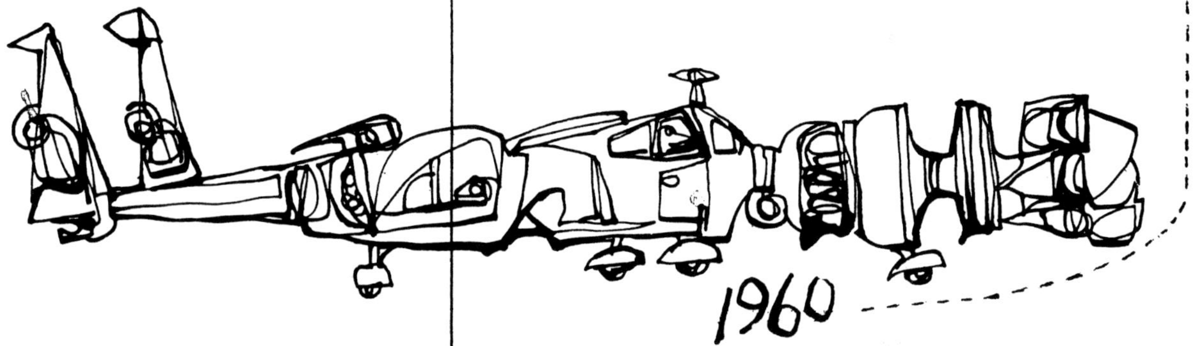

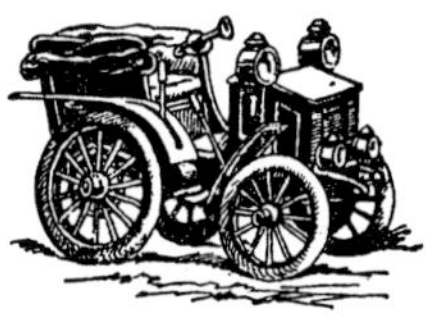

The Racing Motor-car, which seems to be running on shrapnel and is more beautiful than the Victory of Samothrace,

(Non, vous, Marinetti', wrote Apollinaire, 'vous fondez une religion nouvelle établie sur le développement des moyens de locomotion. Au lieu de Divinité vous dites Vélocité; sans le savoir les Allemands ont bien fondé la religion de la Férocité,' – Appollinaire: 'Anecdotiques': 'La nouvelle religion de la Velocité', 16 Oct. 1916).

made Meyerhold invent his biomechanical theatre, a synthesis of drama, gesture rhythm, sound, colour, and technical constructions on the stage;

and Tairov want both to acclaim the concept of spectacle **(the theatre must be theatrical)** and break the footlights dividing the stage from the audience **(a theatre which presented a room from which one had amputated the fourth wall),**

(it was not the marxist artists, it was the marxist philosophers who condemned soviet culture' to at least thirty years of **Bieder**man+ Bummel**meier** Aesthetics).

made Paul Klee fall in love with **a green leaf, a little star, a butterfly wing,**

made the dadaists contradict **the existing world order,**

made Kurt Schwitters invent **MERZ-art.**

select list of books

Christoph Bignens and Jörg Stürzebecher: *Richard P Lohse. Konstruktive Gebrauschgrafik*. Hatje Cantz, 1999

Susan Compton: *The World Backwards. Russian Futurist Books 1912-16*. The British Library, 1978

Susan Compton: *Russian Avant-Garde Books 1917-34*. The British Library, 1992

William J R Curtis: *Modern Architecture Since 1900*. Phaidon, 1996

Magdalena Droste: *Bauhaus*. Taschen, 2002

Johanna Drucker: *The Visible Word. Experimental Typography and Modern Art, 1909-1923*. University of Chicago, 1994

Jeannine Fiedler and Peter Feierabend: *Bauhaus*. Köneman, 1999

Edward M Gottschall: *Typographic Communications Today*. MIT Press, 1989

Richard Hollis: *Graphic Design. A Concise History*. Thames & Hudson, 2001

Richard Hollis: *Swiss Graphic Design. The origins and growth of an international style 1920-70*. In course of preparation

Robert Flynn Johnson: *Artists' Books in the Modern Era 1870-2000*. Fine Arts Museums of San Francisco/Thames & Hudson, 2001

Robin Kinross: *Modern Typography*. Hyphen Press, 1992

John Lewis: *The Twentieth Century Book*. Studio Vista, 1967 and 1984

Richard P Lohse et al (eds): *Neue Grafik/New Graphic Design/Graphisme actuel*. Otto Walter, 1958-65

Ruari McLean: *Jan Tschichold: Typographer*. Lund Humphries, 1975

Ruari McLean: *Jan Tschichold: A Life in Typography*. Lund Humphries, 1997

Ad Petersen and Pieter Brattinga: *Sandberg. Een Documentaire/A Documentary*. Kosmos, Amsterdam, 1975

Rick Poyner: *Typographica*. Laurence King, 2001

John Russell Taylor: *The Art Nouveau Book in Britain*. Methuen, 1966

Herbert Spencer: *Design in Business Printing*. Lund Humphries, 1952

Herbert Spencer: *Pioneers of Modern Typography*. Lund Humphries, 1969

Herbert Spencer (ed): *Typographica*. Lund Humphries, 1949-67

Caroline Tisdall and Angelo Bozzolla: *Futurism*. Thames & Hudson, 1977

Jan Tschichold, trans Ruari McLean: *Asymmetric Typography*. Faber and Faber/Cooper and Beatty, 1967

Richard Weston: *Modernism*. Phaidon, 1996

Fifty Years Bauhaus. Exhibition catalogue, Royal Academy of Arts, 1968

index of designers and printers

Text-only references are in italic